St Teresa of Avila
Her Writings and Life

LEGENDA

LEGENDA is the Modern Humanities Research Association's book imprint for new research in the Humanities. Founded in 1995 by Malcolm Bowie and others within the University of Oxford, Legenda has always been a collaborative publishing enterprise, directly governed by scholars. The Modern Humanities Research Association (MHRA) joined this collaboration in 1998, became half-owner in 2004, in partnership with Maney Publishing and then Routledge, and has since 2016 been sole owner. Titles range from medieval texts to contemporary cinema and form a widely comparative view of the modern humanities, including works on Arabic, Catalan, English, French, German, Greek, Italian, Portuguese, Russian, Spanish, and Yiddish literature. Editorial boards and committees of more than 60 leading academic specialists work in collaboration with bodies such as the Society for French Studies, the British Comparative Literature Association and the Association of Hispanists of Great Britain & Ireland.

The MHRA encourages and promotes advanced study and research in the field of the modern humanities, especially modern European languages and literature, including English, and also cinema. It aims to break down the barriers between scholars working in different disciplines and to maintain the unity of humanistic scholarship. The Association fulfils this purpose through the publication of journals, bibliographies, monographs, critical editions, and the MHRA Style Guide, and by making grants in support of research. Membership is open to all who work in the Humanities, whether independent or in a University post, and the participation of younger colleagues entering the field is especially welcomed.

ALSO PUBLISHED BY THE ASSOCIATION

Critical Texts
Tudor and Stuart Translations • New Translations • European Translations
MHRA Library of Medieval Welsh Literature

MHRA Bibliographies
Publications of the Modern Humanities Research Association

The Annual Bibliography of English Language & Literature
Austrian Studies
Modern Language Review
Portuguese Studies
The Slavonic and East European Review
Working Papers in the Humanities
The Yearbook of English Studies

www.mhra.org.uk
www.legendabooks.com

STUDIES IN HISPANIC AND LUSOPHONE CULTURES

Studies in Hispanic and Lusophone Cultures are selected and edited by the Association of Hispanists of Great Britain & Ireland. The series seeks to publish the best new research in all areas of the literature, thought, history, culture, film, and languages of Spain, Spanish America, and the Portuguese-speaking world.

The Association of Hispanists of Great Britain & Ireland is a professional association which represents a very diverse discipline, in terms of both geographical coverage and objects of study. Its website showcases new work by members, and publicises jobs, conferences and grants in the field.

Editorial Committee
Chair: Professor Trevor Dadson (Queen Mary, University of London)
Professor Catherine Davies (University of Nottingham)
Professor Sally Faulkner (University of Exeter)
Professor Andrew Ginger (University of Bristol)
Professor James Mandrell (Brandeis University, USA)
Professor Hilary Owen (University of Manchester)
Professor Christopher Perriam (University of Manchester)
Professor Philip Swanson (University of Sheffield)

Managing Editor
Dr Graham Nelson
41 Wellington Square, Oxford OX1 2JF, UK

www.legendabooks.com/series/shlc

Boetius Adams Bolswert (1569–1659), after Peter Paul Rubens, *Heilige Teresa*, print, 34mm × 91mm, reproduced with permission, Rijksmuseum, Amsterdam.

St Teresa of Avila

Her Writings and Life

EDITED BY TERENCE O'REILLY,
COLIN THOMPSON AND LESLEY TWOMEY

Studies in Hispanic and Lusophone Cultures 19
Modern Humanities Research Association
2018

Published by Legenda
an imprint of the Modern Humanities Research Association
Salisbury House, Station Road, Cambridge CB1 2LA

ISBN 978-1-78188-501-7 (HB)
ISBN 978-1-78188-502-4 (PB)

First published 2018

All rights reserved. No part of this publication may be reproduced or disseminated or transmitted in any form or by any means, electronic, mechanical, photocopying, recording or otherwise, or stored in any retrieval system, or otherwise used in any manner whatsoever without written permission of the copyright owner, except in accordance with the provisions of the Copyright, Designs and Patents Act 1988, or under the terms of a licence permitting restricted copying issued in the UK by the Copyright Licensing Agency Ltd, Saffron House, 6–10 Kirby Street, London EC1N 8TS, England, or in the USA by the Copyright Clearance Center, 222 Rosewood Drive, Danvers MA 01923. Application for the written permission of the copyright owner to reproduce any part of this publication must be made by email to legenda@mhra.org.uk.

Disclaimer: Statements of fact and opinion contained in this book are those of the author and not of the editors or the Modern Humanities Research Association. The publisher makes no representation, express or implied, in respect of the accuracy of the material in this book and cannot accept any legal responsibility or liability for any errors or omissions that may be made.

Trademark notice: Product or corporate names may be trademarks or registered trademarks, and are used only for identification and explanation without intent to infringe.

© Modern Humanities Research Association 2018

Copy-Editor: Richard Correll

CONTENTS

Acknowledgements ix
Abbreviations x
List of Illustrations xi
Notes on the Contributors xii

Introduction 1
COLIN P. THOMPSON

PART I: ST TERESA AND HER TIMES

1 St Teresa of Ávila and Earlier Carmelite Traditions 14
   PATRICK MULLINS

2 Teresa of Ávila's Theological Reading of History: From her Second Conversion to the Foundation of St Joseph's, Ávila 32
   EDWARD HOWELLS

3 A Clash of Titans: St Teresa in Pastrana 42
   TREVOR J. DADSON

4 Vicente Carducho, Painter and Writer: His Contributions to the *iconografía teresiana* and Reflections on St Teresa and the Perfection of Religious Paintings 59
   JEREMY ROE

PART II: ST TERESA THE MYSTIC

5 Teresa as a Reader of the Gospels 80
   ROWAN WILLIAMS

6 Teresa of Ávila's Picture of the Soul: Platonic or Augustinian? 91
   PETER TYLER

7 St Teresa and her First Jesuit Confessors 108
   TERENCE O'REILLY

8 St Teresa and the Prayer of Offering 124
   IAIN MATTHEW

9 Teresa's Theological-Spiritual Synthesis: What Does it Really Accomplish? 135
   GILLIAN T. W. AHLGREN

PART III: TERESA THE WRITER

10 From Fear to Courage: The Testimonies of Teresa of Ávila and her Early Hagiographers ... 150
ELENA CARRERA

11 The 'Library' of Santa Teresa: Teresa of Ávila's Sources and their Effect on her Writings ... 167
HILARY PEARSON

12 Seeing and Knowing God: Reinterpreting Vision in the Writing of Teresa of Ávila and Other Cloistered Women Writers ... 193
LESLEY K. TWOMEY

13 Traditions of Discourse and Santa Teresa ... 213
CHRISTOPHER J. POUNTAIN

Bibliography ... 232

Index ... 251

ACKNOWLEDGEMENTS

The editors wish to record their deep gratitude to the Embassy of Spain in London, and to TORCH (the Oxford Research Centre in the Humanities), the Spanish Studies Fund of the Faculty of Medieval and Modern Languages, and the John Fell Fund of the University of Oxford, for their encouragement and practical support of the project, from its beginnings to the publication of this book.

ABBREVIATIONS

Books by St Teresa and relevant manuscripts

Camino	*Camino de perfección* [Way of Perfection]
CE	*Camino de perfección* [Way of Perfection, Escorial manuscript]
CV	*Camino de perfección* [Way of Perfection, Valladolid manuscript]
Constituciones	[Constitutions]
Cuentas	*Cuentas de conciencia* [Spiritual Testimonies]
Exclamaciones	*Exclamaciones del alma* [Soliloquies]
Fundaciones	*Libro de las fundaciones* [Book of Foundations]
Meditaciones	*Meditaciones sobre los Cantares* [Meditations on the Song of Songs]
Moradas	*Las moradas del castillo interior* [Mansions of the Interior Castle]
Vida	*Libro de la vida* [Book of her Life]

Works by St Teresa in English translation

Foundations	*Book of Foundations* [*Libro de las fundaciones*]
Interior Castle	*Mansions of the Interior Castle* [*Moradas*]
Life	*Book of her Life* [*Vida*]
Soliloquies	[*Exclamaciones del alma*]
Way	*Way of Perfection* [*Camino*]

Other abbreviations

CSIC	Centro Superior de Investigaciones Científicas
HSMS	Hispanic Seminary of Medieval Studies
LCL	Loeb Classical Library
MHRA	Modern Humanities Research Association
TWAS	Twayne World Author Series

LIST OF ILLUSTRATIONS

FRONTISPIECE. Boetius Adams Bolswert (1569–1659), after Peter Paul Rubens, *Heilige Teresa*, print, 34mm × 91mm, reproduced with permission, Rijksmuseum, Amsterdam.

FIG. 3.1. *St Teresa Confers Habits on Juan Narduch and Mariano Azzaro, in the Presence of the Prince and Princess of Éboli* (1569), seventeenth-century mural painting, Pastrana, Fundación de San Pedro, Museo de San Francisco. Image ceded by Esther Alegre Carvajal.

FIG. 4.1. Vicente Carducho, *St Teresa Beholding the Vision of St Albert of Sicily, who Showed her the Future of the Order; St Teresa Dispenses the Habits of the Discalced Carmelites, St Teresa's Vision of the Virgin and St Joseph* [Santa Teresa de Jesús ante la visión de San Alberto de Sicilia, que le muestra el futuro del Órden; Santa Teresa de Jesús entrega los hábitos del Carmelo Descalzo; Santa Teresa ante la visión de la Virgen y San José], c. 1622–30, ink and grey-brown wash heightened with white lead, 15.7 × 24.6 cm, Unknown location (in 1977 in a private collection), photograph courtesy of the Biblioteca de Catalunya, Barcelona.

FIG. 4.2. Vicente Carducho, *St Teresa Writing* [Santa Teresa escribiendo], date uncertain, oil on canvas (?), 25 × 147 cms, Convento de San José, Ávila.

FIG. 4.3. Vicente Carducho, *The Transverberation* [La Transverberación], date uncertain, oil on canvas (?), 25 × 147 cms, Convento de San José, Ávila.

FIG. 4.4. Vicente Carducho, *The Death of St Teresa* [La muerte de Santa Teresa], oil on canvas (?), date uncertain, 25 × 147 cms, Convento de San José, Ávila.

FIG. 4.5. Vicente Carducho, *St Teresa's Vision of Christ at the Column* [Santa Teresa ante el Cristo a la columna], date uncertain, 1622–25, oil on panel, Convento de las Carboneras del Corpus Christi, photograph courtesy of the Biblioteca de Catalunya, Barcelona.

FIG. 4.6. Jerónimo Dávila, *Christ at the Column* [Santa Teresa ante el Cristo a la columna], date uncertain, Fresco, 164 × 103 cms, Convento de San José, Ávila.

NOTES ON THE CONTRIBUTORS

Gillian T. W. Ahlgren is Professor of Theology and Founding Director of the Institute for Spirituality and Social Justice at Xavier University in Cincinnati, Ohio. A church historian specializing in the Christian mystical tradition, her interests include how historical context influences mystics' insights into God, their theological expression, and their engagement of reform and transformation. She is the author of six books, including *Teresa of Avila and the Politics of Sanctity*, *Entering Teresa of Avila's Interior Castle: A Reader's Companion*, *Enkindling Love: The Legacy of Teresa of Avila and John of the Cross*, and, most recently, *The Tenderness of God: Reclaiming Our Humanity*. She leads retreats and is an experienced spiritual director. Her pastoral commitments include working with the formerly homeless, women in recovery from substance abuse, and women who have experienced domestic violence.

Elena Carrera is Senior Lecturer in Hispanic Studies at Queen Mary University of London, and Director of its Centre for the History of the Emotions. She is the author of *Teresa of Avila's Autobiography: Authority, Power and the Self in Mid-Sixteenth Century Spain* (2005) and editor of *Madness and Melancholy in Sixteenth- and Seventeenth-century Spain* (2010) and *Emotions and Health, 1200–1700* (2013). Her current research projects focus on fear in the context of interfaith conflict in late medieval and early modern Spain, and on women's courage in the early modern Hispanic world.

Trevor J. Dadson is Professor of Hispanic Studies at Queen Mary University of London, having previously held chairs at Queen's University, Belfast, and the University of Birmingham. He is the author of numerous books, articles, and book chapters on Spanish Golden Age literature, textual criticism, and socio-cultural history. Among his recent books are *Epistolario e historial documental de Ana de Mendoza y de la Cerda, princesa de Éboli* (2013); *Tolerance and Coexistence in Early Modern Spain: Old Christians and Moriscos in the Campo de Calatrava* (2014); *Diego de Silva y Mendoza, conde de Salinas, marqués de Alenquer. Cartas y memoriales (1584–1630)* (2015); (with Helen Reed), *Cautiva del rey: Vida de Ana de Mendoza y de la Cerda, princesa de Éboli (1540–1592)* (2015); *Conde de Salinas. Obra completa. I. Poesía desconocida* (2016). He was President of the 'Asociación Internacional «Siglo de Oro»' (1999–2002), Vice-President of the 'Asociación Internacional de Hispanistas' (2004–07), and President of the 'Association of Hispanists of Great Britain & Ireland' (2011–15). In 2008 he was elected a Fellow of the British Academy, and in 2015 he was awarded the 'Encomienda de la Orden de Isabel la Católica' by King Felipe VI of Spain for his services to Spanish culture. In 2016, he was elected a Corresponding Fellow of both the Real Academia Española and the Real Academia de la Historia.

Edward Howells is Senior Lecturer in Christian Spirituality at Heythrop College, University of London. He is author of *John of the Cross and Teresa of Avila: Mystical Knowing and Selfhood*, and has written widely on late medieval mystical theology. He is currently editing the *Oxford Handbook of Mystical Theology* (forthcoming 2018).

Iain Matthew joined the Discalced Carmelites in 1978, having studied at St Joseph's College, Ipswich. Following studies at Ushaw College and Durham University, he made his solemn profession in 1985 and was ordained priest the following year. Doctoral studies at Oxford University and at the *Centro Internacional Teresiano Sanjuanista*, Ávila, Spain, brought together St John of the Cross and contemporary questions in Christology. He has since worked in parish, retreat, and formation ministry, and spent some years with the Carmelites in Venezuela. He currently teaches at the *Teresianum Pontificio Istituto di Spiritualità*, Rome. He has written variously on the theology and spirituality of members of the Carmelite Order.

Patrick Mullins O.Carm. S.T.D., Ph.D., is the Director of Studies of the Carmelite Institute of Britain and Ireland. Specializing in the origins and spirituality of the Carmelite Order, his most recent publication is *The Life of St Albert of Jerusalem: A Documentary Biography*, a study in two parts published by Edizioni Carmelitane.

Terence O'Reilly is Professor Emeritus in the Department of Spanish, Portuguese and Latin American Studies, University College Cork. His principal field of research is sixteenth- and seventeenth-century Spain, especially the history and the influence on literature and art of its religious thought. He has written extensively on spirituality in late medieval and Golden Age Spain.

Hilary Pearson has an Oxford DPhil in Medieval History, with a thesis on the writings of Teresa de Cartagena. Her current research interests are the theology in the writings of Teresa of Ávila and Teresa de Cartagena. She is also working on the life of Lady Annora de Briouze, a thirteenth-century anchoress at Iffley church in Oxford, and her sister Loretta, Countess of Leicester, who was an anchoress outside Canterbury.

Christopher J. Pountain is Emeritus Professor of Spanish Linguistics in the Department of Spanish and Latin American Studies at Queen Mary University of London. His current research interests are register in the history of Spanish, learned syntactic borrowing in the Romance languages, and the role of pragmatic factors in syntactic change.

Jeremy Roe is a Fundação para a Ciência e a Tecnologia Post-doctoral Research Fellow at the Centro de História d'Aquém e d'Além-Mar. His current research explores the representation and projection of political identity in the seventeenth-century visual culture of Portugal and its empire. He has previously worked on the paintings of Velázquez; the treatises on painting by Vicente Carducho and Francisco Pacheco; and the library of the Count-Duke of Olivares. In addition to publishing a number of articles on these subjects, he has co-edited three volumes of essays: *On Art and Painting: Vicente Carducho and Baroque Spain*, *Poder y saber. Bibliotecas y bibliofilia en la época del Conde-Duque de Olivares*, and *Imagery, Spirituality, and*

Ideology in Iberia and Latin America. His co-translation *Francisco Pacheco, On Christian Iconography: Selections from The Art of Painting (1649)* will be published later this year by St Joseph's University Press.

Colin P. Thompson is an Emeritus Fellow of St Catherine's College. He is a specialist in the literature and broader artistic culture of Golden Age Spain and has written articles on a number of its principal writers. He is the author of two books on St John of the Cross and another on Fray Luis de León. He has also been an ordained minister of the United Reformed Church for more than forty years.

Lesley Twomey is Professor in Iberian Art and Literature at the University of Northumbria. She has published on female religious writers, as well as on material culture, particularly textiles and fabrics. Her publications present extensive texts in translation from Latin, French, Catalan and Castilian. She has written on Marian literature in the Peninsula, most recently *The Fabric of Marian Devotion in Isabel de Villena's Vita Christi* and *The Serpent and The Rose: The Immaculate Conception and Hispanic Poetry in Late Medieval Spain*. She has a collection of essays *Christ, Mary and the Saints: Reading Religious Subjects in Medieval and Renaissance Spain* (Brill, forthcoming, co-edited with Andrew Beresford). Her monograph *The Sacred Space of the Virgin Mary in Spanish Literature from Gonzalo de Berceo to Ambrosio Montesino* is in press with Tamesis.

Peter Tyler is Professor of Pastoral Theology and Spirituality at St Mary's University, Twickenham. He is also a spiritual director and registered psychotherapist. His recent publications include *The Pursuit of the Soul: Psychoanalysis, Soul-Making and the Christian Tradition, Teresa of Avila: Doctor of the Soul* and *The Return to the Mystical: Ludwig Wittgenstein, Teresa of Avila, and the Christian Mystical Tradition*. He has contributed much to the on-going debate between psychology and spirituality and is co-editor of *Vinayasadhana*, a new journal for psycho-spiritual formation.

Rowan Williams took up the mastership of Magdalene College, Cambridge, on 1 January 2013. He has published studies of Arius, Teresa of Ávila, and Sergii Bulgakov, together with writings on a wide range of theological, historical and political themes.

INTRODUCTION

Colin P. Thompson

Teresa of Ávila occupies a commanding place in the history of sixteenth-century Spanish literature and spirituality. More than that, she is a central figure in the Western mystical tradition, and in 1970 became the first woman to be proclaimed a Doctor of the Roman Catholic Church. This collection of essays offers the latest thinking on a wide range of approaches to her life and work, from the historical to the theological and the artistic to the literary, as it seeks to re-evaluate her mystical experience and teaching, both in the sense of a critical rereading of her own life and times and of her specific contribution to a theology of the contemplative calling in our own age. If it seems quixotic even to set out on such a quest in a secular age which all too often dismisses religion as a childish fantasy, we might remember that Teresa herself was not without quixotic side. In the first chapter of *The Book of her Life* [Libro de la vida], she recounts how as a child she was inspired by reading heroic tales of the martyrdom of saints, and left home one day with a younger brother to seek to emulate them in Moorish lands. Later tradition has it that an uncle found them on the road out of Ávila and brought them safely back. George Eliot recalled the episode in a preliminary note to her great novel *Middlemarch* (1872) as emblematic of the way a woman's great idea is crushed by domestic reality, as it would be for her heroine Dorothea Brooke.[1] Today Teresa is perhaps best known for her insistence that God is to be found as much among the pots and pans of the kitchen as anywhere else (*Fundaciones* 5.8) or for the little poem which has come to be known as her bookmark, 'Let nothing worry you' [Nada te turbe], though doubt has been recently cast on its authenticity.[2] There is also a much-quoted prayer attributed to her, 'Christ has no hands on earth but your hands', which one looks for in vain in her published works. But there is so much more to her than that, as this book seeks to demonstrate.

Like her first editor, the Augustinian Fray Luis de León (1527–1591), himself one of the great poets and prose writers of the age, we can only know her through what she left behind. He began his dedication to the first edition of her works, which he had been entrusted with preparing, with these moving words: 'I neither knew nor saw Mother Teresa of Jesus while she was on earth; but now that she is in heaven I know and see her almost always in two living images which she left us of herself, that is, her daughters and her books' [Yo no conocí ni vi a la Madre Teresa mientras estuvo en la tierra; mas agora que vive en el cielo la conozco y veo casi siempre en dos imágenes vivas que nos dejó de sí, que son sus hijas y sus libros].[3] His edition was published just six years after her death. The fact that her writing includes substantial teaching on prayer makes this the more remarkable, given that the Pauline injunction against women speaking in church (1 Cor. 14.34) had for centuries been taken to mean that women were excluded from any form of teaching ministry in the Church.

Even in her thwarted childhood adventure two of the qualities which mark Teresa's adult life — the power of an imagination stimulated by reading, together with the firmness of her resolve — were evident. Much later on, she herself would describe with refreshing candour in her *Book of Foundations* the obstacles both physical and institutional which constantly threatened her own great idea, as she travelled through Spain founding convents of her reformed Carmelite observance. She would have been astonished (and probably quite pleased) that her writings are better and more widely known now than they ever were, and that her understanding of the spiritual life has become the bedrock of the faith and practice not only of the communities she founded but of many religious traditions and individual searchers — even among those Christians she invariably refers to with a mixture of horror and concern as misguided 'luteranos'.

Teresa was born into a prosperous and well-connected family, unlike her younger contemporary and fellow-reformer John of the Cross, whose early life was marked by extreme poverty. She was given the kind of education considered appropriate for a girl of her background and grew up surrounded by books. One of the first things she tells us in her *Life* is that her father was a great reader of 'good books' (*Vida* 1.1) [buenos libros], some of which were in Spanish 'so that his children could read them' [para que leyesen sus hijos éstos]. Her mother, who died when Teresa was thirteen, also loved reading, but her preference was for the first popular fiction of the age of printing, the chivalric romance. Though Teresa's early reading of saints' lives had led to her childhood adventure, she soon adopted her mother's tastes and took up these tales of knights and damsels, enchanted castles and monsters, to such an extent that she spent 'many hours of the day and the night in so pointless an exercise' (*Vida* 2.1) [muchas horas de el día y de la noche en tan vano ejercicio]. Later, however, books of a very different kind came to play a significant part in her development, as she found in contemporary works on prayer and translations of some of the Fathers' teaching which clarified her doubts and confusions and encouraged her to persevere.

This early familiarity with books stood her in good stead when she came to write her own. The first of her works was her *Life*, completed in 1562 at the command of one of her confessors, and takes the form of a spiritual autobiography modelled in many ways on Augustine's *Confessions*, a work which had left a deep impression on her when she read it in translation (*Vida* 9.7). In it she gives an account of her young life, her profession as a Carmelite nun, the illnesses and crises through which she passed, the deepening of her prayer life, accompanied by visions and revelations of various kinds and by a growing call to begin a reform of her Order, which would in due course lead to the foundation of the first house of the Discalced Carmelites, San José, in Ávila.[4] She began her *Way of Perfection* at the end of that same year, as a guide on prayer and community life addressed to the sisters of her Reform. The first version of her *Meditations on the Song of Songs* was written in 1566 and a second followed in 1574. This short work is unusual for being a commentary on a biblical book in Latin, a language she did not know, and at a time when translations of such into the vernacular were strictly prohibited. She would, however, have gained some knowledge of it from its use in the Divine Office and from explanations of particular verses given in sermons and devotional literature. Her account of the founding of the seventeen Discalced convents, the *Book of Foundations*, was begun in 1573 and she continued adding chapters until not long before her death. Her last work, the *Mansions of the Interior Castle*, her most mature treatise on the different stages of prayer, was completed in 1577. In addition to these major works, she wrote a number of religious poems in popular metres and several shorter prose works, and carried on an extensive correspondence with a wide range of people, from her own family members and fellow-religious to King Philip II himself. All her writing had to be squeezed into whatever time she could spare from the demands of her travels and other activities, which ranged from fund-raising and acquiring property for her new foundations to participating in the often convoluted internal politics of the Carmelite Order and in delicate negotiations with external bodies in order to achieve her ends. For a saint who devoted herself to the life of contemplation, she was a very busy woman. Not everyone admired her: Filippo Sega, the papal nuncio to Spain from 1577–81, famously described her as a 'restless and obstinate gadabout, who, under the guise of devotion, spreads evil teachings' [fémina inquieta y andariega, desobediente y contumaz que, bajo el color de la devoción, inventa malas doctrinas].[5] He could hardly have been more wrong.

What's a saint? In John Henry Newman's poem 'The Dream of Gerontius', set to music so memorably by Sir Edward Elgar, the chorus of demons shouts derisively 'a bundle of bones which fools adore when life is o'er'. The cult of relics was very much alive in sixteenth-century Spain and well beyond: General Franco famously always travelled with a relic of her right arm. Teresa herself was not immune to it after her death. But that view of sanctity is far removed from the life and work of Teresa. There is a wealth of material available to us from the years following her death in 1582, both from the documents associated with her beatification and canonization, and in three early biographies of her, from the last decade of the sixteenth century and the first of the seventeenth. All include impressions of Teresa by those who had known her and worked alongside her, and together they provide the beginnings of an answer to the question, at least for those who had known her.

The first of her biographers was the Jesuit Francisco de Ribera (1537–1591), who had been one of her confessors. His book, published in 1590, only two years after the first edition of her works, predates the investigations which would lead to her eventual beatification and canonization in 1614 and 1622 respectively.[6] It provides an account of her life and her virtues, before turning to examine the miracles which began to take place after her death. It is quite clear that Ribera is already writing in order to argue for the sanctity of one he often refers to as 'our holy mother Teresa' [nuestra santa Madre Teresa]. It begins with a Spanish translation of the Papal Bull issued by Sixtus V just before the book went to print, confirming the Constitutions which Teresa had written for the Discalced sisters. This document, Ribera states, also confirms much of what he has written, and, he continues, it will be of particular interest to the followers of Teresa to learn what the Holy See feels about her. One thing about his book is different from its successors: he prefaces his account of her life with a long study of the place of visions and revelations in Christian history, to argue that Teresa belongs to a venerable tradition, experienced in the lives of many saints, both male and female. It may be that so soon after her death there were still questions being asked about Teresa's extensive treatment of these phenomena in her own *Life*, and that Ribera is anxious to demonstrate that they were the marks of some of the greatest saints venerated by the Church.

In Teresa's case, the discovery in 1585, three years after her death, that her body was uncorrupted and sweet-smelling added impetus to a cult which was already beginning to grow up around her. It seems macabre to modern sensibilities, but when her tomb was opened, cloths applied to the corpse and impregnated with its secretions were subsequently credited with many miraculous cures. Once an individual began to acquire a reputation for sanctity and miracle-working, the Church invoked procedures to test these claims. These had recently been reformed by Pope Sixtus V, with the creation of the Sacred Congregation of Rites in 1588, one of the responsibilities of which was to oversee the making of saints. The year after Ribera's book was published the formal investigations began, in accordance with the revised requirements.[7] They come in distinct groups: two information-gathering enquiries [*procesos informativos*] in 1591–92 and 1595–96, that is, while many of the people who knew Teresa well were still alive, and two more formal submissions (*procesos remisoriales* 'in genere' and 'in specie'), of 1604 and 1610, which gathered testimonies more clearly aimed at establishing whether or not she was already being regarded as a saint.[8] The second of these consisted of no fewer than 117 questions, though witnesses were only required to answer those they could. These documents were then remitted to Rome for consideration.

Dozens of witnesses testified during these first hearings, conducted in many Spanish towns and cities. Many report the miracle of Teresa's bodily incorruption and its sweet odour, and their accounts contain many miracles attributed to her both while she was alive and after her death, in the latter case usually through the application of cloths which had been in contact with her corpse to particular individuals. These range from near-death experiences, when doctors had given up all hope of recovery, to a fish-bone stuck in a nun's throat, which was dislodged when one of these cloths had been placed on the affected area. But among the accounts of miracles witnessed or experienced there are also more human details, nowhere more so than in the deposition of Ana de Jesús Lobera (1545–1621), who professed in San José, Ávila in 1571, and was the constant companion and favourite daughter of Teresa during the remaining eleven years of the saint's life. It was to Ana that John of the Cross dedicated his commentary on the 'Spiritual Canticle' poem, and she herself was to take the Carmelite Reform into France and the Low Countries.[9] In her deposition in Salamanca in 1595 she tells us that she saw Teresa writing on many occasions, and that it was she who gathered up the originals of her manuscripts from a number of different places to hand them over to the Augustinian Fray Luis de León, who had been entrusted with their publication.[10] She explains that the *Foundations* was omitted from the first edition of 1588 because Fray Luis was too encumbered with other duties to have sufficient time to edit it. That these initial enquiries in 1591 had eventual canonization in view is evident from her record of how the opening of Teresa's coffin came to the King's notice and began the whole process, and of how the Grand Prior of the Order of St John of Jerusalem, don Fernando de Toledo (1527–1591), had left 14,000 ducats in his will to support it.[11]

Ana tells a number of stories which add real warmth and humanity to the picture of Teresa. After meeting her, the Abbess of the Discalced Franciscans in Pastrana, where Teresa made her one foundation which did not survive, exclaimed: 'Blessed be God, because he has let us see a saint whom we can all imitate; who eats, sleeps, and speaks like us, and goes around without any fuss' [Bendito sea Dios, que nos ha dejado ver una Santa a quien todas podamos imitar, que come, duerme, y habla como nosotras, y anda sin ceremonias].[12] She tells us that it was wonderful to hear Teresa singing the Prologue to St John at matins on Christmas night, 'since she did not naturally have a good voice' [no teniendo ella naturalmente buena voz].[13] Another story adds an element of the miraculous as it gives us a delightful glimpse into early Discalced domestic life. The first sisters were very worried about wearing the coarse woollen habit which Teresa had prescribed, because they feared it would become a breeding-ground for fleas. Teresa prayed that they would be spared this discomfort, and since then, Ana adds, no flea has ever been found, despite there now being more than six hundred sisters.[14]

It is her second biographer, Diego de Yepes (1529–1613), who adds two other details.[15] He states that the crystal castle which Teresa imagined for her picture of the soul in the *Interior Castle* came to her in a vision, when she was trying to imagine the beauty of a soul in grace.[16] In her own account Teresa is much less informative; she simply says 'it came to me' (*Moradas* 1.1) [se me ofreció]. The other detail is less flattering, but serves to show that saints were not expected to exhibit physical perfection. Her teeth, he tells us, were worn down and black, yet her breath was sweet as musk. He suspected she must be using perfume, but when he put this to her she laughed it off and said she hated it, because it gave her a headache.[17] Yepes sets forth at length the case for Teresa's canonization, referring to her quite openly and frequently as a saint. The first of the four books tells the story of her life, with direct quotations from Teresa's own account but also much commentary on the saintly qualities which characterized it. The second is the story of her foundations, the third an account of her heroic virtues and supernatural gifts, and the fourth of the miracles she worked in life and after her death. It is these last two books which constitute the basis of the case for canonization, although like several other deponents in the *procesos* he is at pains to argue that the growth of the Discalced Order from such small beginnings, and with so many hardships and obstacles in the way, to so many houses living so perfect a monastic life in so short a period of time is itself nothing less than a miracle.

In his prologue, addressed to Pope Paul V, Yepes states that he is under an obligation to provide His Holiness with an accurate account 'of such incredible perfection and sanctity' [tan increíble perfección y santidad] and of this 'rarest prodigy of holiness' [prodigio de santidad raríssimo]. He stresses her supernatural gifts, her ability to discern spirits and the divine grace which enabled her to perform miracles after her death, all qualities which strongly argue for sanctity. In addition to her foundations, he notes the marvellous fact that 'a woman who according to the common condition of such is excluded from being a teacher to others has been made by the particular grace and inspiration of heaven the master of many, with the Holy Spirit moving her pen [...] so that she wrote books full of heavenly doctrine' [que una mujer a quien la común condición de su estado excluye de ser enseñadora de otros, la particular gracia y aliento del cielo hiciese maestra de muchos, moviendo el Espíritu Santo su pluma (...) escribiese libros llenos de celestial doctrina].[18]

This is a striking confession. The prohibition against women exercising a teaching ministry in the Church also covered the discernment of spirits, likewise the preserve of the male priesthood. The conventional view was that women were particularly susceptible to being misled or deceived if they became involved in such matters. There were a number of cases in the sixteenth century in which nuns famed for their sanctity were exposed as frauds, like the Cordoban Poor Clare Magdalena de la Cruz, whose reputation reached the royal family but who confessed in 1543 that she had been in league with the devil all along. Teresa, like her confessors, would have known of such cases, which helps to explain their fears that she might herself be deluded or, worse still, a victim of demonic deception.[19] This prologue is followed by an account of those learned and holy persons who approved her spirit in life, as well as others renowned for their holiness, all (of course) male priests and religious, further to bolster the case. Only then does Yepes begin his story. Three years later the Discalced Carmelite Juan de Jesús María (1564–1615) produced a Latin account of the life of the saint, his *Compendium vitae beatae Virginis Teresiae*, a work similar to that of Yepes, but in five books, and even more clearly aimed at building up the case for canonization, since it was written in the official language of the Church and therefore more widely available to interested parties who knew no Spanish.[20]

All these witnesses emphasized the miraculous and supernatural elements of Teresa in life and after death because without them there could be no real hope of success in the campaign to make her a saint. The first serious attempt at a critical appraisal of hagiographical writings began later in the seventeenth century through the work of a group of scholars, originally all Jesuits, who have come to be known as the Bollandists, from Jean Bolland (1596–1665), and who continue to this day. It is to them that we owe a more rigorous approach to the lives of saints, which sought to dispense with anything which was legendary or unverified by appropriate evidence. Their fiercest early battle, interestingly, was with the Spanish Carmelites. The Bollandist Daniel van Papenbroeck (1628–1714) published a volume in which he criticized the Carmelite tradition that the Order had been founded by Elijah and Elisha because it was insufficiently grounded in historical evidence. Between

1681 and 1693 some twenty to thirty pamphlets by Carmelites directed abuse at him and culminated in a large volume in the name of Sebastian of St Paul, Provincial of the Flemish-Belgian Province of the Order, which brought together all the errors of which they believed Papenbroeck guilty. They appealed first to Rome, which took a cautious view, and then to the Spanish Inquisition, which did not. In 1695, it condemned not just the offending volume but all fourteen volumes of the Bollandists' *Acta Sanctorum* published up to that point. Rome continued to prevaricate, but it was not until 1715, by which time Papenbroeck was dead, that the Inquisitorial decree was revoked.[21] The whole affair is an early object lesson in the clash between the zealous guardians of a tradition which was not to be questioned and those who believed that all claims should be subject to a full examination of the available facts.

The Teresa whom we encounter in her books, however, is less the miracle-worker of the hagiographers than a very human, sometimes flawed figure who, despite all the barriers placed in her way, reached a level of wisdom in things of the spirit attained by very few others, male or female. She understands human frailties and temptations, and confronts them with grace and good humour, mostly because she has experienced them herself. If we are tempted to explain away her supernatural visions and revelations as the products of a less enlightened age, we would do well to remember that many of her early advisers had serious doubts about their veracity. In any case, it is easy to warm to the painful honesty of her self-analysis, the difficulties her gender caused her as a teacher of prayer, and the sheer common sense which pervades so much of what she writes about prayer and growth in the spiritual life.

These aspects of her writing, and many others besides, will be explored in greater depth in the essays in this volume. But Teresa should also be allowed a word of her own introduction. Her *Way of Perfection*, written for the small band of sisters of the first Discalced House at the very beginnings of the Carmelite Reform, is less well known than her *Life* or her *Interior Castle* but it contains many glimpses of a spiritual wisdom which shapes her writing and transcends the context in which it was written. She insists, for example, that the life of prayer is to be incarnational, that is, that it must bear fruit, thereby offering a fresh perspective on the polemic between Catholics and Protestants in her own time on the relationship between faith and works. She argues strongly for the contribution of women to the life of the Church, against their detractors, and she sees humility and love as the necessary foundation for life in community.

Prayer, she says, should feed active Christian service, even when, as at San José, the sisters live an enclosed life. Women may not be permitted to preach in the formal sense yet 'you must all try to be preachers through works' (23.1) [todas havéis de procurar de ser predicadoras de obras]. For her, the practice of a spiritual life is not an escape from the world in order to retreat into a peaceful space where cares and anxieties fade away. It is a journey into the self which confronts the illusions and deceptions which comfort us and which, when touched by the grace of God, lifts the soul above them and remakes it according to the image of God. The key to a life of prayer for Teresa is meditation, usually on the Passion of Christ, which she describes as 'the starting-point for acquiring all the virtues and something which gives life to all us Christians as soon as we begin it, and no one [...] is to abandon it' (24.3) [principio para alcanzar todas las virtudes, y cosa que nos da vida en comenzarla todos los cristianos, y ninguno (...) lo havía de dejar]. She freely confesses her own failures in this respect: 'I spent fourteen years of never being able to meditate except when reading' (27.3) [Yo estuve catorce que nunca podía tener meditación sino junto con leer]. This is what she means by mental prayer; but from her own experience she knows that some of her sisters will be as unable to practise it as she was: 'so, sisters, mental prayer, and if you can't do that, vocal prayer, readings and colloquies [conversations] with God [...]. And if humility is genuine, blessed such a servant in the active life who does not complain except about herself' (29.2–3) [Ansí que, hermanas, oración mental, y quien no pudiere, vocal y lección y coloquios con Dios (...). Y si es de veras la humildad, bienaventurada tal sierva de vida activa que no mormura sino de sí.]

She can be bold in some of her assertions about the role of women in the Church. Some churchmen argued strongly that nuns should not practise any form of mental or imaginative prayer or meditation, because their imaginations were so prone to being led astray.[22] In a passage well known to scholars because the early censors of her work crossed out the words after 'tanto amor' in thick black ink, Teresa challenges such attitudes with her characteristic blend of self-depreciation and courage:

> Lord of my soul, when you walked abroad in the world, you always particularly favoured women with great mercy and found in them as much love and more faith than in men [...] for you are a just judge and not like the judges of this world, who, because they are sons of Adam and all of them in the end are men, there is no virtue in woman which they do not find suspicious (...). I do not say this for myself, since the world already knows my sinfulness and I rejoice in its being made public; but because I see our times in such a way that it is not right to reject strong and virtuous souls, even if they belong to women. (4.1)

> [Señor de mi alma, cuando andávades por el mundo, las mujeres antes las favorecistes siempre con mucha piadad y hallastes en ellas tanto amor y más fe que en los onbres (...) que sois justo juez y no como los jueçes deste mundo, que como son yjos de Adán, y, en fin, todos varones, no ay virtud de mujer que no tengan por sospechosa (...). No hablo por mí, que ya tiene conoçido el mundo mi rruyndad y yo olgada de que sea pública; sino porque veo los tiempos de manera que no es razón desechar ánimos virtuosos y fuertes, aunque sean de mujeres.]

Writing a little later of the tendency of sisters to address each other in overly affectionate terms, she says: 'It's very much a woman thing, and I wouldn't want my sisters to resemble anything but strong men, for if they do what is in their power, the Lord will make them so manly that they will make men afraid' (11.8) [Es muy de mujeres, y no querría yo mis hermanas pareciesen en nada sino varones fuertes, que si ellas hacen lo que es en sí, el Señor las hará tan varoniles que espanten a los hombres].

She offers her sisters three guiding principles for their life in community: 'the first is love for one another; the second, detachment from every created thing; the third, true humility, which, even though I put it last, is the main one and includes them all' (6.1) [la una es amor unas con otras; otra, desasimiento de todo lo criado; otra, verdadera humildad, que, aunque la digo a la postre, es la principal y las abraza todas]. Lack of humility is a destructive force in a small community. It manifests itself in many ways, but concern for one's own status is especially damaging: 'May God deliver us, by his Passion, from saying "I'm senior", "I'm older", "I've worked harder", "the other sister is being treated better than me". It's necessary to curb these instinctive reactions quickly, because if they're dwelt on or talked about, they're a plague, and become the source of great evils in convents' (18.4) [Dios nos libre, por su Pasión, en decir «Si soy más antigua», «si he más años», «si he travajado más», «si tratan a la otra mijor». Estos primeros movimientos es menester atajarlos con presteza; que si se detienen en ellos, u lo ponen en plática, es pestilencia y de donde nacen grandes males en los monasterios].

Because these things are difficult, perseverance is required. To find the living water of Christ she counsels

> a great and resolute determination not to stop until you reach it [the living water], come what may, pass what will, whatever the hardships, whatever the gossip, whether I get there or not, whether I die on the way or have not the stomach to face its hardships, whether the world collapses; as often happens when people say 'it's dangerous', 'such-and-such a woman went astray here', 'this man was deceived', 'that man who prayed fell', 'they harm virtue', 'it's not for women, they suffer from delusions', 'better that they sew', 'they don't need these fancy things', 'the Our Father and the Ave Maria are enough'. (35.2)
>
> [una grande y muy determinada determinación de no parar hasta llegar a ella (el agua), venga lo que viniere, suceda lo que sucediere, travaje lo que se travajare, mormure quien mormurare, siquiera llegue allá, siquiera me muera en el camino uno tenga corazón para los travajos que hay en él, siquiera se hunda el mundo; como muchas veces acaece con decir: «hay peligros», «hulana por aquí se perdió», «el otro se engañó», «el otro que rezava cayó», «dañan la virtud», «no es para mujeres, que les vienen ilusiones», «mijor será que hilen», «no han menester estas delicadeces», «basta el Paternóster y Avemaría».]

Here again she confronts head-on those churchmen who insisted that women should stick to saying out aloud the prayers the Church prescribed and nothing else. Indeed, the closing chapters of the *Way* are a subtle critique of that conventional view, no doubt rooted in her own earlier experience of being discouraged from this path, since they outline a meditative way in which to pray the most fundamental of all vocal prayers, the Lord's Prayer. She does not mince her words: 'whoever tells you that this is dangerous, consider him to be the real danger, and flee from him' (36.3) [Quien os dijere que éste es peligro, tenedle a él por el mesmo peligro y huid dél]. She confesses that 'I want to cry out and argue — being the person I am — with those who say that mental prayer is not necessary' (37.2) [querría dar voces y disputar — con ser la que soy — con los que dicen que no es menester oración mental].

Less controversially, she provides much guidance about recollection, the process of withdrawing into oneself in order to listen for the word of God in quiet. Recollection is a process which the soul needs to master, whereas true contemplation is a gift from God and requires only to be received: 'She understands without any words sounding that her master is at work in her soul and that her faculties are not working, as far as she can tell. This is perfect contemplation' (41.2) [Entiende que sin ruido de palabras obra en su alma su maestro y que no obran las potencias de ella, que ella entienda. Esto es contemplación perfecta]. But not everyone is called to this state; not even all the sisters of the Carmelite Reform. Confessing again that 'I spent many years struggling with being unable to focus my thought on any particular thing' (42.2) [pasé muchos años por este travajo de no poder sosegar el pensamiento en una cosa], she encourages the sisters to practise one of her own favourite meditations, on Christ tied to the column to be scourged before the Crucifixion, a scene memorably represented by Velázquez in a painting known as 'Christ contemplated by the Christian soul' [Cristo contemplado por el alma cristiana]. 'Imagine the Lord by your side and see with what love and humility he is teaching you' (42.1) [Representad al Señor junto con vos y mirad con qué amor y humildad os está enseñando], she says, and continues:

> look at him tied to the column full of pain, all his flesh torn to pieces because of his great love for you, persecuted by some, spat on by others, denied by others, friendless, with no one to turn back for him, frozen with cold, in such solitude that you may be consoled by each and every scene; or look at him in the garden, or on the cross, or carrying it [...]; he will look upon you with his beautiful, merciful eyes, full of tears, and will forget his sufferings in order to console you in yours, simply because you have gone to him for consolation and turned your head to look at him. (42.5)

> [miralde en la coluna lleno de dolores, todas sus carnes hechas pedazos por lo mucho que os ama, perseguido de unos, escupido de otros, negado de otros, sin amigos, sin nadie que vuelva por El, helado de frío, puesto en tanta soledad que uno con otro os podéis consolar; u miralde en el huerto, u en la cruz, u cargado con ella (...); miraros ha él con unos ojos tan hermosos y piadosos, lleno de lágrimas, y olvidará sus dolores por consolar los vuestros, sólo porque os vais vos con El a consolar y volváis la cabeza a mirarle.]

Above all, she writes of love, as she tells her sisters:

> Whosoever truly loves God, loves all that is good, desires all that is good, favours all that is good, praises all that is good, keeps company with the good and always defends them; embraces every virtue, and loves only truths and whatever is worthy of love. Do you think that anyone who truly loves God can love vanities? She cannot; neither riches, nor worldly things, nor honour; she does not engage in disputes, does not walk with envy; all because her sole aim is to content the Beloved. He goes the way of death in order to love her and so she disposes her life to understand how she may please him more. (69.3)

> [Quien de veras ama a Dios, todo lo bueno ama, todo lo bueno quiere, todo lo bueno favorece, todo lo bueno loa, con los buenos se junta, siempre los defiende, todas las virtudes abraza; no ama sino verdades y cosa que sea digna de amar. ¿Pensáis que quien muy de veras ama a Dios que ama vanidades? Ni puede, ni riquezas, ni cosas del mundo, ni honras, ni tiene contiendas, ni anda con envidias. Todo porque no pretende otra cosa sino contentar a el Amado.

Anda muriendo porque la quiera, y ansí pone la vida en entender cómo le agradará más.]

These glimpses from the *Way* highlight aspects of Teresa's teaching which are pertinent in any age: a spiritual life which is to be expressed in practical ways and belongs to women as well as men; a life of prayer which is gift but also requires perseverance and above all humility; an emphasis on persistence in love, even when it is difficult. None of this could have been written without the struggles she chronicled with such searing honesty in her *Life*, as a woman who was told that her experiences in prayer and visions were demonic. Through them, and with the help of more discerning counsellors, she defied all the odds and herself became the teacher of men. Just as significantly, she emerged from those early trials and tribulations with a vision of a different kind, a call to action the consequences of which she chronicled in her *Book of Foundations* with not a little political acumen in the face of resistance and prevarication on the part of both civil and ecclesiastical authorities.

This book began as a conversation between two of its eventual editors in 2013, as they wondered how it might be appropriate to celebrate the quincentenary of the birth of Teresa of Ávila. That conversation led to a conference in Oxford at the end of March 2015, under the title 'Teresa of Ávila: Writer, Mystic, Saint'. Almost all the papers delivered then form chapters of this book, together with two others originally given as papers at the annual conference of the Association of Hispanists of Great Britain and Ireland in Exeter a few days later. The Oxford conference ended on a high note, with a public concert given in the Chapel of the Queen's College, Oxford, by Contrapunctus, under the direction of Professor Owen Rees, whose own research has been devoted to the early modern period of music in the Iberian Peninsula. The concert, *Songs of Divine Love*, added a valuable musical dimension to the interdisciplinary nature of the conference. The choir performed settings of texts from the Song of Solomon by Iberian composers of the period: Tomás Luis de Victoria (*c.* 1548–1611), Rodrigo de Ceballos (*c.* 1525–1581), Francisco Guerrero (1527/28–1599), and Sebastián de Vivanco (*c.* 1551–1622). These were interspersed with short readings in English from Teresa's works which related to the text in question.

Support for both the conference and collection of essays has been valuable in enabling this volume to be published. The editors hope that this collection of essays may contribute to further conversation about the extraordinary woman who came into this world half a millennium ago and who is still speaking to us across the centuries through her books.

Notes to the Introduction

1. Eliot had almost certainly read Robert Alfred Vaughan, *Hours with the Mystics*, 2 vols (London: John W. Parker, 1856), which records the episode. Vaughan, a Congregationalist minister, brought a wide range of mystical literature to the attention of a Victorian readership through his anthology, which went through many editions.
2. See José Vicente Rodríguez, 'Nada de turbe, / nada te espante... (Parte I)', in *San Juan de la Cruz*, 30 (2013–14), pp. 323–31.

3. *Obras completas de Fray Luis de León*, ed. by Félix García, 4th edn, 2 vols (Madrid: Biblioteca de Autores Cristianos, 1967), I, 902.
4. The reformed Order came to be known as the Discalced or Barefoot Carmelites [Descalzas], not because they went unshod but because they wore no socks or stockings.
5. As quoted by Gillian Ahlgren, *Enkindling Love: The Legacy of Teresa of Ávila and John of the Cross* (Minneapolis, MN: Fortress Press, 2016), p. 131.
6. *Vida de la Madre Teresa de Jesús* (Salamanca: Pedro Lasso, 1590).
7. They are most easily available in *Procesos de beatificación y canonización de Santa Teresa de Jesús*, ed. by Silverio de Santa Teresa, 3 vols (Burgos: El Monte Carmelo, 1934–35), which I follow, or in a new critical edition, *Procesos de beatificación y canonización de la Madre Teresa de Jesús*, ed. by Julen Urkiza, 6 vols (Burgos: El Monte Carmelo, 2015–16).
8. On these *procesos*, see Gillian T. W. Ahlgren, *Teresa of Ávila and the Politics of Sanctity* (Ithaca, NY: Cornell University Press, 1996), pp. 148–56.
9. On Ana, see Anne Hardman, *Life of the Venerable Anne of Jesus* (London: Sands, 1932).
10. *Procesos*, I, 461–86.
11. *Procesos*, I, 483–84.
12. *Procesos*, I, 472.
13. *Procesos*, I, 474.
14. *Procesos*, I, 475
15. *Vida, virtudes y milagros de la bienaventurada virgen Teresa de Jesús* (Zaragoza: Angelo Tauanno, 1606). In fact this seems to have been the work of the Discalced Carmelite Tomás de Jesús Sánchez Dávila (1564–1627), but appeared under the more prestigious name of Yepes, the Jeronymite Bishop of Tarazona and confessor to Philip II; see *Vida, virtudes y milagros de la bienaventurada virgen Teresa de Jesús*, ed. by Manuel Diego Sánchez (Madrid: Editorial de Espiritualidad, 2015).
16. *Procesos*, I, 277.
17. *Procesos*, I, 286–87.
18. Yepes, *Vida, virtudes y milagros*, pp. 9–12; spelling modernized.
19. See, for example, Elena Carrera, *Teresa of Avila's Autobiography: Authority, Power and the Self in Mid-Sixteenth-Century Spain* (London: Legenda, 2005), especially pp. 106–10.
20. *Compendium vitae beatae Virginis Teresiae* (Rome: Stefano Paolini, 1609).
21. See, for example, 'The Bollandists', at <www.newadvent.org/cathen/02630a.htm> [accessed 6 January 2017].
22. Notable among these was the Dominican Juan de la Cruz (not to be confused with his Carmelite namesake), whose *Diálogo sobre la necessidad y provecho de la oración vocal* (Salamanca: Juan de Cánova, 1555) argued strongly for women to be restricted to vocal prayer; that is, those prayers prescribed by the Church to be recited aloud.

PART I

St Teresa and her Times

CHAPTER 1

St Teresa of Ávila and Earlier Carmelite Traditions

Patrick Mullins O.Carm.

Following the development of critical hagiography as a science during the seventeenth century, and especially after the controversies concerning the Bollandist dossier on St Albert of Jerusalem published in 1675, the claim that the Carmelites were part of an historical succession of monks founded by the Old Testament prophet Elijah gradually came to be universally acknowledged as false.[1] The earliest documented evidence of the Carmelites is now recognized as dating from the final decades of the twelfth century or the first years of the thirteenth, and the foundational document was the *Formula of Life* that Patriarch Albert of Jerusalem wrote for some Latin hermits on Mount Carmel, in about 1206–14. This *Formula of Life* united those hermits as brothers living a lay form of consecration under obedience to their chosen Prior. The Carmelites did not become a group of religious until Pope Innocent IV promulgated a modified version of that *Formula of Life* as the Carmelite Rule in 1247. Like the *Formula of Life*, the Rule allowed the Carmelites to own property collectively but not personally, and the modifications made to Albert's *Formula of Life* at that time implicitly permitted the Carmelites to adapt themselves to the style of pastoral ministry that was typical of the other groups of friars that had then emerged, such as the Franciscans and Dominicans.[2]

The Claim to an Elijan Succession

Perhaps the key impetus leading to the development of the Carmelite claim to an Elijan succession took place in the final decade of the fourteenth century, when the Carmelite Philip Ribot published his *Ten Books on the Way of Life and Great Deeds of the Carmelites*. Among the *Ten Books* was *The Book of the Institute of the First Monks* [Liber de institutione primorum monachorum], which Ribot attributed to John, the forty-fourth bishop of Jerusalem (387–417). During the seventeenth century, this work was widely recognized as falsely attributed, and it is now generally assumed that Ribot wrote it himself, or that it was written by one of his contemporary Carmelites.[3]

The *Institute of the First Monks* claims that the reason the group wanted to be known as Carmelites was 'that their Order, and holy association, is derived, and assumed, from those men who, in the said manner, sought, and now still seek, to imitate humbly the religious life of the prophet Elijah on Mount Carmel'.[4] Although Albert's *Formula of Life* used the terms 'hermits' and 'brothers' to describe the group for whom it was intended, and these terms are also found in the Carmelite Rule of 1247, the *Institute of the First Monks* presents them as 'monks' who modelled their way of life on the solitary lifestyle of Elijah. The poverty of Elijah and Elisha and of those who modelled themselves on their way of life, including the Palestinian anchorite St Hilarion, is highlighted in the quotation from Isidore of Seville's *On Church Offices* [De Ecclesiasticis Officiis] (2.16.1), quoted in Chapter Eight of Book Two:

> But from where has emerged this inclination of the monks to poverty, or who was the author of this way of life? Whose conduct are they imitating? In so far as it pertains to the authority of the scriptures of the ancients, the pioneers of this proposed manner of life were Elijah and his disciple Elisha, or the sons of the prophets who were living in solitude; abandoning the cities, they were making little huts for themselves beside the river Jordan. In the Gospel, also, the author of this proposed manner of life was John the Baptist, who lived alone in the desert, nourished only by locusts and wild honey. And finally, the first-born of this way of life are our most noble Princes, Paul, Anthony, Hilarion, Macarius, and the other fathers from whose example there has spread throughout the whole world the holy institution of the Monks.[5]

The fasting, abstinence, and mystical experience of those who followed the example of Elijah are highlighted in Chapter Eight of Book Three:

> The already mentioned monks, however, had been called 'anchorites' by many people because, strengthening their hearts by fasts, abstinences and other bodily difficulties, they were not afraid, as was said, in unceasing imitation of Elijah, to penetrate without ceasing into the extensive recesses of the solitude of Mount Carmel and of the other solitary places of the Promised Land. There, fortified by holy thoughts, with the intention of prayers, and fortified with the other arms of righteousness, they not only conquered the secret schemes of the devil, but trampled down the open attacks of the demons. So much did they strive in imitation of Elijah their leader to raise their minds upwards to the contemplation of God, that they were thought to have been translated into the heavenly choirs, and to be 'with unveiled face beholding the glory of God' (II Corinthians 3.18), enjoying converse with God to whom they clung with pure minds.[6]

The Book of the Institute of the First Monks makes up the first seven of Ribot's *Ten Books*, and the eighth book is an alleged *Letter of Cyril to Eusebius*, which is attributed to Cyril of Constantinople, the alleged third Prior on Mount Carmel (the first two being Berthold and Brocard). During the seventeenth century, this work was, again, widely recognized as falsely attributed, and it was shown to have been written after, rather than before, Albert's *Formula of Life* and the Carmelite Rule of 1247.[7] Contrary to those documents, and to the available historical evidence concerning the first hermitage that was constructed on Mount Carmel in the thirteenth century, Chapter 2 of the *Letter of Cyril* claims that, under the influence of Berthold and Brocard and with the approval of Patriarch Albert of Jerusalem, the form of solitary life that the followers of Elijah had adopted took the form of an enclosed monastic life during the late twelfth century:[8]

> [...] until the said Patriarch Aimeric first obliged them to this thing, at no time before that were they put under the obligation of needing to obey anyone particular, subject to a certain enclosure on Mount Carmel. Among whom there was his very brother, Brother Berthold, you may be sure, an excellent religious and a holy presbyter, whom, with the unanimous assent of all, he instituted as the first prior for them in 1121 AD, and to whom he enjoined the care of the souls of the others.[9] And on that Mount Carmel, in honour of the Blessed Virgin Mary, Mother of God, he had a monastery built, surrounded by a high circular wall, in which, indeed, he intended to enclose them; but before he might have completed that monastery, God took him up from the world. [...] At length, after some time passed, Brother Brocard, an excellent man, being unanimously placed in authority over them, they all promised obedience to him under whose rule they remained for thirty-three years. By whom, presiding over them, they pointed out to Albert, the Patriarch of Jerusalem, that the same ones had desired to live enclosed in a monastery, subject to the observance of the solitary Religious Life instituted by the Prophet Elijah, from the time in which the said Patriarch Aimeric had united them all under the care of one prior through the bond of obedience. Who, although being certain by means of their institution in what manner each one of them ought to live alone according to perfection and strive for the goal of the solitary life, because, nevertheless, they were proposing that they should be enclosed in a monastery on this Carmel, in which they had never been enclosed up to then, for this reason, before they might be enclosed in it, they were resolutely asking from the said Patriarch Albert that, according to their proposed manner of life, he hand down to them a short formula of life that they should keep from then onwards concerning certain articles that were necessary to monastic life then presented to him by them.[10]

Soon after Ribot's *Ten Books* appeared, the Carmelite Constitutions of 1399 established an annual feast in honour of Elisha on the fourteenth of June.[11] Because he was taken up into heaven alive (see II Kings 2.11), there was no date of death for Elijah, and the feast in honour of his successor, Elisha, may originally have been introduced as an indirect means of honouring Elijah.[12]

Teresa and the Alleged Succession from Elijah

After Teresa joined the monastery of the Incarnation in 1535, she was obliged to recite the Divine Office, and she continued to recite it throughout her Carmelite life, until her death in 1582.[13] During that period, the Carmelite liturgical calendar was not uniform throughout the Order, and it is difficult to determine whether or not the feasts celebrated by the Carmelites in one region are an accurate guide to practice elsewhere. Between 1535 and 1543, the breviary Teresa followed would probably have been the Carmelite Breviary of 1504, or something similar. Among the feasts of Carmelite saints included in the Carmelite martyrology at that time were St Peter Thomas (7 January), St Cyril of Constantinople (6 March), St Albert of Jerusalem (8 April), St Angelus of Sicily (5 May), St Elisha (14 June) and St

Albert of Trapani (7 August).[14] The Missal of 1509 celebrated St Hilarion as a Carmelite saint on 21 October.[15] Following the additions to the Carmelite Calendar of Saints introduced by means of the Carmelite Breviary of 1543, St Euphrasia of Constantinople (c. 380–c. 410) was celebrated as a Carmelite saint on 13 March.[16] In the period from 1564 to St Teresa's death in 1582, St Cyril of Alexandria (378–444), St Anastasius [Magundat] of Persia (d. 628), St Berthold, St Brocard, and even the Benedictine, St Gerard Sagredo (c. 980–1046), were celebrated as Carmelite saints (on 23 and 28 January, 29 March, and 3 and 24 September, respectively).[17] St Euphrosyne was also celebrated as a Carmelite on 11 February in the period from 1575 until Teresa's death in 1582.[18] Critical hagiography now recognizes that none of these last seven individuals was ever, as such, a Carmelite, and there is no contemporary historical collaboration of even the existence of the individuals whose fictitious biographies became part of the false tradition of an Elijan succession and who were alleged to have been the first three priors on Mount Carmel, namely St Berthold, St Brocard, and St Cyril of Constantinople.

Teresa mentions some of the individuals just listed. We know that one of the nuns in the monastery that Teresa founded at Malagón was Catalina de San Cirilo,[19] and that one of the Discalced Carmelite friars at the monastery of Manzera during her lifetime was called Nicolás de San Cirilo.[20] Since the Carmelite College at Alcalá de Henares, approved by the Chapter held at Ávila in 1567,[21] was named in honour of St Cyril of Constantinople, whose feast day was celebrated on 6 March,[22] it would seem that the Cyril in question was St Cyril of Constantinople, the alleged third Prior of Mount Carmel. In a letter dated 19 November 1576 and sent to Jerónimo Gracián, Teresa uses the code name 'Cyril' [Cirilo] to refer to him, perhaps to indicate his suitability as a future leader or prior of the Discalced friars.[23] In a letter dated 7 May 1578, Teresa refers to 'the vigil or feast of Saint Angelus' of Sicily, OCarm.[24] In her *Constitutions* (1567–68) and in a letter dated 22 July 1579,[25] Teresa refers to 'our Father St. Albert', and, since she also mentions the feast day of St Albert on 7 August during 1580 and 1581, it seems clear that she was thinking of St Albert of Trapani, OCarm, rather than St Albert of Jerusalem.[26] Teresa's devotion to St Albert of Trapani was well known, and, in a letter dated July 1579, she refers to a book on 'the life and miracles of St Albert' that was eventually published in 1582. The book was dedicated to her in recognition of her devotion to St Albert of Trapani.[27] The feast of St Elisha on 14 June is found in a number of other Carmelite liturgical calendars in the period 1462–1509,[28] and it may have been celebrated in the monastery of the Incarnation during Teresa's early years there. Since this feast became more widely accepted after 1543, however, it is more likely to have been celebrated there after that date.[29] The indirect link between this feast and the Carmelite claim to an Elijan succession can be seen in the second verse of the hymn for the office of St Elisha, which reads: '[He is] of the first Prophets of the Carmelites, whom the great Elijah of Tishbe instituted at the command of the divine will'.[30] We do not know if St Teresa would have had a translation of this Latin hymn available to her, but she notes that the first Mass in her new foundation at Soria was said 'on the day of our father, St Elisha' [día de nuestro padre san Eliseo] (14 June 1581).[31] There is no feast of St Elijah in the 1543 Breviary,[32] or in the

Calendar of Carmelite Saints issued by the General Chapter of 1564,[33] but there are votive Masses for Elijah in the Carmelite Missals of 1551 and 1574.[34] In those places where the feast of Elijah was celebrated in the period between 1551 and Teresa's death in 1582, it was celebrated on 7 June,[35] within the octave of the feast of St Elisha on 14 June. Since she makes no reference to it, however, it would seem that St Teresa had no experience of any feast day for Elijah. On his feast day (21 October) in 1576, Teresa describes St Hilarion as her 'father' [mi padre san Hilarión].[36] Her poem, 'To Saint Hilarion' [A san Hilarión], also highlights this alleged Carmelite's skill as a spiritual warrior, using solitude, 'poverty sublime' and penance to gain eternal life.[37] Teresa refers to St Euphrasia in a letter dated 4 June 1578,[38] but there is no obvious link to that alleged Carmelite's feast day on 13 March, and it is not clear whether she regarded St Euphrasia as a fellow Carmelite. Although she must have been aware of both St Albert of Jerusalem and St Brocard, who was then commonly identified as the 'B.' mentioned in both the *Formula of Life* and the Rule of 1247, there are, as such, no references to St Albert of Jerusalem, St Cyril of Alexandria, St Anastasius [Magundat] of Persia, St Berthold, St Brocard, St Gerard Sagredo, or St Euphrosyne in the extant writings of St Teresa.

Teresa's book, *The Way of Perfection* [Camino de perfección], written for the Discalced nuns in 1566–67,[39] refers to 'our holy fathers of the past, those hermits whose lives we aim to imitate' [nuestros padres santos pasados y ermitaños, cuya vida pretendemos imitar],[40] and she presents her nuns as doing 'what our holy fathers established and observed' [las (cosas) que nuestros padres ordenaron y guardaron].[41] In her book, *Interior Castle* [Moradas], written in 1577 and addressed to the Discalced Carmelite nuns,[42] she mentions 'those holy fathers on Mount Carmel who in such great solitude and contempt for the world sought this treasure, this precious pearl of contemplation that we are talking about' [aquellos santos padres nuestros del Monte Carmelo que en tan gran soledad y con tanto desprecio del mundo buscaban este Tesoro, esta preciosa margarita de que hablamos].[43] She also refers on two occasions to 'our Father Elijah' [nuestro padre Elías].[44] In *The Book of her Foundations* [Libro de las Fundaciones], written between 1573 and 1582, she again uses the phrase 'our Father Elijah' on two occasions,[45] and she also mentions the feast day 'of our Father St. Elisha' [de nuestro padre san Eliseo].[46] Her poem, 'On the Way to Heaven' [Hacia la Patria], describes the 'nuns of Carmel' as 'following the Father Elijah' and as seeking to obtain 'the doubled Spirit of Elisha' [Al Padre Elías siguiendo (...) / procuremos el doblado / espíritu de Eliseo].[47]

Although Teresa adopted Pope Innocent's Rule as the basis for her reform, Otger Steggink recognized in 1965 that the terms 'former Rule' and 'primitive Rule', as used by her, 'have a content more "retroactive" than what the letter of the Innocentian Rule could give one to understand', so that 'her intentions look further back, to the primitive desert of Mount Carmel'.[48] In 1985, Kieran Kavanaugh and Otilio Rodriguez recognized Teresa's devotion to her Carmelite 'fathers' when they wrote that Teresa 'speaks about the life of our holy fathers of the past', and that she 'found inspiration' in the cherished Carmelite traditions of her time, including the mistaken view 'that the *Institute of the First Monks* was the rule given to their forefathers around the year 400 by John, the forty-fourth Patriarch of Jerusalem'.[49]

The fact that Teresa uses the same expression, my/our 'father', to describe the first two Carmelites who were recognized as saints, St Angelus of Sicily (c. 1185–c. 1220) and St Albert of Trapani (c. 1250–1306), and to describe the Old Testament prophets Elijah and Elisha, and the first millennium anchorite St Hilarion, is a clear indication that she accepted the Elijan succession and the Carmelite Order's claim to historical continuity with Elijah and Elisha. The way in which the expression 'our fathers' is used in her writings reflects the way that she used the expression 'my/our father', and it would seem to be a means of referring, not only to the recognized saints, but to all the male Carmelites who preceded her, going back in a continuous procession to the time of Elijah and Elisha.[50]

The Ávila-Rome Codex and the Carmelite Rule

We might wonder to what extent Teresa had been directly influenced by the understanding of the Carmelite tradition presented in Ribot's *Ten Books*, and whether or not she had access to a Spanish translation of that work. Until the middle of the last century, the direct influence of the *Ten Books* might have seemed unlikely. Following the discovery by Otger Steggink in the early 1950s of what is now called the Ávila-Rome Codex, however, the situation has changed.[51] This fifteenth-century collection of earlier Carmelite writings, given both in Latin and in a Spanish translation, which included Ribot's *Ten Books*, had been labelled as coming 'from the Avila convent' [del convento de Avila] when it was brought to the Provincial Archive of the Carmelites of Andalucia at Jérez de la Frontera during the nineteenth-century exclaustration,[52] and Steggink himself has shown convincingly that the Codex came from the monastery of the Incarnation.[53] The contents of the Codex, which are divided into two parts, the first with six sections[54] and the second (Ribot's *Ten Books*) with ten sections,[55] have been described by Gracián de Santa Teresa,[56] and its significance has been recognized by Tomás Álvarez in his magisterial study of the relationship between St Teresa of Ávila and the Carmelite Rule, published in the first volume of his *Estudios Teresianos*.[57]

One of the most significant aspects of the discovery of the Ávila-Rome Codex is that, alongside her extant writings and the other texts of the Carmelite Rule of 1247 to which she had access, it supports the claim that Teresa's acceptance of the Elijan succession influenced her understanding of the Carmelite Rule, as well as helping to clarify which texts of Pope Innocent IV's Rule she used. Recognizing that the Ávila-Rome Codex included a Spanish translation of Albert's *Formula of Life* and two different Spanish translations of Pope Innocent's Rule, one edited by Pietro Riera in the 1330s and one edited by Ribot in his *Ten Books* in the 1390s, Álvarez took a significant step towards clarifying these questions in 1995, when he published in parallel columns those three texts and the Spanish text of the Rule that is found in the Constitutions of 1581.[58] The texts in the Ávila-Rome Codex were not the only versions available to Teresa during the early 1560s, however. It seems likely that the Spanish translation of the Rule that precedes the Constitutions for the male Discalced Carmelites, which were approved in 1568 by the Carmelite Prior General, Giovanni Battista Rossi, was identical with the translation preceding the no-longer extant Constitutions for the female Discalced Carmelites, which he approved in 1567.[59] This text of the Rule was included with the Constitutions of St Joseph's that Teresa gave to John of the Cross and Anthony of Jesus in 1568 as the model for the Constitutions for Duruelo.[60] The similarities between Teresa's text and the Spanish text of the Rule adapted for women that María de Jesús drew up for the reformed Carmelite monastery at Alcalá de Henares, and which she showed to Teresa in 1562, suggest that Teresa had based her version of Pope Innocent's Rule on that of María de Jesús. Teresa, in other words, probably had access to a fifteenth-century Spanish text of the *Formula of Life* as edited by Ribot in the 1390s, and to five different Spanish versions of Pope Innocent IV's Rule, one based on a Latin text from the 1330s, one based on a Latin text from the 1390s, one received from María de Jesús about 1562, one based on the text of María de Jesús that dates from 1567 at the latest, and one that dates from 1581 at the latest.

The Foundation Rescript of February 1562

Teresa, having joined the Carmelite monastery of the Incarnation in 1535, made her profession there in 1537. The form in which she made her profession is not documented, but, if it was done according to the Latin formula used in 1521, she would have promised obedience 'to God and to the Blessed Virgin Mary of Mount Carmel', to 'the Prior General of the Order', and to the 'Prioress of this monastery of Saint Mary of the Incarnation' and her successors 'according to the Rule of the said Order, until death'.[61] We do not know what kind of instruction about the Rule she received when she was preparing to make her profession. Like other Carmelite monasteries in Spain, the monastery of the Incarnation probably had its own constitutions, but, if so, they have not survived.[62] Álvarez notes that the surviving sixteenth-century constitutions from Spanish Carmelite monasteries of nuns do not include the text of the Rule, and that they say nothing about reading or studying the Rule.[63]

Recognizing that Teresa's personal encounter with the Rule was progressive, Álvarez describes her vision of Hell in 1560 as leading to a decision to keep the Carmelite Rule perfectly:[64] 'the first thing was to follow the call to the religious life, which His Majesty had given me, by keeping my rule as perfectly as I could' [lo primero era seguir el llamamiento que Su Majestad me había hecho a religión, guardando mi Regla con la mayor perfección que pudiese].[65] It was probably during a discussion at the monastery of the Incarnation, sometime in the Autumn of 1560, that, as Jerónimo de San José puts it:

> They began to discuss the difficult life they were living in that house on account of there being so many people, contact and hubbub, concerning which the Saint indicated some reasons, born of that great affection that she had for withdrawing to a quieter life, bringing to mind the solitude and retirement of the ancient hermits of her Order, and how, living according to the primitive Rule, they lived a celestial life.[66]

Mother María Bautista de Ocampo later noted that they also discussed 'half in jest, how the Rule that was kept in that monastery might be reformed [...], and how some monasteries might be built for female hermits, like that primitive one that was seen at the beginning of this Rule that our ancient holy fathers founded'.[67] It may be that Teresa had in mind the emphasis on enclosure and on mystical communion with God in solitude that we have already noted as one of the features of Ribot's *Ten Books*, and that she had heard about this through reading the Ávila-Rome Codex in the monastery's library. As Steggink has noted, the association between the 'primitive Rule' and the Elijan succession as presented in the *Institute of the First Monks* is evident in the references in these accounts to the 'celestial life' of 'the ancient hermits' of the Order and to the Rule founded by the 'ancient holy fathers'.[68]

Shortly afterwards, having been commanded by Christ to found a new monastery called St Joseph's,[69] Teresa began the process that would lead to the foundation of that monastery. When her confessor advised her to speak to her superior, Teresa raised the matter with 'the lady who wanted to found this monastery', who spoke to the Carmelite Provincial of Castile, Ángel de Salazar. The Provincial assented 'very readily', and agreed to accept that house under his jurisdiction. As opposition to the project grew, however, the Provincial withdrew his permission. Teresa describes a vision on the feast of the Assumption (15 August) in 1561 in which the Lord told her to seek no longer the approval of the Carmelite friars of Castile for the new monastery, but to appeal directly to Rome.[70] On her behalf, Doña Aldonza de Guzmán and Doña Guiomar de Ulloa sent a petition to Rome, asking for permission to establish the monastery according to the Carmelite Rule, and under the obedience and correction of the Bishop of Ávila.[71] Since she had vowed obedience for life to the Carmelite Prior General, it is not clear how she might have interpreted the relationship between that obedience and the obedience to the Bishop that would be required should she, or others from the monastery of the Incarnation, join the proposed monastery. As summarized by Cardinal Rainucio of Sant'Angelo, the petition began:

> On behalf of Doña Aldonza de Guzmán and Doña Guiomar de Ulloa, illustrious women and widows of the city of Avila, it is explained to Your Holiness that, inflamed with the zeal of devotion, and for the praise and honour of God, they have desired to construct and build in the said city of Avila a Monastery for a number of Nuns of the Rule and Order of the Blessed Mary from Mount Carmel, and under the invocation that might seem favourable to them, and under the obedience and correction of the venerable Father in Christ, by the grace of God, the Bishop for the time being of Avila, with a Church, a bell-tower, bells, a cloister, a refectory, a dormitory, a garden and the other necessary poultry houses,[72] and also to erect in the same Church one chapel or more chapels, and to suitably endow this Monastery and chapel or chapels out of their own goods; they doubt, nevertheless, whether this thing is permitted to them without the special permission of the Apostolic See.[73]

The petition went on to request all the rights and privileges that the other monasteries and nuns of the Order of Blessed Mary from Mount Carmel enjoyed, and the right to draw up suitable statutes for the said monastery and to modify and change those statutes as necessary. It was approved by an apostolic rescript on 7 February 1562, and we know from the account of the meeting between St Teresa and the Prior General in 1567 that the Prior General was not consulted on the matter. This lack of consultation is surprising, given the reference to a 'dormitory' in the petition and in the approval granted by the apostolic rescript. As the following table makes clear, all the versions of the pre-Eugenian Rule to which St Teresa had access had prescribed that there be a separate cell or separate cells for each one:[74]

English Translation	Spanish Text	Translation
... each one of you should have his own separated cell or cells ...	... cada uno de vosotros tenga su çelda o çelldas apartadas ...	fifteenth-century Formula of Life (1206–14)
... each one of you should have separated cells ...	... cada uno de vosotros tengan çelldas apartadas ...	fifteenth-century Rule (1330s)
... each one of you should have his own separated cell ...	... cada uno de vosotros tenga su çelda apartada ...	fifteenth-century Rule (1390s)
... each one of you should have her own cell ... separated and divided from one another ...	Cada una de vosotras tenga su celda ... apartadas y divididas las unas de las otras ...	María de Jesús, 1562
... each one of you should have his own cell ... separated and divided from one another ...	... cada uno de vosotros tenga su celda ... apartadas y divididas las unas de las otras ...	Friars' Constitutions, 1568
... each one of you should have her own separated cell ...	... cada uno tenga su celda apartada ...	Nuns' Constitutions, 1581

Having a common dormitory was not, in other words, consistent with any of these translations of the Carmelite Rule. Having separate cells had also been a feature of the alleged tradition preceding the *Formula of Life*, and *Institute of the First Monks*, which the *Letter of Cyril* had presented as the basis on which Carmelite monks had lived for many hundreds of years, had also described the first monks on Mount Carmel as 'living alone in cells individually'.[75] We know that in the monastery of the Incarnation those nuns who did not bring a dowry were normally assigned a section of the common dormitory.[76] It would seem that, rather than being guided by any actual text of the Rule as such, Teresa was guided more by the tradition she was familiar with on this point, and that, rather than basing herself on any of the extant texts in use at that time, she presumed that that tradition reflected the prescriptions of the Carmelite Rule. It may be also that the proposal of a common dormitory was motivated by the normative use of common dormitories in Clarissan monasteries during the thirteenth and early fourteenth centuries, and by their later revival during the fifteenth and sixteenth centuries, when 'the re-introduction of a common dormitory was frequently a benchmark change, indicating the new Observant regime'.[77]

The apostolic rescript approving the petition quoted the petition in a way that included the word 'dormitory',[78] but, unusually, the word 'dormitory' is not found in any of the extant editions of the parallel text outlining what was formally approved by that apostolic rescript.[79] Since the word 'dormitory' occurs in the summary of the rescript that is found in the papal Bull of 1565, however, this omission would seem to be a typographical error.

The Second Apostolic Rescript, December 1562

In March 1562 Teresa met María de Jesús, who had with her the documents approving the foundation of a new reformed monastery for Carmelite nuns (later known as the monastery *de la Imagen*) in Alcalá de Henares. Describing her encounter with María de Jesús during the Spring of 1562, Teresa later wrote:

> Until I had spoken to her, it had not come to my notice that our Rule — before it was mitigated — ordered that one should own nothing, nor had I been about to found the house without any income. My intention had been that we have no worries about our needs; I hadn't considered the many cares ownership of property brings with it. Since the Lord taught her, this blessed woman understood well (without knowing how to read) what I, after having read over the Constitutions so often, didn't know.[80]

> [Y hasta que yo la hablé, no había venido a mi noticia que nuestra Regla, antes que se relajase, mandaba no se tuviese propio, ni yo estaba en fundarle sin renta, que iba mi intento a que no tuviésemos cuidado de lo que habíamos menester, y no miraba a los muchos cuidados que trae consigo tener propio. Esta bendita mujer, como la enseñaba el Señor, tenía bien entendido (con no saber leer) lo que yo con tanto haber andado a leer las Constituciones ignoraba].[81]

Since Teresa nowhere refers to any mitigations other than those made by Pope Eugene IV, her phrase 'our Rule — before it was mitigated' probably refers to some version of the Rule of Pope Innocent IV. All the versions of the Rule then available to Teresa prohibit personal ownership, and insist that everything is to be held in common:[82]

English Translation	Spanish Text	Translation
... No friar should say that anything is his own, but all things should be common ...	... Ningún frayle diga que es algo suio propio, mas todas las cosas sean comunes ...	fifteenth-century Rule of Life (1206–14)
... No friar should say that anything is for himself or a personal thing that is for himself ...	... Ningún frayle diga que es algo para sy o cosa propia que es para sy ...	fifteenth-century Rule (1330s)
... No friar should say to himself [that] anything is his own, but let all things be common to you ...	... Ningún frayle diga ser algo suyo propio, mas sean a vosotros todas las cosas comunes ...	fifteenth-century Rule (1390s)
... No sister should have anything of her own, but have all things in common ...	... Ningún hermana tenga cosa propia, mas tened todas las cosas en común ...	María de Jesús, 1562
... No brother should have anything of his own, but you [pl.] are to have all things in common ...	... Ningún hermano tenga cosa propia, mas tener todas las cosas en común ...	Friars' Constitutions, 1568

... No religious should say that he has anything proper to him, but let all the things be common ...	... Ningún religioso diga que tiene alguna cosa propria, sino que todas las cosas sean comunes ...	Nuns' Constitutions, 1581

If we compare the way that these same texts describe where the food that was to be eaten came from, however, the text of the Rule that had been approved for the new foundation by María de Jesús and the two later versions (1567 and 1581) imply that there were no common lands and that the monastery was to live on alms, which would seem to correspond to Teresa's reference to owning nothing and living without an income:[83]

English Translation	Spanish Text	Translation
... from those things that God might give you [pl.] ...	... de aquellas cosas que Dios os diere ...	Fifteenth-century Formula of Life (1206–14)
... those things that were held by you [pl.] or that had been contributed [to you] communally ...	... aquellas cosas que a vosotros ayan o fueren sydo erogadas comúnmente ...	Fifteenth-century Rule (1330s)
... those things that we were given ...	... aquellas cosas que nos (¡) fueren dadas ...	Fifteenth-century Rule (1390s)
... that which they might give to you [pl.] to eat as alms ...	... lo que os dieren en limosna para comer...	María de Jesús, 1562
... that which if it were given to you [pl.] to eat as alms ...	... lo que se os diere en limosna para comer...	Friars' Constitutions, 1568
... that which had been given to you as alms ...	... lo que os fuere dado en limosna ...	Nuns' Constitutions, 1581

Article Twelve of Albert's *Formula of Life* specified that, according to need, the person appointed by the Prior would distribute to each one 'out of such things as the Lord will have given you' [ex his quae Dominus vobis dederit]. In its original context, this was probably an implicit reference to the Lord's giving of the Sabbath and double the usual amount of manna on the sixth day (see Exodus 16.29). The reference to the harvest that 'the Lord will have given' [Dominus dederit] in the life of Bishop Atto of Vercelli, which refers to the agricultural produce of lands that were the property of those concerned, is Albert's most likely source for the Latin phrase he used. The implication, therefore, would seem to be that the hermit brothers lived, not only on alms, but on the produce of their land and, in general, on what divine providence provided. The discovery by archaeologists in 1988 of a commercial-sized wine press at the site on Mount Carmel makes it unlikely that the original Latin hermits on Mount Carmel owned no property, or that they lived entirely on alms.[84]

Teresa had been concerned about the question of providing sufficient income for the proposed monastery,[85] but, over time, she became convinced that the nuns in the new monastery should live on alms 'and there never be any income' [jamás haya renta].[86] It would seem that her change of attitude on this question was influenced by what she had recently learned from María de Jesús, and by what she had read in María's version of the Rule. Later, Teresa explicitly recognized the poverty of St Clare of Assisi as the model for the poverty of the monastery of St Joseph.[87] In the light of her change of attitude, Teresa sought a new rescript from Rome that would allow the already approved monastery to live without an income. The monastery of St Joseph was inaugurated in August 1562 on the basis of the first apostolic rescript, and, on 5 December 1562, Cardinal Farnese, again writing on behalf of Pope Pius IV, approved in a second apostolic rescript the request by the nuns that they be allowed not to have or possess, in common or individually, any goods 'according to the norm of the first Rule of the said Order'.[88]

Conclusions

We have seen that, like her contemporaries, St Teresa accepted the Carmelite claim of an Elijan succession, and that, although she never mentions St Albert of Jerusalem in her extant writings, she recognized the Old Testament prophets Elijah and Elisha and the first millennium anchorite St Hilarion as among her Carmelite 'fathers'. The reform initiated by Teresa seems to have sought to restore the essential continuity from Elijah down to Pope Innocent IV's Rule, as proposed by the claim to an Elijan succession, by rejecting the mitigations of Pope Eugene IV, and adopting the norms of the text of that Rule followed by María de Jesús. These Carmelite traditions were not the only influences on Teresa, however, and she herself later acknowledged that the style of poverty followed at St Joseph's had been modelled on St Clare of Assisi. The explicit request for a dormitory in the proposed monastery reflects the norms then practised by the Observant Franciscan Reform. Teresa's knowledge of the traditions associated with the Elijan succession probably came from the traditions of the monastery of the Incarnation, perhaps derived from the Ávila-Rome Codex, which had a Spanish translation of Ribot's *Ten Books*, but there does not seem to be any evidence of a direct citation from that source in her writings. Teresa distinguishes the mitigated Rule promulgated by Pope Eugene IV from earlier 'unmitigated' versions, which she describes as 'primitive', 'first', or 'former' in relation to Pope Eugene IV's Rule. The direct references to particular texts of the Carmelite Rule in Teresa's extant writings do not seem to come from the Ávila-Rome Codex. They seem to be based either on the text of the Rule followed by María de Jesús (c. 1562), or on the text of the Rule that was attached to the Constitutions of 1567. Given the similarity between these two texts, and the fact that Teresa's version did not follow María de Jesús in changing such gendered terms as Prior to Prioress, it may be that Teresa used the Rule of María de Jesús as her normative text after 1562, making her own adaptations cumulatively, and eventually printing her adaptation of María's text to accompany her Constitutions of 1567. Teresa's 1567 text was, presumably, the same as that used for the friars' Constitutions in 1568.

Notes to Chapter 1

1. See Patrick Mullins, *The Carmelites and St Albert of Jerusalem: Origins and Identity* (Rome: Edizioni Carmelitane, 2015).
2. See Patrick Mullins, *St Albert of Jerusalem and the Roots of Carmelite Spirituality* (Rome: Edizioni Carmelitane, 2012), pp. 167–71, 176–79, 199–215, 238–43.
3. See Mullins, *St Albert of Jerusalem*, pp. 212–14.
4. 'Sed et caeteri hujus Religionis Monachi habitantes alibi cupiunt etiam idcirco Carmelitae appellari, quia eorum Religio, et sancta conversatio, est ab illis viris derivata, et sumpta; qui modo predicto satagerunt in monte Carmeli assidue religiosam vitam Prophetae Eliae, et usque nunc satagunt, humiliter imitari'. See *Philip Riboti, Libri decem de institutione et peculiaribus gestis religiosorum Carmelitarum*, 3.5, in Daniel de la Vierge Marie, *Speculum Carmelitanum, sive historia Eliani Ordinis Fratrum Beatissimae Virginis Mariae de Monte Carmelo*, 4 vols (Antwerp: Typis Michaelis Knobbari, 1680), I, 33–34, n. 119.
5. 'Unde autem ad Monachos studium defluxerit paupertatis? Vel quis hujus conversationis extitit auctor? Cujus isti habitum imitantur? quantum enim attinet ad auctoritatem veterum scripturarum, hujus propositi Princepes Elias & discipulus ejus Elisaeus fuerunt, sive filii Prophetarum, qui habitabant in solitudine: urbibusque relictis, faciebant sibi casulas prope fluente jordanis. Hujus etiam propositi in Euangelio Ioannes Baptista auctor extitit, qui eremum solum incoluit, locustis tantum, & agresti melle nutritus. Iam demum progeniti sunt conversationis hujus nobilissimi Principes Paulus, Antonius, Halarion, Macharius, ceterisque Patres, quorum exemplis per universum mundum adolevit sancta institutio Monachorum'. See *Speculum Carmelitanum*, I, 27, n. 88 (2.8). See also *The Ten Books on the Way of Life and Great Deeds of the Carmelites (Including the Book of the First Monks). A Medieval History of the Carmelites Written c.1385 by Felip Ribot, O.Carm.*, ed. and trans. by Richard Copsey (Faversham: British Province of Carmelites, 2005), p. 38.
6. 'Praedicti autem Monachi a plerisque fuerunt Anachorita idcirco appellati; quia corda sua angentes jeiuniorum inediis & caeteris corporis angustiis, non timuerunt, ut dictum est, ab inimatione Eliae incessanter & continue penetrare vastos secessus solitudinis montis carmeli, & aliorum eremorum Terrae promissionis: ubi (a) cogitationibus Sanctis, & intensione orationum, ac caeteris armis justitiae muniti, non solum occultas diaboli insidias vincebant; sed & apertus conflictus daemonum calcantes, tanto conatu (b) mentes suas, ad exemplum Eliae Principis eorum, sursum in Dei contemplatione elevabant, ut in coelestibus choris putarentur translati, & "revelata facie gloriam Deo speculari", perstruentes colloquio Dei, cui puris mentibus inhaerebant'. See *Speculum Carmelitanum*, I, 36, n. 130 (3.8). For a slightly different translation, see *The Ten Books*, p. 53.
7. See Mullins, *St Albert of Jerusalem*, p. 214.
8. See Mullins, *St Albert of Jerusalem*, pp. 40–43.
9. Although both the *Formula of Life* and the Rule present the care of the souls of the members as something to be considered by the community collectively, this text seems to regard the Prior as a monastic Abbot when it presents the care of the souls of the other brothers as the responsibility of the 'Prior' alone.
10. '[...] numquam tamen ad obediendum alicui in monte Carmeli sub certa clausura, se vero speciali prius obligaverant, donec praedictus patriarcha Aymericus eos ad hoc primum astrinxit. Inter quos ipse Fratrem suum habuit, scilicet Fratrem Bertholdum perfectum Religiosum, sanctumque Praesbyterum: quem de unanimi omnium assensu anno Domini MCXXI. In Primum Priorem eis instituit, & cui curam animarum caeterorum injunxit. Et in hoc monte Carmeli, in honore Beatae Mariae Virginis Dei Genetricis, Monasterium aedificari faciebat, muro alto circulariter circumdatum: in quo quidem eos includere intendebat: set priusquam hoc Monasterium consummasset, sustulit eum de mundo Deus. [...] Tandem post lapsum temporis Fratrem Brocardum, virum perfectum, unanimiter praeficientes, ei omnes obedientiam promiserunt, sub regimine cujus triginta tribus annis permanserunt. Quo eis praesidente, Patriarchae Ierosolymitano Domino Alberto proposuerunt, quod a tempore quo praedictus patriarcha Aymericus eos omnes sub cura unius Prioris per obedientiae vinculum colligaverat,

ipsi desideraverant vivere inclusi in Monasterio, sub observantia Religiosae vitae solitariae, per Eliam Prophetam institutae; qui licet per eorum institutionem essent certi, qualiter unusquisque eorum singulariter degens deberet ad perfectionem, & finem vitae solitariae tendere; quia tamen proponebant in hoc Carmelo includi in Monasterio, in quo nequaquam fuerant adhuc inclusi; ideo priusquam in eo includerentur, obnixe requirebant a praedicto Patriarcha Alberto, ut juxta propositum eorum traderet eis de quibusdam articulis, per eos tunc sibi oblatis, conversationi monasteriali necessariis, brevem vitae formulam, quam tenere imposterum deberent'. See *Speculum Carmelitanum*, I, 75, nn. 300–01 (8.2), and *The Ten Books*, pp. 110–11.

11. See Arie Paschalis Kallenberg, *Fontes Liturgiae Carmelitanae* (Rome: Institutum Carmelitanum, 1962), p. 42; Juan Bautista de Lezana and Luca Ciamberlano, *Annales sacri, prophetici, et Eliani Ordinis Beatae Virginis Mariæ de Monte Carmeli*, 4 vols (Rome: Typis Mascardi, 1645–56), I, 287; *Acta Capitulorum Generalium Fratrum B.V. Mariae de Monte Carmelo*, ed. by Gabriel Wessels, 2 vols (Rome: Apud Curiam Generalitiam, 1912, 1934), I, 124.

12. See James Boyce, *Carmelite Liturgical Spirituality* (Melbourne: Carmelite Communications, 2000), p. 30; Arie Paschalis Kallenberg, 'Le Culte liturgique d'Élie dans l'Ordre du Carmel', in *Élie le Prophète*, II, *Études Carmélitaines*, 34 (1956), pp. 134–50; Emanuele Boaga, *Celebrare i nostri Santi* (Rome: Edizione Carmelitane, 2009), p. 44.

13. See *The Collected Works of Saint Teresa of Avila*, trans. by Kieran Kavanaugh and Otilio Rodriguez, 3 vols (Washington, DC: Institute of Carmelite Studies Publications, 1976–85), I, 18–19.

14. See *Missale secundum usum Carmelitarum* (Venice: Lucantonij de Giunta, 1504), calendar; Daniel Papenbroeck, 'De Beato Alberto ex Canonico Regulari Episcopo Primum Vercellensi, dein Patriarcha Hierosolymitano, Legato Apostolico, et Legislatore Ordinis Carmelitici. Ann. Mccxiv', in *Acta Sanctorum*, ed. by Bollandists (Antwerp: Apud Ioannem Meursium, 1643–1794), pp. 769–802 (p. 775).

15. See *Missale secundum usum Carmelitarum ... non paucis imaginibus depictum* (Venice: Lucas Antonius de Giunta, 1509), calendar.

16. See *Breviarium Carmelitanum cum annotationibus in margine ad facillime omnia que in ipso ad alias paginas remittuntur inuenienda* (Venice: Lucantonij de Giunta, 1543), p. 3.

17. See *Speculum Carmelitanum*, ii, p. iii (prefatio), 660, n. 2267; *Breviarium Carmelitanum secundum usum Ecclesiae Hierosolymitanae et Cominici Sepulchri. Nunc recens sub R. P. Ioanne Baptista Rubeo ... solerti cura et diligentia F. Iacobi Maistret ... emendatum ac typu mandatum ...* (Lyons: Apud Ioannem Stratium, 1575), calendar (Januarius, Martius, September); *Breviarium antiquae professionis regularium Beatissimae Dei Genitricis Semperq. Virginis Mariae de Monte Carmelo ex usu et consuetudine approbata Hierosolymitanae Ecclesiae et Dominici Sepulchri superrime iussu ... Ioan. Baptistae Caffardi ... reformatum excusum* (Venice: Apud Iuntas, 1579), pp. 280^r, 304, 77^r.

18. See *Breviarium Carmelitanum secundum usum Ecclesiae Hierosolymitanae* (1575), calendar (Februarius).

19. See *The Collected Letters of St Teresa of Avila*, trans. by Kieran Kavanaugh, 2 vols (Washington, DC: Institute of Carmelite Studies Publications, 2001, 2007), II, 245, 318, n. 26.

20. See Francisco de Ribera, *Vida de Santa Teresa de Jesús, fundadora de las Descalzas y Descalzos Carmelitas*, ed. by Inocente Palacios de la Asunción (Madrid: Librería de Francisco Lizcano, 1863), pp. 77, 533.

21. See Otger Steggink, *La reforma del Carmelo español: la visita canónica del General Rubeo y su encuentro con Santa Teresa (1566–1567)* (Rome: Institutum Carmelitanum, 1965), p. 335.

22. See *Cartas de Santa Teresa de Jesús, Madre y Fundadora de la Reforma de la Orden de Nuestra Señora del Carmen, de la Primitiva Observancia*, ed. by Antonio de San Joseph, 4 vols (Madrid: Don Joseph Doblado, 1771), II, 285, n.1.

23. See *The Collected Letters of St Teresa of Avila*, I, 402 (150.3). Among her other code names for Gracián were 'Paul' [Pablo], 'he of the Cave of Elijah' [el de la Cueva de Elías] and 'Elisha' [Eliseo]: see I, 228 (89.2), 341 (128.4), 369 (136.7), 423 (159.6); II, 72 (292), 209 (303.5), 261 (325.9).

24. 'la víspera o día de San Ángel', II, 65 (244.1).

25. 'nuestro padre San Alberto', *Constitutions*, 5, in *The Collected Works of Saint Teresa of Avila*, III, 320; *The Collected Letters of St Teresa of Avila*, II, 214 (305.1).

26. See *The Collected Letters of St Teresa of Avila*, II, 332 (351.4), 449–50 (403.4). In the letter of 7 August 1581, she refers to the preaching of a Dominican friar on that day, 'the feast of our Father St Albert' [Es hoy día de nuestro padre san Alberto].
27. See Tomás Álvarez, *Estudios Teresianos*, 3 vols (Burgos: Editorial Monte Carmelo, 1995–96), I, 656–71.
28. See Boaga, *Celebrare*, p. 44; *Breviarium iuxta ordinale novarumque ordinationum stilum Fratrum Sacri Ordinis Gloriosissimae Dei Genitricis Semperque Virginis Mariae de Monte Carmeli* (Venice: Bartholomaeus de Blavis & Soc., 1481), calendar; *Missale Ordinis Carmelitarum* (Brescia: de'Bonini, 1490), Junii; *Missale secundum usum Carmelitarum* (1509), calendar, Iunius.
29. *Speculum Carmelitanum*, II, p. iv (prefatio); *Breviarium Carmelitanum* (1543), pp. 295–96; *Breviarium Carmelitanum* (1575), calendar, Iunius; *Breviarium antiquae professionis regularium Beatissimae Dei Genitricis Semperq. Virginis Mariae de Monte Carmelo* (1579), pp. 320–21; Boyce, *Carmelite Liturgical Spirituality*, p. 19, and his article, 'The Feasts of Saints Elijah and Elisha in the Carmelite Rite: A Liturgico-Musical Study', in *Master of the Sacred Page. Essays and Articles in Honor of Roland E. Murphy, O.Carm., on the Occasion of His Eightieth Birthday* (Washington, DC: The Carmelite Institute, 1997), pp. 155–88 (p. 158).
30. 'Carmelitarum principis: Prophetae, quem instituit: Magnus Helias Thesbites Nutu divini numinis': *Breviarium Carmelitanum* (1543), p. 295; *Breviarium Carmelitanum secundum usum Ecclesiae Hierosolymitanae* (1575), p. 883.
31. *Libro de las Fundaciones*, 30 and 30.8, in *Santa Teresa de Jesús. Obras completas*, ed. by Alberto Barrientos, 5th edn (Madrid: Editorial de Espiritualidad, 2000), pp. 480, 483; *The Collected Works of Saint Teresa of Avila*, III, 280, 283.
32. See *Breviarium Carmelitanum cum annotationibus in margine* (1543).
33. See Boaga, p. 61.
34. See Benedict Mary of the Cross Zimmerman, *Ordinaire de l'Ordre de Notre-Dame du Mont Carmel par Sibert De Beka (vers 1312). Publié d'après le manuscrit original et collationné sur divers manuscrits et imprimés* (Paris: Picard, 1910), pp. 346–47.
35. See *Martyrologium Romanum ad novam kalendarii rationem ... restitutum Gregorii XII jussu ditum*, ed. by Caesar Baronius (Rome: Ex Typographia Dominici Basæ, 1586), p. 322.
36. See *The Collected Letters of St Teresa of Avila*, I, 357 (134.6), and Teresa's remarks in her *Life* (*Vida* 27.1), in *The Collected Works of Saint Teresa of Avila*, I, 227.
37. *The Collected Works of Saint Teresa of Avila*, III, 398–99.
38. See *The Collected Letters of St Teresa of Avila*, II, 79 (248.6).
39. See Álvarez, I, 10.
40. Chapter 11.4, in *The Collected Works of Saint Teresa of Avila*, II, 81; *Santa Teresa de Jesús. Obras completas*, p. 687.
41. Chapter 4.4, in *The Collected Works of Saint Teresa of Avila*, II, 54; *Santa Teresa de Jesús. Obras completas*, p. 663.
42. See Álvarez, I, 14.
43. *Moradas* 5.1.2, in *The Collected Works of Saint Teresa of Avila*, II, 336; *Santa Teresa de Jesús. Obras completas*, p. 860.
44. *Moradas* 6.7.8 and 7.4.11, in *The Collected Works of Saint Teresa of Avila*, II, 401, 448; *Santa Teresa de Jesús. Obras completas*, pp. 919, 963.
45. *Fundaciones* 27.17 and 28.20, in *The Collected Works of Saint Teresa of Avila*, III, 247, 257; *Santa Teresa de Jesús. Obras completas*, pp. 450, 460.
46. *Fundaciones* 30.8, in *The Collected Works of Saint Teresa of Avila*, III, 283; *Santa Teresa de Jesús. Obras completas*, p. 483.
47. See *The Collected Works of Saint Teresa of Avila*, III, 387.
48. See Steggink, *La reforma del Carmelo español*, p. 384.
49. See *The Collected Works of Saint Teresa of Avila*, III, 15–16.
50. See Mullins, *The Carmelites and St Albert of Jerusalem*, pp. 107–09.
51. See Graziano di S. Teresa, OCD, 'Il Codice di Avila', *Ephemerides Carmeliticae*, 9 (1958), 442–43. Since 1953, the codex has been in the OCarm. General Archive in Rome, where it has been given the label II.C.O.II.35.

52. See Graziano di S. Teresa, p. 443.
53. See Steggink, *La reforma del Carmelo español*, p. 359, n. 74.
54. The principal works included in the first part, all of which are given in both Latin and Spanish, are the *Constitutions* of Ballester (1369), which take up the first four sections (fols 1–101), and the six works included in section 6: the anonymous *Tractatus de origine* in nine chapters (fols 102–05), apparently a version of *De inceptione ordinis beatae Marie Virginis de Monte Carmelo*, followed by the Rule as promulgated by Pope Innocent IV (fols 106–10), both as edited by Pietro Riera OCarm from the Province of Aragon in the 1330s, the *Compendium* of John Baconthorp (fols 110–18), the *Viridarium* of Giovanni Grossi (fols 118–23), the Question *Utrum religiosi possunt facere testamentum* (fols 123–24), the Carmelite *Privilegia* from Pope Alexander IV to Pope John 22 (fols 124–43), and the tract *Quia novissimo iure plura statuta sunt contra religiosos mendicantes* (fols 144–57). The *Ten Books* of Ribot that make up the second part are also given in both Latin and Spanish. See Graziano di S. Teresa, 'Il Codice', pp. 444–46.
55. The six sections of Part One are marked at the top of the page in red as 'P PS' fols 1–29, 'S PS' fols 29'–72, 'T PS' fols 72'–85', 'Q PS' fols 86–101', 'U PS' or 'V PS' fols 102–05' and 'UI PS' or 'VI PS' fols 106–57. The ten sections of Part Two, which correspond to the *Ten Books* of Ribot, are marked: 'L J° fols 157'–172', 'L IJ°' fols 173–84', 'L. IIJ°' fols 185–97', 'L IIIJ°' fols 197'–207', 'L V' fols 208–15, 'L VI' fols 215'–25', 'L VIJ' fols 226–33', 'L VIIJ' fols 234–57, 'L IX' fols 257'–66', and 'L X' fols 267–74'; see Graziano di S. Teresa, 'Il Codice', p. 443.
56. Graziano di S. Teresa, 'Il Codice', pp. 444–46.
57. Álvarez, I, 169–268. This work represents the fruit of a study for the Discalced Carmelite *Secretariatus pro Monialibus*, edited in a number of languages in 1994, an English language version of which can be found on the following website: <http://www.ocd.pcn.net/nuns/n10_en.htm#N_3> [accessed 29 December 2012].
58. Álvarez, I, 225–27.
59. See Tomás de la Cruz and Simeón de la Sagrada Familia, *La reforma teresiana: documentario histórico de sus primeros días* (Rome: Teresianum-Desclée, 1962), pp. [110]–20 (doc. VI); Steggink, *La reforma del Carmelo español*, p. 388, n. 246.
60. See Álvarez, I, 176.
61. See Álvarez, I, 170; Nicolás González y González, *El monasterio de la Encarnación de Ávila*, 2 vols (Avila: Caja de Ávila, 1976–77), I, 29.
62. See González y González, II, 276, n. 4.
63. See Álvarez, I, 171.
64. Álvarez, I, 172.
65. *Vida* 32.9, in *The Collected Works of Saint Teresa of Avila*, I, 279.
66. '[...] se comenzó a tratar de cuán penosa vida era la que se pasaba en aquella casa, por haver tanta gente, comunicación y bullicio; acerca de lo cual dijo la Santa algunas razones, nacidas de aquel grande afecto que traía de retirarse a vida más quieta, trayendo a la memoria la soledad y retiro de los antiguos ermitaños de su orden, y cómo, viviendo según la Regla primitiva, pasaban una vida celestial.' Jerónimo de San José, *Historia del Carmen Descalzo* [...]. *Tomo Primero* (Madrid: Francisco Martínez, 1637), p. 511 (3.2).
67. 'medio de burla cómo se reformaría la Regla que se guardava en aquel monesterio [...], y se hiciesen unos monesterios a manera de ermitañas, como lo primitivo que se guardava al principio desta Regla que fundaron nuestros santos padres antiguos.' Steggink, *La reforma del Carmelo español*, p. 357, n. 72.
68. Steggink, *La reforma del Carmelo español*, pp. 357, 362.
69. *Vida* 32.11, in *The Collected Works of Saint Teresa of Avila*, I, 280.
70. See Steggink, *La reforma del Carmelo español*, p. 369, n. 131; *Vida* 33.16, in *The Collected Works of Saint Teresa of Avila*, I, 292.
71. See *Vida* 32.13, 16, in *The Collected Works of Saint Teresa of Avila*, I, 281–82; Steggink, *La reforma del Carmelo español*, p. 344.
72. Since the Nuns would do their work in solitude, there would be no need for workshops in the Monastery, but, since the Rule explicitly allowed them to have poultry (to provide eggs), the word *officina* is translated as 'poultry houses' rather than 'workshops'.

73. 'Exponitur Sanctitate vestrae pro parte Domnae Aldoncae de Guzman et Domnae Guiomarae de Ulloa, mulierum illustrium et viduarum abulensis civitatis, quod ipsae zelo dovotionis accensae et ad Dei laudem & honorem desiderant in dicta civitate Abulensi unum Monasterium Monialium, in numero & sub invocatione eis bene visis, Regulae & Ordinis Beata Maria de Monte Carmelo, ac sub obedientia & correctione venerabilis in Christo Patris, Dei gratia, Episcopo Abulensis pro tempore existentis cum Ecclesia, Campanili, Campanis, Claustro, Refectorio, Dormitorio, Horto, & aliis necessariis officinis construere, & aedificare: necnon in eadem Ecclesia unum [sic], seu plures Capellaniam, seu Capellanias erigere; ac Monasterium & Capellaniam, seu Capellanias huiusmodi ex propriis earum bonis competenter dotare; id tamen vobis licere dubitatis, absque Sedis Apostolicae licentia speciali': Tomás de la Cruz and Simeón de la Sagrada Familia, pp. 145–46.
74. See Álvarez, I, 240–43; *Escritos de Santa Teresa*, ed. by Vicente de la Fuente, 2 vols (Madrid: M. Rivadeneyra, 1861–62), I, 270; Tomás de la Cruz and Simeón de la Sagrada Familia, p. 113 [7]; Steggink, *La reforma del Carmelo español*, p. 388.
75. '[...] ipsi sigillatim habitantes soli in cellis', see *The Ten Books*, p. 48; *Speculum Carmelitanum*, I, 33, n. 118 (3.5).
76. See Steggink, *La reforma del Carmelo español*, p. 297.
77. See Bert Roest, *Order and Disorder: The Poor Clares between Foundation and Reform* (Leiden: Brill, 2013), p. 252.
78. The original has not survived, but the notary's copy by Rodrigo Zapata, the major chaplain of the Church of Toledo, who was one of its executors, is preserved in the archive of the Discalced Carmelite nuns of St Joseph's in Ávila. The document was not an apostolic brief or bull, but, rather, an apostolic rescript: see Steggink, *La reforma del Carmelo español*, p. 373, n. 144.
79. '[...] super hoc, vivae vocis oraculo, nobis facto, vobis, ut unum Monasterium, Monialium numero, & sub invocatione vobis benevisis, Regulae & Ordinis Beatae Mariae de Monte Carmelo, ac sub obedientia & correctione dicti domini Episcopi Abulensis pro tempore esistentis, cum Ecclesia, Campanili, Campanis, Claustro, Refectorio, [Dormitorio,] Horto, & aliis neceßariis officinis, in aliquo loco, seu situ, intra, aut extra muros dictae civitatis Abulensis, vobis beneviso, sine tamen alicuius praeiudicio, construere & aedificare; ac in eadem Ecclesia unam, seu plures Capellaniam, seu Capellanias erigere; & Monasterium & Capellaniam, seu Capellanias huiusmodi ex propriis vestris bonis competenter dotare; & postquam Monasterium praedictum constructum, & erectum fuerit, illud, illiusque Moniales pro tempore existentes, omnibus & singulis privilegiis, immunitatibus, exemptionibus, praerogativis, libertatibus, conceßionibus & indultis, quibus alia dicti Ordinis Beatae Mariae de Monte Carmelo Monasteria, & illorum Moniales de iure, usu, consuetudine, vel alias in genere utuntur, potiuntur, & gaudent, ac uti, potiri, & gaudere poterunt quomodolibet in futurum; uti, potiri, & gaudere libere, & licite poßint & valeant, tenore praesentium concedimus & indulgemus'. See Jerónimo de San José, part 3, p. 11 (575); Tomás de la Cruz and Simeón de la Sagrada Familia, pp. 140–41.
80. This refers, presumably, to the *Constitutions* of the monastery of the Incarnation, which, as noted earlier, have not survived. See González y González, II, 76, n. 4.
81. *Vida* 35.2, in *Santa Teresa de Jesús. Obras completas*, p. 240. For a slightly different translation, see *The Collected Works of Saint Teresa of Avila*, I, 303.
82. See Álvarez, I, 244–47; Tomás de la Cruz and Simeón de la Sagrada Familia, p. 115 [13]; *Escritos de Santa Teresa*, I, 270.
83. See Álvarez, I, 242–43, 246; Tomás de la Cruz and Simeón de la Sagrada Familia, p. 113 [8]; *Escritos de Santa Teresa*, I, 270.
84. See Mullins, *St Albert of Jerusalem*, pp. 205–06.
85. *Vida* 32.10, 13, 15–16, 18, in *The Collected Works of Saint Teresa of Avila*, I, 280–82, 284.
86. *Vida* 33.13, in *The Collected Works of Saint Teresa of Avila*, I, 290–91.
87. '[...] horis congruis in eorum ecclesijs et illarum claustris ac per earum ambitus manere et deambulare libere et licite valeant'. See Ludovico Saggi, 'La mitigazione del 1432 della Regola Carmelitana: tempo e persone', *Carmelus*, 5 (1958), p. 21; Steggink, *La reforma del Carmelo español*, p. 389.
88. 'Ex parte vestra nobis oblata petitio continebat, quod licet vos, ex indulto speciali Sedis

Apostolicae, in vim quarumdam litterarum Apostolicarum per officium Sacra Paenitentiariae expeditarum Fundatricibus dicti Monasterii nuper erecti concesso, quaecunque bona in communi, & particulari habere, & poßidere valeatis; nihilominus, ob melioris vitae frugem, cupitis, bona aliqua in communi, aut particulari habere, seu poßidere minime posse, iuxta formam primae Regulae dicti Ordinis, sed ex eleemosynis vobis per Christi fideles pie elargiendis, vos sustentare, prout aliae Moniales dicti Ordinis in illis partibus degunt: id tamen vobis licere dubitatis, absque Sedis Apostolica licentia speciali. Quare supplicari fecistis humiliter, vobis super his per Sedem eandem de opportuno remedio misericorditer provideri. Nos igitur vestris in hae parte supplicationibus inclinati, auctoritate Domini Papae, cuius Poenitentiariae curam gerimus, & de eius speciali mandato super hoc vivae vocis oraculo nobis facto, vobis, ut bona aliqua in communi, aut particulari habere, seu poßidere minime possitis, iuxta formam primae Regulae dicti Ordinis, sed ex eleemosynis, & charitatis subsidiis vobis per Christi fideles pie elargiendis, vos sustentare libere valeatis, tenore praesentium concedimus, & indulgemus'. See Jerónimo de San José, part 4, p. 5 (626); *Bullarium Carmelitanum*, ed. by Eliseo Monsignano and G. M. Ximenes, 4 vols (Rome: Hermathenea, 1715–18, 1768), II, 123 (VIII); *Obras de Santa Teresa de Jesús*, ed. by Silverio de Santa Teresa, 9 vols, Biblioteca Mística Carmelitana (Burgos: Monte Carmelo, 1915–24), II, 159–60.

CHAPTER 2

Teresa of Avila's Theological Reading of History: From her Second Conversion to the Foundation of St Joseph's, Ávila

Edward Howells

The critical question of how history and theology relate to each other is a real one for Teresa of Ávila. It arose with particular force with the onset of frequent ecstatic experiences following her second conversion, which provoked her to question how or whether they were from God and what action should follow on her part. How exactly was her personal history to be properly understood in relation to this theological invasion? In her autobiography or *Life*, she recounts her experience of debilitating ecstasies, which left her paralysed for days at a time. Mystical ecstasy presents the disjunction between history and theology in possibly its most intense form, because it introduces an unavoidable break between the God of these extraordinary events and the ordinary circumstances and progression of life. In classical theological terms, the question concerns the relation of nature and grace: how human nature is changed and affected by the gift of God's grace. The distinction between nature and grace is brought sharply into view: the profound difference between God's intervention and the recipient's previous understanding of human nature cannot be avoided. What I want to examine here is how Teresa develops her own tools for discerning this relationship, particularly in terms of what the soul can do in response to, and in preparation for, the immediate divine presence. Teresa develops a truly critical understanding here, of a kind that I hope to explain.

How to bring history and theology together has always been a prominent theme in Christianity. It was so for Eusebius in his *Ecclesiastical History* of the early Church, and it arose with particular force for modern New Testament scholarship in debates about how to reconcile the 'Jesus of history' with the 'Christ of faith', which continue today. In the case of Teresa, there are enough sources for her history to be known in considerable detail, but these same sources also contain her theological agenda. Her *Life*, unlike a modern biography that might make some claim to be 'objective' and to present facts unaffected by the author's self-understanding, is a work on the model of Augustine's *Confessions*.[1] It is the story not just of Teresa's independent trajectory but also of God's story in relation to her, in terms of how she became part of the journey of the Incarnation to remake a fallen creation. As Marie-Dominique Chenu pointed out in his *Nature, Man and Society* (1957), there is a particular challenge for the historian of spirituality in how to recognize both the strong connections between theology and history in the sources and the critical distinction that must be made in order to study them, at once.[2] I shall suggest that Teresa can help us to make such a critical distinction out of her own resources, while acknowledging the highly theological nature of her view of history.

The relationship of the divine initiative to Teresa's self-understanding is exemplified by an often repeated saying found in her *Soliloquies* [Exclamaciones]: she exclaims, 'May this "I" die, and may another live in me greater than I and better for me than I, so that I may serve him' (*Exclamaciones* 17.3) [Muera ya este yo, y viva en mí otro que es más que yo, y para mí mejor que yo, para que yo le pueda servir].[3] The saying begins by stating the element of opposition between God and the 'I', demanding the loss of the 'I' in favour of the divine. Paralleling Teresa's experience of the onset of mystical ecstasy, the divine is introduced as something wholly other, marked by the lack of continuity with the 'I' of previous experience. But at the same time, looking harder, one notices that she asks for God to 'live in me' and to 'serve him', which must require the continuation of the 'I', even while it dies. The 'death' of detachment turns out to be, simultaneously, entry into new life, in which another level or iteration of the 'I' opens up, which is capable of working positively with God. Later in the *Soliloquy*, she asks for a union in which you 'see yourself drowned in the infinite sea of supreme truth' (*Exclamaciones* 17.6) [te has de ver ahogado en aquel mar infinito de la suma verdad].[4] The overt loss of personal identity in being 'drowned' in a sea is offset by the phrase 'see yourself', which signals a new and deeper engagement between God and the 'I'. Significantly, the divine initiative provides the opportunity to 'see oneself' in a new way, no longer in opposition to God but intimately related to God at a deeper level, and this is the key to Teresa's later view that deliberate good works flow directly from the state of union.

A complicating factor is that Teresa's own understanding of the relationship between the divine initiative and the events of her life developed over time, and she had not reached her mature understanding at the time that she wrote what remains our main source of her history, her *Life* (1562–65). Teresa's excursus on the 'four waters' of prayer in Chapters 11–22 of the *Life* presents an ecstatic model, in which God's role is overwhelming, reducing her human contribution to one mostly of pure passivity, in a kind of total paralysis or, as she says, being 'unable to stir'.[5] There is a strong distinction between history and theology in this view and little room for understanding their interplay. In contrast, by the time that she wrote the *Interior Castle* (1577), Teresa saw such paralysing experiences as transitional, and not even as necessary for all, introducing a more active human role in relation to both the goal of union with God and the preparation for union.[6] It is this account of her mature years, in which divine and human are brought more closely together and work together, while still emphasizing the distinction between the two, that I want to uncover here. I shall look to her *Interior Castle* for this mature understanding, but then use it to shed light on the narrative sections of her *Life*, especially the period from her second conversion to the foundation of St Joseph's. Teresa's developed intellectual clarity serves to uncover intuitions that were already present in the *Life*, in her descriptions of her story, even though they took a while to filter into her teaching.

Turning briefly, then, to the *Interior Castle* for a sketch of her mature understanding, we find her position first summarized succinctly in the image of the silkworm metamorphosing into a butterfly in the Fifth Mansions (*Moradas* 5.2.2–8). The discontinuity of the 'I' in relation to God's work, first of all, is evident in the apparent 'death' of the silkworm in the cocoon: the silkworm 'dies', and the butterfly that emerges is unimaginably different from, and more beautiful than, the cocoon. But the cocoon is life as well as death, and, notably, the 'death' of the cocoon is actively fashioned by the silkworm, which spins the silk to construct the cocoon, to 'build the house wherein it will die' (*Moradas* 5.2.4) [edificar la casa adonde ha de morir]. 'Death' is not simply loss, but something that the soul can 'build' by collaborating with 'the general help given us all by God [...] by going to confession, reading good books' and so on (*Moradas* 5.2.3) [aprovechar del aujilio (*sic*) general, que a todos nos da Dios (...) ansí de acontinuar las confesiones como con buenas liciones]. Therefore, the key moment of 'death' is no longer a wholly passive state, but both passive and active, an active waiting for transformation into the butterfly which God alone can provide, in which one can work with the process.

The combination reappears in Teresa's view of union at the end of the book, in the Seventh Mansions, in the joining of Mary and Martha, the types of contemplation and action, which she relates back to the silkworm image by saying that the 'little butterfly' of ecstatic suspensions now dies.[7] Union is now possible without the element of debilitating passivity, in which the opposition between God and the 'I' is to the fore, because the marriage relationship of bridal union at the centre of the soul unites human activity with passivity in relation to God. The soul's passivity is included in the surrender of the soul as Bride to the divine Bridegroom, while the Bridegroom's reciprocal surrender invites the Bride to share actively in this movement and positively to welcome her own surrender. Activity and passivity are joined in union in an act that is simultaneously both complete self-gift to the other and recognition of one's own positive contribution in this self-gift, because it is valued by the other, in the union of love. There is a kind of self-enhancing dynamism in this mutual surrender, which Teresa describes as 'overflow' from the centre of the soul to the outskirts of the castle, bringing the whole soul and body in all its parts within the ambit of the union, and making virtuous works flow directly from union. Teresa calls this final state one where the soul's life 'is now Christ' (*Moradas* 7.2.5) [su vida es ya Cristo].

Two further examples from the *Interior Castle* help to expand this view. In the Third Mansions, speaking of people who are held back in their preparation for the divine presence by their use of reason, Teresa says:

> Love has not yet reached the point of overwhelming reason. But I should like us to use our reason to make ourselves dissatisfied with this way of serving God, always going step by step [...]. Wouldn't it be best to make this journey all at

once? [...] Let's abandon our reason and our fears into his hands. [...] We should care only about moving quickly so as to see this Lord. (*Moradas* 3.2.7–8)

[No está aún el amor para sacar de razón; más querría yo que la tuviésemos para no nos contentar con esta manera de servir a Dios siempre a un paso paso (...). ¿No valdría más pasarlo de una vez? (...) dejemos nuestra razón y temores en sus manos (...) nosotras, de sólo caminar apriesa por ver este Señor.]

Overtly, Teresa expresses the now familiar contrast between human work and the divine presence: the work of reason stands in the way and must be 'overwhelmed' by love, in a complete self-abandonment to God. Reason produces only a pedestrian 'step by step' mentality that is a hindrance to union and must be bypassed: 'we should only care about moving quickly so as to see this Lord'. Reason is not simply rejected, however, but is drawn into a larger realm by love. In the service of love, we should 'use our reason to make ourselves dissatisfied with this way of serving God'. Reason cannot anticipate the divine presence, and its usual course is to obstruct it, but in view of love it can work constructively in anticipation of God's action. It can actively engage in promoting its own failure. Paradoxically, we need reason to overcome reason.

The paradox is expressed most tightly in Teresa's phrase 'let's abandon our reason'. She implies a discipline, driven by reason, which produces a deliberate act of letting go. Reason and love are, thus, initially contrasted by Teresa, in the same way that the silkworm and the butterfly are contrasted as death and life, but then reunited in the larger view provided by love. Reason and love remain distinct but are joined in a greater unity. The perspective of union is asserted in the possibility of the soul contributing to its own transformation by using reason to *open* itself to the infinite divine presence, even though it cannot grasp this infinite nature. At the end of the Third Mansions, Teresa changes the image to signal this element of continuity: the soul is like a fledgling bird learning to fly, which has now been made 'bold to fly' (*Moradas* 3.2.12) [nos atrevemos a volar]. It cannot fly without the gift of God's immediate presence, but it can do God's will to the extent of boldly desiring to receive the gift, whatever it is, when it is given. To know that one wants to serve God, without any holding back, is itself an active work, in which the soul is already working with God.

By the time that Teresa wrote the *Interior Castle*, she was in no doubt that the soul's work, though wholly unlike God's immediate presence, could be allied with the divine activity *within* the soul's mystical self-understanding, rather than being seen in opposition to it. We cannot transform ourselves, but there is some human activity which contributes to joining us to the one who can. A second significant passage on this point is to be found in the Second Mansions where she discusses the activity of the 'cross' (*Moradas* 2.1.6–7). The cross in this sense means the work of conforming the will to God, understood according to the scriptural metaphor of 'taking up your cross' to follow Jesus. Teresa says that the intellect, for instance, though not yet able to see God as it will in union, strives to remind the soul that Jesus, already present by faith within the 'castle' of the soul, is its 'true lover' who 'never leaves it': it can 'realize that it couldn't find a better friend', because 'outside this castle neither peace nor security will be found' [se le pone delante cómo nunca se quita de con él este verdadero Amador [...] el entendimiento acude con darle a entender que no puede cobrar mejor amigo [...] fuera de este Castillo no hallará siguridad ni paz] (*Moradas* 2.1.4). The cross at this point forms a bridge between the negative associations of self-abandonment, marked by great fears and uncertainties, and the approaching intimate companionship of Christ. To suffer like Christ in the work of giving oneself to God should not, Teresa says, be seen as a war against oneself. The feeling of opposition between the soul and God, though real, is not the whole picture. There is no need to be 'ill at ease', she says, because the soul is sharing in the suffering of the cross, which overcomes the felt opposition between the soul and God in favour of the inner 'peace' of companionship with Christ.[8] To pursue such a path is not easy and requires great determination, as she frequently reminds her readers, but the cross points to a deeper continuity between our work and God's work, as yet hard to see but still capable of freeing us from our fears. She notes the importance of this insight by calling the cross the 'foundation' on which the whole edifice of the soul's transformation will be built (*Moradas* 2.1.7–8).

With this sketch in mind, I would like to return to Teresa's *Life*, to ask whether a similar pattern of discontinuity and continuity between the divine activity and Teresa's activity can be seen. My suggestion is that just as Teresa 'forefronts' the element of discontinuity, with the death of the silkworm and the abandonment of reason, so in the *Life* we hear most prominently about how God overturns the direction of Teresa's life, putting discontinuity in the way of a smooth progression from her past to her present. Most obviously, this is to be seen in what is called her 'second conversion', and also in the dramatic experiences of ecstasy that follow. But whereas this discontinuity remains utterly dominant in her teaching on the 'four waters' of prayer, by contrast in the narrative — especially in the events between her second conversion and the founding of St Joseph, which lie at the heart of the book — there is a deeper attempt to establish lines of continuity: to show how God's action, including the disorientation of painful ecstasies, can be discerned and reconciled in relation to the events of everyday life, in transformed human action. If we look at the *Life* using the mature schematic understanding of the *Interior Castle*, we can see how Teresa is seeking to find the same paradoxical unity between the divine and the human that she asserts there. Indeed, by linking her later schema to her *Life*, we can find a rich development of the same ideas in terms of her autobiography.

Teresa describes her second conversion as a turning point in the direction of her life. The story she tells is that after about twenty years as an unremarkable and not very good nun, one day on entering the oratory of the Incarnation convent in Ávila, she saw a new statue placed there which showed Christ in great suffering. 'My heart broke', she says, and feeling 'how poorly I thanked him for those wounds [...]. I threw myself down before him with the greatest outpouring of tears' (*Vida* 9.1) [Fue tanto lo que sentí de lo mal que havía agradecido aquellas llagas, que el corazón me parece se me partía, y arrojéme cabe El con grandísimo derramamiento de lágrimas]. The period of her life which followed was marked by a series of dramatic ecstasies of a kind which, she says, she began to receive 'habitually' (*Vida* 23.2) [muy ordinario], seeing them as part of the prayer of quiet. She would go into ecstasy, feeling her soul to be torn between heaven and earth; it was an experience in which her soul was 'suspended in such a way that it seems to be completely outside itself' (*Vida* 10.1) [Suspende el alma de suerte que toda parecía estar fuera de sí]. These 'grandeurs' included her famous 'transverberation', described in Chapter 29, the piercing of her heart by the arrow of God's love, and were accompanied by physical swoons which caused her 'deep affliction' [harta pena] (*Vida* 29.14). She clearly saw these experiences, like her second conversion, as a demonstration of the discontinuity that was introduced into her life by the direct intervention of God. They showed that her former religious and spiritual understanding was not enough. A demand was placed on her to reassess everything that she had known of herself and her history up to this point. God did not seem to 'fit' in any of the categories with which she was familiar. As she says in her first mention of 'mystical theology' in Chapter 10, the intellect is 'amazed by all it understands' and yet is also aware that 'it understands nothing' (*Vida* 10.1) [está como espantado de lo mucho que entiende (...) ninguna cosa entiende]. Her life has been turned into a conundrum.

The conundrum, however, is one that sparks a new kind of understanding, which emerges directly in response to her sense of division between life with God and life in the world. Teresa says that although 'I clearly understood that I loved him [...]. I did not understand as I should have what true love of God consists in' (*Vida* 9.9) [Bien entendía yo — a mi parecer — le amava, mas no entendía en qué está el amar de veras a Dios]. Her love of God was enkindled in a new way by her second conversion, which led her to want to reassess what it really is to love God. She notes that there was an immediate effect on her manner of prayer. She began to seek Christ, she says, by picturing him in 'those scenes where I saw him more alone. It seemed to me that being alone and afflicted, as a person in need, he had to accept me [...]. The scene in the garden, especially, was a comfort to me; I strove to be his companion there' (*Vida* 9.4) [las partes a donde le vía más solo. Parecíame a mí que, estando solo y afligido, como persona necesitada me havía de admitir a mí (...). En especial me hallava muy bien en la oración del Huerto: allí era mi acompañarle]. Teresa contrasts this new attempt to find God's presence with her previous way of prayer in which, for those twenty lost years, she was 'having great trouble', because she could only see herself as a 'slave' in relation to the Lord, on account of her failings (*Vida* 7.17) [En la oración pasava gran travajo, porque no andava el espíritu señor, sino esclavo]. Now her attention is drawn to the notion that God shows himself as one 'in need'. This gives her a new insight both into God and into herself: her previous sense of need, which she had seen as a barrier to prayer, because it emphasized her incapacity to love God and her difference from God, is turned on its head by the notion of God's need. Here God is even weaker than Teresa, making it possible for her to understand how she can love him: 'I strove to be his companion there'.

It is not fanciful to see in this transition the first sketch of her mature position in the *Interior Castle*, where God's immediate presence first of all presents the soul with an irreconcilable difference between God's activity and human activity, yet then, on closer examination, opens the soul to a deeper unity which establishes a new form of action. The former barrier that Teresa had set between herself and God in prayer, in terms of her need, turns out not simply to be removed, but to be the essential point of connection between her and God. She experiences God by seeing the continuity between her need and God's. The discontinuity introduced by need is now also the continuity: a sharing with God in a need that has become mutual. This anecdote precisely reflects the logic of her later position, where the discontinuity associated with God's presence becomes, paradoxically, a vital element in the intimate companionship between the soul and God.

Further flesh can be put on this scheme by observing how Teresa structures the narrative between this point and the founding of St Joseph's. Without retelling the whole story, I would like to draw attention to certain elements. First, when Teresa returns to the narrative after the interlude of the 'four waters' of prayer, she reiterates the words also found in the *Soliloquy* with which I began, saying that the life she had lived up to her second conversion 'was mine', whereas now, by contrast, her life was 'the one God lived in me' (*Vida* 23.1) [la de hasta aquí era mía; la que he vivido desde que comencé a declarar estas cosas de oración, es que vivía Dios en mí]. This discontinuity, however, is quickly followed by a reference to the way that the experience has changed her, and changed her gradually, for 'it would have been impossible in so short a time to get rid of so many bad habits and deeds' (*Vida* 23.1) [era imposible salir en tan poco tiempo de tan malas costumbres y obras]. There is a narrative to be told which, even with discontinuity at its heart, relates the old Teresa to the new and reveals a deeper connection.

It is worth noticing that, following her increasingly public experiences of ecstasy, Teresa was forced to seek guidance outside her monastery, against the accusations of devil deception which she knew would inevitably be levelled against her, having seen the fate of other women. She did not remain passive, but actively sought the counsel of wise spiritual persons in the town. The first she consulted, she says, were a 'saintly' layman, Francisco de Salcedo, and a 'learned priest' of the city, Gaspar Daza, who gave a negative verdict, which frightened her very much. She saw danger everywhere, feeling that she was drowning, as if in the middle of a river (not the delightful drowning in the sea of union). But these men also suggested that she consult the Jesuits, recently arrived in Ávila, with whom she gradually gained a more positive view.[9] Teresa emphasizes that it was a slow process, and a struggle between the immense fear of deception and the equally strong sense that God was singling her out for some great work. 'Perfection is not attained quickly' [la perfección no se alcanza en breve], she says, adding that 'many souls want to fly before God gives them wings' [creo se engañan aquí muchas almas que quieren volar antes que Dios les dé alas]. She refers to the active courage required in this work of discerning the will of God, trusting that 'His Majesty will bring it about that what they now have in desires they shall possess in deed' (*Vida* 31.17–18) [La perfección no se alcanza en breve (...). Creo se engañan aquí muchas almas que quieren volar antes que Dios les dé alas (...). Lo que ahora tienen en deseos Su Majestad hará que lleguen a tenerlo por obra]. She intersperses these chapters with guidelines for discernment of the different kinds of locutions and visions, imaginative and intellectual, showing again that there is work for the soul to do in relation to the divine work.

The picture of active cooperation, entirely shaped by God's initiative but nevertheless requiring the soul to play a demanding part, is further developed in terms of the soul's relations with other people. Not only is the soul moving out into activity in response to God's activity but in relation to other people. As Jodi Bilinkoff's book, *The Avila of St Teresa*, nicely points out, Teresa's contacts with the 'reform party' in Ávila, through her quest for authoritative spiritual directors, were vital to her success in founding St Joseph's and starting a new movement of religious reform.[10] Initially, her contact with these powerful men, who were generally inaccessible to a woman religious, was purely a response to the extraordinary ecstatic experiences which had attracted public criticism. The paradox cannot have been lost on Teresa: what started as a divine intervention entirely at the 'interior' level, with feelings of suspension and being cut off from the world, actually led her out to a new public engagement, and that in turn gave her the necessary experience in the public realm that finally enabled her to start a reform. Thus, through her Jesuit directors, Teresa met Doña Guiomar de Ulloa, the influential lady with whom she later sketched out her first plans for St Joseph's (*Vida* 32.10). Through Doña Guiomar, she also met Peter of Alcántara, whom she used as her greatest supporter during her worst periods of opposition in Ávila.[11] We find this paradox again articulated in Teresa's comment on the banning of books on prayer, following the Valdés Index of 1559. She sees it first as a great loss, but quickly moves to point out how God used it to draw her into a new kind of action: 'the Lord said to me, "Don't be sad, for I shall give you a living book"' (*Vida* 26.5) [No tengas pena, que yo te daré libro vivo]. It is the basis for her writing career.[12] The structure is clearly present in the narrative: Teresa identifies precisely those moments where a sharp discontinuity opens up, between the divine initiative and the possibility for human action, as the places in which the divine companionship is discovered at a deeper level, which then leads her to new kind of active engagement in the world.

What is not present in the *Life* is the kind of distillation of this logic in her teaching on union that we find in the *Interior Castle*. At the end of the *Life*, Teresa gives just a brief intimation of what will follow, in two final visions, the first of her soul in union and the second of seeing all things together in God. She draws our attention to the way God and her soul appear as 'mirrors', each reflecting the other, so that 'everything we do is visible' in God, and all things in creation can be seen 'joined together' (*Vida* 40.10), within union [Todo lo que hacemos se ve (...). Ver tantas cosas juntas]. The phrase recurs many times in Teresa's later teaching, that the soul 'sees itself in God' in union. The significance of this phrase is that union is no longer understood simply as the vision of God and how God loves the soul, but of the soul in relation to God, where God lights up and makes room for the soul's contribution. For instance, in the *Interior Castle*, Teresa says that in this union we can 'see God, as well as ourselves placed inside his greatness' (*Moradas* 5.2.6) [vemos a Dios y nos vemos tan metidas en su grandeza]. The soul is aware of a new mutuality in relation to God, which dispels the former sense of opposition and self-loss. The soul finds, instead, space for a new understanding of itself as united with God, and, in turn, for a new sense of vocation and then of action, as this sense of self-understanding shared in relation to God becomes the 'centre of the soul' and flows outwards in world-directed activity.

In the *Life*, the seeds of Teresa's later view are present not in her teaching on union but in the narrative. The experience of conversion and ecstasies is, as we have seen, one in which Teresa finds the space and confidence to examine her own resources. Gradually she examines herself in the light of her new experience of God. What she sees is mostly her failure: her past failure in prayer and her current fears. But these elements are now joined by 'fortitude' and 'courage', because they are found to be compatible with God's intimate companionship with the soul.[13] This is what Teresa later describes as 'taking up your cross', which is actively to use personal failure, not to attack oneself, but to open oneself to God's companionship, in a way that shares in the divine peace and freedom rather than getting stuck in fear.[14]

Conclusion

Teresa's use of history is both a theological and a critical one. We know that her history is not critical in the sense of modern critical scholarship: she has not sifted her sources for the bare bones of a factual account. Rather, she directs her sources towards a theological story — the story of the Incarnation and her own part in it. But neither is she a propagandist, in the sense of turning the facts in any direction to suit a predetermined script. She sees theology as interrupting the life that she would expect to have told, which in turn forces her and her readers to look harder at the facts. To tell the theological story is not so much to find an overarching narrative and to stick to it as to point out where the expected thrust of the narrative seems to have been broken, and to offer theological resources at that point, introducing continuity not merely at the human level but in relation to the divine. Theology provides the critical task of distinguishing the divine from the human, and at the same time of joining them together. So, looking back at her history, Teresa does not see herself as someone who, for instance, ceased to be weak and facing opposition after her second conversion. Her weakness is intensified rather than eradicated by theology: it is more obvious that one is weak as compared with God than as compared with anything else. But theology enables her to see human weakness as positively valued in a larger story, which she understands by bringing in the theological resources of the Incarnation, where weakness can be central to divine companionship. Theology deepens her history, changing the perspective both of the teller and, she hopes, of the reader. She wants us to read her history as critically informed by theology, rather than eradicated or smoothed out. She provides critical resources which are to be appropriated for our own transformation, to enable us to see our own history as better understood — interrupted, yes, but only to be intensified and expanded — in relation to the divine perspective, as 'placed inside God's greatness'.

Notes to Chapter 2

1. *Vida* 9.8. For the manner in which Teresa follows Augustine, see Bernard McGinn, 'True Confessions: Augustine and Teresa of Avila on the Mystical Self', in *Teresa of Avila: Mystical Theology and Spirituality in the Carmelite Tradition*, ed. by Edward Howells and Peter Tyler (London: Routledge, 2017), pp. 9–29. References to Teresa of Ávila's writings are from *Santa Teresa de Jesús. Obras completas*, ed. by Efrén de la Madre de Dios and Otger Steggink, 9th edn (Madrid: Biblioteca de Autores Cristianos, 1997), with English translations from *The Collected Works of St Teresa of Avila*, trans. by Kieran Kavanaugh and Otilio Rodriguez, 3 vols (Washington, DC: Institute of Carmelite Studies, 1976–85).
2. Marie-Dominique Chenu, *Nature, Man, and Society in the Twelfth Century* (London: University of Toronto Press, 1997), pp. xv–xx.
3. Similar statements are to be found in *Vida* 6.9 and 23.1, recalling Galatians 2.20, 'it is no longer I who live, but Christ who lives in me'.
4. *Obras completas*, p. 678; *The Collected Works of St Teresa of Avila*, I, 462.
5. The soul does not work (e.g. *Vida* 14.2; 18 (all); 21.11, 19; 40.7), and is paralysed or unable to stir (e.g. *Vida* 15.1; 20.21; 29.12).
6. I have charted this change in Teresa's thought elsewhere: Edward Howells, *John of the Cross and Teresa of Avila* (New York: Crossroad, 2002), pp. 70–92. Teresa retains some moments of sheer passivity (e.g. *Moradas* 4.1.10–11; *Moradas* 6.4.5; 10.2) and paralysis in her treatment of union (e.g. *Moradas* 6.2.3), but they come earlier in the mystical itinerary and are left behind in the Seventh Mansions.
7. '[...] la mariposilla, que hemos dicho, muere' (*Moradas* 7.2.6), referring back to the 'delightful union' discussed in *Moradas* 3.1–3 and 7.4.10.
8. Her sentiments are captured in these words from her *Interior Castle*: '¿Puede ser mayor mal que no nos hallemos en nuestra mesma casa? ¿Qué esperanza podemos tener de hallar sosiego en otras cosas, pues en las propias no podemos sosegar? [...] Paz, paz [...] dijo el Señor' (*Moradas* 2.1.9).
9. *Vida* 23.2–24.3.
10. Jodi Bilinkoff, *The Avila of Saint Teresa: Religious Reform in a Sixteenth-century City* (London: Cornell University Press, 1989), especially Chapter 5, pp. 110–51.
11. Bilinkoff, *The Avila of Saint Teresa*, p. 120.
12. Gillian T. W. Ahlgren, *Teresa of Avila and the Politics of Sanctity* (Ithaca, NY: Cornell University Press, 1996), pp. 32–84.
13. *Vida* 24.7; 26.5.
14. Teresa uses the image of fear as 'mud' in which the soul gets stuck, obstructing the flowing stream of free and active relationship with God (*Moradas* 1.2.10).

CHAPTER 3

A Clash of Titans: St Teresa in Pastrana

Trevor J. Dadson

In 1529, at the age of fourteen, Teresa Sánchez de Cepeda y Ahumada lost her mother, and this seems to have provoked the first of many profound religious experiences. Her father sent her to the Augustinian monastery of Santa María de Gracia in Ávila to further her education (she had already learnt to read and write at home), and there 'she spent a year and a half under the tutelage of Sor María Briceño and the Augustinian chaplain, Fray Francisco Nieva. While details are few, it is probable that the education she received from the Augustinians mirrored that which she enjoyed in the paternal home'.[1] In late 1535, aged twenty, she entered the Carmelite convent of the Incarnation on the outskirts of Ávila. She would stay there for almost the next thirty years of her life, that is to say, the greater part of it, until she became so disillusioned with the convent's lax rules that she got papal approval to leave and found her own convents under her reformed Rule of the Discalced Carmelites. This early period from 1535 was, however, very important in her life and in the decisions that she would take when it came to reforming the Rule of the Carmelites, and very important in the story of the confrontation between two powerful women, the subject of this essay.[2]

When Teresa entered the Convent of the Incarnation the wall between the convent and the outside world was very permeable: nuns could receive visitors from outside and could leave the convent to make visits themselves; nuns from well-off backgrounds and families could live in various rooms that effectively made up a small apartment, and many of them even had servants to wait upon them.[3] The revenues of a convent depended heavily upon patronage and benefactions, and these came mainly from a nun's dowry when she entered the convent and then from testamentary bequests which often took the form of prayers and Masses, spoken or sung, for the soul of the recently departed to ensure that they spent as little time as possible in Purgatory. Well-off families could leave large sums of money to a convent for these very practical purposes, or could pay for a chantry chapel where prayers and Masses could be said perpetually. Another very powerful reason for taking on the patronage of a new foundation was the need of single, wealthy women for a future burial place. María de Mendoza, daughter of the Counts of Mélito, stipulated in her will of 28 July 1565 that the house that she had bought in Alcalá de Henares and where she lived, in the Calle Santiago opposite the Archbishop's Palace, was to be left to the Dominicans, with sufficient funds to found a convent there to be called 'Madre de Dios'. Her body was to be buried in the middle of the main chapel of the new convent church, once built. In the meantime, she would be buried in the chapel in her own house. In exchange for her financial support, María received patronage over the new foundation.[4]

As with any investment, therefore, the benefactor expected a return on their outlay; this was not a one-way street. In addition to the offering of prayers and Masses, or the guarantee of a burial place, a further way in which the convent could earn its income, so to speak, was by providing a home, comfort and consolation for the widows of benefactors. Many such widows would see the convent as their natural refuge in the aftermath of the death of their husband.[5] As Jodi Bilinkoff has observed: 'The need of elite women for consolation and reassurance in a world filled with strict rules of etiquette, concern over reputation, and the death of loved ones was apparently boundless'.[6]

Widows also held a special legal place in Spanish society at that time. Whereas unmarried daughters and wives depended on their fathers and husbands to act for them in the legal arena, widows could litigate for themselves without recourse to any male. This gave them considerable power which, if allied to financial resources, made them very powerful indeed.[7] At the same time, some widows could feel overwhelmed by the legal and financial demands placed upon them on the death of a husband, especially if they had children under the age of majority (twenty-five years) to care for. Normally, they would become the children's legal guardians. In some noble families we find women effectively running the estates for over one hundred years consecutively, with the estates passing from grandmother to daughter to granddaughter. All of this came as a result of the dangers of everyday life, such as high infant mortality, the death of the male members in battle, journeys overseas, or emigration, which most women were spared.[8] One way in which a widow could escape her legal obligations was precisely by entering a convent; in many cases this was a temporary measure. The widow in question often had no intention of professing, she was simply looking for respite and consolation while she got over the death of her husband and to grips with her new responsibilities.

This was the world into which Teresa of Ávila was born and to which she had to adapt for at least the first forty to fifty years of her life. That she did not find herself entirely comfortable with the convent world she found in the Incarnation is evident from her writings and other sources. As is well known, during the 1560s she set out on a path to reform the Carmelite Order, essentially to bring it back to what she considered its origins, where the emphasis would be on austerity, poverty, and enclosure. Her plan was the revival of the earlier, stricter rules, and the discalceation of the nun. This would eventually become the reformed Order of the Discalced Carmelites. Between 1562 and 1571, reformed female houses were established at Ávila, Medina del Campo, Malagón, Valladolid, Toledo, Pastrana, Salamanca, and Alba de Tormes, with two reformed male houses at Duruelo (province of Segovia) and Pastrana. In total she founded some seventeen convents before her death in October 1582.

The founding of the early convents was not without its problems. Many small to medium-sized towns in Spain already had a good number of convents and monasteries, many of them dependent on the coffers of the local town council for their survival: basically, they lived off alms or *limosna*, and these were often in short supply. The last thing these towns wanted were more convents that were not self sufficient, and yet the principal rationale behind Teresa's foundations was precisely to break them free from noble patronage and benefactions so that her reformed nuns could spend most hours of the day in silent prayer, and not praying or chanting Masses for the souls of the departed, as in the convents she was used to.[9] It has been calculated that the average day for a Discalced Carmelite nun in one of Teresa's convents consisted of some fourteen hours of prayer, and silent prayer at that.[10] Silent prayer was not what benefactors paid for. They needed to know that the souls of their relatives were being prayed for, and they could not do that if the prayer was silent. Who could tell what the nun was praying, or, indeed, if she was praying at all?

Teresa needed the support of the well-off if she were going to establish her new convents, but that support was not going to be easy to find if the very thing they handed money over for was not part of the deal. Very interestingly, all of her early convents, up to 1570 at least, depended on the patronage and good will of the Mendoza family, and in particular of the Mendoza women.[11] The Mendozas, whose natural leader was the Duke of the Infantado, held extensive estates all over Spain, but concentrated mainly in the provinces of Guadalajara and Toledo.[12] Celebrated for the role they had played in the introduction of the Renaissance to Spain, they were great patron of the arts, especially architecture.[13] But aside from their artistic patronage, the Mendozas, and especially their women, also favoured the new religious currents that were sweeping across early sixteenth-century Spain: the reformed Franciscans, the Illuminists, the *alumbrados*, and the followers of Erasmus. Indeed, one of the principal *alumbrado* groups was found in Guadalajara, where it was vigorously protected by the Duke of the Infantado and his family.[14] The Monastery of La Salceda, a reformed Franciscan house near Tendilla in the province of Guadalajara, where Fray Francisco de Osuna wrote his *Abecedario espiritual* (one of the books read by Santa Teresa, and claimed to have had a great influence upon her and her reforming ideas), was a centre for many *alumbrados* in the early sixteenth century.[15]

The Mendozas therefore were very much in the forefront of new ideas and spiritual currents in Renaissance Spain, even at times sailing very close to the wind as far as the Inquisition was concerned, especially over their support of the *alumbrados*. They were to be found with those who defended a less formal and more life-enhancing religious practice, who sought to resolve their pious doubts in a more personal and interior spirituality, eschewing the exterior (and often empty) ritual and ceremonial of the official church, and who supported the various reforming currents of religiosity and mysticism. In time they became identified with the so-called 'Humanist' party at court, later known as the Éboli faction, a group which had strong personal links with men such as the Jesuits Francisco de Borja and

Ignacio de Loyola (St Ignatius), the Dominican preacher and writer Fray Luis de Granada, and the Princess Juana, Philip II's younger sister.[16] Ranged against them was the so-called Imperial party or Alba faction, a noble block which represented the defence of orthodoxy by means of formalism in religious practice and total political intransigence. When Teresa of Ávila began her reform programme, in the 1560s, the Éboli faction was still in the ascendant, hence undoubtedly her seeking out of patrons among the extensive Mendoza family network.

At various times she stayed with one Luisa de la Cerda in her palace in Toledo, and Luisa seems to have acted as Teresa's conduit to the Mendoza women whose support she so desperately needed. Luisa was daughter of the second Duke of Medinaceli, Juan de la Cerda, and his wife María de Silva. The lands of the dukes of Medinaceli bordered those of the Infantado, and there were strong matrimonial, dynastic and political links between the two families. María de Silva was a daughter of the Counts of Cifuentes, whose lands also bordered on those of the Infantado in Guadalajara. Another Cifuentes daughter was Catalina de Silva, mother of Ana de Mendoza y de la Cerda, the celebrated Princess of Éboli. Luisa and Catalina were therefore cousins. In addition, Luisa de la Cerda had had a pre-matrimonial relationship in 1544 with Diego Hurtado de Mendoza, Prince of Mélito and husband to Catalina de Silva, from which illicit relationship was born a daughter, Isabel de Mendoza. Ana de Mendoza y de la Cerda thus had a stepsister.[17]

This obvious stain on her character did not prevent Luisa from making a very good marriage with Marshall Arias Pardo.[18] It was his death in 1561 which brought Teresa and Luisa together, and which introduced Teresa, through her, to all of Luisa's wealthy and very educated connections among the Mendoza women, mostly based in and around Toledo. During Christmas 1561 the Provincial of the Carmelite Order in Castile ordered Teresa to attend on Luisa in Toledo, and she spent the following six months with this wealthy and illustrious aristocrat in her palace. We have little idea of the conversations and meetings that took place then, but the result is very visible: after the first foundation of the Convent of San José in Ávila (1562), five years were to pass before the next foundation of Medina del Campo (1567), but then they succeed each other with great rapidity: Malagón and Valladolid (1568), Toledo and Pastrana (1569). At the same time, Teresa was concerned with the setting up of male foundations, where she was aided by her close friend John of the Cross: reformed male Carmelite monasteries were founded in Duruelo and Pastrana, also in the period 1568–69, and then, in 1571, the Colegio de San Cirilo in Alcalá de Henares, the first Carmelite College, whose students were celebrated for their piety and exemplary behaviour.[19]

Luisa de la Cerda formed part of a very intellectual and well-educated group of women, mostly Mendozas, that met in her palace in Toledo. Among them were her cousin Catalina de Silva, Catalina's daughter Ana de Mendoza (married to the King's principal councillor Ruy Gómez de Silva and leader of the Éboli faction at Court), Luisa's own illegitimate daughter Isabel de Mendoza, and Ana and Isabel's aunt María de Mendoza (sister of Diego, Prince of Mélito, who was father to both girls), who had received lessons in Latin and Greek from the Toledo humanist and poet Alvar Gómez de Castro.[20] Gómez called the group 'gens pliniensis' because they took pleasure in reading and quoting passages from Pliny.[21]

Through these cultured women Teresa was brought into contact with their extensive contacts. The founding of the convent in Medina del Campo undoubtedly owed a lot to the support of don Álvaro Hurtado de Mendoza y Sarmiento, Bishop of Ávila and brother of María de Mendoza y Sarmiento, Marchioness of Camarasa, who also owned land in nearby Olmedo.[22] The triumphal entry into Medina from Olmedo of Teresa and her nuns was made in a Mendoza carriage. For the foundation in Valladolid Teresa could also count on the support of the same María de Mendoza, and another brother, Bernardino de Mendoza, who promised her a house and property at the gates of the city. In the event the house offered turned out to be too unhealthy, and María ceded part of her own palace in Valladolid to the Carmelites until they could occupy a new convent, in February 1569. All this time Teresa was living in some luxury with María de Mendoza in her palace in Valladolid. The convent at Malagón (province of Ciudad Real) was, as we now say, a no-brainer. Malagón belonged to Arias Pardo, recently deceased husband of Luisa de la Cerda, who was willing to spend whatever was necessary to honour the name of her husband. When the nuns arrived there, the works in the convent were still unfinished, so they were lodged in the Pardo fortress.

While Teresa was planning and then negotiating these early foundations she would have met on numerous occasions the young Ana de Mendoza y de la Cerda, Princess of Éboli, wife of the most powerful politician in the country, Ruy Gómez de Silva. Ana and Ruy had palaces in Madrid and Toledo, but by the mid- to late 1560s they were busy accumulating properties in and around Pastrana and refurbishing the palace there, which had originally been built on the orders of Ana's grandmother Ana de la Cerda, Countess of Mélito. By the beginning of 1569 Ruy had finalized the purchase of Pastrana from Ana's uncles, and he and Ana were ready to make it their new, principal residence. They journeyed there in slow stages during the month of March, making their triumphal entry into their new domain on 27 March 1569. In May 1569 a messenger from the Princess arrived at the Carmelite convent of Toledo, along with her own carriage which she had sent to take Teresa back to Pastrana. As the recently installed owners of the town of Pastrana, Ana wanted Teresa to found one of her convents there. Ana had spent quite a lot of time in Toledo with her cousin Luisa de la Cerda, and would have been party to all the talk of reform and new foundations. Her husband was the leader of the humanist or Éboli faction at court, and both were close friends of the reforming Princess Juana (herself a close friend of Francisco de Borja and of Fray Luis de Granada, whom she had known in Lisbon).[23] Ana had seen how other members of her extensive family had aided Teresa in the founding of her convents, and she was keen to follow their lead. There is also no doubt that both she and Ruy were firm supporters of the reform movement, both in Spain and abroad: among Ruy's close political friends were the Counts of Egmont and Horn and the Baron Montigny (Horn's younger brother), reforming nobles from Flanders, whom Ruy had met during his stay in Flanders during the 1550s, alongside the young Prince Philip, and who had lodged with him in Madrid in the 1560s. Whereas this contact had convinced Ruy of the need to allow reform to proceed in Flanders, the same experience had unfortunately convinced Philip of exactly the opposite. All three nobles were secretly murdered on Philip's orders.

The earliest indication of Ana's interest in founding a convent in Pastrana comes from a letter Teresa wrote from Valladolid to don Francisco de Salcedo in Ávila towards the end of September 1568: 'I venture to say that the present year will not pass without my visiting you, as the Princess of Éboli is very urgent about starting the foundation' [que, a usadas sea dicho, si pasa éste sin que yo torne a ver a vuestra merced, sigún da la priesa de la Princesa de Ebuli].[24] These plans had been some time in the making, as we learn from another of Teresa's writings: 'and the fact was that the Princess sent for me, because we had some time ago agreed to found a monastery in Pastrana. I did not think, however, that it would happen so quickly'.[25]

Ana's desire to found a Carmelite convent in Pastrana has to be seen alongside the other foundations she and Ruy were involved in at this time. In 1568 they tried to get the church of Estremera, another of their properties, upgraded to a Collegiate Church; this failed due to the opposition of the local priest, so they turned their attentions to Pastrana.[26] On 18 January 1569 they received a Papal Bull allowing them to turn the parish church of Pastrana into a Collegiate Church with forty-eight prebendaries, more than most Cathedrals.[27] In the following years the Princes, now Dukes of Pastrana, lavished money and attention on their Colegiata, acquiring relics from all over Europe and setting up various financial arrangements which would give it economic stability for generations to come. They also endowed the already existing Convent of St Francis, just outside the city walls and behind their Palace. Religious foundations took up much of their time and resources during the last years of the 1560s.

At the time the messenger from Pastrana arrived, Teresa was busy, still sorting out the recent foundations at Malagón and Toledo, and she was very reluctant, she said, to embark on another foundation, especially one that involved the Princess, who was already well known as a strong-willed young woman. Teresa tried to put her off or at least delay a decision until, she said, she had consulted with God and her confessor. Her confessor, clearly a man of the world, told her that it was a very good thing to have Ruy Gómez on her side, as he was so well connected to the king and everyone else. Teresa duly arrived in Pastrana on 10 June 1569 (in the Princess's carriage), and on 17 June she and her first group of nuns made their triumphal entry into Pastrana, to be received with festivities organized by the Town Council and the Dukes. On 23 June the convent was officially founded, and the nuns went straight to the building that Ana had prepared for them as their new home. About a fortnight later, 9 July, Teresa bestowed habits on two Carmelite friars, Fray Mariano de San Benito and Fray Juan de la Miseria, who were to be the founding members of the male Carmelite monastery of St Peter, situated approximately two kilometres outside of the town walls (Figure 3.1).

After the successful foundation of two convents in Pastrana, Teresa returned, on 21 July, to Toledo, to her new (and still unfinished) convent there and the company of Luisa de la Cerda. Again, she travelled in the Princess's carriage, drawing this

Fig. 3.1. *St Teresa Confers Habits on Juan Narduch and Mariano Azzaro, in the Presence of the Prince and Princess of Éboli* (1569), seventeenth-century mural painting, Pastrana, Fundación de San Pedro, Museo de San Francisco. Image ceded by Esther Alegre Carvajal.

stinging comment from a passing cleric: 'Are you the Saint who deceives everybody and goes around in carriages?' [¿Sois vos la santa, que engañáis al mundo y os andáis en coches?].[28] There is no record of Teresa's reply. From Toledo she wrote on 17 January 1570 to her brother Lorenzo (then living in Lima), bringing him up to date with her latest news, among which is an interesting comment on Pastrana: 'At present I am at Toledo. It will be a year since I came on the eve of Lady-day next March. During this time I visited a town belonging to Ruy Gómez, Prince of Éboli, where a house was founded for friars and another for nuns, both of which are doing well. I returned here to set this house in order'.[29]

In spite of this good start, the Carmelite convent at Pastrana and Teresa's relations with Ana de Mendoza have been the subject of much speculation but little real scrutiny, and a lot of ink has been spilled over what happened there. For Pastrana was the only one of Teresa's foundations that was later closed down, in April 1574; the only failure, so to speak, of her reform programme. For that very reason it has taken up an inordinate amount of space in all discussions of Teresa's foundations and reform movement, but that 'space' has from the start been ideologically charged and highly partial, beginning with Teresa's own so-called recollections on and of the event. Her description of the founding and then closure of the convent at Pastrana comes in Chapter 17 of the *Book of Foundations*, a book which she started to write in 1573 and then continued on and off until 1579. In other words, she was writing about her recollections in autobiographical form, often after the events narrated, and subject of course to later realities and hindsight. In the case of Pastrana it seems that she wrote well after all the events narrated in the book had occurred and when the convent no longer existed, when she had removed her nuns to the new foundation of Segovia, and, perhaps of greatest importance, when her benefactors were no longer the Mendozas. Her description of events in Pastrana, therefore, is highly justificatory as she tries to explain why she listened to God and Ruy Gómez back in May 1569, why she was persuaded by his influence (no longer there in the late 1570s, as he died in July 1573), and why she had given in to the Princess's insistent calls to found a convent in Pastrana. Teresa's defence of her own actions, seen in the light of hindsight, was then taken up by all her supporters, especially her Carmelite hagiographers. And in this portrayal there is one very clear bad guy or, in this case, bad girl — Ana de Mendoza y de la Cerda, who is variously depicted as capricious, wilful, obstinate, selfish, and/or insane. Teresa is of course a model of reason and good behaviour.

In the rest of this essay I wish to put the case for Ana de Mendoza y de la Cerda, a case that has hitherto been largely ignored. So, let us begin at the beginning, and Teresa's decision to go, we are told very much against her will, to Pastrana in June 1569, to found what would be her sixth reformed convent. Teresa apparently anguished over this decision, was appalled at the luxurious festivities put on in her honour when she arrived in Pastrana, and then was upset at the (small) size and living conditions of the house offered to her for her new convent. All of this has been seen by later commentators as clear examples of Ana's pride and extravagance. Not true: 1) Teresa was very happy at the chance to found a convent in Pastrana because Ruy had offered her the opportunity to found also a monastery for reformed Carmelite friars, and Teresa was very keen to push on with the male foundations she had recently begun (this monastery did not close down in 1574 or any time thereafter, and continued functioning as a Carmelite foundation until the nineteenth century when it was taken over by the Franciscans); 2) regarding the festivities put on in Pastrana to welcome Teresa and her nuns, the same had happened in Malagón, where Teresa arrived in a carriage accompanied by Luisa de la Cerda, and in Valladolid, where nuns and friars walked in procession through the streets to the applause of the multitude; similar processions took place in Toledo; 3) none of the original houses offered to Teresa for her convents was found to be suitable: in Medina they were put in a semi-ruined house; in Malagón the house was still undergoing building works and they had to be lodged elsewhere; in Valladolid the first house offered to them was found to be unhealthy and Teresa and her nuns all caught malaria. Only with the foundation in Pastrana are the size and condition of the house taken to be a slight on Teresa and her nuns, an example of the Princess's capricious nature.[30] As had happened elsewhere, the Princess quickly provided a new building outside the city walls, and she took personal charge of the building works, following closely the demands of the founder, which included the erection of a church and the provision of a garden or orchard. In the meantime, Teresa and her nuns were lodged in the ducal Palace, where they lived with the Princess of Éboli, just as they had done with Luisa de la Cerda (in Toledo and Malagón) and María de Mendoza y Sarmiento (in Valladolid), and just as they would do in the future with the Dukes of Alba, her new patrons. Nothing out of the ordinary, so far.

In the foundational documents for Pastrana the Princess set out some conditions: if the Carmelites were unable to sustain themselves, Ana, who had already provided them with a house, orchard, and church, would give them what they needed so that they would not need to live off charity. In exchange for this support, she would have the right of patronage. This has been taken by later commentators as another example of the Princess's meddling in the affairs of the convent, which ultimately led to its closure. Indeed, it was hinted at by Teresa herself in her own recollections in the *Book of Foundations*, when she talks about the Princess demanding 'some things which were not convenient for our religion [i.e. the reformed Carmelites], and so I determined to come away from there without founding a convent' [por pedirme algunas cosas la princesa que no convenían a nuestra religión, y ansí me determiné a venir de allí sin fundar antes que hacerlo].[31] The inconvenient things were undoubtedly the Princess's right of patronage and all that that meant in practice. And yet this was precisely what Teresa had agreed to in the founding of the convent in Malagón with Ana's cousin and close friend and ally, Luisa de la Cerda! In exchange for a house, a church and an annual rent, so that the nuns would not have to live off charity, Luisa had demanded that the nuns celebrate a daily Mass for the repose of the soul of her dead husband Arias Pardo, and that she have the right of patronage. This latter meant in practice that she could go and live in the convent if she wished, where she would expect to find refuge and consolation in her widowhood. None of this was compatible with the reforms Teresa was pushing forward, and yet she accepted all of Luisa's demands in Malagón.[32] Ana de Mendoza was asking for no more than this in her foundation at Pastrana — founded only a few months after that at Malagón — but it has always been interpreted as another sign of her capriciousness, arrogance and possible madness. It was nothing of the sort. Ana was simply following the well-known pattern of aristocratic patronage outlined at the start of this essay: it was a two-way street, in which, in exchange for financial and other support, the benefactors expected some return on their investment. Teresa had been very happy to accept this support at the start of her reform programme, even though apparently it went against all her principles, and Ana's demands were no different to those of María de Mendoza y Sarmiento or her cousin Luisa de la Cerda.[33] No one has seen fit to damn them as they have Ana, nor did Teresa herself see fit to close down her convents at Valladolid, Toledo, or Malagón. Why was Pastrana different?

Much hinges on the events that took place in Pastrana from the end of July 1573 onwards. At eight o'clock in the evening of 29 July, Ruy Gómez died in Madrid, after a short and painful illness. His distraught widow, present at his death, who was only thirty-three years old at the time and the mother of six children under the age of majority (the eldest, Ana, was twelve, the youngest, another Ana, barely a year old), immediately dressed in the garb of one of the Carmelite friars (Fray Baltasar de Jesús), also present at her husband's death, and set off with her mother and some servants, plus two friars, to Pastrana, taking with them the coffin of Ruy Gómez in a cart drawn by mules. News of their imminent arrival reached the convent at two in the morning of 31 July, as one of the two friars went on ahead. The prioress is supposed to have said: 'The Princess a nun? It will be the ruin of this house!' [La princesa, monja! Yo doy la casa por deshecha].[34] The funeral cortege arrived there later that day and, not surprisingly, presented something of a strange spectacle, especially the Princess dressed up as a friar in a very dirty, shabby, and oversized habit. This incident has been used by the Princess's detractors to suggest that Ruy Gómez's death had left her unhinged, and that her arrival at the Carmelite convent in Pastrana was yet another act of a selfish and wilful woman. Again, not true. Ana was doing what any widowed noblewoman was used to doing: seeking refuge, comfort, company and consolation in the convent she patronized. Equally importantly, this refuge offered the young and inexperienced Ana the chance to think and to plan how to rebuild her life after Ruy. Throughout the summer of 1573 the king, Philip II, urged Ana to leave the convent and take on her responsibilities, in particular those of legal guardian of her children. Ana was just as determined not to leave the convent or take on those burdens. The children were not abandoned as some historians have argued. Initially, they were left behind in Madrid in the care of the Duke's large retinue of servants, but they were soon joined by Ana's mother and their grandmother, Catalina de Silva, who quickly returned from Pastrana to look after them. Ana's entry into her convent in Pastrana was not solely nor principally a whim or fancy brought on by uncontrollable grief, but was probably a calculated move on her part to give her time and breathing space. She would have known little of her husband's complex financial matters, but what little she did know would have caused any recently widowed woman to stand back and ask for time. The moment she accepted the legal guardianship of her children she would be responsible for everything, including Ruy's astronomical debts.[35] No wonder she rushed off to what she saw as 'her convent'.

At the beginning it would appear that the prioress, Isabel de Santo Domingo, put up with Ana's demands: she permitted her to have her own servants and slaves; she provided her with a small apartment and meals apart, if she wished; and she allowed her visitors, among them the Bishop of Segovia and officials of her late husband who needed instructions. But the demand that seems to have pushed her over the edge concerned one of Ruy's testamentary bequests, indeed the one that Ana was most concerned to see carried out: he had asked for perpetual prayers, day and night, to be said before the Holy Sacrament, in each of the three religious houses he had patronized in Pastrana: the Convent of St Francis; the Monastery of St Peter (male Carmelites), and the Convent of St Joseph (Carmelite nuns). And these were to be said for all the following: the universal state of Mother Church; the health and life of King Philip and his successors; the souls of Ruy Gómez and his forebears; those of his wife Ana and her forebears; and those of the heirs and successors in their noble house. That is a lot of praying. Ruy and Ana might have been part of the religious reform movement in sixteenth-century Spain and friends of all the major reformers, but they were still very traditional when it came to the health of their souls and Purgatory. Ana was determined that this testamentary bequest would be carried out as her husband had stipulated, and Isabel de Santo Domingo was equally determined that her thirteen Carmelite nuns were not going to spend their time on their knees praying for the soul of Ruy Gómez, or even the welfare of the king.[36]

A clash between these two powerful and determined women was inevitable and it eventually led to so much pressure being put on Ana — by the king, by the Prior of Atocha,[37] by the Carmelite Provincial, by her mother Catalina, and by the local Town Council of Pastrana — that she had no choice but to leave the convent, in early 1574, and take up residence first of all in a hermitage in the gardens of the convent and then, eventually (probably by mid February), in her own Palace. When she left the convent she stopped the regular maintenance payments she and Ruy had agreed to pay the convent so that they would not be solely reliant on charity. With other religious houses in the town all dependent on local charity, Teresa's convent was no longer viable economically, and an alternative plan had to be looked for. It came in the most dramatic fashion.

In March 1574 Teresa finally responded to her Prioress's constant appeals for help. She decided to close the convent and transfer the nuns to the recently opened convent in Segovia. Two men she trusted, Julián de Ávila and Antonio Gaitán, were charged with the business. They left Segovia on 27 March and were to approach Pastrana silently, at night, so as not to arouse suspicion. There they met with Isabel de Santo Domingo, overjoyed to be leaving the place, and she organized five carts and mules to transport the nuns and their belongings out of Pastrana and to the safety, as she saw it, of Segovia. At about midnight on Thursday 1 April they all left the convent, 'with the greatest silence we were capable of', later wrote Julián de Ávila, whose account is the most detailed that we have.[38] However, the Princess got wind of what was going on and sent her steward after them. Amidst scuffles and shouting, and with the aid of a Carmelite friar who came to their rescue, they were able to climb the hill out of Pastrana to where the carts were waiting for them. They travelled all night without stopping in order to get beyond the Princess's jurisdiction. Later they almost all drowned in the swollen waters of the river Henares, but eventually, after five days of travel in the most uncomfortable of conditions, which included a climb through the snows and passes of the Sierra de Guadarrama, they arrived to much rejoicing in Segovia: it was Wednesday of Holy Week, 7 April.

Obviously, this 'heroic' escape and journey has become part of Carmelite folklore. One of Teresa's disciples, María de San José Salazar, wrote about the event in her *Libro de Recreaciones*, and in it the nuns are described as heroines escaping the clutches of no less a personage than the Princess of Éboli.[39] Julián de Ávila's own eyewitness account says much the same, and the dichotomy — good Teresa, bad Ana — has become firmly embedded in Carmelite hagiography of the Saint. Teresa's own account in her *Book of Foundations*, written some years after the event, and thus with the benefit of hindsight, also emphasizes the struggle of wills between the Princess nun (who signed her letters at this time as Sor Ana de la Madre de Dios) and the put-upon Prioress.[40] In other words, Teresa, as she writes the history of her foundations, describes the closure from the point of view of someone trying to justify her only failure, and in so doing she rewrites the actual events. Closure must be seen to be justified as the only possible outcome, hence from the start her description of the founding of the convent in Pastrana is tinged with negative comments. She did not really want to go there, it meant leaving unfinished her work in Malagón and Toledo, she was always aware of the Princess's difficult character, no good could come of this, and so on. From the start she prepares for the end, for the eventual and inevitable closure, and her account, and all those that have followed it faithfully, must be read in this light.

Teresa has had a good press and very good biographers; Ana has suffered from very much the opposite: a bad press and pretty awful biographers, who have concentrated more on the legends and myths that have built up around her (whilst always adding a few more of their own) than on dealing with her historically.[41] As we have seen, Ana's so-called demands were the traditional responses of aristocratic widows in sixteenth-century Spain who expected their foundations to provide them with support, comfort, and consolation. It is quite probable that, with time, Ana would have got over her terrible grief and left the convent of her own accord, or that she would have adopted the stance of her aunt María de Mendoza, who became what is known as a 'pisadera', that is to say, a women who did not profess but entered and left the convent whenever she wanted to, treating it as a sort of 'piso' or flat. Ana's demands were therefore entirely traditional, no different in fact to those of her cousin Luisa de la Cerda, which Teresa had had no difficulty in meeting.

So, why the problems now and with Ana? The answer is possibly two-fold: in the first place, Pastrana was at that time the only town where Teresa had founded both a female and a male Carmelite house, and the male house had been the subject of much scandal and gossip. Discipline was excessive, and there had been complaints from the novices; then the two founding brothers, Mariano de San Benito and Baltasar de Jesús, had gone off with the hermit Catalina de Cardona (a close friend of Ana's as it happens) into the wilderness of the Alcarria, where they set up two monasteries of Discalced Carmelites. The ensuing scandal posed a real problem and threat to the female house, which could easily fall prey to the same contagion.[42] Teresa felt she had to act. In the second place, the answer to our question has to lie also in the changing political landscape that occurred towards the end of the 1560s and accelerated with the death of Ruy Gómez in 1573. During the course of the 1560s Ruy found himself more and more on the margins of political debate. Whereas previously he had been very much the king's prime councillor, the man he always listened to, now he slipped slowly from favour, though not losing any of his privileges or wealth; indeed, they actually increased almost in proportion to his waning influence. The antagonistic, illiberal and warmongering Duke of Alba was now in the ascendant and he had the ear of the king, especially when it came to dealing with the problems of the Low Countries. Teresa of Ávila was a very political animal, and she could see as well as anyone the way the winds were blowing. If she had hitched her reform wagon to the Mendozas (the Éboli faction) at the start of her crusade, from 1571 onwards she moved steadily and decisively into the Alba orbit. The next convent to be founded after Pastrana was in Salamanca, in 1570, where again she benefited from Mendoza patronage, this time in the shape of Bishop Pedro González de Mendoza, son of the Duke of the Infantado. Whilst there, she received a call to found a convent in nearby Alba de Tormes, seat of the Alba dukedom. The call apparently came from Francisco Velázquez and Teresa de Laíz, but this was just a front: the real patrons were the Dukes of Alba, who endowed the new convent with an annual rent and held patronage over it (just as Ana and Ruy had done in Pastrana). The foundation took place without any pomp, ceremony or propaganda. It would appear that Teresa wanted to keep quiet, at least for the time being, her jumping ship from the Mendozas to the Álvarez de Toledo. But by 1574 and the closing of the convent in Pastrana, there was no longer any need for secrecy: Ruy Gómez had died, the Princess no longer mattered, and Teresa was fully involved with her new Alba friends. Her decision to abandon Ana de Mendoza was clearly the right move to make politically, though it says little positive about her religious concerns or motives.[43] Teresa would of course continue founding convents right up to the year of her death, 1582, with new foundations in Granada and Burgos. In September she travelled to Alba de Tormes to be present at the birth of the Duchess's grandson, heir to the dukedom, and there she died on 4 October. By then the Princess had been arrested on the orders of the king, in late July 1579, accused among many other offences of having meddled in state affairs. She was imprisoned in fortresses at Pinto and San Torcaz, and then, in 1582, placed under house arrest in her palace of Pastrana, where she would die, still imprisoned, on 2 February 1592.

Every saint needs a sinner, an 'other', and undoubtedly Teresa (and her later biographers) found hers in Ana de Mendoza y de la Cerda, but whereas history has been kind to Teresa it has not been so to Ana. Referred to in her own day as the Jezebel at court, the one-eyed temptress who is supposed to have had sexual relations with the king, and then with his secretary Antonio Pérez, Ana's story has not been properly told. This essay has been an attempt to put the record straight, at least as regards what really happened with the convent in Pastrana.

Notes to Chapter 3

This essay owes a large debt to Esther Alegre Carvajal and to Helen H. Reed: to the former for her excellent studies on Santa Teresa and the Princess of Éboli: 'El encuentro y la ruptura entre Teresa de Jesús y la Princesa de Éboli: ¿Una cuestión de enfrentamiento personal o un asunto de estrategia política?', *eHumanista*, 24 (2013), 466–78, and 'Ana de Mendoza y de la Cerda, princesa de Éboli y duquesa de Pastrana (Cifuentes, 1540–Pastrana, 1592)', in *Damas de la Casa de Mendoza: historias, leyendas y olvidos*, ed. by Esther Alegre Carvajal (Madrid: Polifemo, 2014), pp. 578–617; to the latter for her co-authorship of our book *La princesa de Éboli. Cautiva del rey: vida de Ana de Mendoza y de la*

Cerda (1540–1592) (Madrid: Marcial Pons Historia-Centro de Estudios Europa Hispánica, 2015), from which I have taken significant material, much of which was originally authored by Helen.

1. Elizabeth Teresa Howe, *Education and Women in the Early Modern Hispanic World* (Aldershot and Burlington, VT: Ashgate, 2008), p. 61.
2. Joseph Pérez offers a very good description of these early years in *Teresa de Ávila y la España de su tiempo*, 2nd edn (Madrid: Algaba Ediciones, 2015).
3. There is much useful information on convent life in early sixteenth-century Spain in Jodi Bilinkoff, *The Avila of Saint Teresa: Religious Reform in a Sixteenth-Century City* (Ithaca, NY: Cornell University Press, 1989), and Mary Elizabeth Perry, *Gender and Disorder in Early Modern Seville* (Princeton, NJ: Princeton University Press, 1990), Chapter 4, 'Walls without Windows'.
4. See Juana Hidalgo Ogáyar, 'La familia Mendoza, ejemplo de patronazgo femenino en la edad moderna', in *Familias, jerarquización y movilidad social*, ed. by Giovanni Levi y Raimundo A. Rodríguez Pérez (Murcia: Editum, 2010), pp. 297–309 (p. 302): 'The patronage that these women in Alcalá de Henares exercised was in the majority of cases related to the search for a place of burial for themselves and, on occasion, for their family [...]. They made use of a formula that had been in existence since the Middle Ages and which consisted in a person with economic means providing the money necessary so that a religious community could build their convent; in exchange, they acquired the patronage of the foundation and a burial place in the convent church' [El patronazgo que ejercieron estas mujeres en Alcalá de Henares estuvo relacionado en la mayoría de los casos con la búsqueda de un lugar de enterramiento para ellas y, en ocasiones, para su familia (...). Se sirvieron de una fórmula que se venía utilizando desde la época medieval y que consistía en que una persona con recursos económicos aportaba el dinero necesario para que una comunidad religiosa pudiera construir su convento, a cambio adquiría el patronazgo de la obra y un lugar de enterramiento en la iglesia del monasterio]. All translations from the original Spanish are mine, unless otherwise stated.
5. Again, Bilinkoff is the authority here: 'Elite Widows and Religious Expression in Early Modern Spain: The View from Avila', in *Widowhood in Medieval and Early Modern Europe*, ed. by Sandra Cavallo and Lyndan Warner (London: Longman, 1999), pp. 181–92.
6. Bilinkoff, *The Avila of Saint Teresa*, p. 104.
7. The now standard work on the subject is Grace Coolidge, *Guardianship, Gender, and the Nobility in Early Modern Spain* (Farnham: Ashgate, 2010).
8. See Allyson M. Poska, *Women and Authority in Early Modern Spain: The Peasants of Galicia* (Oxford: Oxford University Press, 2005), especially Chapter 1, 'Women without Men', and Chapter 5, 'Widowhood'.
9. Alison Weber underlines the opposition that Teresa encountered in many towns to her new foundations, especially the economic consequences and the 'break with the traditional system that bound religious Orders to powerful elites through a system of endowed chaplaincies'. *Teresa of Avila and the Rhetoric of Femininity* (Princeton, NJ: Princeton University Press, 1990), p. 124.
10. For a detailed description of the typical day of a Discalced Carmelite nun, see *María de San José Salazar, 'Book for the Hour of Recreation'*, ed. by Alison Weber (Chicago, IL: University of Chicago Press, 2002), pp. 12–13. As she states in another work: 'twelve of the eighteen hours that constituted the Carmelite day were spent in solitary activities — in prayer, devotional readings, and manual labour'. 'Saint Teresa's Problematic Patrons', *Journal of Medieval and Early Modern Studies*, 29.2 (1999), 357–79 (p. 372, n. 7).
11. See Alegre Carvajal, 'El encuentro y la ruptura entre Teresa de Jesús y la Princesa de Éboli' for the best description of this patronage. For the important role played by Mendoza women in Early Modern Spain, see *Power and Gender in Early Modern Spain: Eight Women of the Mendoza Family, 1450–1650*, ed. by Helen Nader (Urbana and Chicago: University of Illinois Press, 2004), and *Damas de la Casa de Mendoza*, ed. by Esther Alegre Carvajal (Madrid: Ediciones Polifemo, 2014).
12. On the power and the extensive client networks of the Mendozas, see Esther Alegre Carvajal, 'Grupos aristocráticos y práctica urbana: la ciudad nobiliaria de los Mendoza. "Imagen distintiva" de su linaje y de su red de poder', in *Familia, valores y representaciones*, ed. by Joan Bestard and Manuel Pérez García (Murcia: Editum, 2010), pp. 31–47.

13. The standard work remains Helen Nader, *The Mendoza Family in the Spanish Renaissance, 1350–1550* (New Brunswick, NJ: Rutgers University Press, 1979).
14. For a history of the *alumbrados* in Spain, see Antonio Márquez, *Los alumbrados: orígenes y filosofía, 1525–1559* (Madrid: Taurus, 1972). For the role played by some noble families (Mendoza, Pacheco, Enríquez) in the support they offered to these different reformist groups and, in some cases, protection from the Inquisition, see the excellent study by Stefania Pastore, *Una herejía española: conversos, alumbrados e inquisición (1449–1559)* (Madrid: Marcial Pons Historia, 2010).
15. Márquez, *Los alumbrados*, pp. 63–64; Pérez, *Teresa de Ávila*, pp. 205–06. Like Teresa herself, all of the *alumbrados* were Jewish converts or descendants of converts from Judaism (see Pastore, *Una herejía española*, p. 171).
16. For the Éboli faction, see José Martínez Millán, 'Grupos de poder en la corte durante el reinado de Felipe II: la facción ebolista, 1554–1573', in *Instituciones y elites de poder en la Monarquía Hispana durante el siglo XVI*, ed. by J. Martínez Millán (Madrid: Universidad Autónoma de Madrid, 1992), pp. 137–97. For the Humanist party and its links with a number of Portuguese intellectuals, see Reed and Dadson, *La princesa de Éboli*, p. 44, and Alegre Carvajal, who writes that 'The Humanist party, during the reign of Charles V, derived from the Isabeline party, formed with the protection and support of Queen Isabel, and then it became the Éboli faction in the reign of Philip II' [El partido humanista, durante el reinado de Carlos V, derivaba del *partido isabelino*, formado bajo la protección y apoyo de la reina Isabel, y luego se transforma en el partido ebolista en el reinado de Felipe II] ('Ana de Mendoza y de la Cerda', p. 581, n. 9).
17. On this extra-marital affair, see Reed and Dadson, *La princesa de Éboli*, pp. 51–53.
18. He was the nephew of Cardinal Juan Pardo de Tavera, Archbishop of Toledo and Inquisitor General (Pérez, *Teresa de Ávila*, p. 177). There is useful information on Luisa de la Cerda in María Pilar Manero Sorolla, 'La Biblia en el carmelo femenino: la obra de María de San José (Salazar)', in *Actas del XII Congreso de la Asociación Internacional de Hispanistas. Birmingham 1995*, ed. by Jules Whicker, 7 vols (Birmingham: University of Birmingham, 1998), III, *Estudios Áureos II*, 52–58, and 'On the Margins of the Mendozas: Luisa de la Cerda and María de San José (Salazar)', in *Power and Gender in Early Modern Spain*, ed. by Helen Nader, pp. 113–31.
19. This foundation was supported financially by Ruy Gómez de Silva, Prince of Éboli.
20. On this remarkable woman, see María del Carmen Vaquero Serrano, *En el entorno del Maestro Alvar Gómez; Pedro del Campo, María de Mendoza, y los Guevara* (Toledo: Oretania Ediciones, 1996); 'Books in the Sewing Basket: María de Mendoza y de la Cerda', in *Power and Gender in Early Modern Spain*, ed. by Helen Nader, pp. 93–112; 'La ilustre y hermosísima María de Mendoza: nuevos datos de su vida y poemas del humanista Alvar Gómez a ella', *Lemir*, 19 (2015), 9–68; and María Belén Rubio Ávila, 'María de Mendoza y de la Cerda (Utiel, *c*. 1522–Madrid, 15 de julio de 1567)', in *Damas de la Casa de Mendoza*, ed. by Esther Alegre Carvajal, pp. 561–76.
21. On the intellectual environment surrounding these Mendoza women, see Reed and Dadson, *La princesa de Éboli*, pp. 46–50, and Trevor J. Dadson, 'The Education, Books and Reading Habits of Ana de Mendoza y de la Cerda, Princess of Éboli (1540–1592)', in *Women's Literacy in Early Modern Spain and the New World*, ed. by Anne J. Cruz and Rosilie Hernández-Pecoraro (Aldershot and Burlington, VT: Ashgate, 2011), pp. 79–102.
22. She was daughter of the Counts of Ribadavia and the wife of Francisco de los Cobos, Secretary of State to Charles V, until his death in 1547.
23. In 1555, and aided by Francisco de Borja, her confessor, Juana secretly became a Jesuit, in spite of its being a strictly male Order. She adopted the pseudonym of Mateo Sánchez.
24. *The Letters of Saint Teresa. A Complete Edition Translated from the Spanish and Annotated by the Benedictines of Stanbrook*, 4 vols (London: Thomas Baker, 1919–24), I, 38. The original in Spanish can be found in *Santa Teresa de Jesús, Obras completas*, ed. by Efrén de la Madre de Dios and Otger Steggink (Madrid: Editorial Católica, Biblioteca de Autores Cristianos, 2015), p. 880, Letter 13.
25. *Santa Teresa de Jesús, Obras completas*, p. 730: 'y era que [la princesa de Éboli] enviava por mí, porque havía mucho que estava tratado entre ella y mí de fundar un monesterio en Pastrana. Yo no pensé que fuera tan presto'.
26. Trevor J. Dadson and Helen H. Reed, *Epistolario e historia documental de Ana de Mendoza y de la Cerda, princesa de Éboli* (Madrid: Iberoamericana-Vervuert, 2013), pp. 86–91, docs. 11–13.

27. Dadson and Reed, *Epistolario e historia documental*, pp. 92–105, docs. 14–18 and 20. Indeed, it was only exceeded by the Cathedral of Toledo, which had fifty prebendaries.
28. Quoted in Pérez, *Teresa de Ávila*, p. 176.
29. *The Letters of Saint Teresa*, I, 61; the original in Spanish in *Santa Teresa de Jesús, Obras completas*, p. 891, letter 25: 'Al presente estoy en Toledo. Havrá un año por la víspera de nuestra señora de marzo que llegué aquí, aunque desde aquí fui a una villa de Rui Gómez, que es príncipe de Ebuli, adonde se fundó un monesterio de frailes y otro de monjas, y están harto bien. Torné aquí por acabar de dejar esta casa puesta en concierto'.
30. Ironically, it is likely that Ana was trying to anticipate what she knew were Teresa's idealistic principles of living in poverty and off charity, hence the simple lodgings provided for the nuns.
31. *Santa Teresa de Jesús, Obras completas*, p. 733.
32. As Pérez notes, *Teresa de Ávila*, p. 87: 'Luisa de la Cerda organizes everything very well: she offers a house, a church in good condition, an annual rent of 50,000 maravedís, plus an income in goods, sixty-four bushels of wheat and the same of barley, and, in addition, 30,000 maravedís a year for a chaplaincy: a daily Mass will be said for the repose of the soul of Marshall Arias Pardo. In exchange, she reserves to herself the right of patronage over the convent. All of this is contrary to the principles of Teresa's reform, which puts at the forefront the ideal of poverty. Luisa de la Cerda insists; the Jesuits support her. Teresa gives way' [Luisa de la Cerda lo dispone todo muy bien: ofrece una casa, una iglesia acondicionada, una renta anual de ciento cincuenta mil maravedís, más unos ingresos en especie, sesenta y cuatro fanegas de trigo y otras tantas de cebada, y, además, treinta mil maravedís al año para una capellanía: se oficiará una misa diaria por el reposo del alma del mariscal Arias Pardo. En contrapartida, se reserva el derecho de patronazgo sobre el convento. Todo esto es contrario a los principios de la reforma teresiana, que pone en primer plano el ideal de pobreza. Luisa de la Cerda insiste; los jesuitas la apoyan. Teresa cede].
33. For the sometimes uneasy relations between Teresa and her (generally female) patrons, see Weber, 'Saint Teresa's Problematic Patrons'.
34. Quoted in Efrén de la Madre de Dios and Otger Steggink, *Tiempo y vida de Santa Teresa*, 3rd edn (Madrid: La Editorial Católica, Biblioteca de Autores Cristianos, 1996), p. 563.
35. It was later claimed that the Princess had paid some 106,942,202 maravedís to cancel the Prince's debt, and that it took her until 1579 to do so. The sum was equivalent to 285,179 ducats, an extraordinary amount of debt for any woman to take on, and at least four times the annual revenues of the wealthiest noble estate in Spain at the time.
36. For more on the paradoxical nature of their spirituality, see Trevor J. Dadson, 'Tradición y reforma en la vida espiritual de la princesa de Éboli', in *Rostros, relatos e imágenes de Teresa de Jesús: reflexiones en el V Centenario de su nacimiento*, ed. by Esther Alegre Carvajal, *eHumanista*, 33 (2016), 230–45.
37. Fray Hernando de Castillo, Prior de Atocha, made at least two visits to Pastrana to try to persuade the Princess to leave the convent: in November 1573 and again in January 1574. See Reed and Dadson, *La princesa de Éboli*, pp. 241–43.
38. It is related in Efrén de la Madre de Dios and Steggink, *Tiempo y vida de Santa Teresa*, p. 561 et seq.
39. See María de San José Salazar, '*Book for the Hour of Recreation*', ed. by Alison Weber, p. 132.
40. *Santa Teresa de Jesús, Obras completas*, p. 734. An illustration of one of the Princess's letters, where she signs as Sor Ana de la Madre de Dios, can be found in Dadson and Reed, *Epistolario e historia documental*, pp. 588–90, Figure 4.
41. Reed and Dadson, *La princesa de Éboli*, tries to remove all of these legends and myths, concentrating solely on the historical record.
42. See Reed and Dadson, *La princesa de Éboli*, pp. 206–07 for the details of the scandal. There are also some interesting facts about the problems of the male house in *The Letters of Saint Teresa*, I, 116–18, and IV, 379–80.
43. Curiously, however, the 'Pastrana affair' does not seem to have affected relations between the two women in the years following. When John of the Cross was secretly imprisoned in Toledo

by the unreformed Carmelites in 1578, Teresa wrote to her close ally and friend Fray Jerónimo Gracián de la Madre de Dios: 'I feel certain that if some influential person were to plead for Fray John with the Nuncio, were he only entreated to inquire into the father's character and the injustice of his imprisonment, Sega would at once order that he should be sent to one of his own houses. I do not know by what mischance it is that nobody remembers that saint. The Princess of Éboli would intercede for him if Father Mariano stated the case to her' (*The Letters of Saint Teresa*, III, 141; original in *Santa Teresa de Jesús, Obras completas*, p. 1174, dated 19 August 1578: 'Yo le digo que tengo por cierto que, si alguna persona grave pidiese a fray Juan al nuncio, que luego le mandaría ir a sus casas con decirle que se informe de lo que es ese padre y cuán sin justicia le tienen. No sé qué ventura es que nunca hay quien se acuerde de este santo. A la princesa de Ebuli que lo dijese Mariano, lo haría'. See Reed and Dadson, *La princesa de Éboli*, p. 259). In the early summer of 1580, when the Princess was in prison in San Torcaz, she was visited by the same Jerónimo Gracián. The King had given him a special permission to visit her and help her in her business affairs, but it is likely that Philip did so at the request of Teresa, for she wrote to Gracián on 3 June 1580 enquiring after the Princess and her whereabouts: 'Report said that the Princess of Éboli had returned to her home in Madrid: the last news is that she is at Pastrana. I do not know which is true: in either case, it is a very good position for her' (*The Letters of Saint Teresa*, IV, p. 43; original in *Santa Teresa de Jesús, Obras completas*, p. 1276: 'Dijeron estava la princesa de Ebuli en su casa en Madrid; ahora dicen está en Pastrana. No sé lo que es verdad; cualquiera de estas cosas es harto buena para ella'. See also Reed and Dadson, *La princesa de Éboli*, p. 348).

CHAPTER 4

Vicente Carducho, Painter and Writer

His Contributions to the *iconografía teresiana* and Reflections on St Teresa and the Perfection of Religious Paintings

Jeremy Roe

In a now not so recent publication, Margit Thøfner highlighted the contrast between the relatively few studies of visual representations of St Teresa's life and the wealth of studies on her writings and life, as well as the many hagiographical texts.[1] A comprehensive bibliographical survey is beyond the scope of this essay, but, as the titles listed below reveal, this situation has since changed, and research has been undertaken on a range of lines of enquiry.[2] The centenary celebrations of 2015 will undoubtedly have prompted further scholarship on the range of visual representations of St Teresa, and in this regard the aim of the present essay is to contribute to the study of the saint's iconography by examining a series of representations of St Teresa by Vicente Carducho (*c.* 1576–1638), the Florentine-born painter, who led a highly successful career as court painter under Philip III and Philip IV.[3] To date this modest yet significant corpus of images has not been studied as a whole, and none of the individual images has been examined within the context of St Teresa studies. However, the focus of the essay is not solely iconographical: the final part analyses Carducho's discussion of St Teresa, in his treatise *Dialogues on Painting* [*Dialogos de la pintura*] (1633), as an exemplar of the devout contemplation of religious images.[4] The study of this literary source in conjunction with other documentary evidence offers a valuable testimony of the spiritual and cultural significance of St Teresa at the Madrid court during the first two decades of the reign of Philip IV, as well as Carducho's own knowledge of Teresa's *Life* and other hagiographical texts.

As will be seen below, from perhaps as early as 1605 St Teresa figured as a subject for Carducho's drawings, and over the course of his career he returned to different episodes of her life in the form of drawings, paintings, and finally writing. In the case of Carducho it may also be argued that his lifelong artistic interest in St Teresa was combined with his devotional affiliations. When drawing up his will, he swore it to be true in the name of the Trinity, the Holy Spirit, the Virgin Mary, Queen of Angels, as well as St Francis and St Teresa of Jesus.[5] Then with regard to the distribution of his legacy, he left one third to the Third Order of St Francis, but stated that if Fray Joan de Piña de Salcedo were not able carry out his wishes this should be done by 'Mother Beatriz de Jesús, niece of the Holy Mother Teresa, prioress of the Discalced Carmelites of this City'.[6] Carducho's devotion to St Teresa was seemingly kindled by his reading: the inventory of his library lists two copies of 'Saint Teresa of Jesus on the Song of Songs', each valued at three *reales*, and a 'life of Saint Teresa', valued at eight *reales*.[7] A detailed study of Carducho's library is beyond the scope of this essay, but a closer study of the thirty-nine religious titles listed would offer a clearer idea of the place of Teresa in Carducho's devotions. For example, a further indication of an interest in the Carmelite reform is suggested by a 'life of Ana de Jesús'.[8] The first of the two books by St Teresa may be provisionally identified as her meditations on the Song of Songs, published in 1611 under the title *Conceptions of the love of God* [*Conceptos del amor de Dios*].[9] Meanwhile, the 'life' owned by Carducho could have been her own autobiographical account, or any one of a number of early biographies, such as those published by Francisco de Ribera in 1590, Diego de Yepes in 1606, and Pablo Verdugo de la Cueva in 1615. What is clear from Carducho's *Dialogos* is that he considered three episodes from St Teresa's life to be of special significance with regard to his reflections on the practice and art of religious painting. However, before turning to his discussion of the Carmelite his knowledge of both textual and visual accounts of St Teresa's life must be considered with regard to his depictions of her life and spiritual significance.

The 1638 post-mortem inventory of Carducho's estate also lists a painting of St Teresa, which remains to be traced. The work was keenly sought after at his death. In the inventory it is titled '*Saint Teresa and Angel*' [Vna Sta Teresa con vn Ángel en lienço de Vara y tres quartas], which suggests that this scene might have been a depiction of the transverberation or another mystical scene, rather than merely a devotional portrait. No value is given for the work in the inventory, which indicates that it had been reserved by an aspiring buyer, the identity of whom is revealed later as Jerónimo de Villanueva, whose political responsibilities included membership of the Supreme Council of Aragon and Secretary to Philip IV. Furthermore, Luisa Caturla refers to him as the 'Count-Duke's [of Olivares] right-hand man'.[10] He paid three hundred *reales* for the work, but the significance of this price is hard to gauge without knowing the work's dimensions and other characteristics. No further evidence of this work has been found, nor is anything further known about Villanueva's art collection. However, this painting was just one of a number of depictions of St Teresa painted and drawn by Carducho during his career in Madrid, as well as other Castilian cities including Ávila. A chronological survey of this corpus reveals how Carducho developed novel themes in the iconography of St Teresa and also how other patrons at the court of Philip IV shared Villanueva's devotion to St Teresa. With regard to this latter point, further contextualization of Villanueva's interest in Carducho's painting of St Teresa is provided by the fact that the 1630 Plantin edition of *Las obras de la Santa Madre Teresa de Jesús* was dedicated to the Count-Duke of Olivares, whom Carducho would single out for praise in his *Dialogos*.[11] In addition to this, Olivares's brother-in-law, Don Manuel de Zúñiga y Fonseca, Count of Monterrey, is understood to have had a *Bust-reliquary of Saint Teresa* [Busto-relicario de Santa Teresa] made for the Church of the *Purísima*, which forms part of Convent of Augustinian Recollect Nuns in Salamanca.[12] Finally, Lope de Vega, who submitted both a poem and a defence of painting to Carducho's treatise, is considered to have written as many as three plays on St Teresa.[13] Further study of the devotion to St Teresa at the Madrid court cannot be undertaken here, but the discussion that follows offers further insight into the role played by art in disseminating the saint's spiritual importance.

The recent publication of Álvaro Pascual Chenel and Ángel Rodríguez Rebollo's *catalogue raisonné* of Carducho's drawing has provided a key foundation for this study. It includes detailed entries on four drawings depicting St Teresa by Carducho. The first and earliest of these, *The Virgin Accompanied by Saint Teresa of Jesus and Saint Gertrude the Great* [La Virgen entre santa Teresa de Jesús y santa Gertrudis la Magna] (1604–14), is conserved in the Galleria degli Uffizi and is dated to between 1605 and 1614.[14] The drawing, which shows St Teresa standing on the right-hand side of the Virgin while writing in a book, has been marked out with a grid to enable the image's transfer to a panel or canvas for painting, or perhaps for engraving, and this indicates that it was part of a specific commission. Regrettably, nothing further is known about the fate of the drawing. Pascual and Rodríguez have discussed this image in the context of the promotion of St Teresa's case for canonization at the court in Madrid, and they suggest that the Hieronymite friar and biographer of St Teresa, Diego de Yepes, may have been involved in the commission, as he records his involvement in the patronage of a painting of a dual portrait of the two saints.[15] Pascual and Rodríguez have also drawn attention to the specific references to St Gertrude made in Francisco de Ribera's 1590 biography of St Teresa, and this signals an important facet of Carducho's work, which is that his compositions are not merely devotional works but also engagements with the hagiographical literature. Needless to say, such themes would most likely have been set by the patrons, and Carducho should not necessarily be credited with inventing this novel iconography of the two saints, although, as was stated above, he clearly pursued his own reading on the saint's life.

The second drawing by Carducho is *St Peter of Alcántara Giving Communion to St Teresa of Jesus* [San Pedro de Alcántara dando la comunión a Santa Teresa de Jesús] (c. 1620–30).[16] The drawing, which is once more marked out with a grid for transfer to another medium, is today held in the Spanish royal collection. It was clearly intended as a compositional guide as there is little to indicate its specific subject: all the haloes are absent, for example, and this led to it being misidentified for many years, until Ordax identified the scene as a combination of both fact and legend from the life of St Teresa.[17] In 1560 Peter of Alcántara and Teresa of Avila met, and, as the latter recounts in her *Life*, their encounter led to a close bond of spiritual companionship and guidance (*Vida* 30.1–7).[18] However, later this gave rise to the legend that on one occasion St Francis of Assisi and St Anthony of Padua appeared before them to act as deacon and sub-deacon during Mass.[19] In the drawing Saints Francis and Anthony can be seen on either side of the officiating St Peter, who offers

St Teresa the Eucharist. Pascual and Rodríguez have suggested that the drawing may have been intended as the main scene of an altarpiece, and they cite Palomino's statement that 'in the church of the *Convento del Carmen* [amongst other convents [...] there are a number of chapels painted by his [Carducho's] hand' [En la iglesia del Convento de Carmen de este corte (entre otros conventos) (...) hay diferentes capillas de su mano].[20] Besides the fact that its transformation into painting would have heightened the legibility of Carducho 'design', within the context of an altarpiece devoted to the saint the scene shown would have been more immediately apparent. Future research may reveal more about these chapel decorations. To date, besides specific depictions of St Teresa, one other painting by Carducho identified with the devotion to the Carmelite Order has come to light, which is a full-figure portrayal of St Albert, today conserved in a private collection. Pérez Sánchez praised it for its Zurbaranesque qualities, and dated it as contemporaneous with the series of paintings Carducho produced for the Convent of El Paular.[21] There is also evidence that Carducho's treatment of *St Peter of Alcántara giving communion to St Teresa of Jesus* gained a degree of renown in Madrid, as it has been argued that its composition, either from the finished painting or a preparatory drawing such as this one, was borrowed by Juan Martin Cabezalero in his version of this same subject painted for a private patron in *c.* 1670.[22]

Carducho's final two drawings, dated to between 1622 and 1630, can seemingly offer a further insight into the form and content of these now lost altarpieces, although in this case the final image would probably have been intended for a smaller, lateral scene, to accompany a larger painting of a subject such as that of the previous drawing. Given the wealth of significant episodes from the saint's life, patrons and artists faced a challenge, not merely which to choose, but, on occasions such as this, how to integrate various scenes together. The two drawings discussed here reveal Carducho's experimentation with two combinations of three episodes from St Teresa's *Life*, which he represented as a simultaneous narrative. The drawings are today held in an untraced private collection and in the Museo del Prado. As the Prado drawing is missing several centimetres from the right-hand side, the former drawing is illustrated here (Figure 4.1).

The three scenes show: St Teresa Beholding the Vision of St Albert of Sicily, St Teresa Dispenses the Habits of the Discalced Carmelites, St Teresa's Vision of the Virgin and St Joseph [Santa Teresa de Jesús ante la visión de san Alberto de Sicilia, que le muestra el futuro del Órden; Santa Teresa de Jesús entrega los hábitos del Carmelo Descalzo; Santa Teresa ante la visión de la Virgen y San José] (*c.* 1622–30). As it is not known whether these were actually developed into a painting, and in this case neither work has had a grid superimposed on it, it is not clear whether either of the two combinations of episodes was finally decided on. Evidently the choice was between prioritizing one of two key subjects, both of which foregrounded Teresa's importance for her Order.

What is clear is that these drawings were based on a visual source, *The Life of the Blessed Virgin Teresa of Jesus* [*Vita Beata Virginis Teresiae a Iesu*], the visual biography produced by the printmakers Adriaen Collaert and Cornelis Galle, which was in fact promoted by the aforementioned Ana de Jesús.[23] The foreground scene in

Fig. 4.1. Vicente Carducho, *St Teresa Beholding the Vision of St Albert of Sicily, who Showed her the Future of the Order; St Teresa Dispenses the Habits of the Discalced Carmelites, St Teresa's Vision of the Virgin and St Joseph* [Santa Teresa de Jesús ante la visión de San Alberto de Sicilia, que le muestra el futuro del Órden; Santa Teresa de Jesús entrega los hábitos del Carmelo Descalzo; Santa Teresa ante la visión de la Virgen y San José], c. 1622–30, ink and grey-brown wash heightened with white lead, 15.7 × 24.6 cm, Unknown location (in 1977 in a private collection), photograph courtesy of the Biblioteca de Catalunya, Barcelona.

Figure 4.1 is evidently a reworking of the twenty-second plate of the visual life of St Teresa, which is based on the vision, recounted in the final chapter of her autobiography, of 'the Holy Man' [el santo] who instructed her to read from the book he held out to her: 'In the time to come this Order will flourish: it will have many martyrs' (*Vida* 40.13) [En los tiempos advenideros florecerá esta orden; habrá muchos mártires].[24] In the first drawing, included here, Carducho made no effort to indicate that the subject is a vision, while in the Prado drawing, where it is relegated to the left-hand background scene, St Albert is depicted as immersed in a bank of clouds. In the first treatment of the scene Carducho adheres to Collaert and Galle's printed source, while in the second, no doubt to underscore the visionary nature of the scene when compressed to a smaller scale, he makes a significant modification to Teresa's text. However, this is the only significant difference noted between the two drawings.

The left-hand background scene, *St Teresa of Jesus Dispenses the Habits of the Discalced Carmelites* [Santa Teresa de Jesús entrega los hábitos del Carmelo Descalzo], appears to take place outside a church or convent, in contrast with the Prado version, where it is the foreground scene and seems to be set inside a church or convent.

However, as Pascual and Rodríguez note, in both cases Carducho departs from his visual sources as well as his textual ones. In the engraving, which the British Museum catalogues as 'Teresa as patron saint', St Teresa protects the kneeling nuns and friars with her mantle in a manner which echoes depictions of the Virgin of Mercy, but Carducho suppresses this Marian theme by giving the image a more worldly sense, and shows the saint with her head down, unlike in the traditional representation of the Virgin, and giving out habits to friars and nuns.[25] Nonetheless, the drawing still adheres to the sense of the print's caption, which reworks the final part of Proverbs 31.16, 'with the fruit of her hands she hath planted a vineyard'. Although the Marian allusion is suppressed, the image clearly sought to affirm St Teresa's role in the growth of the Discalced Carmelites. The right-hand background scene in both drawings is seemingly the same, as it can only be fully appreciated in Figure 4.1, which reveals it to be the saint's vision of the Virgin and St Joseph as recorded in her *Life* (*Vida* 33.14).[26] The presence of the Virgin in this final scene was perhaps another reason for avoiding any blurred identity between the saint and the Virgin in the rear left-hand scene. To date no visual source is known for this final scene, other than images conjured up by Carducho's reading of St Teresa's autobiography.

Whether these two drawings went on to become a painting that adorned one of the chapels referred to by Palomino can only be a matter for speculation. Regrettably, Carducho's paintings remain to be studied in depth, and his *oeuvre* of paintings has not been authoritatively catalogued, a process which would no doubt shed further light on compositions such as these. With regard to Carducho's paintings there are a number of works that undoubtedly merit further study, and three of them were painted for an altarpiece in the Chapter Room of the Convent of San José in Ávila.[27] As well as an image of God the Father, Martín González identified in 1979 *St Teresa Writing* [Santa Teresa escribiendo], the *Transverberation* [la Transverbaración] and the *Death of St Teresa* [la muerte de Santa Teresa] (Figures 4.2, 4.3, 4.4).

Martín González's attribution cannot be discussed in depth, but, on the one hand, they provide an excellent example of the composition of smaller-scale paintings used in altarpieces, as mentioned above, and, on the other, if the attribution is certain, Figure 4.4 provides a precedent for the work bought by Villanueva at Carducho's death. Furthermore, they indicate a parallel with another work identified with Carducho. In their study of Spanish painting published in 1969, Diego Angulo Íñiguez and Alfonso E. Pérez Sánchez listed a depiction of St Teresa by Carducho that showed her '[...] seated at a table upon which is a skull, inkwell and paper; her eyes gaze up and in her hand she holds a quill while listening to the Holy Spirit' [(...) sentado ante una mesa con cráneo, tintero y papel: los ojos levantados y la pluma en la maño escuchando el Espíritu Santo]. Regrettably, nothing further is known about this painting, which was recorded as being in the collection of Cardinal Despuig in Palma de Mallorca.[28]

Besides contributing a further work to the corpus of representations of the transverberation, Carducho's depictions of the saint both as author and in the moment

VICENTE CARDUCHO, PAINTER AND WRITER 65

FIG. 4.2. Vicente Carducho, *St Teresa Writing* [Santa Teresa escribiendo], date uncertain, oil on canvas (?), 25 × 147 cms, Convento de San José, Ávila.

FIG. 4.3. Vicente Carducho, *The Transverberation* [La Transverbaración], date uncertain, oil on canvas (?), 25 × 147 cms, Convento de San José, Ávila.

Fig. 4.4. Vicente Carducho, *The Death of St Teresa* [la muerte de Santa Teresa], oil on canvas (?), date uncertain, 25 × 147 cms, Convento de San José, Ávila.

of death are significant in terms of their affinity with works by contemporaneous painters. The former can be contrasted with works such Alonso Cano's *St Teresa's Vision of the Crucifixion* [Aparición de Cristo crucificado a santa Teresa de Jesús], now in the Museo del Prado, and the latter with depictions by Zurbarán and Alonso del Arcos of Saint Teresa by her desk with quill in hand, which are in Seville Cathedral and the Fundación Lazaro Galdiano respectively. With regard to Carducho's representation of the saint's death, the subject is much rarer, and, given the intended location, its significance would no doubt be closely linked to the keen sense of loss felt by St Teresa's own nuns.

The final painting to be discussed here is *St Teresa's Vision of Christ at the Column* [Santa Teresa ante el Cristo a la columna] (Figure 4.5), which forms part of the altarpiece Carducho painted for the Convent of Corpus Christi (or *Las Carboneras*), along with a series of other paintings, as well as sculptures by Antón de Morales.[29]

The central scene of the *Last Supper* [Última Cena] is the best-known painting of this altarpiece, and it is the only painting Tovar Martín discusses in his survey of the extant documentary evidence related to the decoration of the convent.[30] The significance of the altarpiece's iconography as a whole remains to be studied. The other works that make up the altarpiece are as follows: along the lower first tier, full-figure painted portrayals of St Augustine, St Dominic Guzmán, St Clare of Assisi, and St Gregory the Great; the second tier is dominated by the central scene, the *Last Supper*, with, on its right, a sculpture of St Jerome and the aforementioned painting of the *Vision of St Teresa*, while on the left there is a sculpture of St John the Baptist and a painting of the *Apparition of Christ to Saint Francis* [Aparición de Cristo a San Francisco]; finally, in the top tier there are sculptures of the *Archangel Saint Michael* [San Miguel Arcángel] and the *Guardian Angel* [Ángel de la Guardia] flanking the central sculpture of the *Crucifixion with the Virgin and St John* [La Crucifixión con la Virgen y San Juan], which is crowned with a sculpture of *God the Father and the Holy Spirit* [Padre Eterno y el Paráclito]. The final tier also includes the shields of the Count and Countess of Castelar, who founded the convent in 1607.[31] With regard to the present discussion, Carducho's representation of St

Fig. 4.5. Vicente Carducho, *St Teresa's Vision of Christ at the Column* [Santa Teresa ante el Cristo a la columna], date uncertain, 1622–25, oil on panel, Convento de las Carboneras del Corpus Christi, photograph courtesy of the Biblioteca de Catalunya, Barcelona.

Teresa's vision is doubly significant, first because it indicates his concern to develop new iconographical subjects based on accounts of St Teresa's own life, which will be discussed below, and secondly because he considered this vision to be of particular significance, and he later commented on it when he came to discuss St Teresa as a spectator of religious art in his *Dialogues on Painting* [Dialogos de la pintura].

Before turning to discuss Carducho's *Dialogos*, the significance of his comments can be contextualized by considering the cursory discussion of St Teresa given in the *Art of Painting* [Arte de la pintura], the other landmark Spanish Baroque treatise on painting written by a painter, Francisco Pacheco. The writing of the definitive version of this second treatise was contemporaneous with Carducho's, between 1634 and 1638, although it was published posthumously in 1649. As in Carducho's treatise and for similar reasons, religious art is given a predominant place, in fact Pacheco devoted much of his life to studying and compiling erudite debates on the nature of religious imagery, as well as the decorum to be applied to a range of religious subjects.[32] Therefore it might be expected that when he finally came to write his treatise he would have discussed images of St Teresa as well as her writings. In fact he only mentions her name once, and he does so to cite the renowned portrait of her made by Fray Juan de la Miseria, which is cited as part of a catalogue of nobles and saints who practised painting: he was essentially concerned with Miseria's painting of the portrait and not its sitter.[33] Pacheco's silence is all the more

Fig. 4.6. Jerónimo Dávila, *Christ at the Column* [Santa Teresa ante el Cristo a la columna], date uncertain, Fresco, 164 × 103 cms, Convento de San José, Ávila.

surprising as in the manuscript entitled *Learned Treatises by Various Authors* [*Tratados de Erudición de varios autores*], which contains a selection of texts that he compiled and wrote, there is a short piece entitled *By Francisco Pacheco in favour of St Teresa of Jesus* [*Francisco Pacheco Pintor en favor de Santa Teresa de Jesús*], one of Pacheco's two forays into religious polemic (in 1620 he published a text on the Immaculate Conception).[34] This manuscript has been identified as a response to Francisco de Quevedo's *Memorial* of 1628 opposing the proposal to make St Teresa a co-patron of Spain, but no further reference to this debate was made when Pacheco came to write his *Art of Painting* [*Arte de la pintura*].[35]

In comparison with Pacheco's *Art of Painting*, the *Dialogues on Painting* [*Dialogos de la pintura*] is a more accomplished literary work, and Carducho clearly valued himself as a writer: when he later painted his self-portrait he depicted himself with a pen, rather than a brush, in hand.[36] The conjunction of art and literature is apparent from the outset, as the allegorical frontispiece suggests, and each of the eight dialogues on painting that follow concludes with an allegorical engraving designed by Carducho; seven of these are accompanied by a poem by one of a number of contemporary writers, including Lope de Vega and José de Valdivieso.[37] His treatise is divided into eight dialogues, in which a master and his disciple discuss aspects of the art of painting. Each dialogue has a broad theme within which a number of topoi in the early modern discourse on art are addressed. However, Carducho's treatise was by no means merely a courtly display of erudition and literary style, but was motivated by a number of specific contemporaneous concerns: first and foremost, a legal suit defending painters against the levying of the *alcabala* tax on their earnings, and secondly, moral concerns about lascivious painting, which led a number of theologians to jointly publish their views on this matter.[38] Carducho, a seasoned courtier, combines a defence of painters' rights and a critique of immoral artworks and of lapses in the decorum of religious art with deferential approval of the royal and noble patrons and collectors of Madrid, despite the fact that noble tastes often included the type of works targeted by the theologians. However, he kept discussion of religious art and secular patronage separate. His penultimate dialogue focuses on the issues of religious decorum, while the final one provides a tour of Madrid's noble art collections, during which he does not list a single church or convent, thereby seeming to draw a clear distinction between the profane concerns of the nobility and the sacred aims of the Church.

In Dialogue Seven, *On the differences and manner of painting sacred events and histories with the decency that is required* [Las diferencias y modos de pintar los sucessos e historias sagradas con la decencia que se deve], the Master and Disciple discuss a range of themes, such as the precedent of God as the first painter, the *Deus Artifex*, and the validity of depicting spiritual themes through metaphorical allusions that depart from historical verisimilitude. Over the course of the dialogue a number of ancient authorities are cited, including St Basil and the Venerable Bede, along with contemporaneous authorities, such as Fray Luis de León, anecdotes taken from the Annals of the Society of Jesus, the aforementioned 1632 publication on lascivious imagery by theologians of Salamanca and Alcalá, and also St Teresa herself. As the dialogue's title suggests, decorum and decency is a central element of this chapter, but the particular section to be examined here is a response to a specific issue raised by the Disciple. Having listened to the Master insist on the importance of perfection in art and cite God as the first painter, the Disciple puts the Master on the spot by stating that he has seen many images of the Virgin, the Crucifixion, as well as the most devout saints, through which the Lord works *grandíssimos* miracles, but that if judged with the eyes of an artist they are works that lack proportion and art.[39] What is more, he raises the point that in works that are of artistic merit God rarely works marvels. The Master answers the first point by stating that it does not matter whether an image prayed to is made with or without art, 'because it is neither the form, nor material that works [miracles], but what the [images] represent, and so it does not matter if they are made with or without perfection' [porque no obra ni la forma ni la materia (sino lo que representa, y no más) y assí no importa para esto que sea hecha con perfección o sin ella]; what is more, 'a contrite and humble heart is what God requires for such miracles: miracles are not attributed to man's skills so that nothing miraculous should be attributed to his skill, by making an idol of it' [para obrar estas maravillas (Dios) no quiere de nosotros más que el coraçón contricto y humillado, no fiando del hombre, porque no se atribuya a su ciencia (haziendo ídolo della) algo del milagro].[40] He then goes on to state that none of these images is in fact 'discomposed nor indecent' [descompuestas ni indecentes], unlike 'some of those made by the great men of this profession' [algunas de las que hizieron grandes hombres en la facultad], and he justifies his insistence on artistic perfection by stating that 'it is certain that God does not dislike sacred images made with art and perfection, but [he does dislike] the attitude with which Art is celebrated, and at times with discourtesy and scant attention to what is represented: thereby God looks to the heart and the intention' [es cierto que no le desagradan a Dios las pinturas sagradas hechas con arte y perfección, sino el afecto con que acuden a celebrar el Arte, y quiçás con descortesía, y poca atención a lo que representan; de suerte que Dios mira al coraçón e intención].

Nonetheless, Carducho continues to give a demonstration of the importance of good painting that displays 'propriety and decorum' [propiedad y conveniencia], as 'it causes the most devotion and moves the spirits to most fervent emotions, love and ardent desires to act virtuously' [las tales causen mayor devoción, y que muevan los ánimos a los afectos a mayor fervor, amor y encendidos deseos de obrar en la virtud]. Carducho's *Maestro* acknowledges that even the unvirtuous have reformed their ways through images, but the discussion then focuses on the exemplary figures of the Franciscan Juana de la Cruz (1481–1534) and St Teresa of Ávila as examples of a fervent response to art. With regard to Juana de la Cruz, he cites the request she made to Christ that he amend an image of Our Lady that was 'so badly made that it used to put the nuns off their devotions' [una imagen de nuestra Señora de tan mala mano (...) que antes quitava la devoción a las devotas], a request which Christ carried out for her. Carducho then turns to St Teresa. He offers a succinct summary of the following scene from Teresa's *Life*:

> It happened that, entering the oratory one day, I saw an image which had been procured for a certain festival [...]. It represented Christ sorely wounded; and so conducive was it to devotion that when I looked at it I was deeply moved to see Him thus, so well did it picture what He suffered for us. So great was my distress when I thought how ill I had repaid Him for those wounds that I felt as if my heart were breaking, and I threw myself down beside Him, shedding floods of tears and begging Him to give me strength once [*sic*] for all so that I might not offend Him. (*Vida* 9.1)

> [Acaecióme que, entrando un día en el oratorio, vi una imagen que habían traído allá a guardar, que se había buscado para cierta fiesta (...). Era de Cristo muy llagado y tan devota que, en mirándola, toda me turbó de verle tal, porque representaba bien lo que pasó por nosotros. Fue tanto lo que sentí de lo mal que había agradecido aquellas llagas, que el corazón me parece se me partía,

y arrojéme cabe Él con grandísimo derramiento de lágrimas, suplicándole me fortaleciese ya de una vez para no ofenderle.]⁴¹

No comment is made on the quality of this first image which Carducho claims showed Christ as 'covered in wounds' [mui llagado], and Peers states that is thought to have been either an *Ecce homo* or *Christ at the Column*.⁴² Nonetheless, it is for Carducho a clear example of the saint's 'fervent emotions, love and ardent desires to act virtuously' [afectos a mayor fervor, amor y encendidos deseos de obrar en la virtud], signalling that it was this that moved the saint, and he states how this encounter initiated a process of spiritual improvement.⁴³

The issue of quality is returned to in the following anecdote, drawn from the saint's life. Carducho summarizes the thirtieth of her *Spiritual Relations* [*Relaciones*]:

> I had read in a book that it was an imperfection to have nice pictures, so I did not want to keep one which I had in my cell. Even before reading this I had thought it a sign of poverty to have no pictures other than paper ones; and ever since then I have not wanted pictures of any other kind. Once, however, when I was not thinking of this at all, I heard the Lord say that this mortification was not good. For which, He asked me, was better: poverty or charity? If love was better, I must not give up anything that awakened love in me, nor take any such thing from my nuns — and the book spoke of nice devices and adornments in images, and not of images or pictures in themselves. What the devil was doing with the Lutherans was taking from them all means of awakening greater love, so that they were being lost. 'My Christians, daughter', He added, 'must now, more than ever, do the reverse of what the Lutherans do'. I understood that I was under great obligation to serve Our Lady and Saint Joseph, because often, when I was going in quite the wrong direction, God would hear their prayers and restore me to health again.
>
> [Había leído en un libro que era imperfección tener imágenes curiosas, y así quería no tener en la celda una que tenía, y también antes que leyese esto me parecía pobreza no tener ninguna sino de papel; y como después un día de estos leí esto, ya no las tuviera de otra cosa. Y entendí esto estando descuidada de ello: que no era buena mortificación, que cuál era mejor: la pobreza o la caridad; que pues era lo mejor el amor, que todo lo que me despertase a él, no lo dejase, ni lo quitase a mis monjas; que las muchas molduras y cosas curiosas en las imágenes decía el libro, no la imagen; que lo que el demonio hacía en los luteranos era quitarles todos los medios para más despertar, y así iban perdidos. 'Mis cristianos, hija, han de hacer, ahora más que nunca, al contrario de lo que ellos hacen'. Entendí que tenía mucha obligación de servir a nuestra Señora y a san José; porque muchas veces yendo perdida del todo, por sus ruegos me tornaba Dios a dar salud.]⁴⁴

This passage was published in 1630 along with other *papeles* as an epilogue to the *Life* that made up the first volume of the *Obras completas* published by the Plantin Press.⁴⁵ Carducho uses this quotation to warn his disciples that 'painting that was not well formed or prints' [la pintura que no fuesse bien formada, o la estampa de papel] would not have the aforementioned spiritual effects, and he underscores this by concluding with a reminder that God has perfected works of art without even lifting a brush, as his final discussion of St Teresa demonstrates. In this Carducho offers a further demonstration of the divine approval of perfectly painted images that echoes the miracle worked for Juana de la Cruz. St Teresa, having had a vision of Christ after the flagellation (the subject depicted in Figure 8), instructed a painter to depict her vision, and insisted on a laceration being included on Christ's arm. Despite the saint's advice and guidance, the painter found this detail a challenge to paint, and it was only completed by way of a miraculous intervention as the painter turned away in a moment of distraction.[46] Carducho specifies that this image, 'the Christ which the saint commissioned in Ávila [...] in the way in which he had appeared to her, tied to the column' [el Christo que la Santa hizo pintar en Ávila (...) al modo que se le avía aparecido a la columna atado] was painted for a hermitage in the Convent of St Joseph's in Ávila, from which it has been deduced that he refers to the painting of this subject by Jerónimo Dávila (Figure 8), studied by Martín González and Christopher Wilson. The former has argued that the painting was retouched by Francisco Rizi in 1674, which may be why this key detail is lost. Although, regrettably, it has only been possible to study the image as a photograph, the reproduction included here gives a striking sense of the confined setting of the hermitage for which this work was painted, and where it continues to be contemplated. Martín González cited Silverio de Santa Teresa's history of the Discalced Carmelites as stating that the aforementioned laceration was the result of Christ giving a piece of his flesh from his arm to the saint in her vision.[47] Wilson subsequently identified the earliest references to this collaboration between the saint and painter, which is recorded in another work of Silverio's, his two-volume collection of documents relating to the processes of beatification and canonization.[48] However, neither of the two witnesses, Luis de Pacheco and Isabel del Santo, makes any reference to the aforementioned visceral vision, nor do they comment on any form of miraculous intervention.[49]

Despite not commenting on the vision, both witnesses testify to the devotion inspired by the work, and de Luis de Pacheco, who actually mentions Dávila by name, refers to the special devotion Teresa had for this key detail in the painting. Isabel del Santos's account refers to the role of a 'a very good painter' [muy buen pintor], and places an emphasis on Teresa's guidance on the painting of the 'ropes binding Christ, the wounds, the face, the hair, especially a tear in his flesh near the elbow' [las ataduras, las llagas, el rostro, los cabellos, y especialmente un rasgón en el brazo izquierdo junto al codo], underscoring the advisory role played by Teresa as well as the role of prayer in this work. Teresa is quoted as saying, 'I tell you my daughter that it was painted with unceasing prayer and that the Lord made me desire greatly that this figure would be painted right; blessed is he that he wanted to be amongst us in this way' [Yo le digo, hija, que se pinto con hartas oraciones y que el Señor me puso gran deseo que se arcertase a pintar esta figura; bendito El sea, que así quiso ponerse por nosotros].[50] Her account thus offers a further example of Teresa's keen interest in painting as a spiritual aid, which complements Carducho's comments above. The latter point is significant as it indicates how Carducho's discussion also reflects a more popular discourse on devotional art, and that he was not merely articulating theoretical or literary concerns. Isabel del Santo's testimony also affirms that the painting was produced for the hermitage dedicated to *Christ at the Column*, and therefore this work can be related to a reference to the hermitage and its decoration in the saint's *Life*, where Teresa recounts an experience of God speaking to her (*Vida* 39.3).[51]

One highly probable source for Carducho's discussion of this episode is Diego de Yepes's biography, published in 1606, where he recounts the vision described in the *Life*: 'Christ revealed Himself to me, in an attitude of great sternness [...]. I saw Him with the eyes of the soul more clearly than I could ever have seen Him with those of the body' (*Vida* 7.6) [representóseme Cristo delante con mucho rigor (...). Vile con los ojos del alma más claramente que le pudiera ver con los del cuerpo].[52] On this he comments, 'then Our Lord revealed himself to her bound to the column sorely wounded, and particularly in one arm, near the elbow, with a piece of flesh torn away' [Entonces se le mostro nuestro Señor atado a columna muy llagado, y particularmente en un brazo junto al codo desgarrado un pedaço de carne].[53] He goes on to state how the saint had it painted for a hermitage at St Joseph's in Ávila, and then declares, 'I have seen the work, and it is so lifelike, that all who behold it tremble with fear and devotion' [yo lo he visto, y está tan al vivo que estremece con gran pavor, y devoción a quien le mira], adding that it was painted with the saint's assistance. Later, in Chapter Fifteen, Yepes returns to the theme of St Teresa's recurring visions of Christ, and records how she asked Juan de la Peña, a *racionero* [prebendary] of Salamanca who was a skilled painter as well as a friend, to paint a vision she had of Christ crowned with thorns, following her guidance.[54]

Carducho may well have consulted other sources that were disseminated in both print and manuscript during the beatification and canonization of St Teresa, as well as the efforts made to have her named a patron of Spain. However, there is also the possibility that Carducho went to Ávila, either prior to undertaking the commission for the convent or later to oversee the installation of his paintings, and there he could perhaps have seen Dávila's painting for himself. The contrast between Figures 7 and 8 suggests that he did not adhere to Dávila's painting in his depiction of St Teresa's vision for the convent of *Las Carboneras*, although the chronology of these works remains to be studied, as well the possible involvement of Carducho's studio.

Carducho concluded his discussion by stating:

> I know all too well that this matter is absolutely not for those that are merely skilled artificers, who will not be convinced by these arguments, because philosophers always look for the natural causes for things, and not finding such a cause, they would do well to leave it to God, who knows everything. What has been said is sufficient to infer how differently the emotions of devotion and the will are moved by Painting, when guided by greater perfection rather than uneducated and crudely painted works.

> [Bien conozco que esta materia no es absolutamente para los que son meros científicos artífices, y que no quedarán convencidos con estas razones, porque siempre los Filósofos buscan la causa natural de las cosas, y no alcançando esta causa, harán bien dexarlo a Dios que lo sabe todo. Basta que de lo dicho se infiere con quánta diferencia mueve los afectos de la devoción y disposición la

Pintura, con mayor perfección conducida que no la que inculta y toscamente fuere pintada.][55]

His comments underscore the need for perfection in painting, but also foreground the role of the emotions. He thereby distinguished himself not only from artists, such as Pacheco, who placed an overwhelming emphasis on historical verisimilitude based on textual authority, but also from painters who based their practice exclusively on the study of nature, and who, as he states elsewhere in his treatise, would consequently not be able to find a basis for representations of spiritual figures and their emotions. In this he adhered to Archbishop Paleotti's view on this matter, succinctly stated in his quotation from St Augustine, 'to delight is a matter of sweetness, to instruct a matter of necessity, to sway a matter of victory'.[56]

Carducho's discussion of St Teresa as an exemplar of pious spectatorship is true to the spirit of her own use of art, above all with regard to how the emotional and spiritual effects of beholding images lend support in the quest of perfection. However, the divergences as well as the parallels between the saint's views and those of the worldly Carducho and his artistic concerns should also be noted, and this final quotation from St Teresa provides a timely reminder that the perfection of art bears little comparison with a genuinely spiritual vision. Describing her own visions, she wrote:

> I would think the vision was an image, though it was like no earthly painting, however perfect, and I have seen a great many good ones. It is ridiculous to think that the one thing is any more like the other than a living person is like his portrait: however well the portrait is done, it can never look completely natural: one sees, in fact, that it is a dead thing. (*Vida* 28.7)
>
> [me parecía imagen, no como los dibujos de acá, por muy perfectos que sean, que hartos he visto buenos; es disparate pensar que tiene semejanza lo uno con lo otro en ninguna manera, no más ni menos que la tiene una persona viva a su retrato, que por bien que está sacado no puede ser tan al natural, que, en fin, se ve es cosa muerta.][57]

Notes to Chapter 4

1. I would like to express my thanks to the Convento de San José, Ávila, for generously supplying photographs of three of the paintings discussed in this essay, as well as giving permission for them to be reproduced here. Likewise, I would like to thank the Convento de las Carboneras del Corpus Christi for permission to reproduce Figure 4.5. See Margit Thøfner, 'How to Look Like a (Female) Saint: The Early Iconography of St Theresa of Avila', in *Female Monasticism in Early Modern Europe: An Interdisciplinary View*, ed. by Cordula van Wyhe (Aldershot: Ashgate, 2008), pp. 59–80 (pp. 59–60). Thøfner does not offer an exhaustive bibliography, and a number of works cited below supplement her list.
2. Works published since 2008 include Christopher Wilson, 'Teresa of Ávila vs. the Iconoclasts: Convent Art in Support of a Church in Crisis', in *Imagery, Spirituality, and Ideology in Baroque Spain and Latin America*, ed. by Jeremy M. N. Roe and Marta Bustilllo (Newcastle: Cambridge Scholars Press, 2010), pp. 45–57; María José Pinilla Martín, 'Arte efímero en Valladolid con motivo de la beatificación de Teresa de Jesús', *Boletín del Seminario de Estudios de Arte*, 75 (2009), 203–14; 'Dos "Vidas Gráficas" de Santa Teresa de Jesús: Amberes 1613 y Roma 1655', *Boletín del Seminario de Estudios de Arte*, 79, (2013), 183–202; 'La ilustración de los escritos teresianos:

grabados de las primeras ediciones', *Boletín del Seminario de Estudios de Arte*, 74 (2008), 185–202; 'Una aproximación a la iconografía de Santa Teresa', *Patrimonio Histórico de Castilla y León*, 54 (2015), 63–66; Fernando Moreno Cuadro, 'En torno a las fuentes iconográficas de Tiepolo para la "Visión teresiana" del Museo de Bellas Artes de Budapest', *Archivo Español de Arte*, 82 (2009), 243–58; 'Iconografía de los testigos de los procesos teresianos: a propósito de Adrian Collaert y la iconografía de la Capilla Cornaro', *Archivo Español de Arte*, 87 (2014), 29–44; 'La serie de la transverberación de Santa Teresa con las dos Trinidades derivada de Wierix: acerca de una pintura de Francisco Rizi', *Goya: Revista de Arte*, 341 (2012), 312–23; 'San Pedro de Alcántara y la transverberación teresiana en la estampa alemana del último Barroco', *Cauriensia: Revista Anual de Ciencias Eclesiásticas*, 7 (2012), 421–32.

3. On Carducho's life and work, see George Kubler, 'Vicente Carducho's Allegories of Painting', *The Art Bulletin*, 47 (1975), 439–45; Mary Crawford Volk, *Vicente Carducho and Seventeenth-century Castilian Painting* (London and New York: Garland Publishing, 1977); Vicente Carducho, *Dialogos de la pintura: su defensa, origen, esencia, definicion y differencias*, ed. by Francisco Calvo Serraller (Madrid: Ediciones Turner, 1979); Werner Beutler, *Vicente Carducho en El Paular* (Cologne: Verlag Locher, 1998); Eduardo Barceló de Torres and Leticia Ruiz Gómez, eds, *La recuperación de El Paular* (Madrid: Ministerio de Educación, Cultura y Deporte, 2013); Álvaro Pascual Chenel and Ángel Rodríguez Rebollo, *Vicente Carducho. Dibujos. Catálogo razonado* (Madrid: Centro de Estudios Europa Hispánica, Biblioteca Nacional de España, Museo del Prado, 2015), pp. 15–16; Jean Andrews, Oliver Noble Wood, and Jeremy Roe, eds, *On Art and Painting: Vicente Carducho and Baroque Spain* (Cardiff: University of Wales Press, 2016).
4. Vicente Carducho and Francisco Martínez, *Dialogos de la pintura: su defensa, origen, ess[n]cia, definicion, modos y diferencias* (Madrid: Francisco Martínez, 1633). All further references made to this work are to this edition.
5. María Luisa Caturla, 'Documentos en torno a Vicente Carducho', *Arte Español*, 26 (1968), 145–221 (p. 147).
6. Caturla, p. 167.
7. Caturla, p. 195.
8. Caturla, p. 196. See Ana de Jesús, *Escritos y documentos*, ed. by A. de Fortes and R. Palmero (Burgos: Monte Carmelo, 1996), p. 251.
9. The text is edited in *Santa Teresa. Obras completas*, ed. by Tomás Álvarez (Burgos: Monte Carmelo, 2014), pp. 1343–96, and translated in *The Complete Works of St Teresa of Avila*, trans. by E. Allison Peers, 3 vols (London and New York: Burns & Oates, 2002), II, 357–99.
10. J. H. Elliott, *The Count-Duke of Olivares: The Statesman in an Age of Decline* (New Haven, CT: Yale University Press, 1986), pp. 260–61.
11. See Carducho, *Dialogos*, fol. 59^v. In a forthcoming publication Fernando Bouza Álvarez addresses the 1630 publication of St Teresa's works along with its historical context.
12. The sculpture is today in the Museo Lázaro Galdiano, inventory number 5584. See Ignacio Miguéliz Valcarlos, 'Bustos relicarios italianos en el Museo Lázaro Galdiano', *Goya: Revista de Arte*, 310 (2006), 3–10; A. Madruga Real, *Arquitectura barroca salmantina: las agustinas de Monterrey* (Salamanca: Centro de Estudios Salmantinos, 1983).
13. See Barbara Mujica, 'Performing Sanctity: Lope's Use of Teresian Iconography in *Santa Teresa de Jesús*', in *A Companion to Lope de Vega*, ed. by A. Samson and J. Thacker, Colección Támesis, Serie A, 260 (Woodbridge: Tamesis, 2008), pp. 183–98; Lope de Vega, *Vida y muerte de Santa Teresa de Jesús. Commedia inédita. Introduzione, edizione e commento a cura di Elisa Aragone* (Florence: Casa Editrice d'Anna, 1970).
14. Pascual Chenel and Rodríguez Rebollo, *Catálogo razonado*, pp. 78–79.
15. Pascual Chenel and Rodríguez Rebollo, *Catálogo razonado*, p. 78.
16. Pascual Chenel and Rodríguez Rebollo, *Catálogo razonado*, pp. 150–52.
17. See Salvador Andrés Ordax, 'Iconografía Teresiana-Alcantarina', *Boletín del Seminario de Estudios de Arte*, 48, (1982), 301–26.
18. *Complete Works of St Teresa*, I, 194–97; *Santa Teresa. Obras completas*, pp. 296–300.
19. Ordax cites, amongst other sources, Fray Juan de San Bernardo's *Chronica de la vida admirable y milagrosas haçanas de el Admirable Portento de la Penitencia S. Pedro de Alcántara* [...] (Naples: En la

empresa de Geronimo Fasulo, 1667), p. 601. This source recounts how Teresa was accompanied by Isabel de Ortega. The only vision linked to Peter of Alcántara is one of him alone, p. 357. No hagiography of St Teresa is cited. On the iconography of these two saints see also Juan Nicolau Castro, 'Santa Teresa en el arte español', *Toletum: Boletín de La Real Academia de Bellas Artes y Ciencias Históricas de Toledo*, 15 (1984), 111–25 (p. 113).

20. Pascual Chenel and Rodríguez Rebollo, *Catálogo razonado*, pp. 150–51; Antonio Palomino de Castro y Velasco and Nina A. Mallory, *Vidas* (Madrid: Alianza Editorial, 1986), p. 113.
21. Alfonso Emilio Pérez Sánchez, 'Pintura madrileña del siglo XVII: "Addenda"', *Archivo Español de Arte*, 49 (1976), 293–326 (p. 301). Carducho was working on his series of fifty-six paintings for the Convent of El Paular between 1626 and 1627: see *La recuperación de El Paular*.
22. Pascual Chenel and Rodríguez Rebollo, *Catálogo razonado*, p. 151.
23. It was first published in Antwerp in 1613. On this visual biography, see Pinilla Martín, 'Dos "Vidas Gráficas", pp. 184–86.
24. *Santa Teresa. Obras completas*, p. 434; *The Complete Works of St Teresa of Avila*, I, 295. See also the following link: <http://www.britishmuseum.org/research/collection _online/collection_ object_details/collection_image_gallery.aspx?assetId=429022001&objectId=3025021&partId= 1> [accessed 17 March 2017].
25. See <http://www.britishmuseum.org/research/collection_online/collection_object_details/ collection_image_gallery.aspx?assetId=429040001&objectId=3024955&partId=1> [accessed 17 March 2017].
26. *Santa Teresa. Obras completas*, p. 346; *Complete Works of St Teresa*, I, 230.
27. Juan José Martín González, 'El Convento de San José de Ávila (patronos y obras de arte)', *Boletín del Seminario de Estudios de Arte*, 45, (1979), 349–76.
28. Diego Angulo Íñiguez and Alfonso E. Pérez Sánchez, *Historia de la pintura española. Escuela madrileña del primer tercio del siglo XVII* (Madrid: Instituto Diego Velázquez, 1969), p. 175.
29. This painting is discussed in Angulo Íñiguez and Pérez Sánchez, pp. 113–14.The decoration of this church is also discussed in Vicente Benítez Blanco, 'Evocación de la santidad: los relicarios del convento madrileño del Corpus Christi, vulgo "Las Carboneras"', in *El culto a los santos cofradías, devoción, fiestas y arte*, ed. by F. Javier Campos y Fernández de Sevilla (San Lorenzo del Escorial: Ediciones Escurialenses, 2008), pp. 739–58, accessible online at <https://dialnet. unirioja.es/servlet/articulo?codigo=2826320>; Eduardo Delgado and Eduardo Lamas, 'La serie de dibujos de Vicente Carducho con los Padres de la Iglesia: nuevos elementos', *Anales de Historia del Arte*, 23 (2013), 89–97; Virginia Tovar Martín, 'Noticias documentales sobre el convento madrileño de Las Carboneras y sus obras de arte', *Boletín del Seminario de Estudios de Arte*, 38 (1972), 413–25.
30. Tovar Martín, 'Noticias documentales', pp. 442–45.
31. On the Countess, see Elvira M. Melián, 'Santiago contra Santa Teresa: Beatriz Ramírez de Mendoza o la redención de cautivos', *Clepsydra: Revista de Estudios de Género y Teoría Feminista*, 8 (2009), 29–46.
32. See Bonaventura Bassegoda i Hugas, 'Observaciones sobre el *Arte de la Pintura* de Francisco Pacheco como tratado de iconografía', *Cuadernos de Arte e Iconografía*, 2 (1989), 185–96, and 'Las tareas intelectuales del pintor Francisco Pacheco', *Symposium Internacional Velázquez: Actas*, ed. by Alfredo J. Morales and Carlos Sánchez de las Heras (Seville: Junta de Andalucía, Consejería de Cultura, 2004), pp. 39–46.
33. Francisco Pacheco, *Arte de la pintura*, ed. by Bonaventura Bassegoda i Hugas (Madrid: Cátedra, 1990), p. 225.
34. See Bassegoda, 'Las tareas', p. 40; *Tratados de erudición de varios autores*, MS 1713, Biblioteca Nacional (Madrid), fols. 246^r–2449^v.
35. Francisco de Quevedo, *Memorial por el patronato de Santiago y por todos los santos naturales de España*. Madrid, 1628. The manuscript is conserved in the Biblioteca Nacional (Madrid), MS R/11465.
36. Carducho's self-portrait dated *c.* 1633–38 is today conserved in Pollok House, Glasgow.
37. See Kubler, 'Vicente Carducho's Allegories of Painting'; Jeremy Lawrance, 'Vicente Carducho and the Spanish Literary Baroque', and Javier Portús, 'Painting and Poetry in the *Diálogos*', in *On Art and Painting: Vicente Carducho and Baroque Spain*, ed. by Jean Andrews, Oliver Noble

Wood and Jeremy Roe (Cardiff: University of Wales Press, 2016), pp. 71–90 (pp. 19–70 and 71–90).

38. In terms of this debate, focused in part on the claim of painters for an intellectual status, the following passage from Chapter 8.3 of St Teresa's *Libro de las fundaciones* [*Book of Foundations*] offers a seemingly radical view on such matters. She recounts how 'the very learned Dominican, Fray Domingo Báñez, [said] [...] wherever we see a representation of Our Lord it is right for us to reverence it, even if it has been painted by the devil himself; for he is a skilful painter, and, though trying to harm us, he is doing us a kindness if he paints us a crucifix or any other picture in so lifelike a way as to leave a deep impression upon our hearts. This argument seemed to me excellent; for, when we see a very fine picture, we always value it even if we know it has been painted by a wicked man, we should not stop appreciating the image nor should we allow the identity of the painter to hinder our devotion' [un gran letrado dominico, el maestro fray Domingo Báñez, le dijo que (…) adonde quiera que veamos la imagen de nuestro Señor es bien reverenciarla, aunque el demonio la haya pintado, porque él es gran pintor, y antes nos hace buena obra quiriéndonos hacer mal, si nos pinta un crucifijo u otra imagen tan al vivo que la deje esculpida en nuestro corazón. Cuadróme mucho esta razón, porque cuando vemos una imagen muy buena, aunque supiésemos la ha pintado un mal hombre, no dejaríamos de estimar la imagen ni haríamos caso del pintor para quitarnos la devoción]. *The Complete Works of St Teresa*, III, 4; *Santa Teresa. Obras completas*, p. 1047.
39. *Dialogos*, fol. 124^r.
40. *Dialogos*, fol. 124^v.
41. *Complete Works of St Teresa*, I, 54; *Santa Teresa. Obras completas*, pp. 92–93.
42. *Complete Works of St Teresa*, I, 54, note.
43. *Dialogos*, fol. 125^v.
44. *Complete Works of St Teresa*, I, 349; *Santa Teresa. Obras completas*, p. 1314.
45. *Las obras de la Santa Madre Teresa de Jesús fundadora de la reformación de las descalças y descalços de N. Señora del Carmen*, 3 vols (Antwerp: Plantin, 1630), I, 456–57.
46. *Dialogos*, fols 125^v–26^r.
47. González, p. 352; Silverio de Santa Teresa, *Historia del Carmen Descalzo en España, Portugal y América*, 15 vols (Burgos: Monte Carmelo, 1935–52), II, 644.
48. Wilson, p. 50.
49. *Procesos de beatificación y canonización de Santa Teresa de Jesús*, ed. by P. Silverio de Santa Teresa, 3 vols (Burgos: Monte Carmelo, 1934–35), II, 210–11 and 495–96.
50. *Procesos de beatificación y canonización*, II, 496.
51. *Complete Works of St Teresa*, I, 280; *Santa Teresa. Obras completas*, pp. 414–15.
52. *Complete Works of St Teresa*, I, 40; *Santa Teresa. Obras completas*, p. 74.
53. Diego de Yepes, *Vida, virtudes y milagros, de la Bienaventurada Virgen Teresa de Jesus, Madre y fundadora de la nueva Reformación de la Orden de Los Descalços y Descalças de Nuestra Señora del Carmen* (Zaragoza: Angelo Tauanno, 1606), p. 46.
54. Yepes, p. 98.
55. *Dialogos*, fol. 126^r.
56. Gabriele Paleotti, *Discourse on Sacred and Profane Images* (Los Angeles, CA: Getty Research Institute, 2012), p. 111.
57. *Complete Works of St Teresa*, I, 181; *Santa Teresa. Obras completas*, p. 279.

PART II

St Teresa the Mystic

CHAPTER 5

Teresa as a Reader of the Gospels

Rowan Williams

For a sixteenth-century nun, access to the text of Scripture would almost certainly have been restricted for the most part to what was available in liturgical books; nuns were not professional commentators on Scripture, as were those engaged in University teaching or canonical processes of formation for male clergy and religious, and only those employed in this context would have habitually used full texts of the Bible. A very brief glance at St John of the Cross's pattern of biblical citation will illustrate the point: John draws from a wide range of Old Testament books, including most of the prophets, and quotes verbatim, often quite copiously. The same holds for Francisco de Osuna's biblical references, though he has rather fewer word-for-word citations. In contrast, it is not surprising that, when Teresa refers to texts from Hebrew Scripture, they are usually paraphrased and come from a relatively narrow range of books: the Psalms are of course the best-represented book, followed by the Song of Songs, but apart from these, the majority of references are to fairly well-known incidents (the Burning Bush of Exodus 3, the crossing of the Red Sea, events in the life of Elijah), with a scattering of prophetic texts, all but one, an allusion in her *Way of Perfection [Camino]* 42.3 to Malachi 3.20, undoubtedly derived from a liturgical source, as it simply mentions the image of Christ as 'Sun of Righteousness' to Isaiah and Ezekiel. Job (quite frequently quoted by John of the Cross) appears a few times, reflecting probably the regular homiletic use of his story; but there is only one actual quotation. The pattern of reference is exactly what we would expect from someone with no access to a complete vernacular Bible, accustomed to pick up phrases and narratives from liturgical, devotional, and homiletical contexts.[1] Interestingly, she refers in chapter 16.11 [CE 26.4] of the *Way* to 'reading the Passion' in a way which might suggest that this is a personal devotional activity as well as a liturgical observance.[2] And this liturgical background to the use of texts makes sense of the pattern of Teresa's habits of allusion to the New Testament as well — most notably in the absence of anything reliably identifiable as an independent citation of Mark's Gospel: although the biblical indices to the standard editions and translations (including those in the Institute of Carmelite Studies translations) include putative references to Mark, the texts in question are all paralleled in Matthew or Luke, and it is very unlikely indeed that Teresa derived anything directly from a Gospel that was barely visible in liturgical usage, since it was generally regarded as an epitome of Matthew.

However, Teresa does undoubtedly cite Gospel texts with some regularity; and it is instructive to see exactly which she utilizes most and what picture they help to form of her own sense of where she saw herself and the vocation of her sisters in the Gospel framework. In the brief survey offered here, it will be clear that she has strong preferences in her habits of quotation, and that these sketch a distinctive biblical theology of the contemplative calling. For reasons that will emerge, she tends to use Lucan parables and narrative passages, although in strict quantitative terms it is Matthew that she quotes most often (over fifty times in the *Life*, *Way*, and *Interior Castle* all together). The Fourth Gospel is cited over twenty times in the *Interior Castle*, but is used a good deal less frequently in the *Way* (eleven times) and the *Life* (six times). As we shall see, quotations and allusions fall into 'clusters' — groups of texts regularly associated together in Teresa's mind — and these give us our best clues as to how Teresa sought to deploy Gospel citation and allusion to illuminate the essentials of the Carmelite life. Thus, in what follows, I have not tried to give a complete catalogue of all her Gospel references, but only to pick out the most frequent and telling concentrations of textual and narrative reference, to draw into better focus the theological priorities which she brings to bear on her reading of the Gospels.

The *Way* gives us the context in which she is working.[3] In the wake of the Inquisition's unprecedentedly severe restrictions (in the Index of 1559) on spiritual literature in the vernacular, the challenge for a community of laywomen unversed in Latin was a serious one. Teresa, in her *Life* (*Vida* 26.5) as well as — by implication — in the *Way* (e.g. *Camino* 21.3–4 [CE 35.3–4], with its reference to the books that cannot be taken away), laments the way in which communities like hers are deprived of theological and spiritual sustenance; but her response is to insist that all that is necessary can be drawn out of the texts that everyone knows and habitually uses — the Our Father and the Hail Mary — and from 'the words of the Gospels' (*Camino* 21.4 [35.4]) [las palabras de los Evangelios].[4] Books can indeed be dangerous and distracting, she disarmingly admits, but the text of the Gospels and of the familiar prayers, properly understood, will lead to recollection and interior prayer. She claims in the same passage that she has no intention of writing 'commentary' on the prayers; she is careful to use vocabulary which makes it plain that she is not setting herself up in the kind of role restricted to ordained males. All she intends is to persuade her sisters to go forward in the way of prayer, whatever risks there may seem to be, since in her view the life of the sisters in her communities is a necessary witness and reparation in an age of violent religious conflict and the widespread rejection (as she sees it) of sacramental life and devotion by the emerging churches of the Reformation, 'Lutherans' [luteranos], as she characterizes them all with a fine indiscriminate hostility. This life *needs* to be lived in the Church at such a period, and so there is need for resource that will enable it to be lived with intelligence and integrity (see especially *Camino* 1.2–5). Later (37.1 [CE 65.3]), she describes the Our Father as an 'evangelical prayer' [oración evangélica] — meaning, it seems, not just that it is literally found in the Gospels but that it can act as a summary of the Gospel itself. So her aim in the *Way* is to clarify the ground and trajectory of contemplative prayer with reference to nothing but what the layperson might know and hear or read. This provides a 'living book' (*Vida* 26.5) [*libro vivo*] where Christ speaks directly; and it is part of the process by which the community itself becomes a 'text' to communicate to the world God's promise and purpose at a time when — as she has spelled out at the beginning of the *Way* — the world is racked by religious confusion and rebellion.

As we have already noted, Matthew is the most frequent source for Gospel citations; only in the *Interior Castle* do quotations from John outnumber those from Matthew. In the *Way*, Matthew is cited twenty-two times altogether; and the most pronounced 'cluster' of references is from the Sermon on the Mount — Jesus's commendation of prayer in solitude (Matthew 6.6) and the clauses of the Lord's Prayer. Elsewhere we find allusions to Matthew 11.28 ('Come to me all you who are weary and burdened [...]') in the *Life* (*Vida* 11.16), the *Soliloquies* (VIII.2) and possibly the *Way* (*Camino* 19.15 [CE 32.7]), though this sounds more like John 7.37, 'Let anyone who is thirsty come to me and drink', recast in a slightly Matthean form — as the same text is also in *Soliloquies* IX. Jesus's prayer in Gethsemane from Matthew 26 is referred to twice in the *Way* (*Camino* 30.2 and 32.6), to alert us to what is implied in praying 'Thy will be done', and is also referenced in *Meditations on the Song of Songs* (3.11); *Interior Castle* (*Moradas* 2.11) alludes to the same episode in Gethsemane, but with reference to Jesus's injunction to the disciples to pray not to be brought into temptation. The *Way* (*Camino* 18.6, 29.4, and possibly also 34.10 [CE 61.6]) and *Interior Castle* (*Moradas* 2.8 and 6.11) refer to the request of James and John to sit on either side of Jesus in the Kingdom (Matthew 20.22), and Jesus's reproach to them because they have not counted the cost of what they pray for.

These are the most significant allusions to Matthew's text — significant in the sense that they appear more than once in important contexts to make important points. Teresa's exegesis of the Lord's Prayer sets out the rationale for her insistence that the community must disregard considerations of social or ethnic status in their common kinship as adopted brothers and sisters of the eternal Son, sharing with him the liberty of approaching the Father (see particularly *Camino* 27.6 [CE 45.2]); her use of Christ's invitation ('Come to me all you who are weary [...]') underlines the priority of Christ's action in leading us into this adoptive relationship; and the references to the prayer in Gethsemane and the appeal of the sons of Zebedee warn of the cost of the contemplative life as a sharing in Christ's own bearing of the cross. Her quotation of Johannine texts comes at the basic theme of sharing Christ's intimacy with the Father by a slightly different route. Here, the most noticeable concentrations of reference — apart from allusions to the conversation with the Samaritan woman in John 4, to which we shall be returning — are to chapters 14, 17, and 20. The *Interior Castle* has five references to John 14, one (*Moradas* 1.1) to Christ's description of the place to which he goes as having 'many rooms' or 'many dwelling places' (John 14.2), also referred to in *Way* (*Camino* 20.1 [CE 33.1]) and *Life* (*Vida* 13.13), the others to later verses touching on Jesus as the way to the Father and on the Father as 'seen' in Jesus: and there are also four references to John 17.20–23, on the mutual indwelling of Father and Son and their indwelling in the community of the faithful. Especially in *Interior Castle* (*Moradas* 7.7–9), this indwelling is understood as the goal of our own journey towards the centre of ourselves, where Son and Father 'encounter' each other in the created soul, for example *Spiritual Testimonies* [*Cuentas*] 52. In short, the citations of Matthew and John by Teresa are predominantly to do with emphasizing that the relation between Christ and the Father as shown and enacted in the Gospel narrative is the form of our own relation to Christ's Father; and that this implies both the risk of following in the way of the cross and the radical spiritual and communal egalitarianism of a community united simply by the invitation of Christ.

When we turn to Teresa's use of Luke's Gospel, there is a noticeable shift of focus, although there are important continuities with the themes so far outlined. The frequency of Lucan material overall is not far short of her use of Matthew (indeed, in the *Interior Castle* Luke is slightly more often quoted than Matthew, sixteen as opposed to fifteen times, where John is quoted twenty-five times in all), and it is strongly focused on specific *narratives* (including parables) rather than teaching passages. It is also worth noting that her Lucan citations have very limited overlap with those to be found in John of the Cross or Osuna, who does not refer to Teresa's two favourite texts, the Mary and Martha story (Luke 10.38–42) and the incident at the house of Simon the Pharisee involving a 'sinful woman' (Luke 7.36–50), though he does, like Teresa, make use of the Lucan parables, notably the Prodigal Son and the Pharisee and the Publican (8.1).[5] Teresa's favoured narratives are regularly about Jesus's relation to women followers and about God's acceptance of sinners. The Mary and Martha story from Luke 10 is the most frequently quoted (seven times overall, four of these in the *Way*, two in the *Interior Castle*, one in the *Soliloquies*), followed closely by the story of the sinful and penitent woman (Luke 7) who anoints the feet of Jesus when he visits the house of Simon the Pharisee (five references, two in the *Way*, three in the *Interior Castle*). In addition to this, we have mention of the parables of the Prodigal Son and the Pharisee and the Tax-Collector (Luke 15 and 18), the woman who touches the hem of Jesus's garment (Luke 8), and the penitent thief on the cross (Luke 23). Twice (*Camino* 42.1 [CE 72.3], *Moradas* 5.2.13) there is a quotation of Luke 22.15 (I have eagerly desired to eat this Passover with you): Jesus longs to be released from the sufferings of this world, praying like us to be 'delivered from evil'; he responds just as any spiritually sensitive person must, says Teresa in the *Way*. But in the *Interior Castle*, she deploys this differently in order to underline what must have been the strength of his desire to save our souls if it could overcome the natural fear and shrinking from profound pain and death.

One of the governing themes of this array of Lucan texts is thus Jesus's welcome of and passion for the sinner. But there is a more complex subtext to Teresa's citations. As we have noted, it is an obvious enough point about Teresa's rhetoric that she has to insist that she is not trying to 'teach' about the life of prayer, being a woman and therefore unqualified to do so; yet she cannot resist reminding her readers that Christ 'found as much love and more faith' [tanto amor y más fe] in women as opposed to men, and that every virtue in women is automatically suspected by men (*Camino* 3.7 [4.1]).[6] Women are intimidated, she says, in this world; but they may still pray that God will allow them to receive the good things merited by the prayers of the Virgin, recalling that Christ invariably met women with compassion. Behind Teresa's exegesis of specific passages lies this conviction, that the status accorded to women, especially women contemplatives, is at odds with the Gospel record in essential respects; and so she is especially concerned to make use of Gospel texts which make the point. Luke is uniquely well provided with these; but it is not surprising that she uses the Samaritan woman from John 4 in much the same way (three times in the *Way*, once in the *Interior Castle*). Famously, in the *Vejamen*,[7] in her comments on the responses of various clerical associates to the words 'Seek yourself in me' [Búscate en mí], she implicitly reproaches John of the Cross for implying that no one can approach Christ without prior self-emptying and purification: 'The Magdalene was not dead to the world when she found him, nor was the Samaritan woman or the Canaanite woman' [No lo estava (muertas al mundo) la Madalena, ni la Samaritana, ni la Cananea, cuando le hallaron]; the Canaanite woman of Matthew 15 is cited more indirectly in *Foundations* (*Fundaciones* 8.2), but is absent from other works. Jesus regards women without that 'suspicion' that is shown by the 'sons of Adam' (*Camino* 4.1) [yjos de Adán].[8] And what is more, he can be relied upon to *defend* the female contemplatives for whom Teresa writes.

This is one of the more distinctive arguments in Teresa's work. Like practically all her Catholic contemporaries, she assumes that the sinful woman at the house of Simon is identical not only with Mary of Bethany, Martha's sister, but with Mary Magdalene; and this enables her to present a figure whose relation to Jesus is repeatedly characterized by risk or scandal, *from which Jesus protects her*. So in *Way* (*Camino* 15.7 [CE 23.2]), Teresa discusses how the sisters should react to criticism and blame, and appeals to Christ's defence of 'Magdalene' both from Simon the Pharisee and from her sister. This is at first sight simply about dealing with unmerited criticism as an individual; but when the theme recurs in chapter 17, the emphasis has moved somewhat. Mary is being criticized *for being a contemplative*: so the contemplative must be silent, waiting for Jesus to defend her. And Teresa, characteristically, adds that it will not do for the contemplative to look down on those who perform necessary practical tasks, since there are diverse callings at diverse moments, depending on the divine will (17.5–6 [27.5–6]). The *Interior Castle* (*Moradas* 7.4.13) imagines 'Magdalene' abandoning her dignity and social status to go and perform a menial task for Jesus (washing his feet), living through a very public change of behaviour (and 'dress and everything else' [vestido y todo lo demás]), so that her contemplative life is grounded in the visible sacrifice of reputation and dignity that takes her to the feet of the Lord in action as well as contemplation (and prepares her for the dreadful suffering of witnessing Christ's Crucifixion). Already in the *Interior Castle* (*Moradas* 6.11.12), Teresa has promised her sisters that Jesus will answer for them 'as he did for the Magdalene' [como hacía por la Magdalena] when the intensity of spiritual longing brings about extreme conditions or behaviours. And all of this suggests that the discussion in *Way* (*Camino* 15 [CE 23]) is not only about individual faults in the course of the common life but about the sense that the contemplative life itself is in some sense 'scandalous'.

In the context especially of the *Way*, this is a significant complex of ideas. We know that Teresa begins this work by articulating the insecurity of her position as a woman obliged by circumstance to provide some kind of spiritual formation for contemplatives who are not literate in Latin, and who are in any case widely regarded as incapable of contemplation because of their sex. As she says, what would otherwise be called good is suspect in a woman; the contemplative calling is regarded as a matter of danger for a woman, and thus also for the Church as a whole, and the female contemplative becomes a 'transgressive' figure, rebelling against her role and status (or lack of status). In Teresa's environment, the role of the female religious house was closely bound to a set of concerns about status. A little later, the Counter-Reformation was to intensify restrictions on female enclosure as an aspect of its interest in consolidating the discipline and uniform behaviour of consecrated persons, priests, brothers, and religious sisters; but this has not yet, in Teresa's day, become the issue it would be by the last quarter of the century. Teresa's problem is that the typical women's religious house of her era was — as so much of Teresa's correspondence and comments in the *Way* and the *Foundations* confirms — an institution that offered a clear 'contract' to its secular environment in terms of intercession, public recognition of patronage and reinforcement of family solidarity and dignity by provision for the unmarried without loss of standing.[9] It would be extreme to say that a distinctive theology of contemplative vocation for women was absent from the Church's vocabulary; but the intense suspicion directed at anyone who might be regarded as a *beata*, an unauthorized female religious teacher, meant that the spiritual expectations of a female religious had to be modest.[10] Claims about a calling to interior prayer, 'mental' prayer, had about them, in the ears of clerical authority, especially in Spain, an unacceptable flavour of appeal to a realm outside the mediations of grace in the life of the Church, grace as administered by a visibly authorized system of sacramental and doctrinal discipline. And a community that — like Teresa's — refused the 'contract' of local usefulness, declining the usual forms of patronage and so threatening to be a financial burden on top of all its other ambivalent features, was manifestly a problem: Teresa's frequently declared hostility to large-scale benefactions with strings attached meant that the financial situation of her houses was unusual, creating difficulties for local administrators, secular and religious.

All this is fairly familiar as a characterization of what Teresa faced; but what makes her so theologically interesting in this context is precisely what she does with the common and authorized currency of liturgical prayer and scriptural narrative to create a rationale for both the contemplative calling as such and her own particular version of it as involving certain standards of simplicity and financial quasi-independence. If our reading of her practice as an interpreter of the Gospels is accurate, she is constructing just that theology of the contemplative calling — especially for women — that was occluded or discouraged in much of current teaching. Thus she lays general foundations in her meditations on the Our Father and related texts from Matthew, where, as we have seen, she (i) elaborates her convictions about how kinship with Christ relativizes other kinship claims;

(ii) emphasizes the priority of Christ's call; and (iii) insists on the costliness of following this call. This is further refined in her use of John's Gospel, in particular the Farewell Discourses: here the emphasis is on the abiding presence within the contemplative of the Trinitarian life, and the reality of the promised indwelling of Christ — with also a recognition (through the use of the 'many dwelling-places' passage of John 14.2) of (i) the need for the soul to advance through a series of such 'dwelling-places', the rooms of the interior castle, and (ii) the diversity of routes by which the soul moves Godwards, so that no soul with genuine desire for union with God is excluded, even if they are not in the conventional sense contemplatives.

And when Teresa turns to her Lucan material, this last point is given a further and potentially radical refinement. The general affirmation of diversities of calling turns into an affirmation of diversities that will appear problematic to some authorities: specifically, the calling of women to be both contemplative and active in the way they were meant to be in the reformed Carmels of Teresa's foundation is grounded in Jesus's own affirmation of women who resisted convention in order to be in direct contact with him, both in practical service and in contemplative listening. Teresa does not set out to negate the hierarchical order in which she finds herself, but in effect challenges that order to recognize what the Christ of the Gospel narratives recognizes: that women may be invited to the spiritual intimacy with him that is fulfilled in contemplation within an apostolic community. When, in the *Way* (*Camino* 27.6 [45.2]), she apostrophizes the 'college of Christ, where St Peter, being a fisherman, had more authority [...] than St Bartholomew, who was a king's son' [colesio de Cristo, que tenía más mando san Pedro con ser un pescador (...) que san Bartolomé, que era hijo de rey], she is underlining the fact that the original apostolic community represented a refusal of pre-existing kinship and status patterns: thus, when contemporary women embark on journeys that appear as scandalous as that of 'Magdalene' to the house of Simon the Pharisee, we must see it in the context of that primitive refusal. The Carmelite calling may be suspect in the eyes of the current ecclesiastical world, but its advocate is Jesus himself.

Contemplation — especially in its 'Teresian' manifestation, accompanied by poverty and the repudiation of what I earlier called the 'contract' around religious life — becomes in this framework a place of 'otherness' in regard to the social order and its ecclesiastical reflections and accommodations. And it is even more confusing for the critic to the extent that Teresa refuses to settle with a clear traditional hierarchy of contemplative and active; what she has to say about this is often unclear, but what is plain is her unease with any typology that reinscribes in the community a difference between high and low status. Thus in one of the passage where she addresses this (*Camino* 17 [CE 27–28.1]), she begins by reflecting on aspiration to contemplative prayer as an offence against humility: contemplation is precisely what cannot be planned or earned by human excellence, so we should not be seeking contemplative gifts as a way to reinforce our self-opinion. 'Not because all in this house practice prayer must all be contemplatives: that's impossible' [no porque en esta casa todas traten de oración, han de ser todas contemplativas. Es imposible] (*Camino* 17.2 [CE 27.2]). The life as a whole, the life of *all* in community has as its rationale the nurture of proper response to contemplative gifts from God. And one 'proper' response to these gifts in others is to accept that they are not, or not yet, for oneself. It is again a 'proper' response to assume that the lack of such gifts is caused by one's own failings (*Camino* 17.4 [CE 27.4]), but equally proper not to conclude that one is fixed in inferiority: God requires all kinds of service. So if the gifts of mental prayer are not forthcoming, we do not despair but assume that the Lord is working with us in the way best suited to us at this particular moment. With a very Teresian touch she adds: 'I don't say that we shouldn't try' [No digo yo que quede por nosotras, sino que lo provéis todo] (*Camino* 17.7 [CE 28.1]). Contemplation is what we can rightly pray for, it seems, and it seems to be given when we are detached from any issues of status or success around it. The point is that the entire scheme of community life is both designed to pave the way for contemplative union *and* designed to make sense of the absence or delay of contemplative gifts, in the light of a strong belief in the dignity of any and every task performed in the convent for the service of Christ. Our individual spiritual growth is woven in to the complex of tasks that make the community work; and one of the central paradoxes of this is the implied notion that 'active' service is justified by what it makes possible for the contemplative. Its 'usefulness' is to do with creating the ambience in which the 'useless' loving contemplation of God in Christ may flourish, whether in myself or in my neighbour.

Action is useful insofar as it allows uselessness; the disciplined life of the convent is not 'useful' because it guarantees prayerful support for kindred or city (not that these are in any way simply denied or disallowed by Teresa), but because it creates the environment in which something that is an end in itself, something that is not useful in terms of anything but itself, is made more attainable, at least for some. Precisely by withdrawing attention and attachment from the various kinds of social solidarity available outside the community — the solidarities of actual family relationship, the reinforcing of status and influence by conspicuous patronage — the community's discipline nurtures contemplation in a context that is in important respects spiritually and practically egalitarian. And so the awkward and embarrassing 'otherness' of the female contemplative, challenging conventions and boundaries, comes to be a sign of the deeper and unsettling otherness of the contemplative life as such, its refusal to be instrumentalized in the service of a divided social order. Teresa's typology intriguingly brings together the scandal of 'Magdalene' as a displaced gentlewoman, abandoning her family and the walls of her household to go in search of Jesus, with the scandal of her listening to Jesus in contemplative silence. As we have noted, *Interior Castle* evokes this vividly:

> Do you think it would be a small mortification for a woman of nobility like her to wander through these streets (and perhaps alone because her fervent love had made her unaware of what she was doing) and enter a house she had never entered before and afterward suffer the criticism of the Pharisee and the very many other things she must have suffered? [...] If nowadays there is so much gossip against persons who are not so notorious, what would have been said then? (*Moradas* 7.4.13)

> [Y ¿pensáis que le sería poca mortificación a una señora como ella era, irse por

esas calles, y por ventura sola, porque no llevava hervor para entender cómo
iva, y entrar adonde nunca havía entrado, y después sufrir la mormuración del
fariseo, y otras muy muchas que debía sufrir? (...) Pues ahora se dice a personas
que no son tan nombradas, ¿qué sería entonces?]

Her humiliation as a transgressive woman is part of her preparation for contemplative silence, a suffering that detaches the soul from obsession with its solidity and status.

Notice that Teresa suggests that Mary's intense love makes her unaware of what she is doing; it is not a casual point. If a woman causes scandal by adopting a religious life on Teresa's model, this is because she is overwhelmed by the divine imperative. As elsewhere, Teresa wants to stress that her actions are not a deliberate campaign against ecclesiastical discipline, but primarily a response to the initiative of Christ. And the imagery of 'wandering through the streets' — imagery intriguingly paralleled in the use of the Song of Songs (3.2: 'I will get up now and go about the city, through its streets and squares; I will search for the one my heart loves') in the liturgy for St Mary Magdalene's feast — tacitly recognizes the gravity of the reproach: Magdalene may be a repentant prostitute, but in this respect at least she continues in her old habits.[11] Only Christ's welcoming gestures and words will establish her identity as a transformed sinner; her behaviour appears ambiguous. Teresa is being bold here, anticipating the most destructive criticism possible and turning its flank. For her sisters, clarity about the reputational risk of this life is essential and she deliberately underlines it: if the search for God in the reformed Carmel will be compared by critics to the humiliation of prostitution, this is all part of the preparation for that ultimate displacement of the self and its images that occurs in interior prayer.

Teresa's biblical models allow her here to make some very strong points about contemplation, not only for women but for all believers. From the point of view of ordinary social exchange and the mutual securing of status and power, contemplation will sooner or later appear as a dangerous and suspect affair. And when the socially constrained figure of a woman (especially a woman of putatively 'good' family) is involved, the otherness and unsettling character of contemplation is particularly marked. For men, the issues of exposure and scandal are not the same; and Teresa's response to John of the Cross about access to Jesus has so strong a gendered character that it is as if she is saying that there is something about the contemplative calling which only women — and particularly women who are or have made themselves marginal to their inherited systems or structures — can demonstrate; not because of some 'essentialist' notion of the female as more naturally contemplative (an idea that would not have made sense in Teresa's day) but because of the issues of status and danger that arise where the female contemplative is concerned. She is not constructing a general theology of the standing of the contemplative in the Church, but she is unmistakeably constructing a foundation for such a theology, if only by the close linkage she makes between the contemplative community's repudiation of 'honour' as a social marker and the possibility of growth towards union. For the further stages of the *Interior Castle*'s journey to happen, what is needed is a dissolution of secure and enclosed images of identity over against God;

the rupture with a society obsessed with managing and negotiating such images is a beginning for this deeper rupture.[12] And the scheme leads us to recognize that the contemplative as such is always 'other', not in the sense of superiority on a single scale but as representing the novelty of the society that Christ creates, the 'college' of the Apostles.

As a reader of the Gospels, then, Teresa is in search of material that will provide a theological account of this novelty, and also a narrative and imaginative rationale for the disruption that response to a contemplative calling entails — most dramatically through the figures to which she returns so many times, the problematic and challenging female figures who approach Jesus and are welcomed. Part of her theological legacy is here in this subtle use of such figures to suggest an ecclesiology as well as a theology of the contemplative calling. The Catholic Church is from its beginnings a community in which kinship with Christ is the supreme defining category, so that any other natural distinction of race, family or indeed gender is put in question. And the contemplative life is at the heart of the unremitting task of reminding the Church to be what it is in relation to Christ's invitation, because it is a life that requires the most fundamental loss of self-based solidity or security, a faithful and sacrificial response to divine fidelity. As I hope to show elsewhere at greater length, this can be connected with the foundations of a Teresian theology of the Eucharist as the sacrament of divine fidelity within the Church and the soul, the tangible promise of God's refusal to abandon world, self, or Church.[13] But in our present context of thinking about Teresa and the Gospels, it is clear that contemplative life in poverty, outside the familiar forms of the patronage system, is being highlighted as one of those things that most clearly reminds the Church of its very identity as the 'kindred' of Jesus. The contemplative calling in the Church, making the Church other to its habitual, routinized self, recalls the basic otherness of Church to fallen creation (especially status-ridden society); and its living-out by women under the Teresian discipline makes this particularly clear. If the sixteenth-century Spanish Church wanted to deny women the contemplative life in its full Teresian radicality, something essential for both Gospel and Church is lost in Teresa's eyes; the unsettling universalism of the 'college of Christ' is to a significant extent absorbed back into the habits of a rivalrous and anxious society.

And if that radical vision does not inform the understanding of the contemplative calling wherever it is responded to, contemplation will be in danger of becoming a search for just the wrong sort of 'interiority' and just the wrong sort of achievement — a private spiritual journey with only a tangential relation to the integrity of the Church as a whole, and, at worst, a programme of individual spiritual refinement which could create new kinds of hierarchy and new kinds of division. Teresa clearly finds it impossible to separate out her theology of contemplation from her ecclesiology — even though she would probably not have wanted to use such terms of her own thought. The priority of Christ's invitation is what creates both the new community of grace and the new de-centred subject that emerges in the long process of contemplative maturation. It would be worse than eccentric to separate them, and a proper 'evangelical' understanding of both is needed (now as then) to prevent the theology of interior prayer from becoming indulgent or sentimental and the theology of transfigured community from becoming activist and self-reliant.

Notes to Chapter 5

1. References to Teresa's writings are to *The Complete Works of St Teresa of Ávila*, ed. and trans. by Kieran Kavanaugh and Otilio Rodriguez, 3 vols (Washington, DC: Institute of Carmelite Studies, 1980–87). All contain scriptural indices, though these need to be used carefully as, for example, they sometimes ascribe a citation or allusion as being to St Mark's Gospel, where it is much more likely that Teresa is using a Matthean parallel (see below, p. 81).
2. There are two different versions of the *Way*, the El Escorial codex [CE] and the Valladolid codex [CV], which reduces the number of chapters from 73 to 42. The translators normally follow the latter, but occasionally, as here, insert material found only in the former. For the sake of completeness, references to the El Escorial codex [CE] are given in square brackets.
3. See the excellent treatment in Gillian T. W. Ahlgren, *Teresa of Avila and the Politics of Sanctity* (Ithaca, NY: Cornell University Press, 1996), especially Chapter 4; see also Rowan Williams, *Teresa of Ávila* (London and New York: Continuum, 1991), Chapters 1 and 4.
4. Spanish text from *Obras completas de Santa Teresa*, ed. by Efrén de la Madre de Dios and Otger Steggink, 2nd edn (Madrid: Biblioteca de Autores Cristianos, 1967), p. 261.
5. Francisco Osuna, *Tercer abecedario espiritual*, ed. by Melquiades Andrés Martín (Madrid: Editorial Católica, 1972), 1.1, 4.1, 13.2.
6. The greater part of this passage in defence of the faith of women and critical of male suspicion of them was crossed out by Teresa's confessor, García de Toledo, in the Escorial codex and was omitted by her in the Valladolid codex. The translators have restored it in full. On Teresa's relationship with her confessors, see also Terence O'Reilly in this volume (p. 108).
7. A *vejamen* was a kind of comic or satirical competition, in which individuals were invited to submit their answers to a particular problem, in expectation of a critical but humorous response.
8. *The Complete Works*, ed. and trans. by Kavanaugh and Rodriguez, pp. 360–61; *Obras completas*, ed. by Efrén de la Madre de Dios and Otger Steggink, p. 1135.
9. On the role of religious houses in civic life, see Jodi Bilinkoff, *The Avila of St Teresa: Religious Reform in a Sixteenth-century City* (Ithaca, NY: Cornell University Press, 1989). See also, more recently, Joseph Pérez, *Teresa de Ávila y la España de su tiempo*, 2nd edn (Madrid: Algaba Ediciones, 2015).
10. See especially Ahlgren, *The Politics of Sanctity*, pp. 86–97.
11. The new Tridentine liturgy of 1570 finally established the use of the Song of Songs as the first reading for the Mass on St Mary Magdalene's feast, replacing the widespread medieval use of Proverbs 31. It is not clear whether the new usage was current in Spain before the completion of the Tridentine reform, and if so whether the Carmelite rite was affected. James Boyce, *Carmelite Liturgy and Spiritual Identity: The Choir Books of Krakow* (Turnhout: Brepols, 2008), contains much useful information on the medieval Carmelite liturgy including (pp. 133 et seq.) the antiphons for the feast of St Mary Magdalene: one of these (*Dum esset Rex*) is drawn from the Song of Songs (1.12), but this is not unique (as far as I know) to Carmelite usage.
12. Michel de Certeau, *The Mystic Fable*. I: *The Sixteenth and Seventeenth Centuries* (Chicago, IL, and London: Chicago University Press, 1992), pp. 188–200, discusses Teresa's rhetoric as seeking an answer to the question, 'Who am I?' within a 'Catholic space' that has become fractured and problematic.
13. Publication details are as yet unknown.

CHAPTER 6

Teresa of Ávila's Picture of the Soul: Platonic or Augustinian?

Peter Tyler

Introduction

Teresa of Ávila's debt to St Augustine (345–430 CE) is well known. She begins her writing with a *hommage* to the Bishop of Hippo by choosing the genre of 'confession' to shape her first exposition of her understanding of theology, in *The Book of her Life* (*Life*) [*Libro de la vida*]. However, as well as being heir to the Augustinian tradition, she is equally in debt to the medieval exposition of the work of Dionysius the Areopagite as transmitted to her through the work of the Victorines, Jean Gerson, and the person she declared to be her 'master' — Francisco de Osuna (c. 1492/97–c. 1540). In the fourth chapter of the *Life* she describes the crucial encounter with her uncle Pedro during a time of physical, emotional, and spiritual crisis, when he gave her a copy of Osuna's *Third Spiritual Alphabet* [*Tercer abecedario espiritual*]:

> When I was on my way, that uncle of mine I mentioned who lived along the road gave me a book. It is called *The Third Spiritual Alphabet* and endeavours to teach the prayer of recollection. [...] I did not know how to proceed in prayer or how to recollect myself and therefore I was very delighted with it and determined to follow this way with all my strength. And so I was very happy with this book and resolved to follow that path with all my strength. [...] For during the twenty years after this period of which I am speaking, I did not find a master, I mean a confessor, who understood me, even though I looked for one. (*Vida* 4.6)
>
> [Cuando iva, me dio aquel tío mío — que tengo dicho que estava en el camino — un libro; llámase Tercer Abecedario: que trata de enseñar oración de recogimiento (...) No sabía cómo proceder en oración ni cómo recogerme, y ansí holguéme mucho con él y determinéme a siguir aquel camino con todas mis fuerzas (...) Porque yo no hallé maestro — digo confesor — que me entendiese, aunque le busqué.]¹

Her uncle Pedro was clearly a wise spiritual director. In giving the young woman Osuna's text he was effectively placing in her hands a primer of late medieval *theologia mystica* and by studying it Teresa was able to gain a grounding in that tradition denied her by the fact that, unlike John of the Cross, she could not study theology at university.

One of the principal elements of Osuna's structure in his *Third Spiritual Alphabet*, a work which owed a great deal to Jean Gerson, is the division made in Chapter Six between speculative theology [*theologia speculativa*] and mystical theology [*theologia mystica*]. Osuna defines the former in the following terms:

> [It] uses reasoning, argumentation, discourse, and probability, as do the other sciences, hence it is called scholastic theology, the theology of learned people [*letrados*], and if someone wishes to acquire it, he needs a good mind, continual exercise, books, time, attentiveness, and work, having a learned teacher to study under, as is required for any other of the sciences. (*Tercer abecedario* 6.2)

> [Usa de razones y argumentos y discursos y probabilidades según las otras ciencias; y de aquí es que se llama teología escolástica y de letrados, la cual, si alguno quiere alcanzar, ha menester buen ingenio y continuo ejercicio y libros y tiempo, y velar, trabajar teniendo enseñado maestro, lo cual también es menester para cualquiera de las otras ciencias.][2]

Theologia mystica, on the other hand, is unlike other sciences or learning, for it is a 'hidden' [*escondida*] theology. It is pursued not through learning, books, and teachers but through 'pious love and exercising the moral virtues' (*Tercer abecedario* 6.2) [*por afición piadosa y ejercicio en las virtudes morales*][3] No book can teach it, including, he says, his own:

> I do not presume to teach it in this alphabet nor can any mortal do so, for Christ reserves to himself the ministry of secretly teaching the hearts where that theology lives hidden like divine science, more excellent by far than the other theology [...] that may be called searching or analytical. (*Tercer abecedario*)

> [No que en él presuma yo enseñarla, pues ninguno de los mortales la enseñó, porque Cristo guardó para sí este oficio de enseñar en secreto a los corazones en que viviese aquesta teología escondida como ciencia divina y mucho más excelente que la otra teología (...), que se llama escudriñadora.][4]

We can trace this 'mystical theology' ultimately back to the Parisian schools of the twelfth and thirteenth centuries, when we see the rise of a type of discourse that has been referred to as *Affective Dionysianism*.[5] Central to this movement was the group of theologians centred on the Abbey of Saint-Denis near the Schools of Paris. This group of writers and commentators associated with the Abbey of St Victor took particular interest in the Dionysian *corpus*, which was in the process of being re-translated by theologians such as Sarracenus and Robert Grosseteste, in a manner which addressed the deficiencies of the older translations by Hilduin and John Scotus Eriugena.[6] From its inception this distinctive Victorine tradition was concerned with questions about the relationship between the mind [*intellectus*] and the emotions [*affectus*] which would in due course find expression in the works of St Teresa.

The Neoplatonic Schema for the Deliverance of the Soul

I have noted that, alongside her debt to the Augustinian tradition, Teresa was also immersed in the medieval Neoplatonic tradition of mystical theology inherited from the Victorines and their twelfth-century interpretation of the *corpus* of Dionysius the Areopagite. I have traced that lineage in an earlier work, and do not intend to pursue it here.[7] Rather, I would like to sketch what I see as two patterns or schemata for the union of the soul with God that predominate in the Western tradition. I have termed these the Augustinian and Plotinian, following the two authors who shaped their utterance. In so doing I want to detail their approaches as foundational schemes that continued to persist in the Christian imagination throughout the Middle Ages and well into the early modern period. Although Teresa's debt to Augustine is well known and easily traced, it may appear more problematic to link her work with the Neoplatonist Plotinus (*c.* 204–70 CE), whom she cannot have read. However, as I have already suggested, a clear lineage can be established from her 'master' Francisco de Osuna, back through Gerson and the Victorines, to the influence of Dionysius the Areopagite himself. Dionysius is not firmly in the Plotinian tradition, but there is sufficient 'family resemblance' (to use Wittgenstein's term) between the two to make his work useful as a cipher to point towards a way of understanding the soul that is manifest in all late medieval thought. The importance of Plotinus to our purpose is that his schema acts as a convenient summary of many of the strands of Neoplatonic interpretation which were prevalent in the late Classical world and presents it in a digestible fashion. Accordingly, I shall begin by presenting the main outlines of the two schemata before proceeding to my analysis of Teresa's approach.

The Plotinian Schema

The principal features of the Plotinian/ Neoplatonic schema for the formation of the soul may be summarized in the following way:

(i) It is primarily based on the teachings of Plato and the Greek philosophers. Plotinus sees himself as offering a system that derives from and exemplifies the teachings of the great master, Plato. Although he has clearly assimilated the earlier Neoplatonic schools and their interpretations, he sees himself as directly encountering Plato and his text making it accessible to his contemporaries. Later Neoplatonism, as in the case of Iamblichus of Chalcis (*c.* 242–327 CE), will emphasize once again the role of the gods in achieving unity with the One, whereas Plotinus tends to downplay the role of theurgy and liturgy in the life of the seeker and gives renewed emphasis to the truth that is found in the sacred writings of the Greek masters, especially Plato.

(ii) We come from a source beyond this world, we contain that source within ourselves and long to return to it through expression of our *eros*. Kenney calls the higher part of the Plotinian soul 'the unitive or erotic soul', emphasizing the role of *eros* in returning the higher part of psyche to the world soul.[8] *Eros*, and the practice and pursuit of *eros* through art, culture, beauty, and love, are thus essential parts of the return 'of the alone to the Alone'.[9] The whole cosmos for Plotinus, says Kenney, 'crackles with synaptic life as these intelligible minds contemplate their inter-relationships'.[10]

(iii) Contemplation is the means by which we return to this source. Because of our ambivalent natures, living between matter and spirit, the human soul [*psyche*] is essentially unstable: 'our focus shifts up and down, now highly temporal and fractured, now informed by the intelligible, the stable and the authentic'.[11] It is through contemplation [*theoria*] that the soul discovers its 'more ancient nature'.[12] This *theoria* seeks to stabilize the soul so that it can be present to its true origins in the One. Porphyry tells us in his *Life of Plotinus* that it seems as though the master achieved this state of unity with the One at least four times in his life, following, says Porphyry, the road to contemplation set out by Plato in *The Symposium*.[13]

(iv) The source of our selves is non-material. We have 'fallen' into the world of matter. The soul has 'cooled' (Greek term, *psyche*) from its origins in the higher realm but this still retains the imprint of its origin to which it is determined to return.[14] We are 'weighed down' in our present body but the process of contemplation will enable us to be 'born aloft' again.[15] As Philo of Alexandria, one of Plotinus's important precursors, states: 'the soul in the body is like a foreigner, a sojourner in a strange, hostile land', for the body is the prison or tomb of the *psyche* and the soul carries the body around like a corpse: 'Therefore man must not settle down into the body as if it were his own native land'.[16]

(v) Certain actions and ways of living, such as moral purification and intellectual training, will help the process of the return of the soul to its true origin. Contemplation in itself is insufficient for Plotinus we must also engage in ethical action and right conduct to form our souls. This is coupled with moderate ascetical practices (nothing too extreme): Plato's constant injunction to *sophrosyne* [moderation, prudence, self-control] is taken seriously, together with the importance of philosophical dialogue, which becomes part of a wider religious and spiritual practice which Pierre Hadot has termed 'a way of life'.[17]

(vi) 'Inner' contemplation will lead to the 'ascent' of the soul. As Plotinus states: 'We must withdraw from all the external, pointed wholly inwards, not leaning to the outer; the total of things ignored, first in their relation to us and later in the very idea'.[18] The One lies not outside but within. Such an introspection will, Plotinus assures us, lead inevitably to the in-breaking of the Divine *Nous* such that 'the soul taking that outflow from the divine is stirred; seized with a Bacchic passion, goaded by these goods, it becomes love'.[19] This internal turn will also be reflected in Augustine's writing, where the 'inward' search will lead eventually to the truths he is seeking.

(vii) The Ascent can be experienced in sudden 'ecstasies'. In this respect Plotinus was once again reflecting the great Neoplatonic tradition to which he was heir. Plotinus describes the choreography of the contemplative life as being rather like a 'choral dance'.[20] The natural movement of the soul 'is in circle around something, something not outside but a centre, and the centre is that from which the circle derives'.[21] At times we see the One and are caught up in its ecstasy, at other times we move around the circle and the vision is obscured:

> We are always around it but do not always look at it; it is a like a choral dance: in the order of the singing the choir keeps round its conductor but may sometimes

turn away, so that he is out of sight, but let it but face aright and it will sing with beauty [...] when we do but turn to him then our term is attained; this is rest, this is the end of discordance, we truly dance our god-inspired dance around him.[22]

(viii) The Plotinian search for the soul is essentially an erotic process. As the soul yearns for its origin through *eros*, so *eros* must play a significant role in its return to the source. As we have seen, the lover, the musician and, inevitably, the philosopher, are deeply embedded in the search for truth and the soul, he tells us at the end of his *Enneads*, 'loves God and longs to be at one with Him in the noble love of a daughter for a noble father'.[23]

(ix) The goal of the process is deification. By following the practices of contemplation, the exercise of moral virtue and engaging in the dialectic of the philosophers, we shall reach the Plotinian goal of identification with the *Nous* and ultimately the One: 'You must become first of all godlike and beautiful if you intend to see God and beauty' and thus the soul will end up becoming love itself.[24] Discovery of self becomes discovery of the Divine.[25]

We may therefore summarize the characteristics of a picture of the soul and its redemption that we can call Plotinian or Neoplatonic thus:

1. It is primarily based on the teachings of Plato and the Greek philosophers;
2. it suggests that we are from a source beyond this world;
3. that contemplation is the best means by which we can return to this source;
4. that the source of our selves is non-material;
5. that intellectual and moral training can lead us back to that source;
6. that 'inner' contemplation will lead to the 'ascent' of the soul;
7. that this ascent can be experienced in sudden 'ecstasies';
8. that the Plotinian ascent is primarily an erotic process;
9. and that the goal of the process is deification.

St Augustine's Picture of the Soul

St Augustine was no stranger to the writings of Plotinus and the Neoplatonists. As he explained in his *Confessions*, he encountered practitioners of Neoplatonism and the Neoplatonic writings whilst seeking God in Rome and Milan as a young man. Raised by pagan and Christian parents, he embodies the tensions between one world ending (late paganism) and a new one emerging (medieval Christianity), and his own struggle to find expression of his picture of the soul is no less convoluted. The Plotinian schema described above was clearly attractive to the young Augustine and one he sought to pursue as a young man in Italy. However, the mature Augustine of *On the Trinity* [De Trinitate] seeks a synthesis between the Neoplatonic and the Christian before arriving at what is effectively a new distinctly Christian way of talking of the soul.

According to Trapè, 'the essential task of Augustinian spirituality is the restoration of the image of God to man', or as Augustine himself puts it in *Literal Commentary on Genesis* [De Genesi ad litteram]: 'It was in the very factor in which he surpasses non-rational animate beings that man was made in God's image. That, of course, is *ratio* [reason] itself, or *mens* [mind] or *intelligentia* [intelligence] or whatever we wish to call it' [In eo factum hominem ad imaginem dei in quo irrationalibus animantibus antecellit. Id autem est ipsa ratio uel mens uel intelligentia uel si quo alio uocabulo commodius appellatur].[26] As we have already seen, the chief aim of the Neoplatonic ascent to the divine was to develop the individual *psyche* such that it could contemplate the World *Nous* and thus ultimately the One. Whilst clearly influenced by the Platonic model, Augustine presents us with a significantly modified picture. In the first place, as we have seen, he places the Greek and Hebrew Scriptures at the origin of his search. For Plotinus the contemplative insight [*theoria*] of the intellect will lead us to the *Nous*. Augustine, on the other hand, gives priority to memory as the attribute of the *psyche* most likely to bring us to the divine.

As well as reflecting the triune life in its constituent parts Augustine, in contrast to the Platonists, places Christ as the key mediator and educator of the soul. Christ, for Augustine, is 'the way, the truth and the life' (John 14.6) and, as he says in his *Homily on the Psalms*: 'The Lord himself heals the eyes of our hearts to enable us to see what he shows us' (*Enarrationes in Psalmos* 84.1) [Sed quia ipse sanat oculos cordis ad uidendum se].[27]

Intimacy with the person of Christ will thus lead to the divinization of the soul, not through our own efforts or merits, but simply through the love and grace of God freely given (in contrast to the Platonic way, in which our own effort, in contemplation [*theoria*], will inevitably lead to union with the Divine): 'The Son of God was made a sharer in our mortal nature so that mortals might become sharers in his Godhead' [Filius enim Dei particeps mortalitatis effectus est, ut mortalis homo fiat particeps diuinitatis][28] and 'It is quite obvious that God called human beings 'gods' in the sense that they were deified by his grace, not because they were born of his own substance [...] he alone deifies who is God of himself, not by participation in any other' (*Enarrationes in Psalmos* 49.1.2) [est ergo, quia homines dixit deos, ex gratia sua deificatos, no de substantia sua natos (...) et ille deificat qui per seipsum non alterius participatio Deus est].[29] Thus God deifies us only by adoption, through no quality inherent in our own natures (unlike the Plotinian schema). Although there is clearly an overlap with and dependence upon the Neoplatonic schema in Augustine's picture of the soul, there is sufficient difference for us to contrast it with the Plotinian schema. As with Plotinus, I will characterize Augustine's schema as having nine basic elements:[30]

(i) As Plotinus bases his schema on the books of Plato and the Greek philosophers, so Augustine's primary sources are the Hebrew and Greek Scriptures. For example, the first books of *On the Trinity* [De Trinitate] concentrate on what God reveals concerning God's self in the sacred texts.

(ii) The impetus for the creation and transformation of the soul lies with God. Unlike Plotinus's One, which is to be sought by us, Augustine's God seeks us out: the Divine is proactive in pursuing our salvation. Augustine's God seeks each person out individually. As the dynamo for Plotinus's schema was primarily *eros*, for Augustine it is primarily grace [*gratia*]. In his *Confessions* he reiterates a common theme in his writing: 'Who shall deliver him from the body of this death, but only your grace, through Jesus Christ our Lord' (7.21.27) [Quis eum liberabit de corpora mortis huius, nisi gratia tua per Iesum Christum dominum nostrum] for, as he continues in the same passage, such grace is not contained in the writings of the Platonists.[31]

(iii) Creation is broken or flawed. Unlike the Plotinian scheme, in which a beautiful soul is held imprisoned in corrupting matter, the soul itself is corrupted in some way that Augustine finds difficult to pin down (see *De Trinitate* 8.2.3). But he has no doubt that sexuality and concupiscence have a large part to play in this corruption. We can contrast this with the Plotinian schema where, as we saw, beauty and *eros* are both vital engines in the mechanism by which we return to the *Nous*. As Augustine puts it elsewhere: 'For no-one can cross the sea of this world unless he is carried by the cross of Christ' (*Homilies on John* 2.2) [Nemo enim potest transire mare huius saeculi, nisi cruce Christi portatus].[32]

(iv) Although Augustine's schema is not primarily driven by *eros*, he nonetheless considers that we have a longing for the source implanted in us and that this desire will drive our earthly search for the Divine. This impels Augustine's stress on the interior search, so tellingly described in the *Confessions*, which will, he assures us, ultimately lead us to knowledge and experience of God. As in Plotinus's scheme, this search is primarily directed within. As McGinn expresses it: 'Augustine taught that "to go within is to go above", that is, the movement into the soul's ground would lead to a discovery of God within who is infinitely more than the soul'.[33] Or, as Augustine puts it in the *Homily on the Psalms*:

> God is within, spiritually within, but also spiritually on high, though not in a spiritual sense, as high places are distant from us [...] God who is within us is most high, spiritually exulted, and the soul cannot reach him unless it transcends itself. (*Enarrationes in Psalmos* 130.12)

> [Sed intus est Deus eius, et spiritaliter intus est, et spiritaliter excelsus est; non quasi interuallis locorum, quomodo per interualla loca altiora sunt (...) Ergo intus Deus altus est, et spiritaliter altus; nec peruenit anima ut contingat eum, nisi transierit se.][34]

(v) Sudden ecstasies are possible on our journey to the Divine. In such an experience in Milan, recorded in *Confessions* Augustine writes of the *ictus cordis* — the sudden 'blow on the heart' (7.17.23) of the ecstasy. Likewise, in *Literal Commentary on Genesis* [De Genesi ad litteram], he explains: 'When however the attention of the mind is totally turned aside and snatched away from the senses of the body, then you have what is more usually called ecstasy' (12.12.25) [Quando autem penitus auerititur atque abripitur animi intentio a sensibus corporis, tunc magis dici extasis solet.][35] The same idea occurs in the *Confessions*:

> From time to time you lead me into an inward experience quite unlike any other, a sweetness beyond understanding. If ever it is brought to fullness in me my life will not be what it is now, though what it will be I cannot tell you. (10.40.65)

> [et aliquando intromittis me in affectum multum inusitatum introrsus ad nescio quam dulcedinem, quae si perficiatur in me, nescio quid erit, quod vita ista non erit.][36]

Such ecstasy is a *foretaste* of the bliss to come, which cannot be attained in full in this earthly realm.

(vi) Augustine's path is a way of ascent from the material to the spiritual, as famously described in the Ostia Vision:

> Step by step we [Monica and Augustine] traversed all bodily creatures and heaven itself, whence sun and moon and stars shed their light upon earth. Higher still we mounted by inward thought and wondering discourse on your works, and we arrived at the summit of our minds; and this too we transcended to touch that land of never failing plenty. (*Confessions* 9.10.23–24)
>
> [perambulavimus gradatim cuncta corporalia, et ipsum caelum, unde sol et luna et stellae lucent super terram. Et adhuc ascendebamus, interius cogitando et loquendo et mirando opera tua, et venimus in mentes nostras et transcendimus eas, ut attingeremus regionem ubertatis indeficientis.][37]

Withdrawal from the world, therefore, is necessary to find God.

(vii) For the Platonists, the development of *theoria* was essential to enter into the mind of the Divine. For Augustine, the equivalent role is played by *memoria* which is the subject of the tenth book of the *Confessions*. Augustine's famous art of *confessio* is in itself a play of memory and much of the book is concerned with the art of memory and how its cultivation brings us closer to the divine: 'Confession is Augustine's way of understanding — a special divinely authorized speech that establishes authentic identity for the speaker and is the true and proper end of mortal life'.[38]

(viii) The human soul reflects the triune nature of the Divine. The human soul is the image of God for Augustine. As God is Triune (demonstrated in the first six books of *On the Trinity*) the soul, which is created in his image and likeness (Genesis 1.26) must therefore also be triune in nature, as its attributes of memory, will, and understanding, demonstrate. These are discussed in *On the Trinity* 8–10; for example in 10.11.18 or 9.5.8, where the soul is divided up into mind [*mens*], knowledge [*notitia*], and love [*amor*]. As Andrew Louth puts it, for the later Augustine 'the image of God is man, or to be precise, man's rational soul. And since God is the Trinity, the image of God in man's soul is trinitarian'.[39] Augustine famously elaborates on this in Books 8 and 9 of *On the Trinity* as the relationship in the soul between lover, loved, and love.

(ix) Christ is the divine mediator to the soul. When we have the humility to accept Christ's presence in the soul we can have the true contemplation of the Trinity:

> The Son of God came [in the form of] a man and became humble; you are therefore instructed to be humble, it does not teach you to become a brute animal instead of a man [...]. He who comes to me, is incorporated in me, he who comes to me is made humble.
>
> [Venit Filius Dei in homine, et humilis factus est; praecipitur tibi ut sis humilis, non tibi praecipitur ut ex homine fias pecus; ille Deus factus est homo; tu, homo, cognosce quia es homo; tota humilitas tua, ut cognoscas te.][40]

The moment of baptism is the beginning of this process of renewal in Christ, but the full extent of our union with Christ in the Godhead will be achieved only after a life-long commitment to, and identification with, Christ:

> So then the man who is being renewed in the recognition of God and in justice and holiness of truth by making progress day by day, is transferring his love from temporal things to eternal, from visible to intelligible, from carnal to spiritual things; he is industriously applying himself to checking and lessening his greed for the one sort and binding himself with charity to the other. And his success in this depends upon divine assistance. (*De Trinitate* 14.23)
>
> [In agnitione igitur dei iustitiaeque et sanctitate ueritatis qui de die in diem proficiendo renouatur transfert amorem a temporalibus ad aeterna, a uisibilibus ad intellegibilia, a carnalibus ad spiritalia, atque ab istis cupiditatem frenare atque minuere illisque se caritate alligare diligenter insistit. Tantum autem facit quantum diuinitus adiuuatur Dei quippe sententia est: Sine me nihil potestis facere.][41]

Central to this process is the role of the Church and its sacraments which is Christ's presence on earth.[42] For ultimately 'we will be like God, but only like the Son, who alone in the triad took a body in which he died and rose again' (*De Trinitate* 14.24) [Et in hac quippe similes erimus deo sed tantum modo filio quia solus in trinitate corpus accepit in quo mortuus resurrexit atque id ad superna peruexit].[43]

We may therefore summarize these characteristics of the Augustinian picture of the soul as follows:

1. It is primarily based on the Christian Scriptures;
2. Augustine's God actively seeks us out;
3. we live in a flawed and broken cosmos;
4. we have a longing to reunite with our Divine maker;
5. union with the Divine can occasionally be experienced in sudden 'ecstasies';
6. 'inner' contemplation will lead to the ascent of the soul;
7. memory and confession will play an important role in this journey;
8. the human soul reflects the Triune nature of the Divine;
9. Christ is the divine mediator to the soul.

Teresa of Ávila's Picture of the Soul

I now turn to examining how far these two models accord with the picture of the soul and of deification as presented by Teresa, especially in the *Life* and the *Interior Castle* [Moradas]. In doing so, I will structure my interpretation around the nine points above.

1. Sources of Interpretation

It seems clear enough that Teresa's work is based on the Christian Scriptures rather than the Platonic tradition. She was not familiar with the Platonic texts as, unlike John of the Cross, who would have studied them at Medina and Salamanca, she never refers to them. Yet her relationship to the Christian Scriptures is far from straightforward. As she tells us in her *Life*:

> When a number of books in Spanish were taken away from us and we were not allowed to read them, I felt it very much because the reading of some of them had given me great recreation, and I could no longer do so since they were only available in Latin. Then the Lord said to me: 'Don't be upset, for I will give you a living book'. (*Vida* 26.6)
>
> [Cuando se quitaron muchos libros de romance, que no se leyesen, yo sentí mucho, porque algunos me dava recreación leerlos, y yo no podía ya, por dejarlos en latín; me dijo el Señor: 'No tengas pena, que yo te daré libro vivo'.]

In this passage we learn of one of the most significant events to have affected her: the prohibition of many spiritual books in the vernacular on which she had relied in her early life, the Index of Prohibited Books promulgated under the name of Archbishop Fernando de Valdés y Salas (1483–1568) in 1559. Scripture in the vernacular had in any case never been available. Her knowledge of Scripture, therefore, would be mediated through the mystical writers she had read, other devout reading, and the Divine Office.

2. Origins of the Soul

The Augustinian schema involves a flawed creation that needs God's grace for its perfecting. The Neoplatonic schema, on the other hand, uses the power of *eros* in its contemplation of *Nous* to find its goal in the One. Where does Teresa's picture fit on this continuum? The first 'apparition' of the soul in the *Interior Castle* is not one of a flawed or broken self, as she describes it so eloquently at the beginning of the exposition:

> While I was beseeching our Lord today to speak through me, as I was unable to find a thing to say or how to begin to comply with this obedience, what I will say now presented itself with this starting point: that we consider our soul to be like a castle, totally of diamond or very clear crystal, where there are many abodes as in heaven there are many mansions. Now if we consider it carefully, sisters, the soul of a just person is nothing else but a paradise where He says he takes his delights. Well then, what do you think such an abode would be like where a King so powerful, so wise, so pure, so full of good things, takes his delight? I cannot find anything with which to compare the great beauty and capacity of the soul; and truly our intellects will no more be able to grasp this than they can comprehend God, no matter how keen they are, for He Himself said that He created us in his own image and likeness. (*Moradas* 1.1.1)
>
> [Estando hoy suplicando a nuestro Señor hablase por mí, porque yo no atinaba a cosa que decir ni cómo comenzar a cumplir esta obediencia, se me ofreció lo que ahora diré para comenzar con algún fundamento: que es considerar nuestra alma como un Castillo todo de un diamante o muy claro cristal, adonde hay mucho aposentos, así como en el cielo hay muchas moradas. Que si bien lo consideramos, hermanas, no es otra cosa el alma del justo sino un paraíso adonde dice El tiene sus deleites. Pues ¿qué tal os parece que será el aposento adonde un Rey tan poderoso, tan sabio, tan limpio, tan lleno de todos los bienes se deleita? No hallo yo cosa con que comparar la gran hermosura de un alma y la gran capacidad; y verdaderamente apenas deben llegar nuestros entendimientos, por agudos que fuesen, a comprenderla, así como no pueden llegar a considerar a Dios, pues El mismo dice que nos crió a su imagen y semejanza.][44]

Admittedly, this picture of the perfect soul will soon be replaced by a darker one overrun by toads, vipers, and other venomous creatures (1.2.14), just as in her *Life* we are presented with visions of corruption, the stench of sin and Hell that would have met with Augustine's approval (notably in *Moradas* 32.1–5). Yet the overriding impression given by this perfect vision of the soul at the beginning of the *Interior Castle* is of an initial state of unity and bliss which we lose but can regain through the methods the book presents.

3. God seeks us out

Even when we stray, God is trying hard to seek us out. In the Fourth Mansion of the *Interior Castle*, she describes how, when we have lost our way in the journey to reunion with God, the shepherd's pipe of the Lord can be heard blowing and leading us back to where we need to be:

> I don't know in what way or how they heard their shepherd's whistling. It wasn't through the ears, because nothing is heard. But one noticeably senses a gentle drawing inward as anyone who goes through this will observe, for I don't know how to make it clearer. It seems to me I have read that it is like a hedgehog or tortoise, when they withdraw into themselves; the one who wrote this must have understood it well. (*Moradas* 4.3.3)
>
> [No sé por dónde ni cómo oyó el silbo de su pastor, que no fue por los oídos — que no se oye nada, mas siéntese notablemente un encogimiento suave a lo interior, como verá quien pasa por ello, que yo no lo sé aclarar mejor. Paréceme que he leído que como un erizo o tortuga, cuando se retiran hacia sí; y devíalo de entender bien quien lo escrivió.][45]

In clear contrast to the Platonic schema, Teresa's vision of the action of God is closer here to Augustine's notion of the God of grace who acts on the soul to rescue us in our fallen state.

4. The role of eros

As I have argued elsewhere, the experience of *eros* is central to Teresa's understanding of the search for union with the Creator.[46] The Divine Platonic *eros* plays a central stage in Teresa's work in a way we do not find in Augustine, who, I would argue, is suspicious of *eros* and its role in the spiritual life. One example will suffice: the account given in Chapter 29 of the *Life* usually referred to as the Transverberation and immortalized in Bernini's famous statue at Santa Maria della Vittoria in Rome. Here is her first account of it in the *Life*:

> Sometimes (when I was at this place) the Lord wanted me to see this vision: I saw an angel close to me on my left side in corporeal form, something I only see occasionally. Although angels are represented to me many times I don't see them, at least not in the sense of 'vision' of which I spoke at first. It pleased the Lord that I should see this vision in the following manner: he was not large but small, very beautiful, the face so enflamed that he appeared to be one of the very high angels that appear to be totally aflame (I believe they are called Cherubim although they don't tell me their names, but I see clearly that there is

a great difference between certain types of angels and others, and between these and others still, of a kind that I could not possibly explain). I saw in his hands a long golden spear [*un dardo de oro largo*], and at the end of the iron tip there appeared a little flame, this he seemed to put into my heart several times so that it reached my entrails [*y que me llegava a las entrañas*]. As he removed it, they seemed to be drawn with it so that I was left totally on fire with a great love of God. The pain I felt was so great that I uttered several moans, and so excessive was the sweetness [*suavidad*] caused by this pain that one would never want to lose it, nor would the soul be content with anything less than God. It is not a bodily pain, but spiritual, although the body has a share in it — considerably so. It is such a sweet love-exchange [*requiebro*] which passes between the soul and God that I beg Him out of His goodness to give this delight] (*Vida* 29.13)

[Quiso el Señor que viese aquí algunas veces esta visión: vía un ángel cabe mí hacia el lado izquierdo en forma corporal, lo que no suelo ver sino por maravilla. Aunque muchas veces se me representan ángeles, es sin verlos, sino como la visión pasada que dije primero. Esta visión quiso el Señor le viese ansí: no era grande, sino pequeño, hermoso mucho, el rostro tan encendido que parecía de los ángeles muy subidos que parecen todos se abrasan (deven ser los que llaman cherubines, que los nombres que los nombres no me los dicen; mas bien veo que en el cielo hay tanta diferencia de unos ángeles a otros, y de otros a otros, que no lo sabría decir). Víale en las manos un dardo de oro largo, y al fin de el hierro me parecía tener un poco de fuego; éste me parecía meter por el corazón algunas veces y que me llegava a las entrañas. Al sacarle, me parecía las llevava consigo, y me dejava toda abrasada en amor grande de Dios. Era tan grande el dolor, que me hacía dar aquellos quejidos, y tan excesiva la suavidad que me pone este grandísimo dolor, que no hay desear que se quite, ni se contenta el alma con menos que Dios. No es dolor corporal sino espiritual, aunque no deja de participar el cuerpo algo, y aun harto. Es un requiebro tan suave que pasa entre el alma y Dios, que suplico yo a su bondad lo dé a gustar a quien pensare que miento.][47]

If we look at the strikingly similar passage in Mansion Six of the *Interior Castle*, we can appreciate how Teresa is using the erotic tradition (inherited ultimately from the Neoplatonic influences of Dionysius) to demonstrate the role of *eros* in mystical union, in itself a deeply Platonic theme:

So powerful is the effect of this on the soul that it dissolves with desire and doesn't know what to ask for, for clearly it seems that it is with its God. You will ask me: Well, if it knows this, what does it desire or what pains it? What greater good does it want? I don't know. I do know that it seems that this pain reaches to the soul's entrails [*entrañas*] and that when He who wounds it draws out the arrow, it indeed seems, in accord with the deep love the soul feels, that God is drawing these very entrails after Him. I was thinking now that it is as though, from this fire enkindled in the brazier that is my God, a spark [*centella*] jumped out and so touched the soul that the flaming fire was felt by it and since it was not enough to set the soul on fire, and it is so delightful, the soul is left with that pain; and this produced by it just touching the soul. (*Moradas*, 6.2.4)

[Hace en ella tan gran operación, que se está deshaciendo de deseo y no sabe qué pedir, porque claramente le parece que está con ella su Dios. Diréisme: pues si esto entiende, ¿qué desea, u qué le da pena?, ¿qué mayor bien quiere? No lo sé; sé que parece le llega a las entrañas esta pena, y que, cuando de ellas saca la saeta el que la hiere, verdaderamente parece que se las lleva tras sí, según el sentimiento de amor siente. Estava pensando ahora si sería que en este fuego del brasero encendido que es mi Dios, saltava alguna centella y dava en el alma, de manera que se dejava sentir aquel encendido fuego, y como no era aún bastante para quemarla y él es tan deleitoso, queda con aquella pena y a el tocar hace aquella operación.]⁴⁸

When the two passages are juxtaposed in this way it becomes possible to interpret the passage in keeping with Teresa's mystical theology. Bernini's statue is, of course, a magnificent artefact of Baroque statuary, but its effect has been to take this passage from the *Life* entirely out of its mystical context, thereby distorting its significance within her text. What is remarkable is the consistency of the language between the two passages written over ten years apart. The only significant word that does not reappear in the second account is 'delight' [*gustar*]. As I explored in an earlier work, this pivotal word is one of Teresa's favourites for describing the spiritual gifts of the life of prayer, especially in the earlier *Life*; however, in the later passages of the *Interior Castle* she suggests that the mature spiritual life moves away from 'delight' [*gusto*] to the wordless and intimate embrace of the Trinity.⁴⁹ The flame of the cherubim remains (so essential for the Victorine tradition). However, Teresa introduces the all-important word 'spark' [*centella*] into the later passage, in clear reference to the *synderesis* (literally, 'the little spark') of the medieval mystical tradition. This, according to this tradition, is the part of the soul where the divine touches the human — the spark she mentions arising from the 'brazier'. This little spark gently touches the heart and causes the ecstasy of fire. It does not 'penetrate', as some translators suggest, and although sexual connotations are present in the passage this sexualized interpretation cannot detract from the fact that these passages are referring to the workings of the heart rather than anything specifically sexual. The other expression common to both passages is *las entrañas* [entrails or bowels, the seat of the emotions]. Both, then, are good examples of Teresa taking the later medieval Dionysian (Neoplatonic) tradition and cloaking it with her own original interpretation. The Plotinian *eros* is clearly present but Teresa has decked it out with late-medieval clothes suitable for her time and audience.

5. *The role of contemplation in Teresa*

Although, like Augustine, Teresa firmly insists on God's action through grace to lead to mystical union, like the Platonists, she equally emphasizes the role of contemplation. Augustine's vision, as we have seen, insists on an inner vision leading to an ascent, and we find in her a similar emphasis on the 'inner contemplation' that will lead to God. In Teresa's version, however, we do not so much see ascent as a breaking through of the person of Christ into the essence of the soul. As she puts it at the end of the *Life*:

> Once, during the recitation of the Office with all the Sisters, my soul suddenly became recollected and it seemed to me to be like a totally clear mirror without having back, sides, top or bottom that weren't totally clear, and in the centre of

it Christ Our Lord was represented to me, as I generally see Him. It seemed to me I saw Him in all parts of my soul, clear as a mirror, and also this mirror — I don't know how to say it — was engraved all over upon the same Lord by a communication which I cannot explain but which was very loving. (*Vida* 40.5)

[Estando una vez en las Horas con todas, de presto se recogió mi alma, y parecióme ser como un espejo claro toda, sin haber espaldas ni lados ni alto ni bajo que no estuviese toda clara, y en el centro de ella se me representó Cristo nuestro Señor, como le suelo ver. Parecíame en todas las partes de mi alma le veía claro como en un espejo, y también este espejo — yo no sé decir cómo — se esculpía todo en el mismo Señor por una comunicación que yo no sabré decir, muy amorosa.][50]

This dissolution of the personality through contemplation is one of the most puzzling and challenging aspects of Teresa's account. In it she seems to introduce a new schema, one not found in her masters in either the Platonic or Augustinian traditions.

6. Moral and ascetical training

As with Plotinus, we see in Teresa's schema an emphasis on the moral and ascetic training required in the spiritual journey. The spiritual search cannot be an end in itself for Teresa, but as she reassures us at the end of the *Interior Castle*, the aim of prayer, contemplation, and union is 'good works':

This is the reason for prayer, my daughters, the purpose of this spiritual marriage: the birth always of good works, good works [...]. I repeat it is necessary that your foundation consist of more than prayer and contemplation. If you do not strive for virtues and practice them, you will always be dwarves. (7.4.6, 10)

[Para esto es la oración, hijas mías; de esto sirve este matrimonio espiritual: de que nazcan siempre obras, obras (...). Torno a decir, que para esto es menester no poner vuestro fundamento sólo en rezar y contemplar; porque, si no procuráis virtudes y hay ejercicio de ellas, siempre os quedaréis enanas.][51]

What she learns from Augustine is the need to temper good works with the ascetic practice of purification of memory and the act of confession. The act of making the confession, admitting all the wayward movements of the soul to another person, through the practice of such humility, will lead us, like her and like Augustine before her, to the union we seek.

7. The union can occasionally be experienced in sudden 'ecstasies'

In common with Augustine and Plotinus, Teresa stresses that it is possible for the soul to experience union on earth for short bursts of time. As she says in the *Interior Castle*, these are possible for short periods of time. The *exstasis* as she describes it, like the description of the Transverberation (above; 6.4.13–14), owes much to the medieval descriptions of the mystical theology that she inherits from Gerson and the Victorines via her source in Osuna's *Third Spiritual Alphabet*. However, where she develops the tradition in passages of the *Interior Castle* (see, for example, *Moradas* 6.4.13–14) is to distinguish the moment of ecstasy, in its Plotinian or Augustinian sense, from the after-effect which she says can last several days and which opens the whole self to God's love.⁵²

8. The role of Christ

For Teresa, as for Augustine, Christ is the *sine qua non* for mystical union. Without the practice of the imitation of Christ the union is not possible. Yet although in the final mansions of the *Interior Castle* she emphasizes the growing intimacy with Christ, this is also accompanied by a Dionysian apophasis, a state of unknowing and of the inability to communicate the experience. As she puts it in *Interior Castle*:

> You will ask how, if nothing is seen, one knows that it is Christ, or a saint, or His most glorious Mother. This the soul will not know how to explain, nor can it understand how it knows, but it does know with the greatest certitude. (*Moradas* 6.8.6)
>
> [Diréis que si no se ve, que cómo se entiende que es Cristo, u cuándo es santo, u su Madre gloriosísima. Eso no sabrá el alma decir, ni puede entender cómo lo entiende, sino que lo sabe con una grandísima certidumbre.]⁵³

Teresa stipulates throughout a 'divine unknowing' — the Dionysian *stulta sapientia* [foolish wisdom] she inherited from the medieval tradition, which, for her, is implicit as we move into the realm of the supernatural (see *Moradas* 6.9.18).

9. Picture of the Trinity

In holding this balance between the *persona Christi* and the divine unknowing of our encounter with the Source, Teresa is following Augustine throughout these final Mansions in emphasizing how the picture of the soul reflects the picture of the triune Christian God. She characterizes the state of the soul here as a time of quiet, 'like the building of Solomon's temple when no sound was heard [...] There is no reason for the intellect to stir or seek anything, for the Lord who created it wants to give it rest here' (*Moradas* 7.3.11) [como en la edificación del templo de Salomón, adonde no se había de oír ningún ruido (...)], as the faculties, she says, are now quietened in amazement.⁵⁴ In these final remarkable passages of the *Interior Castle*, I would argue that Teresa is able to combine the Augustinian tradition of representation of *theosis* [deification] as life in the Trinity with the Dionysian and Platonic tradition of *apophasis* [unknowing] to present a theological strategy of returning us to Christ through the processes of *theologia mystica*.

Conclusion

In this essay I have sought to map onto Teresa's picture of the soul two classic pictures from the Western tradition: the Augustinian and the Neoplatonic. My conclusion is that we find in Teresa's work a fascinating and highly original blend of the two. Whereas she follows closely many of the tropes of the Augustinian tradition, not least in its emphasis on the role of confession, inner contemplation, and identification with the *persona Christi*, from her Neoplatonic sources she also renders her vision alive to the possibility of new dimensions, most notably in her exposition of the roles of *eros* and *apophasis*. Her remarkable achievement in the *Interior Castle* is to blend the linguistic strategies of the *theologia mystica*, to which she was heir, with her own theological imagery, to present a radical proposal of how the Christian should act in the world through embodied unknowing in selfless action. The final result is a sophisticated spiritual text with an unprecedented experiential force in the literature of Western Christian spirituality.

Notes to Chapter 6

1. The Spanish text is taken from *Obras completas de Santa Teresa*, ed. by Efrén de la Madre de Dios and Otger Steggink (Madrid: Biblioteca de Autores Cristianos, 1997), pp. 42–43. English translations are mine, unless otherwise indicated.
2. *Tercer abecedario espiritual de Francisco de Osuna*, ed. by Saturnino López Santidrián (Madrid: Biblioteca de Autores Cristianos, 1998), p. 200. My translation.
3. *Tercer abecedario*, p. 200.
4. *Tercer abecedario*, pp. 199–200.
5. For this, see especially P. Rorem, *Pseudo-Dionysius. A Commentary on the Texts and an Introduction to their Influence* (Oxford: Oxford University Press, 1993), pp. 214–19, and Bernard McGinn, 'Thomas Gallus and Dionysian Mysticism', *Studies in Spirituality*, 8 (1998), 81–96.
6. The twelfth-century scholar John Sarracenus produced his version of the *corpus* in 1166–67, the first full translation since Eriugena's, some three hundred years earlier.
7. Peter M. Tyler, *The Return to the Mystical: Ludwig Wittgenstein, Teresa of Ávila and the Christian Mystical Tradition* (London: Continuum, 2011).
8. John P. Kenney *Contemplation and Classical Christianity: A Study in Augustine* (Oxford: Oxford University Press, 2013), p. 23.
9. *Enneads*, 6.9.11, p. 345.
10. John P. Kenney, *The Mysticism of Saint Augustine: Rereading the 'Confessions'* (London: Routledge, 2005), p. 21.
11. Kenney, *The Mysticism of Saint Augustine*, p. 23; compare Plotinus, *Enneads*, 4.8.8.
12. *Enneads*, 6.9.8, pp. 331–35.
13. *Vita Plotini*, 23, p. 71.
14. The Greek term, *psyche*, has links with the Greek *psykhein* 'to blow, cool' as well as various terms for life-force, ghost, spirit and even butterfly. For more on these connections, see Peter M. Tyler, *The Pursuit of the Soul: Psychoanalysis, Soul-Making and the Christian Tradition* (Edinburgh: T&T Clark, 2016).
15. *Enneads*, 6.9.7, pp. 327–31.
16. Philo of Alexandria, *On the Confusion of Tongues*, trans. by F. Colson and G. Whitaker, Loeb Classical Library, 227 (London: Heinemann, 1929), 17.77; *Allegorical Interpretation of Genesis 2, 3*, trans. by F. Colson and G. Whitaker, Loeb Classical Library, 226 (London: Heinemann, 1929), 3.22.69.
17. Pierre Hadot, *Philosophy as a Way of Life: Spiritual Exercises from Socrates to Foucault* (Oxford: Blackwell, 1995).
18. *Enneads* 6.9.7, pp. 327–31.
19. *Enneads* 6.7.22, pp. 155–59.
20. *Enneads* 6.9.8, pp. 331–35.
21. *Enneads*, 6.9.8, pp. 331–35.
22. *Enneads* 6.9.8, pp. 331–35.
23. *Enneads*, 9.9.9, pp. 335–39.
24. *Enneads* 1.6.9, pp. 259–61; 6.7.22, pp. 155–59; 6.9.9, pp. 235–39.
25. *Enneads* 5.1.1, pp. 11–13. In this Plotinus follows Plato's *Theaetetus* (176b).
26. Agostino Trapè, in *The Golden Age of Latin Patristic Literature from the Council of Nicea to the Council of Chalcedon*, ed. by Angelo Di Berardino (Westminster: Christian Classics, 1986), IV, 454;

On Genesis. A Refutation of the Manichees, Unfinished Literal Commentary on Genesis. The Literal Meaning of Genesis, in *The Works of Saint Augustine. A Translation for the Twenty-First Century*, ed. by John E. Rotelle, trans. by E. Hill, 3 vols (Hyde Park, NY: New City Press, 1996), 1.13, p. 234; *Sancti Aureli Augustini, Corpus Scriptorum Ecclesiasticum Latinorum*, 36, ed. by J. Zycha (Prague: Tempsky, 1894; repr. 1972), p. 86.

27. *Exposition on the Psalms*, in *The Works of Saint Augustine*, 3.18, p. 204; *Corpus Christianorum, series Latina*, 39, ed. by E. Dekkers and J. Fraipont (Turnholt: Brepols, 1955–), pp. 1161–62. See also *Confessions* 7.18.24.
28. *Exposition on the Psalms*, 3.17. *The Works of St Augustine: A Translation for the Twenty-first century*, ed. by John E. Rotelle, trans. by Maria Boulding (Hyde Park, NY: New City Press, 2000), pp. 38–40; *Corpus Christianorum, series Latina*, 39, p. 642.
29. *The Works of St Augustine*, trans. by Boulding, 3.16, p. 381; *Corpus Christianorum*, 38, p. 575.
30. As will be clear by now, the complexity and range of Augustine's thought makes it difficult to summarize simply. In this schema I am drawing primarily on the descriptions of the self given in the *Confessions* and *On the Trinity*.
31. *Confessions*, pp. 398–99; (LCL, 26).
32. *The Works of St Augustine*, trans. by Hill, 3.12, p. 37; *Corpus Christianorum*, 36, p. 12.
33. Bernard McGinn, *The Presence of God: A History of Western Christian Mysticism*, 6 vols (London: SCM Press, 1991 to the present), I, 242.
34. *The Works of St Augustine*, trans. by Boulding, III.20, pp. 150–01; *Corpus Christianorum*, 40, pp. 1907–08.
35. *The Works of St Augustine*, trans. by Hill, 1.13, p. 477; *Corpus Scriptorum Ecclesiasticum Latinorum*, 36, ed. by Zycha, p. 395.
36. LCL 2, p. 196.
37. LCL 2, p. 48.
38. *Confessions*, trans. by James J. O'Donnell, 3 vols (Oxford: Clarendon Press, 1992), I, xliii.
39. Andrew Louth, *The Origins of the Christian Mystical Tradition: From Plato to Denys* (Oxford: Oxford University Press, 2007), p. 147.
40. *The Works of St Augustine*, trans. by Hill, 3.12, p. 123; *Corpus Christianorum*, 36, p. 257.
41. *The Works of St Augustine*, trans. by Hill, 1.5, pp. 137–38; *Corpus Christianorum*, 50, pp. 454–55.
42. See, for example, *Confessions* 7.10.16, 7.18–19, pp. 24–25.
43. *The Works of St Augustine*, trans. by Hill, 1.5, pp. 137–38; *Corpus Christianorum*, 50, pp. 454–55.
44. *Obras completas*, p. 472.
45. *Obras completas*, p. 503. Teresa is referring here to the same example that Osuna uses in the *Tercer abecedario* 4.4. Teresa's 'drawing inward' [*encogimiento*] is an interesting variant on 'recollection' [*recogimiento*].
46. See *Sources of Transformation: Revitalizing Christian Spirituality*, ed. by Peter M. Tyler and Edward Howells (London: Bloomsbury Continuum, 2010), pp. 135–47.
47. *Obras completas*, pp. 157–58.
48. *Obras completas*, p. 529.
49. See Tyler, *Teresa of Avila: Doctor of the Soul* (London: Bloomsbury Continuum, 2013), especially Chapters 4–6.
50. *Obras completas*, p. 224.
51. *Obras completas*, pp. 579–80.
52. Also described in *Vida* 38.3.
53. *Obras completas*, p. 554.
54. *Obras completas*, pp. 576–77.

CHAPTER 7

St Teresa and her First Jesuit Confessors

Terence O'Reilly

St Teresa is remembered now as the author of influential books on prayer, and as the founder of the Discalced Carmelite Reform. These achievements, however, belong to the last part of her life, to the years between *circa* 1560, when she was forty-five, and 1582, when she died. For three decades before that she led the humble life of a Carmelite nun in Ávila. Looking back later on this period, she described it as fraught. Her health was poor, and at one point she fell gravely ill. She also encountered serious problems in prayer. Though settled in her vocation and devout, she lacked the advice of a wise confessor, and she was therefore obliged to seek guidance instead in books on the spiritual life. When her prayer became mystical, however, these proved unable to help, and she found herself stuck and confused, unable to interpret her experience, and unsure how to proceed. This anguished state of affairs lasted for almost twenty years. It was not resolved, in fact, until the mid-1550s, when she came into contact with members of a new religious order, recently arrived in Ávila: the Society of Jesus. The Jesuit confessors she consulted then, Diego de Cetina and Juan de Prádanos, understood her problems, and the advice they gave her resolved them decisively.[1] Their intervention raises two questions. First, what was the nature of the crisis Teresa endured? Her account of it is confusing at times, and it has given rise to conflicting interpretations.[2] And second, to what extent was the advice of her Jesuit confessors shaped by the *Spiritual Exercises* of their founder, St Ignatius Loyola? The pages that follow consider these questions in turn.

Teresa's Experience of Prayer

When Teresa became a nun in 1535, at the age of twenty, she did not know, she tells us, how to practise mental prayer.[3] This changed, however, a few years later, in 1538, when she read the *Tercer abecedario spiritual* [The Third Spiritual Alphabet] (Toledo, 1527), a book on prayer by a Franciscan, Francisco de Osuna.[4] She took its teachings as a guide, and in accordance with them she turned her attention inwards, to the presence of Christ in her soul: 'I tried as hard as I could to think of Jesus Christ, our Good and our Lord, as present within me, and it was in this way that I prayed. If I thought about a scene from his Passion, I would picture it within' (*Vida* 4.7)

[Procuraba lo más que podía traer a Jesucristo, nuestro bien y Señor, dentro de mí presente, y esta era mi manera de oración. Si pensaba en algún paso, le representaba en lo interior]. This simple form of meditation, affective rather than discursive, was succeeded at times by something different, a direct apprehension of the presence of God:

> When picturing myself close to Christ in the way I have mentioned, and sometimes even when reading, I used to experience unexpectedly a feeling of God's presence of such a kind that I could not possibly doubt that he was within me, or that I was entirely engulfed in him. (*Vida* 10.1)
>
> [acaecíame en esta representación que hacía de ponerme cabe Cristo (...), y aun algunas veces leyendo, venirme a desora un sentimiento de la presencia de Dios que en ninguna manera podía dudar que estaba dentro de mí o yo toda engolfada en Él.]

She adds that 'this was not like a vision: I believe they call it mystical theology' [Esto no era manera de visión: creo lo llaman mística teología]. The profound experience that she describes was, as she indicates, the beginning of mystical prayer or contemplation, the terms used later to describe it by St John of the Cross: 'contemplation, in which the understanding has the most exalted knowledge of God, is called mystical theology, which means secret wisdom of God' [la contemplación por la cual el entendimiento tiene más alta noticia de Dios llaman teología mística, que quiere decir sabiduría de Dios secreta].[5] What followed in Teresa's prayer during the remaining years of her life was not an addition to this gift, but its deepening and expansion in her soul. She observed: 'What is given to those who are more advanced is the same as what is given at the start' (*Vida* 22.16) [(es) todo uno lo que se da a los que más adelante van que en el principio]. To make her point, she used a vivid image: as food gives life to the body, so contemplation gives life to the soul:

> It is like food that many people consume, and those who eat a little are left for a brief moment with just a pleasing taste; those who eat more, it helps to sustain; to those who eat a lot, it gives life and strength.
>
> [es como un manjar que comen de él muchas personas, y las que comen poquito, quédales solo buen sabor por un rato; las que más, ayuda a sustentar; las que comen mucho, da vida y fuerza.]

In her own case, the experience of contemplation was at first brief (it lasted, she notes, no longer than a *Hail Mary*), but with the passing of time it became more frequent and prolonged, and in the process it transformed her. Her experience of its growth, however, was not serene. On the contrary, she found herself within a short time troubled and perplexed in three distinct areas of her life.

A Divided Heart

Teresa tells us that during her time as a novice she realized she was happy to be a nun, and her happiness deepened when she learned how to practise mental prayer (*Vida* 4.2, 7). A few years later, however, she discovered that prayer was a source of distress as well as joy, because it made her aware, acutely, of conflict within. She was by nature charming and affectionate, and she enjoyed many friendships as a result, but this aspect of her personality, she came to see, was disordered: in her relationships she lacked *discreción* (discretion), meaning balance and right judgement:

> I had a most great fault, which caused me great harm, and it was this: when I began to realize that someone was fond of me, and if I liked them, I would become so attached to them that my memory would be largely tied down by thoughts of them, though without any intention of offending God; but I delighted to see them and to think of them and in the good things I saw in them. This was so harmful that it brought my soul to a most ruinous state. (*Vida* 37.4)

> [Tenía una grandísima falta de donde me vinieron grandes daños, y era esta: que como comenzaba a entender que una persona me tenía voluntad, y si me caía en gracia, me aficionaba tanto que me ataba en gran manera la memoria a pensar en él, aunque no era con intención de ofender a Dios, mas holgábame de verle y de pensar en él y en las cosas buenas que le veía. Era cosa tan dañosa, que me traía el alma harto perdida.]

The problem was accentuated by the fact that her convent was not enclosed. She had frequent contact, therefore, with outsiders, whose concerns were shaped, not by the Rule of her Order, but by their lives in the world. At this time, she wrote, her religious practice was flawed: 'It was full of imperfections and very faulty' (*Vida* 6.7) [era lleno de imperfecciones y con muchas faltas]. Her behaviour was imperfect too: 'In wrongdoing, punctiliousness, and vanity I was most skilful and assiduous' [Para el mal y curiosidad y vanidad tenía gran maña y diligencia]. The result was inner tension: 'I had neither joy in God, nor contentment in the world. When I was in the midst of worldly contentments, I was distressed by the memory of what I owed God; when I was with God, I was made restless by worldly affections' (*Vida* 8.2) [ni yo gozaba de Dios ni traía contento en el mundo. Cuando estaba en los contentos del mundo, en acordarme lo que debía a Dios era con pena; cuando estaba con Dios, las aficiones del mundo me desasosegaban]. It was in prayer, especially, that the tension surfaced:

> My life was most burdensome, because in prayer I understood my faults more keenly. On the one hand God was calling me; on the other, I was following the world [...]. It seems I wished to reconcile these two contrary things — so opposed to each other — namely the spiritual life, and the contentments, joys and pastimes of the senses. (*Vida* 7.17)

> [Pasaba una vida trabajosísima, porque en la oración entendía más mis faltas. Por una parte me llamaba Dios; por otra, yo seguía al mundo (...). Parece que quería concertar estos dos contrarios — tan enemigo uno del otro — como es vida spiritual y contentos y gustos y pasatiempos sensuales.]

Her distress was extreme, and so much so that she wondered in retrospect how she had coped: 'This is a war so painful that I do not know how I managed to endure it for one month, let alone so many years' (*Vida* 8.2) [Ello es una guerra tan penosa, que no sé cómo un mes la pude sufrir, cuanto más tantos años].

Teresa's account of her problems might lead one to suppose that she was lax in the observance of her Rule, and inclined to be neglectful of the demands of community life. Her contemporaries, however, record that such was not the case. The Dominican Domingo Báñez, for instance, testified that in her youth her faults in such matters were not exceptional. On the contrary, he affirmed, she was considered above average in her care for the sick and her dedication to prayer.[6] There is no reason to doubt that this was so, but if his remarks are accurate, how does one account for the anguish Teresa felt? The answer lies, it would seem, in the nature of her prayer. In the *Noche oscura del alma* [Dark Night of the Soul], John of the Cross describes how contemplation, slowly but surely, purifies the soul of imperfection:

> This dark night is an inflowing of God into the soul, which purges it of its imperfections, habitual, natural and spiritual, and which contemplatives term infused contemplation or mystical theology. In it God teaches the soul secretly, and instructs it in the perfection of love, without her doing anything or understanding how this occurs.
>
> [Esta noche oscura es una influencia de Dios en el alma, que la purge de sus ignorancias e imperfecciones habituales, naturales y espirituales, que llaman los contemplativos contemplación infusa o mística teología, en que de secreto enseña Dios al alma y la instruye en perfección de amor, sin ella hacer nada ni entender cómo].[7]

Exposed to this divine inflowing, Teresa became aware, intensely, of her failings, and of her inability, unaided, to correct them. This knowledge, understandably, she found hard to bear: 'When I recalled the gifts the Lord was giving me in prayer and the great deal I owed him, and how badly I was repaying him, I could not endure it' (*Vida* 6.4) [como se me acordaba los regalos que el Señor me hacía en la oración y lo mucho que le debía, y veía cuán mal se lo pagaba, no lo podía sufrir]. So great was her pain, indeed, that for a period of eighteen months she gave up mental prayer altogether, with the intention of not resuming it until her behaviour had improved, and though she came to repent of her decision, which she saw as the greatest temptation she had faced, prayer continued to be a torment. Her suffering would have been less, perhaps, if she had understood its causes, but she did not, partly because of the nature of contemplation itself. According to John of the Cross, God uses it to teach the soul 'secretly', meaning in a way hidden even from the soul, so that it is, truly, in the dark. And matters were made worse for Teresa by the confessors on whom she depended for advice. They made light of her imperfections, and failed to warn her against the occasions of venial sin that beset her. One whom she consulted replied, 'that even if I were experiencing lofty contemplation, such occasions and relationships would not harm me' (*Vida* 8.11) [que aunque tuviese subida contemplación, no me eran inconveniente semejantes ocasiones y tratos], a judgment that she came to see was untrue.

A lack of wise guidance is one reason why Teresa's agony lasted so long. Another is the fact that she needed time to become convinced of her weakness, of her incapacity to attain by her own striving the wholeness for which she longed. On more than one occasion in her writings she asks why it should take so long to pass from the beginnings of contemplation to freedom of soul, and she answers that the impediment lies not in God, but in ourselves:

> We think we are giving everything, but in fact we are offering God the income or the fruits, and keeping the property and its ownership for ourselves. [...]. And so, because the gift is not complete, we are not given this treasure completely. May his Majesty be pleased to give it to us drop by drop, even if this costs us all the trials in the world. (*Vida* 11.2)
>
> [parécenos que lo damos todo, y es que ofrecemos a Dios la renta o los frutos y quedámonos con la raíz y posesión (...). Así que, porque no se acaba de dar junto, no se nos da por junto este tesoro. Plega al Señor que gota a gota nos le dé su Majestad, aunque sea costándonos todos los trabajos del mundo].

Teresa's trials came to a head in the mid-1550s. Then, on reading the *Confessions* of St Augustine, recently printed in Spanish translation, she saw herself reflected in his account of how he longed to give himself wholly to God, but felt unable to do so until, mysteriously, the Lord called to him in a garden. She wrote: 'When I reached his conversion, and read how he heard that voice in the garden, I could not but think that the Lord was calling *me*, so keenly did my heart feel it' (*Vida* 9.8) [Cuando llegué a su conversion y leí cómo oyó aquella voz en el huerto, no me parece sino que el Señor me la dio a mí, según sintió mi corazón]. At about the same time she was moved to tears before an image of Christ wounded in his Passion: 'So great was my distress at how poorly I had repaid those wounds, that my heart, it seems, broke apart, and I threw myself down beside him, shedding floods of tears, and begging him to give me strength once for all not to offend him' (*Vida* 9.1) [Fue tanto lo que sentí de lo mal que había agradecido aquellas llagas, que el corazón me parece se me partía, y arrojéme cabe Él con grandísimo derramiento de lágrimas, suplicándole me fortaleciese ya de una vez para no ofenderle]. It was only at this point, when she came to the end of her strength, that she was granted what she desired.

The Humanity and Divinity of Christ

After reading Osuna's book on prayer, Teresa's method of meditation was to ponder affectionately the presence of Jesus within her, as we have seen. She loved to dwell on his Passion, especially his solitude in Gethsemane (*Vida* 9.4). Then, when contemplation came, and she could work no longer with her reason and her imagination, her mental images of Jesus disappeared: 'When that was my prayer', she wrote, 'I could think of nothing at all' (*Vida* 23.12) [que no podía pensar nada cuando tenía aquella oración]. Osuna's book gave clear advice about how to prepare for this experience. He recommended clearing the mind of all images, even images of Jesus, so that when contemplation was granted, the soul would be ready to receive it:

> It is well for those who wish to attain high and pure contemplation to set aside created things and the sacred humanity [of Christ] in order to mount higher and receive more fully the communication of things that are purely spiritual.
>
> [conviene a los que se quieren allegar a la alta y pura contemplación dejar las criaturas y la sacra humanidad para subir más alto y recibir más por entero la comunicación de las cosas puramente espirituales.]

To explain what he meant, Osuna referred to the experience of the Apostles, who were so attached to the human nature of Jesus that they did not perceive his divinity until his bodily presence was withdrawn at the Ascension. Christians who practise mental prayer, he concluded, should learn from this, and turn their attention away from the human nature of Christ:

> Since it was well for the Apostles to cease for a time the contemplation of Our Lord's humanity, so as to more freely occupy themselves entirely with the contemplation of the divinity, it seems most suitable also for a time in the case of those who wish to mount to a greater state.
>
> [Pues que a los apóstoles fue cosa conveniente dejar algún tiempo la contemplación de la humanidad del Señor, para más libremente se ocupar por entero en la contemplación de la divinidad, bien parece convenir también aquesto algún tiempo a los que quieren subir a mayor estado.][8]

Teresa, having no one else to guide her, followed his counsel, and savoured the joy she found in prayer. Soon, however, her happiness became clouded in two ways. First, when she emptied her mind of images, the cares and distractions caused by her divided heart flowed in to replace them. And second, she began to feel that somehow it was wrong to exclude in this way images of Christ. She later wrote: 'Can it be, Lord, that for so much as an hour I could have thought you would impede my greatest good? From where did all good things come to me, if not from you?' (*Vida* 22.4) [¿Es posible, Señor, que cupo en mi pensamiento ni una hora que Vos me habíais de impedir para mayor bien? ¿De dónde me vinieron a mí todos los bienes sino de Vos?]. Her words imply that to separate in one's mind the two natures of Jesus is to deny or forget that he is, in the words of St Paul, 'the one mediator between God and humankind' (1 Timothy 2.5). Such, certainly, is the view she later came to hold. It accords with the teaching of the Council of Chalcedon (AD 451) that in Christ the two natures, human and divine, remain distinct, but are never divided.[9] At the time, however, Teresa continued to follow Osuna's advice, and the joy that contemplation gave made her reluctant to return to meditation on Christ's humanity. It seemed to her, indeed, an obstacle: 'It is a delicious form of prayer, if God sustains it, and the delight is great. And seeing that profit and that joy, no one could have made me go back to the Humanity. On the contrary, it seemed to me, in truth, to be a hindrance' (*Vida* 22.3) [es oración sabrosa, si Dios allí ayuda, y el deleite mucho. Y como se ve aquella ganancia y aquel gusto, ya no había quién me hiciese tornar a la Humanidad, sino que, en hecho de verdad, me parecía me era impedimento]. Looking back years later, she reflected ruefully that her attraction to contemplation had led her astray. 'The mistake it seemed to me I was making', she wrote, was 'not delighting so much in the thought of our Lord Jesus Christ, but continuing in that stupor, while awaiting that gift' (*Moradas* 6.7.15) [El engaño que me pareció a mí que llevaba (era) andarme en aquel embebecimiento, aguardando aquel regalo].

Discernment of Spirits

Teresa records in the account of her life that during the 1550s she began to fear that the source of her prayer might not be the Lord, but instead the devil. She had never intended, however, to do wrong. It followed, therefore, that she was being deceived (*Vida* 23.2). Her anxiety becomes explicable when we bear in mind the alarm felt in Spain at the time, by senior members of the clergy, the Inquisition, and the king's ministers too, about the level of religious enthusiasm in certain religious Orders and among the laity. Conscious of Protestantism in Europe, they feared it might lead before long to schism and heresy in Spain itself. Matters came to a head in 1558, when Protestant cells were discovered in Seville and Valladolid, and in 1559 the Inquisition issued an Index of Prohibited Books in which many works on mental prayer written in Spanish were banned. Women who were mystics were a particular concern because they were revered, and therefore influential, but had no formal training in theology. Teresa alludes to this situation when she writes 'At that time there had been cases of women falling prey to great illusions and deceptions at the hands of the devil' (*Vida* 23.2) [en estos tiempos habían acaecido grandes ilusiones en mujeres y engaños que las había hecho el demonio].[10]

Two aspects of her prayer caused Teresa to worry. First, the joy that contemplation conferred: 'I began to be afraid, because the delight and sweetness that I felt was so great, and often beyond my control' (*Vida* 23.2) [comencé a temer, como era tan grande el deleite y suavidad que sentía, y muchas veces sin poderlo excusar]. Certain theologians in Spain were arguing in the same period that such joy was suspect, especially when it was not matched by a life of great perfection. In a book on prayer printed in Salamanca in 1555, the Dominican Fray Juan de la Cruz (not to be confused with his Carmelite contemporary) observed that on occasion, 'those fervours come to sinful people, stirred up by the malice of the enemy of our souls' [vienen aquellos fervores a los viciosos atizados por la malicia del enemigo de nuestras almas], the devil's purpose being to deceive, 'so that by them the sinful person might be caught on the bait of a spiritual joy, and think he is not rejected entirely by God or estranged from intimacy with him, and thus not consider it a great evil to persevere in sin' [para que en ellos se cebe el pecador de algún gusto de espíritu, y le parezca que no es del todo desechado de Dios, ni anajenado de su familiaridad, para que con esto no tenga por grande mal perseverar en pecado].[11] Teresa, who accepted that contemplation and exemplary virtue were normally linked, was only too aware of the gap in her own case between her behaviour and her prayer. The second cause of worry was her practice of Osuna's advice to clear the mind of images. She had believed it was a means of deepening her prayer, but was it instead a devilish ruse to curtail her prayer, and to take her away from Christ? She wrote 'I began to fear again, and to wonder if the devil wished to suspend my understanding, and to make me think this was a good thing, in order to deprive me of mental prayer and stop me thinking of the Passion' (*Vida* 23.2) [tornaba a temer y a pensar si quería el demonio, haciéndome entender que era bueno, suspender el entendimiento para quitarme la oración mental y que no pudiese pensar en la Pasión]. The same theologians held that Osuna's teaching, misunderstood, might weaken the attachment of the faithful to the liturgy and sacraments of the Church.[12]

Conscious of her need of spiritual direction, Teresa requested the advice of a devout layman and close friend, Francisco de Salcedo, and he consulted in turn with a priest who also knew her, Gaspar Daza. To help them, she prepared a written account of her prayer, probably the first redaction, now lost, of her *Life*.[13] Their judgement, when it came, that her prayer was indeed the work of an evil spirit, was devastating. It had, however, a positive outcome. Daza and Salcedo urged her to speak with a member of the Society of Jesus, and to describe her prayer in detail in the context of a general confession. In their view this was the best course, because in spiritual matters the Jesuits were 'most experienced' (*Vida* 23.14) [muy esperimentados].

Diego de Cetina

The date of Teresa's first contact with the Society of Jesus is not certain, but it was probably the early summer of 1555.[14] The Jesuit she met then, Diego de Cetina, was twenty-four years old, and only recently ordained. He was taking a break in Ávila from his studies at university in Salamanca, where he was reading for a degree in theology. The break was needed, it seems, because his health was delicate.[15] The fact that he was able to help Teresa is, at first sight, surprising, given his youth, his limited formation, and his frailty. It is natural, therefore to ask: on what resources did he draw to give her advice? The answer appears to be: the *Spiritual Exercises* of Ignatius Loyola.

As a novice in Salamanca, in his early twenties, Cetina had made the lengthy retreat that the *Exercises* involve, under the direction of a close friend of St Ignatius, Miguel de Torres.[16] At the time Ignatius allowed the *Exercises* to be given only by people who, in his view, understood their spirit profoundly, and Torres was one of these. Before joining the Society, Torres taught in the University of Alcalá de Henares, where Ignatius had been a poor student at an earlier date. They had friends in common in the town, including Manuel Miona, who had been Ignatius's confessor, but they did not meet until 1540, when Torres visited Ignatius in Rome.[17] Two years later he made the *Exercises* under the direction of Ignatius himself, a rare privilege: we know of only one other person to whom Ignatius gave the *Exercises* during the 1540s and 1550s.[18] He then continued in Rome, it seems, for a further four years, living with Ignatius in community, and helping to administer the young Society.[19] Later, in 1548, when the *Exercises* were printed privately, Torres was one of the few to whom Ignatius entrusted a copy.[20] So close were they, in fact, that Ignatius used to say, 'the person who touches Dr Torres touches me in the apple of my eye' [El que tocare al Doctor Torres, me toca a mí en las niñas de los ojos].[21] It is reasonable to suppose, therefore, that Cetina's understanding of the *Exercises* was not far removed from that of Ignatius, their author. Let us consider in the light of this the advice Cetina gave.

First and foremost, Cetina removed Teresa's fears about the spirit informing her prayer. She had been concerned about the joy it gave her, but he told her that her prayer was 'very evidently' the work of the Spirit of God (*Vida* 23.16). In the *Exercises* the word used for joy, consolation, has a central place. The term itself, *consolación*, and its cognate *consolar*, occur forty times. It is associated throughout with the action of God, which inspires the soul with a love, intensely felt, into which all other loves are gathered, and its significance is underlined by Ignatius, who warns in the *Sixth Annotation* that if the retreatant does not feel consolation at all, he or she may not be practising the *Exercises* properly (*Exercises* 6).[22] The value accorded in this way to spiritual joy made the *Exercises* suspect in the eyes of the Spanish Inquisition.[23] It enabled Cetina, however, to steady Teresa's nerves.

Second, Cetina brought Teresa back to meditation on the humanity of Christ, confirming her intuition that it had been a mistake to put it aside. He told her that her prayer lacked a proper foundation, that she should dwell each day on a scene of the Passion, and that she should focus on the human nature of the Lord (*Vida* 23.17). In the *Exercises*, attention is drawn throughout to the union of the two natures in Jesus, the Creator who became man (*Exercises* 53). The retreatant bears in mind, for instance, that in the Passion the divine nature was concealed while the human nature suffered: 'consider how the divinity hides itself: that is to say, it could destroy its enemies, but it does not do so; and how it leaves the most sacred humanity to suffer most cruelly' (*Exercises* 196) [considerar cómo la Divinidad se esconde, es a saber, cómo podría destruir a sus enemigos, y no lo hace, y cómo dexa padescer la sacratíssima humanidad tan crudelíssimamente]. He reflects also that the union of the two natures did not cease when Jesus died: 'After Christ expired on the Cross, when his body was left separated from his soul yet always united with his divinity, his soul descended into Hell, likewise united with the divinity' (*Exercises* 219) [después que Christo espiró en la cruz, y el cuerpo quedó separado del ánima y con él siempre unida la Divinidad, la ánima beata descendió al infierno, asimismo unida can la Divinidad]. He considers, finally, how the divine nature shone forth at the Resurrection in the very human scene of Christ meeting his mother: 'consider how the divinity, which seemed to hide itself during the Passion, appears and manifests itself now so miraculously' (*Exercises* 223) [considerar cómo la Divinidad, que parescía esconderse en la passión, paresce y se muestra agora tan miraculosamente]. At no point does Ignatius allow the two natures of Christ to be separated, and Cetina, no doubt prompted by this, warned Teresa against Osuna's teaching.

Third, Cetina counselled Teresa to fight against her attraction to contemplation: 'He told me [...] that I should resist those experiences of recollection and joy as much as I could, and in such a way as to give them no room, until he should tell me otherwise' (*Vida* 23.17) [Díjome (...) que aquellos recogimientos y gustos resistiese cuanto pudiese, de manera que no los diese lugar hasta que él me dijese otra cosa]. His advice in this matter has been interpreted by some commentators as evidence that he did not have full confidence in the authenticity of Teresa's prayer.[24] It makes sense, however, when one bears in mind the importance Ignatius attaches to 'indifference' [*indiferencia*], as defined in the *Principle and Foundation* (*Exercises* 23). Indifference, however, is not an end in itself, but a means of becoming open to deeper union with God. Later in the *Exercises*, Ignatius writes that when discerning the divine will it is crucial: 'I must be [...] indifferent, without any disordered attachment [...], as though at the centre of a pair of scales, ready to follow whatever I sense to be more to the glory and praise of God our Lord and the salvation of my soul' (*Exercises*

179) [es menester (...) hallarme indiferente, sin affección alguna dessordenada (...), que me halle como en medio de un peso para seguir aquello que sintiere ser más en gloria y alabanza de Dios nuestro Señor y salvación de mi alma].[25] Cetina, it would seem, wished Teresa to become detached from her attraction to contemplation by reacting against it, a procedure described in the Latin version of the *Exercises* as *agendo contra*, but only so that in the long run she might be more sensitive to God's presence in prayer, and respond more fully to his gifts.[26] Hence the implication in his advice that at some point he would tell her to resist no longer ('*hasta que él me dijese otra cosa*'). Teresa records that for the next two months she fought as hard as she could against 'the gifts and favours of God' (*Vida* 24.1) [los regalos y mercedes de Dios], and in the process she learned a valuable lesson. Osuna had led her to believe that she could do something to prepare for contemplation, but she came to see that this was mistaken. Her resistance was met, despite her efforts, with greater favours in prayer: 'In the past I had thought that to receive gifts in prayer much seclusion was required, and I hardly dared to stir. Afterwards I saw how little this mattered; for the more I sought distraction, the more the Lord enveloped me in that sweetness and glory' (*Vida* 24.2) [antes me parecía que para darme regalos en la oración era menester mucho arrinconamiento, y casi no me osaba bullir. Después vi lo poco que hacía al caso; porque cuando más procuraba divertirme, más me cubría el Señor de aquella suavidad y gloria]. She came in this way to understand that resistance 'was no longer in my power' [que no era más en mi mano].

The wisdom of Cetina's advice was underlined a short time later, when she met at his suggestion Francisco de Borja, the close associate of Ignatius, who was making a brief visit to Ávila.[27] He confirmed that her spirit was 'of God': 'díjome que era espíritu de Dios' (*Vida* 24.3), and that she should always begin prayer with thoughts of Christ's Passion. He indicated too that Cetina's advice to resist contemplation had been good. But now, he added, it was time to change: 'If [...] the Lord should carry my spirit away, I should not resist, but let His Majesty carry it off, without striving after this myself' (*Vida* 24.3) [que si (...) el Señor me llevase el espíritu, que no lo resistiese, sino que dejase llevarle a Su Majestad, no lo procurando yo]. Here the key phrase is, 'without striving after this myself': the lesson that Cetina had wanted her to learn. The line taken by both Jesuits accords in this respect with the later teaching of St John of the Cross in the *Ascent of Mount Carmel* [*Subida del Monte Carmelo*], where he affirms that if contemplative gifts are granted in prayer: '[the soul] must not strive to attain them, or long to receive them' (2.3 2, 4) [no ha de procurarlas ni tener gana de admitirlas]. Instead she must accept them with detachment: 'Let her respond to them with resignation, humbly, and passively: for since she receives them passively from God, he will communicate them to her when it pleases him, if he sees her humble and detached' [Háyase resignada, humilde y pasivamente en ellas: que, pues pasivamente las recibe de Dios, él se las comunicará cuando él fuere servido, viéndola humilde y desapropiada].[28]

Cetina, finally, sought to narrow the gap between Teresa's prayer and her behaviour. He helped her to discern when exactly her conduct was sinful and when it was not, a matter in which she had become confused. According to her first biographer, the Jesuit Francisco de Ribera, Cetina gave her at some point 'part of the *Exercises*'.[29] He is not specific, but the part she received may have included the rules for examining one's conscience (*Exercises* 24–44), or those for dealing with scruples (*Exercises* 345–51), both of which train the retreatant to distinguish between venial and mortal sin.[30] Cetina encouraged her, in addition, to practise penance, and though she found this unpalatable, she obeyed him because of the gentleness with which he directed her. She wrote: 'He did not put me under pressure; instead he seemed to consider it all of slight importance. And this moved me the more, for he led me by the way of loving God, and as if to leave me free' (*Vida* 24.1) [no me apretaba, antes parecía hacía poco caso de todo. Y esto me movía más, porque lo llevaba por modo de amar a Dios y como que dejaba libertad]. Her words call to mind the harshness of an earlier director, who had insisted she mend her ways instantly, a command she had found impossible to obey (*Vida* 23.8). Cetina's lighter touch is the approach recommended by Ignatius when dealing with people who are vulnerable, as Teresa certainly was: 'If the person giving the exercises sees that the one receiving them is in desolation and tempted, let him not treat them severely or harshly, but gently and with kindness, giving them courage and strength for what lies ahead' (*Exercises* 7) [el que da los exercicios, si vee al que los rescibe que está desolado y tentado, no se haya con él duro ni desabrido, mas blando y suave, dándole ánimo y fuerzas para adelante]. Cetina, in keeping with this advice, encouraged Teresa by urging her to persevere in prayer, 'for', he said, 'who knows? The Lord may want you to be of help to many people' (*Vida* 23.16) [que qué sabía si por mis medios quería el Señor hacer bien a muchas personas], words that proved prophetic, as Teresa notes.

Juan de Prádanos

Cetina's stay in Ávila was brief: after a few months he left, to resume his studies at university. Teresa was bereft. But the following year she was put in touch with another Jesuit, Juan de Prádanos. He was twenty-six years of age, and, like Cetina, recently ordained. Like him too, he had made the thirty-day retreat under Miguel de Torres.[31] He began by placing before Teresa the highest possible ideal: 'He told me that to please God entirely it was necessary to leave nothing undone' (*Vida* 24.5) [Decíame que para del todo contentar a Dios no había de dejar nada por hacer]. Ignatius, at the start of the *Exercises*, does the same:

> It greatly helps the person receiving the exercises to enter them with great courage and generosity towards their Creator and Lord, offering him all their desire and freedom, so that His Divine Majesty may avail of him and all he has according to his most holy will. (*Exercises* 5)

> [al que rescibe los exercicios, mucho aprovecha entrar en ellos con grande ánimo y liberalidad con su Criador y Señor, ofreciéndole todo su querer y liberalidad, para que su divina majestad, así de su persona como de todo lo que tiene, se sirva conforme a su sanctíssima voluntad.]

Prádanos then helped her to face the difficulties caused by disorder in her friendships, the one remaining problem she had. The matter was a delicate one, because Teresa was unsure where true virtue lay. She was attached to certain friends, and to abandon them seemed to her unkind. She therefore asked her confessor: would it not be ingratitude to give these relationships up, since they were not, intrinsically, offensive to God? The answer he gave is interesting. He did not tell her what to do. Instead he encouraged her to seek God's will: 'He told me to commend the matter to God for a few days, and to recite the hymn *Veni, Creator*, so that God might give me light to see what was best' (*Vida* 24.5) [Él me dijo que lo encomendase a Dios unos días y rezase el himno de *Veni, Creator*, porque me diese luz de cuál era lo mejor]. In the *Exercises*, similarly, the retreatant, when faced with a decision, asks God to guide him: 'I should beg God our Lord to deign to move my will and put into my soul what I should do, in connection with the matter at hand, that would most redound to his praise and glory' (*Exercises* 180) [pedir a Dios nuestro Señor quiera mover mi voluntad y poner en mi ánima lo que yo debo hacer acerca de la cosa propósita, que más su alabanza y gloria sea]. Teresa followed his advice, with unexpected results. While saying the *Veni, Creator*, and making her own its prayer for divine inspiration, she was caught up in a rapture, and heard the Lord speak deep within her soul: 'I began the hymn, and while I was saying it, a rapture came upon me so suddenly that it almost took me out of myself [...]. I heard these words: *I no longer wish you to converse with men, but with angels*' (*Vida* 24.5) [comencé el himno, y estándole diciendo, vínome un arrebatamiento tan súbito que casi me sacó de mí (...). Entendí estas palabras: *Ya no quiero que tengas conversación con hombres, sino con ángeles*]. The experience as she describes it corresponds with one that Ignatius evoked in a letter, written in 1536 to a friend in Barcelona, Sor Teresa Rejadell:

> It often happens that our Lord moves and impels our soul to one action or another by opening our soul, that is, by speaking inside it without any noise of voices, lifting up everything to his divine love, so that even if we wished to resist his meaning, we could not do so.
>
> [Acaece que muchas veces el Señor nuestro mueve y fuerza a nuestra ánima a una operación o a otra abriendo nuestra ánima; es a saber, hablando dentro della sin ruido alguno de voces, alzando todo a su divino amor, y nosotros a su sentido, aunque quisiésemos, no pudiendo resistir.][32]

Teresa, like Ignatius, found the inner command irresistible, and transformative too: suddenly, and unexpectedly, she was granted the inner freedom for which she had longed: 'In one moment he gave me the liberty that I myself, despite all the efforts I had made over many years, could not attain alone' (*Vida* 24.8) [en un punto me dio la libertad que yo, con todas cuantas diligencias había hecho muchos años había, no pude alcanzar conmigo]. She discovered that the disorder in her affections had been healed, and from this point onwards her friendships no longer disturbed her intimacy with God. The words she had heard were 'substantial words' [palabras sustanciales], in the terminology of St John of the Cross: they had effected, in the depths of her being, what they signified.[33] Dramatic and profound change of this kind is described by Ignatius in the *Exercises* when explaining how God's will is sometimes made known: 'The first time is when God our Lord so moves and attracts the will that the soul concerned, without hesitating or being able to hesitate, follows what is shown' (*Exercises* 175) [El primer tiempo es cuando Dios nuestro Señor así mueve y atrae la voluntad, que sin dubitar ni poder dubitar, la tal ánima sigue lo que es mostrado]. Teresa, reflecting on this moment, praised the wisdom her confessor had shown in refusing to give her question a direct answer: 'Because [he] saw I was so attached in this matter, he had not dared to tell me firmly what to do. He had to wait for the Lord to act, as indeed he did' (*Vida* 24.7) [como me veía (...) tan asida en esto, no había osado determinadamente decir lo que hiciese. Debía aguardar a que el Señor obrase, como lo hizo]. Ignatius would have approved also, for the guidance Prádanos gave accords with the approach recommended in the retreat of thirty days.[34] There the 'giver' of the *Exercises* (Ignatius does not use the term 'director') is urged to stand aside, and to allow God and the soul to interact, without coming between them: 'the person giving them should not incline or lean to one side or the other, but, staying in the centre like the point of a balance, he should allow the Creator to deal directly with the creature, and the creature with its Creator and Lord' (*Exercises* 15) [que el que los da no se decante ni se incline a la una parte ni a la otra; mas estando en medio como un peso, dexe immediate obrar al Criador con la criatura, y a la criatura con su Criador y Señor].

Conclusion

The study of Teresa's encounter with the Ignatian tradition of prayer throws light on two matters: the nature of her spiritual crisis, and the early history of the *Exercises*. Teresa's problems were connected intimately with her experience of infused contemplation, which began towards the end of the 1530s, when she was a young nun. The experience initiated a long process of inner transformation that St John of the Cross would later describe as 'the dark night of the soul'. It made her painfully conscious of disorder in her personal relationships and in her response to spiritual gifts, and her distress deepened as she became aware that her own efforts were not sufficient to put matters right. Over time her love of God and of others became more intimate, heartfelt, and cleansed of self-regard, until eventually, in the 1550s, she was set free of the inner constraints that had impeded her prayer and made her suffer. The realization that she had been granted contemplation before, rather than after, her inner disorder had been healed gave her an abiding sense of indebtedness to God's mercy that would later inform the account of her crisis in *The Book of her Life* [*Vida*].

The resolution of Teresa's problems was facilitated by her first Jesuit confessors, who guided her in the light of the *Exercises*. The fact that they understood her so well, and gave her helpful advice, confirms that in the time of Ignatius the *Exercises* were open to mystical prayer. After his death, however, in 1556, the contemplative aspect of the *Exercises* was overshadowed gradually by an ascetical reading of the text that gathered momentum in the 1560s. It came to a head in the 1570s, during the generalate of Everard Mercurian (1573–80).[35] The development of such a reading explains some of the difficulties faced by Teresa's third Jesuit confessor, Baltasar

Álvarez, who directed her between 1558, when Prádanos left Ávila, and 1562. In these years the divisions in the Spanish Church caused by the reaction against mysticism were acute.[36] The ascetical emphasis left its mark subsequently on the official *Directory* of the *Exercises*, which was completed in 1599, and it received fresh impetus in the nineteenth century, when the suppression of the Society (1773–1814) came to an end.[37]

Though the contemplative dimension of the *Exercises* never disappeared from view, it was not recovered fully until modern times.[38] Its occlusion for so long was made possible by a number of factors, including the terms used in the text itself to describe prayer. These differ, in a number of respects, from those used by Teresa, which became normative in the Western Church after her death, largely through the influence of her writings. The word *contemplación*, for instance, which for her denotes mystical prayer, is used by Ignatius to denote meditation on the life of Christ, its meaning in the *Vita Christi* of Ludolph the Carthusian, which he read in 1521, at the time of his conversion in Loyola.[39] He was aware of its mystical sense, which informs the *Imitation of Christ*, his preferred reading the year following in Manresa, but he did not adopt it.[40] Such differences of concept and vocabulary, however, did not prevent the first Jesuits from understanding Teresa. Their experience of receiving the *Exercises* equipped them to respond sensitively to her needs, and she in turn acknowledged readily how much she owed them,[41] especially Diego de Cetina, of whose wise guidance she wrote, 'What a great thing it is to understand a soul!' (*Vida* 23.7) [¡Qué gran cosa es entender un alma!]

Notes to Chapter 7

1. Ignacio Iparraguirre, *Historia de los Ejercicios de San Ignacio*, 3 vols (Bilbao: Mensajero; Rome: Institutum Historicum Societatis Iesu, 1955), II, 124–32.
2. See E. W. Trueman Dicken, *The Crucible of Love: A Study of the Mysticism of St Teresa of Jesus and St John of the Cross* (London: Darton, Longman and Todd, 1963), pp. 277–88.
3. 'no sabía cómo proceder en la oración ni cómo recogerme', *Vida* 4.7, in Santa Teresa, *Obras completas*, ed. by Tomás Álvarez (Burgos: Monte Carmelo, 2014), p. 50; henceforth *Vida*.
4. Francisco de Osuna, *Tercer abecedario spiritual*, ed. by Saturnino López Santidrián (Madrid: Biblioteca de Autores Cristianos, 2005).
5. *Subida del Monte Carmelo* 2.8.6, in Juan de la Cruz, *Obras completas*, ed. by Eulogio Pacho (Burgos: Monte Carmelo, 1997), p. 258. Cited in *Libro de la vida*, ed. by Otger Steggink (Madrid: Castalia, 1986), pp. 174–75.
6. Quoted in *Libro de la vida*, ed. by Steggink, p. 140: 'que en la vida que hizo en la Encarnación en su mocedad no entiende que hubiese otras faltas en ella más de las que comúnmente se hallan en semejantes religiosas que se llaman mujeres de bien. Y que en aquel tiempo, que tiene por cierto se señaló siempre en ser grande enfermera y tener más oración de la que comúnmente se usa'.
7. *Noche oscura*, 2.5.1, in *Obras completas*, ed. by Pacho, p. 599.
8. *Tercer abecedario spiritual*, ed. by López Santidrián, pp. 90–91.
9. *Decrees of the Ecumenical Councils*, ed. by Norman P. Tanner, 2 vols (London: Sheed and Ward, 1990), I, *86. See entry 'Jesucristo en la vida y la enseñanza de Teresa', in *Diccionario de Santa Teresa: doctrina e historia*, ed. by Tomás Álvarez (Burgos: Monte Carmelo, 2006), pp. 363–74.
10. See Henry Kamen, *Spain, 1469–1714: A Society of Conflict*, 2nd edn (London: Longman, 1991), pp. 118–20, 187–90.
11. Juan de la Cruz, *Diálogo sobre la necessidad y obligación y prouecho de la oración y diuinos loores* [...]

(Salamanca: Juan de Cánova, 1555), ed. by Vicente Beltrán de la Heredia, in *Tratados espirituales* (Madrid: Biblioteca de Autores Cristianos, 1962). The passage quoted is on p. 340 in the modern edition.

12. Juan de la Cruz, *Diálogo*, pp. 373–74.
13. See 'Historia del texto', in *Santa Teresa de Jesús, Libro de la vida*, ed. by Fidel Sebastián Mediavilla (Madrid: Real Academia Española, 2014), pp. 477–79.
14. Cándido de Dalmases, 'Santa Teresa y los jesuitas. Precisando fechas y datos', *Archivum Historicum Societatis Iesu*, 35 (1966), 347–78 (p. 356).
15. On Cetina, see Enrique Jorge, 'El P. Diego de Cetina confiesa y dirige a Santa Teresa de Jesús', *Manresa*, 24 (1952), 115–25; Cándido de Dalmases, 'Cetina, Diego de', in *Diccionario Histórico de la Compañía de Jesús*, ed. by Charles O'Neill and Joaquín María Domínguez, 4 vols (Rome: Institutum Historicum Societatis Iesu; Madrid: Universidad Pontificia Comillas, 2001), I, 742.
16. Victoriano Larrañaga, *La espiritualidad de San Ignacio de Loyola. Estudio comparativo con la de Santa Teresa de Jesús* (Madrid: A. C. N. de Casa de San Pablo, 1944), pp. 73–74; Dalmases, 'Santa Teresa y los jesuitas', pp. 349–51.
17. *Fontes narrativi de S. Ignatio de Loyola et de Societatis Iesu initiis*, ed. by Fernández Zapico, Dionysius, and Cándido de Dalmases, 4 vols (Rome: Monumenta Historica Societatis Iesu, 1943), I, 530, n. 5; Marcel Bataillon, *Les Jésuites dans l'Espagne du XVIe siècle*, ed. by Pierre-Antoine Fabre (Paris: Les Belles Lettres, 2009), pp. 148–49, 203–22.
18. Ignacio Iparraguirre, *Historia de los Ejercicios de San Ignacio*, I: *Práctica de los Ejercicios [...] en vida de su autor (1522–1556)* (Bilbao: Mensajero, 1946), p. 9.
19. Marcel Bataillon, *Les Jésuites dans l'Espagne du XVIe siècle*, pp. 218–20.
20. Iparraguirre, *Historia de los Ejercicios de San Ignacio*, I, 159.
21. Pedro de Ribadeneira, *Historia de la Compañía de Jesús en las provincias de España y parte de las del Perú, Nueva España y Philipinas*, 1.8, quoted in Ignacio Iglesias, 'Santa Teresa de Jesús y la espiritualidad ignaciana', *Manresa*, 54 (1982), 291–311 (p. 300).
22. References to the *Exercises* are to the text as it appears in *San Ignacio de Loyola, Obras completas. Edición manual*, ed. by Ignacio Iparraguirre and Cándido de Dalmases (Madrid: Biblioteca de Autores Cristianos, 1982). On consolation, see Jesús Corella, 'Consolación', in *Diccionario de Espiritualidad Ignaciana*, ed. by José García de Castro (Burgos: Monte Carmelo, 2007), pp. 413–24, and Michael Ivens, *Understanding the Spiritual Exercises: Text and Commentary* (Leominster: Gracewing, 1998), pp. 7–8, 136–37, 227–33.
23. Terence O'Reilly, 'The Spiritual Exercises and Illuminism in Spain: Dominican Critics of the Early Society of Jesus', in *Ite Inflammate Omnia. Selected Historical Papers from Conferences Held in Loyola and Rome in 2006*, ed. by Thomas M. McCoog (Rome: Institutum Historicum Societatis Iesu, 2010), pp. 210–15.
24. See, for instance, Tomás Álvarez, *Comentarios a las Obras de Santa Teresa: Libro de la Vida, Camino de Perfección, Castillo Interior* (Burgos: Monte Carmelo, 2005), p. 173, and Daniel de Pablo Maroto, *Lecturas y maestros de Santa Teresa* (Madrid: Editorial de Espiritualidad, 2009), p. 244. For a different approach, see Jean-Claude Dhôtel, 'Les Confesseurs jésuites de Thérèse de Jésus', in *Mystique et pédagogie spirituelle: Ignace, Thérèse, Jean de la Croix*, ed. by Centre Sèvres (Paris: Médiasèvres, 1992), pp. 21–27.
25. On indifference, see Pierre Emonet, 'Indiferencia', in *Diccionario de Espiritualidad Ignaciana*, pp. 1015–22; Michael Ivens, *Keeping in Touch: Posthumous Papers on Ignatian Topics*, ed. by Joseph A. Munitiz (Leominster: Gracewing, 2007), pp. 138–39.
26. Ivens, *Understanding the Spiritual Exercises*, p. 12; *Keeping in Touch*, pp. 63–66.
27. See Efrén de la Madre de Dios and Steggink, *Tiempo y vida de Santa Teresa*, pp. 110–11, n. 65; Barbara Mujica, 'Encuentro de santos: Francisco de Borja y Teresa de Jesús', in *Francisco de Borja y su tiempo: política, religión y cultura en la Edad Moderna*, ed. by Enrique García Hernán and María Pilar Ryan (Valencia: Albatros; Rome: Institutum Historicum Societatis Iesu, 2012), pp. 745–53; and, in the same volume, Alison Weber, 'Los jesuitas y las carmelitas descalzas en tiempos de San Francisco de Borja: amistad, rivalidad y recelos', pp. 103–13.
28. *Obras completas*, ed. by Pacho, pp. 402–03; cited in Larrañaga, *La espiritualidad de San Ignacio de Loyola*, pp. 85–86.

29. Francisco de Ribera, *La vida de la Madre Teresa de Jesús*, ed. by José A. Martínez Puche (Madrid: Edibesa, 2004), 1.9, p. 133.
30. Ivens, *Understanding the Spiritual Exercises*, pp. 33–43, 242–47.
31. See the entry under 'Prádanos, Juan de', in *Diccionario de Santa Teresa*, ed. by Tomás Álvarez, pp. 1088–89; Dalmases, 'Santa Teresa y los jesuitas', pp. 352–57; Larrañaga, *La espiritualidad de San Ignacio de Loyola: estudio comparativo con la de Santa Teresa de Jesús*, p. 91.
32. *Obras completas. Edición manual*, p. 662; quoted in Larrañaga, *La espiritualidad de San Ignacio de Loyola*, p. 95.
33. *Subida del Monte Carmelo*, 2.28, 2, in *Obras completas*, ed. by Pacho, p. 386: 'Palabras sustanciales [...], las cuales en la sustancia del alma hacen y causan aquella sustancia y virtud que ellas significan'.
34. Dhôtel, 'Les Confesseurs jésuites de Thérèse de Jésus', pp. 24–25.
35. See Joseph Veale, 'Dominant Orthodoxies', *Milltown Studies*, 30 (1992), 43–65, reprinted in his collected essays, *Manifold Gifts* (Oxford: Way Books, 2006), pp. 127–49.
36. M. Ruiz Jurado, 'Álvarez, Baltasar', in *Diccionario Histórico de la Compañía de Jesús*, I, 91–93.
37. Terence O'Reilly, 'Joseph Veale and the History of the Spiritual Exercises', *Milltown Studies*, 66 (2010), 1–18.
38. Rob Faesen, 'A French Mystic's Perspective on the Crisis of Mysticism: Jean-Joseph Surin (1600–1665)', in *Mysticism in the French Tradition: Eruptions from France*, ed. by Louise Nelstrop and Bradley B. Onishi (Farnham: Ashgate, 2015), pp. 149–67.
39. Veale, *Manifold Gifts*, pp. 47–48; Ivens, *Keeping in Touch*, p. 68; Terence O'Reilly, 'Early Printed Books in Spain and the *Exercicios* of Ignatius Loyola', *Bulletin of Spanish Studies*, 89.4 (2012), 635–64 (pp. 643–44).
40. See the entries under 'contemplari', 'contemplatio', and 'contemplativus', in *Concordance to the Latin [...] De imitatione Christi*, ed. by Rayner Storr (London: Oxford University Press, 1910), and on the Spanish translation Ignatius read, see O'Reilly, 'Early Printed Books', pp. 657–60.
41. Ignacio Elizalde, 'Teresa de Jesús y los jesuitas', in *Teresa de Jesús. Estudios histórico-literarios* (Rome: Teresianum, c. 1982), pp. 151–75; Iglesias, 'Santa Teresa de Jesús y la espiritualidad ignaciana'.

CHAPTER 8

St Teresa and the Prayer of Offering

Iain Matthew

Once we deny God's three-foldness, 'we immediately are left with a lustreless and joyless (and also humourless!) — in short, an uncomely God'.[1]

Whatever descriptions we could properly use for St Teresa, 'lacklustre, joyless and humourless' are not among them. It may be then that her lustre and joy and humour have their root in her experience of the Blessed Trinity. And, in short, they do. St Teresa's life in the Trinity is also 'comely', beautiful, and I am hoping to capture a ray of that beauty, the beauty of her life in the Trinity, in this essay. What I am aiming at particularly is her prayer of offering: her offering of herself to God; how that happens within the Trinity, and so is a source of joy and freedom.

For one thing, this movement of offering in Teresian prayer suggests how a certain duality in her teaching on prayer should be reconciled. On the one hand, she describes prayer as friendship with Christ and proposes him, in his humanity, as the focus. On the other hand, her 'how-to-pray' book, *The Way of Perfection*, directs its attention to the Pater Noster, where the key is 'knowing [...] where to seek your most sacred Father' (*Camino* 28.1 [CE 46.1]) [saber (...) adónde se ha de buscar vuestro sacratísimo Padre].[2] No surprise that the duality is reconciled in the relationship: approaching Christ, he stands us beside him in his movement of return to the One who sent him.

Biblically, this takes us to John 17, where the reader witnesses Jesus's prayer to his Father; and to the pivotal passage in the letter to the Hebrews (9.14): 'Christ appeared as a high priest [...]. How much more shall the blood of Christ, who through the eternal Spirit offered himself without blemish to God, purify your conscience from dead works to serve the living God'.[3] We are looking at that Christian priesthood so emphasized in the first letter of St Peter: 'Come to him — to Christ — [...] and be yourselves built into a spiritual house, to be a holy priesthood, to offer spiritual sacrifices acceptable to God through Jesus Christ' (1 Peter 2.4–5).[4] For Teresa, conformity to Christ consists in wanting what he wants, in having one's will united to his, in saying with one's whole being to the Father, 'Thy will be done'. *Way* and *Interior Castle* clearly show this. The author finds the key to prayer in the petition, 'Thy will be done':

> Everything I have drawn your attention to in this book is leading up to this point: it's about giving ourselves completely to the Creator, and placing our will in his [...] so that we become available very quickly to reach the journey's goal and to drink the living water. (*Camino* 32.9 [CE 55.3])
>
> [Todo lo que os he avisado en este libro va dirigido a este punto de darnos del todo a el Criador y poner nuestra voluntad en la suya [...] porque nos disponemos para que con mucha brevedad nos veamos acabado de andar el camino y beviendo del agua viva de la fuente que queda dicha.]

Such a commitment to wanting and doing what God wants also crowns her *Interior Castle*: at the climax of the book, Teresa famously affirms that the point of the journey of prayer, including its astonishing mystical manifestations, has been for the sake of service: 'obras, obras' (*Moradas* 7.4.6); works not just as productivity, but as love in action: 'The Lord doesn't look so much at how great our works are but at the love with which we do them' [el Señor no mira tanto la grandeza de las obras como el amor con que se hacen]; what Teresa describes a few lines later as what we 'offer to the Lord' (*Moradas* 7.4.18) [ofrezcamos en el Señor].

A lot is at stake. Repeatedly, Teresa proposes this offering to her readers as the part they can play in changing the world, in remedying the world's evils which she feels so acutely, in bringing people who don't know what's good for them to wake up to the blessings on their doorstep; in saving souls. And, more joyously, the upshot of this will be that God, who is for Teresa so praiseworthy, will indeed be praised and loved. Hence, still in that final chapter of the seventh mansions, she assures us that the mystical fire in St Francis's belly drove him to seek to 'bring souls so that God might be praised' [allegar almas para que fuese alabado]. The prayer of Mary must go hand in hand with the service of Martha, if the Lord is actually to get any food on the table — and 'his food is that in any way that we can we should bring souls that they might be saved and forever praise him' (*Moradas* 7.4.11–12) [Su manjar es que de todas las maneras que pudiéramos lleguemos almas para que se salven y siempre le alaben].

For Teresa this means praying for, caring about, and often writing in the small hours to, specific people. It also means caring about the divisions in the Church in sixteenth-century Europe, and the plight of the native Americans who had yet to hear of Christ. This wide geography of salvation has a mystical depth, revealed for instance in Teresa's account of her vision of hell, shortly before the foundation of San José in Ávila, from which came 'the intense pain [...] and the great impetus to benefit souls' (*Vida* 32.6) [la grandísima pena (...) y los impetus grandes de aprovechar almas].

This is intense stuff, not lacking in anguish, the price of her super-heightened awareness. Self-awareness is painful: 'when you let the sunlight into a room, no cobweb stays hidden' (*Vida* 19.2) [en pieza adonde entra mucho sol no hay telaraña ascondida]. This applies too as she looks out to the world. Her mystical sensitivity sheds light on the cobwebs, indeed on the tarantulas, in society and in the Church. 'The world is in flames! [...] No, my daughters: this is no time to be treating with God of matters of small importance!' (*Camino* 1.5) [Estáse ardiendo el mundo (...).

No, hermanas mías; no es tiempo de tratar con Dios negocios de poca importancia]. So, the heart of her project is to offer one's will to God; and a lot hangs on that — others' salvation and the praise of God.

Teresa's discourse is intense; but it is not tense. It is serious, but not manic. Teresa's letters, for instance, are filled with fresh air; this is not a woman obsessed with a cause, but someone wholesome and broad in her vision. When her cause is on the verge of collapse, it is she who is telling others to calm down: for instance, in late 1578, she is writing to one of her contacts at the Imperial court, Roque de Huerta: 'Let us do our part, and God will then do what he wills. This is God's cause, and all will end well. My hope is in him; do not be distressed' (*Letters* 270.3; *Cartas* 261.7) [hagamos lo que es de nuestra parte y haga Dios lo que sea servido. Causa suya es, y todo parará en bien; yo lo espero en Él; vuestra merced no tenga pena]. Another letter to Roque reads: 'I am sorry about the distress our affairs cause you. You should know that they do not disturb me that much, for I understand that they are from God and that His Majesty looks after our affairs more than we do [...]. You shouldn't be disturbed about anything. The world is not about to end' [Pena me ha dado la que a vuestra merced le dan los negocios. Sepa que no los tomo yo con esa pesadumbre, porque entiendo que son de Dios y que su Majestad tiene más cuenta con ellos que nosotros (...); y así vuestra merced no tenga pena de nada; no se acaba luego el mundo].[5] And in 1579, with options narrowing for Teresa's reform, she gives serious directives to the serious Nicholas Doria; but her postscript reveals her delightful heart: 'But what a letter this is, so characteristic of an old woman with little humility and full of advice! May it please God that some of it be correct; if it isn't, that we still be friends' (*Letters* 286.4; *Cartas* 276.4) [Mas que ¡propria de vieja poco humilde!, va ésta llena de consejos. Plega a Dios que en alguna acierte; y si no, tan amigos como antes].

Teresa's offering of self, then, is total and urgent, for the sake of mission and praise; but the intensity and scope of her gift does not make her an extremist. I want to seek the source of this lightness of touch and great-heartedness, even under such stresses. How did she manage to be serious but not 'obsessive'?

Her sense of humour itself offers a key. Typical of her humour is a kind of irony or banter which is a backhanded way of expressing great affection. 'Give my regards to Padre Antonio de Jesús, and ask him if he has made a vow not to answer me!' (*Letters* 167.4; *Cartas* 163.8) [(...) dé mis encomiendas, en especial al padre Antonio de Jesús, y que si tiene prometido de no me responder]. Or to Gracián, who had had some health issues, 'God forgive you for the days you made me go through with your fevers!' (*Letters* 291.2; *Cartas* 281.4) [Dios se lo perdone que tales días me han hecho pasar con sus calenturas]. Or, sending regards to Rodrigo, 'tell him I think he is more of a friend through deeds than through words, for he has never written to me...!' (*Letters* 319.5; *Cartas* 308.8) [dígale que me parece es más verdadero amigo en hacer las obras que las palabras, pues nunca me ha escrito]. Or to Maria de San José, after noting that Doria has a good opinion of her: 'I am amazed at how you have fooled him!' (*Letters* 335.2; *Cartas* 322.2) [Espántame cuán engañado le tiene]. This is humour making room, expanding confidence, creating more space to move around in the relationship.

The mutual confidence that brings fresh air is central to Teresa's idea of community. She manifests to Jerónimo Gracián, at the time that the text of the nuns' legislation is being revised in 1581, her concern that the Constitutions should not 'seem stricter than they are. I fear more the nuns' loss of the great joy in which our Lord is leading them than those other things [...]' (*Letters* 372.2; *Cartas* 358.2) [(...) la constitución, porque no parezca las aprieta más; que yo temo más que no pierdan el gran contento con que Nuestro Señor las lleva que esotras cosas]. The same tenor is evident in *The Way of Perfection*, which Rowan Williams calls Teresa's 'most consciously mischievous book'.[6] There, the mutual love of Teresa and the sisters of her community creates extra room, like propping up the marquee from inside the tent so that there is more space to move about. Others will express themselves with more precision and depth; but, let's face it: we know each other and love each other and so I may just be able to hit the mark where learned men have had to rush ahead (I paraphrase the Prologue to the *Camino*). Here is an instance of her confidentiality when discussing temptations, from the end of the work:

> I want to tell you something else that helps: if we think the Lord has given us strength in a certain area, realize that it is a gift, and that he can take it away again [...]. Haven't you ever seen this for yourselves sisters? Well, I have! Sometimes I feel I am really free, and when the challenge comes, indeed I am; another time I am so dependent on things — things I would have laughed at the day before — that I scarcely know myself [...]. Sometimes I feel I couldn't care less what they say about me or whatever the gossip; and when it comes to it that sometimes proves to be true — in fact, the criticism makes me happy. There will be other days when one little word wounds me so much that I want to leave the world behind since everything is a weariness to me. I'm not the only one like this. (*Camino* 38.5)[7]

> [También os quiero decir otro alguno, que si nos parece el Señor ya nos la ha dado, entendamos que es bien recibido, y que nos le puede tornar a quitar (...). ¿Nunca lo havéis visto por vosotras, hermanas? Pues yo sí: unas veces me parece que estoy muy desasida, y en hecho de verdad, venido a la prueba, lo estoy; otra vez me hallo tan asida, y de cosas que por ventura el día de antes burlara yo de ello, que casi no me conozco (...). Ansí, unas veces me parece que de ninguna cosa que me mormurasen ni dijesen de mí, no se me da nada; y provado, algunas veces es ansí, que antes me da contento. Vienen días que sola una palabra me aflige y querría irme del mundo, porque me parece me cansa en todo. Y en esto no soy sola yo.]

There is an analogous spaciousness, the marquee held up wide and high, in the way Teresa relates to the Blessed Trinity; the way that she will speak up for the Father in addressing Christ, or for the Son in addressing the Father. This is not scientific language; it is the language of one who is at home in the relationship, and so can stretch it wide with love. So for Teresa the Pater Noster is more than a formula: it is a gift, of the Son, to us, and so of his relationship with his Father, to us. Hence the commentary on the opening words, 'Our Father': 'Oh Son of God and Lord of mine! How can you give us so much with the first word?' (*Camino* 27.2 [CE 44.2]) [¡Oh Hijo de Dios y Señor mío!, ¿cómo dais tanto junto a la primera palabra?].

She goes on then to ask the Son how he could possibly risk exposing his Father to our mishandling — a question which would be spiritually suicidal if meant literally, but which here is a mark of love, a play of confidences, stretching the space of the relationship. The text addresses the Son:

> See, my Lord, that since you stop at nothing, given the love you have for us and your humility — at the end of the day it's true that you, Lord, are on earth and clothed with the earth, since you have our nature, — it seems that you do have some reason to look out for us; but see that your Father is in heaven; you yourself say so. It is only right that you should be concerned about his honour. Since you have committed yourself to lose honour for our sakes, leave your Father in peace; don't oblige him to so much for people as hopeless as me who will give such inadequate thanks. Oh good Jesus, how clearly have you shown that you are one with him, and that your will is his and his yours! What a transparent confession, my Lord! What an amazing love you have for us! (*Camino* 27.3–4 [44.3–4]).

> [Mirad, Señor mío, que ya que Vos con el amor que nos tenéis y con vuestra humildad no se os ponga nada delante (en fin, Señor, estáis en la tierra y vestido de ella, pues tenéis nuestra naturaleza, parece que tenéis causa alguna para mirar nuestro provecho); mas mirad que vuestro Padre está en el cielo, Vos lo decís; es razón que miréis por su honra. Ya que estáis Vos ofrecido a ser deshonrado por nosotros, dejad a vuestro Padre libre; no le obliguéis a tanto por gente tan ruin como yo, que le ha de dar tan malas gracias. ¡Oh buen Jesús, qué claro havéis mostrado ser una cosa con El y que vuestra voluntad es la suya y la suya vuestra! ¡Qué confesión tan clara, Señor mío! ¡Qué cosa es el amor que nos tenéis!]

There is the same play of confidences in the commentary on 'give us this day our daily bread', this time putting the onus on the Father to stand up for his Son. For Teresa, the request for bread is made by Jesus on our behalf, and, in making it, he is asking his Father to give us Jesus in the Eucharist. Teresa writes with heightened anguish as well as trust, in view of reports of desecration of the Eucharist. But there is, too, the same confidence born of her sense of being welcomed within the Trinity, of being at home in the relationship of Father and Son. In the following passage, it is first Jesus who is addressed, and later the Father:

> What father could there be, Lord, who having given us his Son, and such a son, [...] would want to consent to him remaining among us every day to suffer? None, for sure Lord, but yours. You know well the one you are petitioning! God help me! What great love in the Son, and what great love in the Father! Maybe I'm not so shocked at the good Jesus: since he had already said fiat voluntas tua, he had to fulfil it, being the kind of person he is. Yes indeed — for he is not like us. As he knows that he fulfils it by loving us as himself, he went about seeking how to fulfil this commandment in the fullest possible way, even at cost to himself. But you, eternal Father, how could you agree to it?' (*Camino* 33.3 [58.2])

> [Pues, ¿qué padre huviera, Señor, que habiéndonos dado a su hijo — y tal hijo — (...) quisiera consentir se quedara entre nosotros cada día a padecer? Por cierto, ninguno, Señor, sino el vuestro; bien sabéis a quién pedís. ¡Oh, válgame Dios, qué gran amor del Hijo, y qué gran amor de el Padre! Aun no me espanto

tanto del buen Jesús, porque como había ya dicho "fiad voluntas tua", havíalo de cumplir como quien es. Sí, que no es como nosotros, pues como sabe la cumple con amarnos como a Sí, ansí andava a buscar cómo cumplir con mayor cumplimiento — aunque fuese a su costa — este mandamiento. Mas Vos, Padre Eterno, ¿cómo lo consentistes?]

While Teresa's words here are deeply pained, they also reveal her sense of the playfulness of God, of how within the Trinity there is room to breathe, of how full of vitality is the space between Father and Son; and so there must be:

> for however scattered our thinking may be, between such a Son and such a Father, there cannot but be the Holy Spirit, who will move your will to love and keep it held with such a very great love — supposing that your great gain in all this were not enough to hold you. (*Camino* 27.7 [CE 45.3])
>
> [por disbaratado que ande el pensamiento, entre tal Hijo y tal Padre, forzado ha de estar el Espíritu Santo que enamore vuestra voluntad y os la ate tan grandísimo amor, ya que no baste para esto tan gran interese.]

It is this sense of divine delight over and above anything we may do that colours Teresa's prayer of offering. The belief she expressed to Roque de Huerta that the work is not theirs, but God's, points us in this direction. Specifically, the work is Christ's, and the offering is his offering to his Father; and Teresa's offering, if it is to be any use, must ride on the back of his. This is clear from the conclusion to her *Interior Castle*. If indeed 'the Lord doesn't look so much at how great our works are but at the love with which we do them' [el Señor no mira tanto la grandeza de las obras como el amor con que se hacen], we are being called 'inwardly and outwardly [to] offer to the Lord what sacrifice we can, as his Majesty will join it to the sacrifice he made on the cross for us to the Father, so that it might have the value won for it by our will, even though the works be small' (*Moradas* 7.4.15) [interior y exteriormente ofrezcamos a el Señor el sacrificio que pudiéremos, que Su Majestad le juntará con el que hizo en la cruz por nosotras al Padre, para que tenga el valor que nuestra voluntad huviere merecido, aunque sean pequeñas las obras]. What makes our offering significant is its place within the current of giving between the Son and the Father.

Christ's joining of our offering to his could sound like a merely external association. But the relationship between the two — the offering of the sisters and that of Jesus — has all the tenderness and realism of time spent together, like long sitting at the bedside of a sick loved one. The sisters and Christ have spent time together; long hours, in silence and without pay. There they have learned to go beyond a quid pro quo approach to faith; they have let the relationship expand through obedience in suffering. What should a person do, Teresa asks in the *Life*, if their attempt to pray results in barren dryness? Her answer is:

> Rejoice and take comfort and see it as the greatest gift to be working in the garden of so great an Emperor. And since she[8] knows that she pleases him in so doing, and her aim has to be not pleasing herself but him, let her praise him greatly that he shows her such confidence, seeing that without payment she is so careful with what has been entrusted to her [...]. So let her be determined,

even if this dryness should last her whole life long, not to let Christ fall with the cross. (*Vida* 11.10)

[Alegrarse y consolarse, y tener por grandísima merced de travajar en el huerto de tan gran Emperador; y pues sabe (el hortelano) le contenta en aquello, y su intento no ha de ser contentarse a sí, sino a El, alábele mucho, que hace de él confianza, pues ve que sin pagarle nada tiene tan gran cuidado de lo que le encomendó (...) y ansí se determine — aunque para toda la vida le dure esta sequedad — no dejar a Cristo caer con la cruz.]

That is the privileged offering the person is making by persevering in prayer: 'the Lord allows her to be at the foot of the Cross with St John' (*Vida* 22.5) [le consienta el Señor estar al pie de la Cruz con San Juan]. Remain with him there, even if you feel nothing and cannot come up with a single good thought. In fact, whether one feels fulfilled in this prayer, or useless, whether one has a sense of progress, or of bewilderment, is not the point. The point is that there is a work of love going on, the Son's gift of himself to his Father, which does not depend on us at all, but which matters more than anything else in the universe. The disciples' mission, saving souls, putting out the flames, bringing people to praise him, helping the Indians, re-uniting the church, protecting the Eucharist from desecration, surviving the opposition of the nuncio Sega and the visitator, Tostado, putting up with the ineptitude of the Discalced friars, all of this is held within a work of love which does not depend on us at all. To know that love, to witness it mystically, and to believe it in faith, is, for Teresa, the reality which governs her existence.

One of her *Soliloquies* expresses this magnificently. These prayers, written for herself, not for readers, perhaps after Holy Communion, in 1569, take us directly to the mainspring of her life. At this point we shall let Teresa do the talking:

My hope! My Father! My Creator and my true Lord and Brother! When I think of how you say that your delight is to be with the children of men [Proverbs 8.31], greatly does my soul rejoice. O Lord of heaven and of earth, how could any sinner lose hope when these are the words he hears? Had you no one to delight in, Lord, that you should seek such a foul-smelling worm as me? That voice heard at the baptism says that you find your delight in your Son [Luke 3.22]. Lord, are we all to be on the same level? What incredible mercy and what unmerited kindness, more than we could ever deserve! And we mortals forget all this. Remember my God how wretched and weak we are, you, the knower of all.

Oh my soul! Consider the great delight and the great love which the Father has in knowing his Son and the Son in knowing his Father, and the glowing fire in which the Holy Spirit unites himself with them, and how none can be separated from this love and knowledge, since they are one reality. These sovereign Persons know each other, they love each other, and they delight in one another. So what need for my love? Why do you want it, my God, or what good is it to you? Blessed are you, O blessed are you, my God, for ever! Let all things praise you, Lord, without end — since there can be none in you!

Rejoice, my soul, that there is one who loves your God as he deserves; rejoice, that there is one who knows his goodness and how much he is worth; give him thanks that he gave us someone to know him on earth, gave us his only Son. Cared for like this, you can come and beg him that, since his Majesty delights in you, nothing in the world suffice to draw you away from finding your delight and your joy in the greatness of your God, and in how worthy he is of love and praise; and that he help you to play albeit a tiny part in making his name blessed, and that you might say in truth: My soul magnifies and praises the Lord [Luke 1.46]. (*Exclamaciones* 7)[9]

[¡Oh esperanza mía y Padre mío y mi Criador y mi verdadero Señor y Hermano! Cuando considero en cómo decís que son vuestros deleites con los hijos de los hombres, mucho se alegra mi alma. ¡Oh Señor del cielo y de la tierra, y qué palabras éstas para no desconfiar ningún pecador! ¿Fáltaos, Señor, por ventura, con quien os deletéis, que buscáis un gusanillo tan de mal olor como yo? Aquella voz que se oyó cuando el bautismo, dice que os deleitáis con vuestro Hijo, Pues, ¿hemos de ser todos iguales, Señor?

¡Oh, qué grandísima misericordia y qué favor tan sin poderlo nosotras merecer! ¡Y que todo esto olvidemos los mortales! Acordaos Vos, Dios mío, de tanta miseria y mirad nuestra flaqueza, pues de todo sois sabidor.

¡Oh, ánima mía!, considera el gran deleite y gran amor que tiene el Padre en conocer a su Hijo y el Hijo en conocer a su Padre, y la inflamación con que el Espíritu Santo se junta con ellos y cómo ninguna puede apartar de este amor y conocimiento, porque son una mesma cosa. Estas soberanas Personas se conocen, éstas se aman, y unas con otras se deleitan. Pues ¿qué menester es mi amor? ¿Para qué le queréis, Dios mío, o qué ganáis?

¡Oh, bendito seáis Vos!; ¡oh, bendito seáis Vos, Dios mí, para siempre! Alaben os todas las cosas, Señor, sin fin, pues no lo puede haver en Vos.

Alégrate, ánima mía, que hay quien ame a tu Dios como El merece. Alégrate, que hay quien conoce su bondad y valor. Dale gracias, que nos dio en la tierra quien ansí le conoce como a su único Hijo. Debajo de este amparo podrás llegar y suplicarle que, pues Su Majestad se deleita contigo, que todas las cosas de la tierra no sean bastantes a apartarte de deleitarte tú y alegrarte en la grandeza de tu Dios, y en cómo merece ser amado y alabado, y que te ayude para que tú seas alguna partecita para ser bendecido su nombre, y que puedas decir con verdad: 'Engrandece y loa mi ánima al Señor'.]

The energy in this piece of writing suggests an image of Teresa as a child confident in the love of her parents, a child who is running ahead, waiting behind, spinning around, while Mum and Dad are unhurriedly walking forward, enjoying too their child's company. So Teresa here explores all the points of the compass — sinners' trust, stark self-knowledge, mankind's forgetfulness, Teresa's joy in God's joy, her mission to make him praised — all around the delight and love which is the Blessed Trinity, which she sees as 'happening' in our midst thanks to the Son made flesh.

There is one who loves the Father as he deserves; he is our brother. What could be more worthwhile, more productive, or more beautiful, than to say 'yes' to that love, to cheer it on, to applaud it and to be lifted in its slipstream! This is what makes Teresa's call to enter within, to recollection, so powerful: the 'within' is no closed space, but rather the spaciousness of the love of Son for Father. Go there, she says:

> Let's have none of the shyness of some people, which they think is humility [...]. Be with him as with a father, and with a brother, and with a lord and with a spouse; sometimes in one way, sometimes in another; he will teach you what you have to do to please him [...].

> This way of praying [...] is called recollection, because the soul collects all the faculties and enters within herself with her God, and her divine Master comes more quickly to teach her and to give her prayer of quiet than in any other way. For there, in a place within herself, she can think of the Passion and be present to the Son and offer him to the Father and not tire out the mind by going off to look for him on mount Calvary or in the garden, or at the column. (*Camino* 38.3–4 [CE 46.3–47.1])

> [Se deje de unos encogimientos que tienen algunas personas, y piensan es humildad (...). Tratad con Él como con padre y como con hermano y como con señor y como con esposo — a veces de una manera, a veces de otra — , que Él os enseñará lo que havéis de hacer para contentarle (...).
> Este modo de rezar (...) llámase recogimiento, porque recoge el alma todas las potencias y se entra dentro de sí con su Dios; y viene con más brevedad a enseñarla su divino Maestro y a darla oración de quietud que de ninguna otra manera. Porque allí metida consigo misma puede pensar en la Pasión y representar allí al Hijo y ofrecerle a el Padre y no cansar el entendimiento andándole buscando en el monte Calvario, y al huerto, y a la coluna.]

This prayer of offering — joining ours to Christ's, or offering Christ to the Father — was confirmed for Teresa both mystically and sacramentally. Mystically, she speaks in the Sixth Mansions of how the Lord consoled 'a certain person' [a una persona] who felt she never had anything to give to God or to give up for him:[10]

> The Crucified himself said to her, consoling her, that He was giving her all the sufferings and trials which he had gone through in his Passion, that she should consider them hers, to offer to his Father. That soul remained so consoled and so enriched [...] that she can never forget it; indeed, whenever she sees herself so wretched, remembering this experience, her soul is consoled. (*Moradas* 6.5.6)

> [Díjole el Crucificado consolándola, que Él la dava todos los dolores y trabajos que había pasado en su Pasión, que los tuviese por propios para ofrecer a su Padre. Quedó aquel alma tan consolada y tan rica (...) que no se le puede olvidar, antes cada vez que se ve tan miserable, acordándosele, queda animada y consolada.]

Sacramentally, Teresa understood that she could indeed 'be present to' [representar] the Son and offer him to the Father in the Mass. A feature of St Teresa's description of eucharistic life is the way it mirrors the language she also uses of personal prayer: 'be with him', '[s]he entered with him' (*Camino* 34.6, 10 [not in CE]) [estaos con Él; entrábase con Él]. Prayer seeks the presence of the Gospel Jesus, enters to be with him, to be at his feet like Magdalene, acquiring the habit of accompanying him;[11] Holy Communion invites us to be with him, to enter within with him, like Magdalene, acquiring the habit of looking at him and spending time with him.[12] Whenever we think of him, the *Life* tells us, it is his great love that should fix our attention, since love draws out love (*Vida* 22.14). The Eucharist fixes our attention for us: it is Jesus's way of showing us 'how extreme his love is for us' (*Camino* 33.1 [CE 57.1]) [el estremo de amor que nos tiene].

This 'Eucharist' happens precisely in the spaciousness which is the Trinity. Teresa believes that it is the Father who gives his Son to us, in the Mass; as it is the Son who gives us the Father, through the Lord's Prayer. The Eucharist is not peripheral;

rather, it is the communion of love between Father and Son, real in the Lord's flesh. One of Teresa's Testimonies [Relaciones] expresses this belief with breathtaking innocence:

> Once when I had received Communion, I was given to understand how the Father receives this most holy Body of Christ within our soul, as I understand and have seen that these divine Persons are present, and how pleasing this offering of his Son is to him since he delights and rejoices in him (we may say) here on earth. (*Relaciones*, 57)[13]

> [Una vez acabando de comulgar, se me dio a entender cómo este santísimo Cuerpo de Cristo le recibe su Padre dentro de nuestra alma, como yo entiendo y he visto están estas divinas Personas, y cuán agradable le es esta ofrenda de su Hijo porque se deleita y goza con Él — digamos — acá en la tierra.]

The world is perhaps not in flames, but certainly in great need. Teresa's urgent sense of mission is as pertinent as ever. And humanity is as weak as ever, restless and waiting for life to begin. Into this Teresa shines light: there is something worthy of a person's life, something worth doing, worth being part of, which in fact does not derive from us, but into which we are graciously invited. At the core of the universe there is a mystery of infinite spaciousness, the Father's delight in his Son, the Son's offering to his Father.

Teresa was encouraging Roque de Huerta not to be anxious, for the tangle of jurisdictions and antagonisms which was snarling up her reform was in God's hands, and they could trust him. That assurance echoes an earlier testimony of hers to one of her directors:

> One day when I was particularly anguished, longing for the situation in the Order to be remedied, the Lord said to me: 'Do your part, and let me do mine and do not be disturbed about anything; rejoice in the good which has been given to you, which is very great: my Father delights in you and the Holy Spirit loves you.' (*Relaciones* 13)[14]

> [Estando un día muy penada por el remedio de la Orden, me dijo el Señor: 'Haz lo que es en tí y déjame tú a Mí y no te inquietes por nada; goza del bien que te ha sido dado, que es muy grande, mi Padre se deleita contigo y el Espritu Santo te ama.']

Notes to Chapter 8

1. Hans Urs von Balthasar, *The Glory of the Lord: A Theological Aesthetics*, 7 vols (Edinburgh: T. & T. Clark, 1982–89); here *Seeing the Form*, trans. by Erasmo Leiva-Merikakis, ed. by John Riches, I, pp. 55, which refers to Karl Barth, *Church Dogmatics* (London: T. & T. Clark, 1962), vol. II, part I.
2. Quotations from the works of St Teresa will be referred to as follows: *The Book of her Life*, *Vida*; *The Way of Perfection* [*Camino de Perfección*] (Valladolid codex [CV]), *Camino*; *Las moradas del castillo interior*, *Moradas*; her letters, *Cartas*. Translations from the Spanish are mine, except for the Letters, for which I use *The Collected Letters of St Teresa of Avila*, trans. by Kieran Kavanaugh, 2 vols (Washington, DC: Institute of Carmelite Studies Publications, 2001–07). Quotations from the Spanish are from *Obras completas de Santa Teresa*, ed. by Efrén de la Madre de Dios and Otger Steggink, 2nd edn, Biblioteca de Autores Cristianos (Madrid: Editorial Católica, 1967). References for the El Escorial codex (CE) of the *Camino* are given in square brackets.

3. Albert Vanhoye regards Hebrews 9.11–14 as the central axis of the letter: see Vanhoye, *El mensaje de la Carta a los Hebreos* (Estella, Navarra: Editorial Verbo Divino, 1993), pp. 31, 43.
4. Revised Standard Version.
5. *Letters* 287.1, translation adapted; *Cartas* 270.1.
6. Rowan Williams, *Teresa of Avila* (London: Geoffrey Chapman, 1991), p. 78.
7. This passage does not appear in CE.
8. The Spanish here is masculine, as the soul is 'the gardener' at work.
9. My fairly literal translation follows her lilting syntax closely; biblical allusions are given in square brackets.
10. The person in question is almost certainly Teresa herself.
11. *Vida* 9.2, 4; *Camino* 28.4 [CE 47.1]; 29.4 [CE 49.3]; 26.2 [CE 42.2].
12. *Camino* 34.3, 6, 10, 12 [CE 60.3, 61.2, 6, 8].
13. Probable date: 1575; see Teresa of Ávila, *Obras completas*, ed. by Tomás Álvarez (Burgos: Monte Carmelo, 1994), p. 1177.
14. Probable date February 1571; see Teresa of Ávila, *Obras completas*, p. 1143.

CHAPTER 9

Teresa's Theological-Spiritual Synthesis: What Does it Really Accomplish?

Gillian T. W. Ahlgren

As we recognize the profound gift of Teresa of Ávila's life and works on this five-hundredth anniversary of her birth, I set for myself the task of holding up for us a synthesis, *her* synthesis, of how God comes alive in the person who gives herself over to partnership with God.[1] As Segundo Galilea once observed:

> Whenever I read a passage from St Teresa of Avila, I am convinced that God and the experience of God are as real as any object I can touch, or as any historical event I have witnessed. To read St. Teresa is to perceive that God truly exists and can be experienced in our life, and not just as a rather convincing idea.[2]

I think many of us experience Teresa in a way that is similar to what Galilea describes. In this essay I will consider some of Teresa's most significant and thought-provoking theological statements with ten principles (in bold) that I have derived from her work, resulting in what I hope is both a synthesis and an invitational challenge to us today to embrace the same kind of authentic partnership with God that she herself modelled for us.

> Some books on prayer tell us where one must seek God. Particularly, the glorious St Augustine speaks about this for neither in the market place nor in pleasures nor anywhere else that he sought after God did he find Him as he did when he sought Him within himself. Within oneself, very clearly, is the best place to look; and it's not necessary to go to heaven, nor any further than our own selves. (*Vida* 40.6)

> [(E)n algunos libros de oración está escrito adónde se ha de buscar a Dios. En especial lo dice el glorioso San Agustín, que ni en las plazas, ni en los contentos, ni por ninguna parte que le buscaba le hallaba, como dentro de sí. Y esto es muy claro ser mijor; y no es menester ir al cielo, ni más lejos que a nosotros mismos (...).]

Teresa's deep honesty, her humour, her humility, and her radical self-disclosure have made her writings accessible to generations of readers, especially those seeking authentic relationship with God. Her words stimulate both a deep introspection and a hopeful sense that no genuine thirst for God comes solely from us. As Scripture suggests, we love because we have been loved (1 John 4.19); indeed, we *are* because we have been loved into being. For Teresa, relationship with God not only transforms us; it also draws us beyond ourselves and into a whole vital process of godly activity, so that, with God, we become part of the work of renewing, working for dignity, renouncing and denouncing sin and injustice, growing in truth and love and fidelity, and drawing others into this life-giving, creative activity: 'What matters most is to have a very determined determination not to stop until we arrive at perfection' (*Camino* 21.2) [Importa mucho, y el todo, una grande y muy determinada determinación de no parar hasta llegar a la perfección].

Although we often approach them as separate things, Teresa shows us that theology and spirituality are inseparable — and both are neither more nor less than growing toward collaborative relationship with the One who gives life. In my essay, I want to contemplate the legacy of this gadabout woman [*mujer andariega*], this sojourner, this determined seeker, this authoritative teacher, this remarkable human being, this wise woman, this generous mother, sister, spouse and friend.[3] I have organized it around ten basic principles derived from Teresa's life and writings — principles to ponder and discuss but, most importantly, principles to apply to our own lives and work, so that, like Teresa, we might collaborate more fully in making this world a fit dwelling-place for God, the One who is constantly calling us to 'love one another' and to 'remain in My love' (John 15.17, 10).

1. Teresa makes it clear that spirituality is a process entailing and requiring constant growth and development of the human person

Even if you have forgotten or do not yet know Teresa's classic observation that 'whoever does not grow, shrinks' (*Moradas* 7.4.9) [quien no crece, descrece], all you have to do is read through that work to see that growth forms a constant in spirituality and in life.[4] Teresa show that the journey toward both deepest self-knowledge and self-realization-in-God asks us constantly to let go of what holds us back from developing our gifts as human persons and cultivating with God the space in which creativity, goodness and wisdom can come alive, in us and in our world. Teresa's *Interior Castle* gives us a mirror in which to glimpse the brilliance of our inner beauty, a path to recover our dignity, and a method for moving toward the One who gives us life. As Teresa reminds us:

> The things of the soul must always be considered as plentiful, spacious, and large; to do so is not an exaggeration. The soul is capable of more than we can imagine, and the sun that is in this royal chamber shines in all parts. It is very important for any soul that practices prayer, whether little or much, not to hold itself back and stay in one corner. Let it walk through these dwelling places which are up above, down below, and to the sides, since God has given it such great dignity. (*Moradas* 1.2.8)[5]

> [(...) las cosas del alma siempre se han de considerar con plenitud y anchura y grandeza, pues no le levantan nada, que capaz es de mucho más que podremos considerar, y a todas partes de ella se comunica este sol que está en este palacio. Esto importa mucho a cualquier alma que tenga oración, poca u mucha, que lo la arrincone ni apriete. Déjela andar por estas moradas arriba y abajo y a los lados; pues Dios la dio tan gran dignidad (...).][6]

Appropriation of our soulfulness is appropriation of our dignity as human persons; it is not just 'growth' in an abstract way. Teresa teaches that genuine spirituality is measurable in terms of growth in character, in virtue, in goodness, kindness, integrity, concern for others, discretion, wisdom, and a host of other qualities that are not ethereal but are genuinely apparent to others. We have yet to truly leverage what Teresa teaches us spiritually in ways that help us grow as human beings. But we should notice that what Teresa teaches about 'spirituality' is constantly applicable to our becoming more humane, more dignified, and more authentically human.

2. Teresa teaches that spirituality can never be separated from action on behalf of others

While this leads to the obvious understanding that contemplation and action are inseparable, there is something else deeply worth noticing here. Teresa's insistence on the union of spiritual growth and action on behalf of others makes clear that spirituality is never simply an individual pursuit. I am not going to engage here the rather worn debate about whether or not there is spirituality without religion. What seems even more critical, to me, is that there is no spirituality without a concern for others — for their well-being and for the conditions in the world that support the well-being of all humankind: 'The Lord does not look so much at the greatness of our works as at the love with which they are done' (*Moradas* 7.4.18) [El Señor no mira tanta la grandeza de las obras como el amor con que se hacen].[7]

Spirituality without an active concern for social justice and the flourishing of each member of the human family is an absolute *non sequitur*. We cannot pretend that the state of the world we live in pleases God, and Teresa teaches quite clearly:

> All its [the soul's] concern is taken up with how to please God more and how or where she will show God her love. This is the reason for prayer, the purpose of this spiritual marriage: the birth always of good works, good works. (*Moradas* 7.4.6)
>
> [Toda la memoria se le va en cómo más contentarle, y en qué u por dónde mostrará el amor que le tiene. Para esto es la oración, hijas mías; de esto sirve este matrimonio espiritual, de que nazcan siempre obras, obras.][8]

3. Spiritual growth is measured, in large part, by our increased sensitivity to the presence of God and, consequently, to how God is appreciated and esteemed or, conversely, how God is disdained, ignored, or abandoned

This point builds on the first two, and it suggests the underlying reason for the intrinsic connection between spirituality and social justice. From the fourth dwelling-place onward, the progress of the soul is measured in terms of its tenderness, its capacity to love, and therefore in terms of its capacity to respond to suffering. I would argue that our responsiveness to suffering, like Christ's own, must be two-fold: there must be both a deepening compassion capable of expressing itself across all barriers of race, class, gender, ethnicity and all that might divide us, and there must be a keenness of moral analysis and prophetic action to transform injustice. In fact, I would suggest that the 'good works' born of our deepening relationship with God, which Teresa spoke of earlier, are works that bear fruit in restoring human dignity and ensuring that no one in our world is trampled down by others. For nowhere in her writings is Teresa interested in piety (or charity, for that matter — especially when charity translates effectively to alms-giving or other forms of superficial solidarity):

> I hold that love, where present, cannot possibly be content with remaining always the same. (*Moradas* 7.4.9)
>
> [El amor tengo por imposible contentarse de estar en un ser, adonde le hay.][9]
>
> Love is always stirring and thinking about what it will do. It cannot contain itself. (*Vida* 30.19)
>
> [Siempre esta bullendo el amor y pensando qué hará; no cabe en sí.]

Teresa's clarity about love's constant activity leads me to think that, in today's context, whenever spirituality serves a kind of religiosity that is severed from a suffering world, Teresa would say that it is a false spirituality, a work of deception and not light. As she herself reminds us: 'It benefits me little to be alone making acts of devotion to our Lord, proposing and promising to do wonders in God's service, if I then go away and when the occasion offers itself I do everything the opposite' (*Moradas* 7.4.7) [Poco me aprovecha estarme muy recogida a solas, haciendo actos con nuestro Señor, propuniendo y prometiendo de hacer maravillas por su servicio, si en saliendo de allí, que se ofrece la ocasión, lo hago todo al revés].

Today's world provides us with infinite opportunities for prophetic action, and while we might naturally feel rather daunted by the challenges of service in such a deeply suffering world, Teresa is quick to remind us that 'what cannot be done all at once can be done little by little' (*Moradas* 7.4.7) [la que no pudiere por junto, sea poco a poco].

4. Teresa helps us to see that our lives are to be one long prayer, that prayer is life, a life to be lived in the constant presence of God, no matter what our circumstances, roles or vocations

Teresa's vision of life in partnership with God helps us to see that what we are accustomed to call various 'spheres' of our lives (what we do in our family lives, for example, or our professional lives, or our spiritual lives) are all ultimately done in one single sphere, illuminated by the presence of God which constantly invites us to godliness and challenges us to bring God into some rather ungodly spaces. 'The true lover', she writes, 'loves everywhere and is always thinking of her beloved! It would be a thing hard to bear if we were able to pray only when off in some corner' (*Fundaciones* 5.16) [Cuánto más, que el verdadero amante en toda parte ama y siempre se acuerda del amado. Recia cosa sería que solo en los rincones se pudiese traer oración!][10] An honest reading of Teresa moves us from thinking of mysticism as a phenomenon separable from life itself. She causes us to sense more strongly God's invitation to 'the mystical life', which Teresa teaches is 'an [intimate] communication of friendship [and love] above anything we can even imagine: the only life that deserves to be lived with intensity'.[11]

5. Teresa teaches that prayer is a thoroughly and absolutely dialogical process

Teresa's fundamental definition of prayer is that 'mental prayer is nothing more than intimate conversation with a friend. It means taking time frequently to be alone with the One whom we know loves us' (*Vida* 8.5) [No es otra cosa oración mental, a mi parecer, sino tratar de amistad, estando muchas veces tratando a solas con quien sabemos nos ama] immediately dismantles the convoluted polemics about mental and vocal prayer that were so divisive during her day.[12] Instead, Teresa locates prayer in the practice of ever-deepening intimacy with God, a practice we often call 'colloquy' or familiar conversation. The reminder here, for us, is that, just like authentic conversation, prayer involves moments of speaking and moments of listening — both of which are grounded in attentive familiarity and caring.

If this is so, then what begins in honest and sincere conversation becomes a relationship capable of teaching us everything worth knowing. Teresa revolutionized the spirituality of the sixteenth century by opening up for us what it is to be in deep and direct relationship with God. Not only does she outline the mechanics of how this relationship deepens, she reveals the inner life of a genuine partnership with God, forged moment by moment, day by day, like every real relationship, which is always a work in progress and is constantly changing us insofar as we let it.

But the point I want to stress is not so much that this partnership with God transforms *us*. More important for Teresa, I think, is that we take in the truth that we are created to be God's collaborative partners — partners, that is, with God in the work of transforming the world. What does that suggest about God?

6. Teresa's theological corpus requires us to evaluate our inherited notions of God and reject those that render impossible or unimaginable God's radical generosity, availability, and closeness

As we are drawn into deepening friendship with God and invited to 'taste and see' (Psalm 34.8) God's goodness, we are likely to see an increasing dissonance between what people say about God and what God reveals about God's self. Our experience of God shows us a God who is far more tender, far more generous, far more concerned about the details and grit of our lives, and far more joyful than our tradition has led us to believe; a God who draws us in not so much to spaces of mystery but to spaces of delight and wonder and awe; and a God who does not shrink from the messiness of where our lives may have led us.[13] Indeed, a careful review of our lives, done at the side of the One who loves us, shows us that God has been with us even in the darkest moments of our being, even if we weren't entirely aware of that presence or didn't know how to benefit from it during that time of challenge. As we come to know God more experientially, the proverbial 'mystery' of God becomes the more concrete and yet equally unfathomable mystery of God's familiarity and tenderness: the incredible generosity of the One who chooses to share with us a love that thoroughly undoes and remakes us.

The first challenge, then, of the relational life that Teresa opens up for us is that it requires radical theological openness on our part. We cannot allow anything to stand in the way of coming to know God in the ways God chooses to reveal God's self. And these ways are probably going to surprise and even disarm us. Teresa begs the question for us: who are we really in relationship with? And just how willing are we to allow that One to take form and shape in us?

By showing us God's familiarity and even the naturalness of intimacy with God, Teresa encourages us to see a God whose constancy, tenderness, and loving kindness draws *us*, too, into greater friendship with God — a friendship with the capacity to anchor and orient our lives, give us new purpose, and constantly to provide meaning life, and joy. Teresa's God wants to be our companion and partner in life. Choosing toward relationship with this God by definition changes everything, as Pedro Arrupe (1907–1991), former Superior General of the Jesuits, captured so brilliantly in a poem attributed to him, which has become very well known:

> Nothing is more practical than finding God,
> That is, than falling in love in a quite absolute, final way.
> What you are in love with, what seizes your imagination,
> Will affect everything.
> It will decide what will get you out of bed in the morning,
> What you do with your evenings,
> How you spend your weekends,
> What you read, who you know,
> What breaks your heart,
> And what amazes you with joy and gratitude.
> Fall in love, stay in love,
> And it will decide everything.

Ultimately, Teresa is asking us: are we willing to fall in love with God and be changed?

7. God's familiarity, kindness, patience, and fascination with us are illuminated in real and concrete terms through the Incarnation — which means through us, through our senses, and through our embodiment

To live in the constant presence of God would seem, at first, to take us out of the world in which we live. But that is not the way of Incarnation — not the way of the God who chooses to take flesh and share life with us. The disconcerting message of Christianity is that God comes alive in us — in our world and in our lives, in our stories, and therefore in human history. Here again, Segundo Galilea is helpful when he observes:

> Teresa, like many mystics, reminds us that the experience of God in history — which we are sincerely searching for today — is something essential to Christian identity. But locating God in history is an arduous process, with its own special demands.[14]

Teresa shows us this reality over and over, in the concreteness of her experience as the drama of her relationship with God draws us in and leaves us wondering what will happen next. This is not just a living God; this God is the foundation, and source, and companion of all life worth living, all experiences worth wanting. The vividness of Teresa's own life begins to make us wonder if there isn't something very real occurring at the core and heart of her daily life; and something critically missing from our own. She teaches us that the desire for Something More that is lasting; absolutely, infinitely precious; and very, very real is an echo of the *Eros* that gave us life in the first place. Finding and loving this God means engaging the vividness of God alive in our world. As she writes rather tartly in her *Interior Castle*: 'To be always withdrawn from corporeal things and enkindled in love is the trait of angelic spirits, not those who live in mortal bodies' (*Moradas* 6.7.6) [apartados de todo lo corpóreo, para espíritus angélicos es estar siempre abrasados en amor, que no para los que vivimos en cuerpo mortal].[15] Teresa asserts here that searching for and seeing Christ in life experiences is seeing God; indeed she suggests in the same place that this is the only way she has found true and meaningful union with God.

How do we do this? We might start, as Teresa encourages us to do, by praying with Scripture. Teresa suggests this concrete practice because she knows that it will help us to see God in new ways and to understand ourselves differently. Seeing how Jesus interacted with others, taking their sorrows seriously, ministering to their pain and grief, restoring their personal dignity and affirming the fundamental kinship of all human persons shows us a deeply caring God — one who constantly interacts in human affairs. Further, as we let Gospel stories speak to us, it becomes easier to locate ourselves in some of them, and in the parallels and resonances of our own experience we begin to see the constancy of divine activity, then and now. Is it possible, we can then ask ourselves, that God is somehow an embedded part of *my* life, *my* lived experience, and, indeed, of the world around me? If so, then the critical question becomes: what will my response to the God of my life be? What loving response can I make to God and how can I enter more fully into collaborative partnership with the God who wants to come alive in me and, through me, to come alive in the world around me?

In this way Teresa encourages us to understand our own lives as another way in which God's love — God's companionate friendship — plays itself out in the world. This is the context for all genuine prayer: as we take time frequently to be with the One whom we know loves us and experience the strength, dignity, compassion, and courage that such love gives us, we grow in our capacity to love others and to become part of the loving activity of God in the world. Such activity is not entirely like the love we here extol on mass-produced greetings cards, although it will be at least as beautiful — heartbreakingly beautiful, this gritty, I-will-not-leave-you love. Dedicating ourselves to constantly learning that love (rather than assuming that we know what it is and how best to participate in it) is the task of every person of faith. Teresa describes this work beginning in the fifth dwelling-place of her *Interior Castle*, as our partnership with God moves into greater fruition, but the partnered life is, of course, 'normalized' in the seventh dwelling-place, as the soul 'perceives [...] this divine company' (*Moradas* 7.1.8) [siente (...) esta divina compañía] constantly.[16]

> You may think that as a result the soul will be outside itself and so absorbed that it will be unable to be occupied with anything else. On the contrary the soul is more occupied than before with everything pertaining to the service of God, and once its duties are over it remains with that enjoyable company. (*Moradas* 7.1.9)
>
> [Pareceros ha que, según esto, no andará en sí, sino tan embebida que no pueda entender en nada. Mucho más que antes, en todo lo que es servicio de Dios, y en faltando las ocupaciones, se queda con aquella agradable compañía.]

In my conversations with Jesuit friends, we speak of learning this love directly from God as an integral part of the 'pedagogy of God' that Ignatius Loyola's 'Spiritual Exercises' supports. It is a faithful love that is continually expressing itself in the multiple challenges of each day. It is the source of a new kind of fidelity, a 'radical fidelity' that begins to orient and ground our lives, and it is this kind of fidelity that I would like to explore in the remainder of this essay.

As we consider and contemplate our own life narratives as a story of God's love, we become more aware of our own experience of grace and the peace that forgiveness and change bring. The memory of God's love, contained in the intellect, inflames the will with desire; and this is hardly a disembodied process, as the memory of love is mediated by incarnated experiences of love and encoded in the body. So Teresa advises her readers continually to seek out God incarnationally, 'as the Bride did in the Song of Songs' (*Moradas* 7.1.8) [como lo hacía la esposa en los Cantares]. In other words, we need not wait for revelation or infused prayer: we can always benefit here from discursive meditation on moments in the life of Christ and their meaning in contemporary life experiences (*Moradas* 6.7.10) or from remembering how other human beings have somehow mediated for us Christ incarnate. Such an approach to prayer allows a person to walk 'continually in an admirable way with Christ, our Lord, in whom the divine and the human are joined and who is always that person's companion' (*Moradas* 6.7.9) [muy contino no se apartar de andar con Cristo nuestro Señor por una manera admirable, adonde divino y humano junto es siempre su compañía].

In Teresa, God is experienced through transformative companionship. While unitive encounters change us by giving us profound insights and other graced favours, we do not have to wait passively until such experiences come to us. We can enter the divine presence through reflection on the humanity of Christ. Teresa suggests that human–divine encounters are both exterior and interior to us, and that both humanity and divinity serve as mediums for union. An important, if implicit, theological argument is forming here: the incarnate God provides the vehicle to explore the fullness of humanity and the fullness of divinity as a single, integrated whole.[17]

8. Teresa asks us to explore God and love in ways that we have not yet explored, as individuals and as communities

Teresa gives us a vision not only of love as a transformative power but also of how we are to collaborate, with God and with one another, in incarnating that love in our world. The challenge of this theological and practical reality is far greater than we have yet taken on, because as soon as we begin to speak of love we tend to move toward sentimentality, not power; heart, not truth. But Teresa elegantly and thoroughly collapses such false dichotomies. She presents us with a God who empowers us in love and who asks us to collaborate in the work of transforming the world by loving it into greater life.

Teresa's life and works capture and convey the raw power of love to create new worlds. She shows us the blessing and grace of being drawn relationally into a collaborative partnership that empowers us to transform and be transformed. In fact, Teresa ends her *Interior Castle* with something of an admonition:

> In sum, my Sisters, what I conclude with is that we shouldn't build castles in the air. The Lord doesn't look so much at the greatness of our works as at the love with which they are done. And if we do what we can, God will enable us each day to do more and more, provided that we do not quickly tire. (7.4.18)

> [En fin, hermanas mías, con lo que concluyo es que no hagamos torres sin fundamento, que el Señor no mira tanto la grandeza de las obras como el amor con que se hacen, y como hagamos lo que pudiéremos, hará Su Majestad que vamos pudiendo cada día más y más, como no nos cansemos luego.][18]

For Teresa, theological insights matter only when their implications are applied to human behaviour, that is, to what we do and who we are, as human persons. As she explains at the end of her life's work, the inner peace of the seventh dwelling-place is not an ethereal tranquillity, rooted in avoidance or escapism. Teresa's political and ecclesiastical circumstances were at least as troubling as our own, and Teresa understood it to be both her duty and her desire to be engaged actively in working for the greater good of Church and society. Thus, for her, revelations, ecstasy, and all of the forms of divine communication in the sixth dwelling-place are not simply experiences to be savoured but rather transformative activity within the human person that we then move into the world. An ecstatic life, as Teresa helps us to understand it, is participation in human–divine transformative activity in the world, and it is as much a privilege and a joy as a work that both costs and changes us. Indications of the celebratory nature of incarnating include Teresa's identification of the soul with the father of the prodigal son, who rejoices in a presence that works constantly toward the good. Recalling the joy inherent in the process of transformation toward the good is critical if we are to accompany one another and bring about the greater good within the human community. Teresa's insights, I suggest, allow us to move beyond stereotypical Christian expressions of self-abnegation and resignedly 'taking up the cross' in order to engage in deeper explorations of the pleasures of enabling human flourishing.[19]

Teresa invites us to see a love that is not just tender and dissolving but is also muscular, active, and capable. It is not *a* love so much as it is *the* love: the love that matters; the love that makes a difference; the love that changes things; that gives us the courage and backbone to stand up to injustice and to denounce evil; that gives us the creativity to imagine new avenues for a more just world; the love that helps us find the words and actions that incarnate God's presence relationally in all that we do.

9. Teresa clarifies for us that reform and prophetic action are a natural outgrowth of a deepening relationship with God

As we grow more able and accustomed to see things *with* God, we grow troubled about much of what we see: children hungry; human persons bought and sold, used and disposed; senseless, even despicable forms of violence, cruelty and brutality; women and children terrorized in their own homes; hopelessness and fear, with the callousness, apathy, and paralysis that set in as a natural, human response to such overwhelming problems. In the face of the realities of our fallen world, another of Teresa's poignant and pithy truths can cut in either of two directions: 'However enclosed you are, never think that the good or evil you do will remain a secret' (*Camino* 15.7) [Nunca penséis ha de estar secreto el mal o el bien que hiciereis, por encerradas que estéis].

As Teresa describes the spiritual maturity of God's closest friends, she speaks of courage, commitment to truth, tenderness, and extreme sensitivity to the presence or absence of God. A very deep 'purity of conscience' [limpieza de conciencia] is the normal state of the soul as it grows into the unitive life. The experience of God's companionship in daily life 'makes the soul pay attention to everything' (*Moradas* 6.8.4) [hace advertir a todo], she tells us. And so the soul walks 'in deep concern about avoiding anything displeasing to God' (*Moradas* 6.8.3) [con un miramiento grande de no hacer cosa que le desagradase], with a heightened sensitivity to sin — personal, social, or institutional.[20] The dissonance between the love of God that the soul now knows so personally and the injustices of the world is increasingly intolerable at this level of growth, and insofar as the individual can serve as an instrument of the loving activity of God in the world, he or she seeks to do so.

If God chooses to take form in us and share life with us then the challenge of the mystical life — a challenge we are invited to embrace as part and parcel of the joy of living — is how to live in the kind of intimacy with God that ignites us and the relational web of people around us with dignity, kindness, and courage. Through that grounding relationship of intimacy and ever-present grace, we are called to grow toward the intellectual, affective, and moral excellence that enriches the world because of our loving presence.[21]

Where do these observations lead us? What is their relevance for our work in the world today?

10. In a world increasingly characterized not only by individualism, but also by crushing isolation and despair, harsh callousness and even extreme forms of violence and human degradation, Teresa provides the hopeful antidote that our authenticity, our integrity, and our joy as human beings is bound

up in dedicating ourselves to the relational identity that we uncover through intimacy with God and collaborative work with one another

When I explore this message with formerly homeless women in recovery from substance abuse through the Ignatian Spirituality Project, Teresa proves to be thoroughly and absolutely reliable as a witness to subjective human truths. Her familiarity with her readers conveys God's familiarity. Her uncertainties, doubts, and candour about herself make her trustworthy. Her clarity that so much of what we do, especially when we are unaware of God's companionate presence, displeases God rings true in a way that is not so much condemnatory but ultimately hopeful, for it contains the promise that, with God, things can be different. What things? *Every*thing: our behaviours, our lives, the quality of our relationships, our communities, our world.

Teresa's sense that she and God are a 'we' makes it easier for us to trust that perhaps God is inviting us to explore the 'we' that God wants to create with each of us. In opening up the world of 'we' Teresa offers us new ways of relating, to God, self, and others.

Teresa provides a space for safe relational exploration, which is particularly powerful (and particularly necessary) when persons have been violated within relational contexts — and when daily life or intimate relations have proven to be more like active minefields than safe spaces within which we can grow. Teresa's insights into the process of personal and social transformation are not just theoretical, spiritual, or ethereal. They illuminate concrete and practical realities about us: our malleability, our changeableness, and the hopeful reality that, in right and loving relationship and with determination and support, human beings can truly change.

The stages of growth articulated in Teresa's *Interior Castle* for those who are trying to put the pieces of their lives together after disruption, trauma or distress are truly life-giving. As I work with women who have survived domestic violence and are sifting through layers and layers of questions about the meaning of their lives, the trustworthiness of love, and the core of their personal identities, I find that they respond with relief, gratitude, and joy at the spiritual and, just as importantly, the human truths that Teresa has to offer them. Empowered by spiritual practices that allow them to make new or renewed contact with God, people emerge with new possibilities, new options that previously had not appeared possible. The newness of vision, purpose and potential that these women experience is something that we, all of us, deeply need. The basic point is this: any tool that is helpful in the formation of identity is also helpful in the re-formation of identity. When life has broken us down, how will we put ourselves back together? Teresa's vision of life as a deepening love relationship, with God and with others, provides us with the core principles to take heart, embrace change, and begin anew.

As Albert Einstein is reported to have said, 'No society can solve problems from the same consciousness that created them'. Teresa gives us the tools with which to engage relationship with the divine, such that the paradigm shifts that we so deeply need can begin to happen. Many of us are accustomed to (and comfortable with) associating change (especially change of great magnitude or unexpected depth) with God. We call that grace. But Teresa gives us to see the interior workings of grace. She gives us a privileged view of the intricate dance of God and the soul as they grow together and become one. She gives us this privileged view — her view — not because she considers herself so exemplary but because she keenly wants to do two things: spend her life telling people about God's loving kindness and demonstrate, through her own lived experience, the reality that God profoundly wants loving partnership with each one of us. If Teresa is exemplary in anything, she would argue, she is exemplary of how long God waits for us, how hard God works to whisper our name and capture our attention in ways that each of us will recognize and respond to, and what a true and authentic relationship with God might look like — insofar as she has insight into the path toward that relationship. After favour after favour, moment after moment with God, Teresa gradually grew more confident of God's deep kindness, a distinctive loving-kindness that left its own imprint, time after time, one so transforming that Teresa herself could learn and imitate and manifest that same kindness, especially as she engaged more and more in 'conversation with the One Whom we know loves us' (*Vida* 8.5) [tratando a solas con quien sabemos nos ama].[22]

All of this seems to me to be a great testimony to the genius of the Spirit: God's Spirit of truth and light and love as it works collaboratively with the human spirit to forge new paths in the world. Teresa's wisdom and insights, speaking across the centuries to us today, communicate anew God's desire to make use of human ingenuity toward the good of the human community, with generosity of spirit. They illuminate for us God's continuing invitation to us to collaborate with God in transforming all in our world that is small-minded — all that is discriminatory, hostile, violent, avaricious, exploitative, and ultimately unworthy of us — so that all of us might find and take our rightful place at God's table. Teresa's deep and practical wisdom gives us insight into who we are as human beings. Hers are insights into our humanity, after all, not just insights about God, else they would not be able to translate across five centuries and into worlds Teresa herself could not have imagined.

Notes to Chapter 9

1. This essay was originally presented as a paper in Oxford on the five-hundredth birthday of Teresa. At that time, I used a PowerPoint presentation, with passages and illustrative photos, to support it. The PowerPoint presentation is available at <www.enkindlinglove.com>.
2. Segundo Galilea, *The Future of Our Past: The Spanish Mystics Speak to Contemporary Spirituality* (Notre Dame, IN: Ave Maria Press, 1985), p. 26.
3. Filippo Sega, the Apostolic nuncio to Spain, in 1578 famously described Teresa as a restless, gadabout, and stubbornly disobedient woman [fémina inquieta, andariega, desobediente y contumaz].
4. The full text reads 'I repeat, it is necessary that your foundation consist of more than prayer and contemplation. If you do not strive for the virtues and practice them, you will always be dwarfs. And, please God, it will be only a matter of not growing, for you already know that whoever does not increase decreases' [Torno a decir que para esto es menester no poner vuestro fundamento solo en rezar y contemplar; porque si no procuráis virtudes, y hay ejercicio de ellas, siempre os quedaráis enanas; y aun plega a Dios que sea sólo no crecer, porque ya sabéis que quien no crece, descrece].

5. English translations from *The Collected Works of Saint Teresa of Avila*, trans. by Kieran Kavanaugh and Otilio Rodriguez, 3 vols (Washington DC: Institute of Carmelite Studies, 1976–85), p. 42.
6. *Las moradas del castillo interior*, ed. by Dámaso Chicharro, 2nd edn, Clásicos de Biblioteca Nueva, 11 (Madrid: Biblioteca Nueva, 2015), p. 226–27.
7. *Moradas*, ed. by Chicharro, p. 458.
8. *Moradas*, ed. by Chicharro, p. 453.
9. *Moradas*, ed. by Chicharro, p. 455.
10. *Libro de las fundaciones*, ed. by Salvador Ros García (Madrid: San Pablo, 2012), p. 76.
11. On Teresa's words Enrique Llamas Martínez comments '[...] conversation between friends far above anything we can wish for or imagine; the only life worth fully living' [(...) comunicación de amistad, por encima de cuanto podemos desear e imaginar: la única vida que merece ser vivida con intensidad]. In his 'Introducción' to the *Libro de la vida*, in *Teresa de Jesús. Obras completas* (Madrid: Editorial de Espiritualidad, 1984), p. 2.
12. *Moradas*, ed. by Chicharro, p. 188.
13. Compare Julian of Norwich: 'For God does not despise what God has made, nor does God disdain to serve us in the simplest natural functions of our body, for love of the soul which was created in God's own likeness', in *Julian of Norwich. Showings*, trans. by Edmund Colledge and James Walsh (Mahwah, NJ: Paulist Press, 1978), p. 185.
14. Galilea, *The Future of Our Past*, p. 26.
15. *Moradas*, ed. by Chicharro, p. 387.
16. *Moradas*, ed. by Chicharro, p. 431.
17. See Gillian Ahlgren, *Entering Teresa of Avila's 'Interior Castle': A Reader's Companion* (Mahwah, NJ: Paulist Press, 2005), pp. 102–03.
18. *Moradas*, ed. by Chicharro, p. 458.
19. Ahlgren, *Entering Teresa of Avila's 'Interior Castle'*, pp. 124–25.
20. *Moradas*, ed. by Chicharro, p. 396.
21. Pope Francis's apostolic exhortation *Evangelii Gaudium* [*The Joy of the Gospel* (JG)] reminds us that Christ invites each and every one of us to companionship which through intimate moments of daily encounters then 'blossoms into an enriching friendship [...] and liberates us from our narrowness and self-absorption' (*JG*, para. 3). 'The Gospel offers us the chance to live life on a higher plane, but with no less intensity,' writes Pope Francis. 'May the world of our time, which is searching, sometimes with anguish, sometimes with hope, be enabled to receive the good news [...] from ministers of the Gospel whose lives glow with fervor, who have first received the joy of Christ' (*JG*, 10). 'Everyone needs to be touched by the comfort and attraction of God's saving love, which is mysteriously at work in each person, above and beyond their faults and failings' (*JG*, 44).
22. *Libro de la vida*, ed. by Dámaso Chicharro, 17th edn, Letras Hispánicas, 98 (Madrid: Cátedra, 2014), p. 188.

PART III

Teresa the Writer

CHAPTER 10

❖

From Fear to Courage: The Testimonies of Teresa of Ávila and her Early Hagiographers

Elena Carrera

In a sermon preached on 5 October 1614 in Perpignan, as part of the celebrations in honour of Teresa of Ávila, after her beatification, the Jesuit priest Geronymo Ballester referred to Teresa as 'a courageous and strong woman, who sets a disturbing example to the men who wrongly believe they are strong' [una muger valerosa y fuerte, y exemplo y confusión de varones, que se tienen por fuertes y no lo son].[1] Offering an exegetical commentary on the concluding passage of Proverbs, which depicts a 'mulierem fortem' (Proverbs 31), he compared Teresa of Ávila both to Job and to Judith.[2] He also drew on the *Summa theologiae* of Thomas Aquinas, in which *fortitudo* (II–II, quest. 123, art. 6) is defined as a virtue which could be demonstrated in two principal ways: one involved undertaking (or 'tackling', *acometer*) great things; the other involved 'knowing how to endure great suffering' [saber sufrir muy duros travajos].[3]

Fortitudo (courage and fortitude) was one of the four crucial moral qualities, alongside wisdom, justice, and temperance, expected of philosophers since antiquity (as we see in Plato's *Phaedo*). These four qualities became the four cardinal virtues which all Christians were expected to cultivate.[4] Nonetheless, despite the egalitarian potential of Christian ideas, medieval texts tended to refer to these virtues as qualities associated with male excellence. For instance, the very influential *Siete partidas* (written during the reign of Alfonso X [1252–84] and published at least eighteen times, with additions and comments, between 1491 and 1611) suggests that these four virtues are most suitable for knights 'because it is their duty to defend the church, and kings and everybody else' [porque ellos han a defender la iglesia, et los reyes et a todos los otros] and explains that 'fortitude will make them remain firm in what they do and not be changeable' [la fortaleza que estén firmes en lo que fecieren et que non sean camiadizos].[5]

Medieval female Christian writers did subvert the misogynistic prejudices which prevailed in their cultural contexts.[6] After all, among early followers of Christ, women had displayed as much, if not more, courage than men: women had stayed by Christ's side throughout his Passion and were the first to see him risen.[7] Nonetheless, women continued to be portrayed as the 'weaker sex' and, consequently, when a woman rose above prevailing perceptions of gender by displaying a strong mind, this was often explained as the result of divine grace.[8]

In her writings, Teresa of Ávila repeatedly emphasized her bodily weakness, while using the term *ánimo* to refer to a wide notion of courage, which included the notions of intention and determination.[9] According to Ballester, Teresa embodied two types of fortitude, both of which were captured by the Spanish term he used, *fortaleza*. As we see in Covarrubias's dictionary, published in 1611 (four years before Ballester's sermon), the term *fortaleza* was used to refer to the notions of 'courage, bravery, constancy, firmness, tolerance, vigour and strength' [ánimo, valor, constancia, firmeza, tolerancia, vigor y fuerza]. As Covarrubias noted, *fortaleza* 'is to be understood as both courage of mind and bodily strength' [se entiende así del valor del ánimo como de las fuerzas corporales].[10]

In this essay, I will examine Ballester's account of Aquinas's discussion of courage, against the background of claims made in her first two biographies, and during the inquests for Teresa's beatification and canonization. I will then examine Teresa's views on courage and its relationship to fear both in the *Book of her Life* [*Libro de la vida*], written in 1562, and in *The Way of Perfection* (*Way*) [*Camino de perfección*], written in the mid-1560s in the convent of St Joseph, her first Discalced foundation. I will seek to build on the work of Gillian Ahlgren, whose book *Teresa of Avila and the Politics of Sanctity* ends by showing how Teresa was singled out in hagiographical accounts which stressed her 'manliness'.[11] For instance, in 1591, in one of the declarations made in favour of Teresa's beatification and canonization, Domingo Báñez recounted how the Dominican Provincial had been warned not to trust in a woman's virtue, but had then met Teresa and concluded that she was not a woman, but a very manly man: 'you must have been joking when you told me that she was a woman; I can tell you that she is but a most respectable [bearded] manly man' [Habíadesme engañado, que decíades que era mujer; a la fe no es sino hombre varón y de los más barbados].[12] The idea that Teresa was a manly woman was also emphasized in her earliest biographies. For instance, in the account of Teresa's life published in 1590, Francisco de Ribera argues that, unlike other women who had revelations, Teresa should be taken seriously because she was 'manlier' than many great men:

> This is why we do not pay heed to the revelations of women, that is to say, of weak people who are subject to passions. Nonetheless, we must indeed pay heed to the revelations of a woman who is so courageous and brave, that she is manlier than many great men, and to those of similar women.
>
> [Así que no hagamos caso de revelaciones de mujeres, que quiere decir de personas flacas y rendidas a sus pasiones; pero de las de una mujer más varonil que muchos grandes varones, tan animosa y tan valerosa, y de las que a ella se parecieren, mucho caso se debe hacer.][13]

The term *varonil* had traditionally been used to praise great women, including Queen Isabella.[14] Thus, drawing on a longstanding association between strength and virility, Ribera explains that the true distinction between men and women lies not in their bodily differences but in the extent to which they are able to control their passions:

> Why are [some men] surprised to see women who have the strength which they themselves lack because they are not fully committed to God, if God does not distinguish between men and women, but sees all people as his creatures, and commits himself more to those who commit themselves to him? I will not pay much attention to their arguments, if they think carefully about what they say, since the women who control their passions and subject them to God should be called men, and the men who are controlled by their passions should be called women. This is not a question of bodily differences, but of moral strength.

> [¿por qué se espantan (algunos hombres) que tengan ellas lo que no tienen ellos, por no haberse así entregado a Dios, pues delante de Dios no hay hombre ni mujer, todos son criaturas suyas, y a quien más se le da, más se da él también? Tampoco no se me dará mucho que lo digan así, si miran bien lo que dicen, porque las que con fortaleza vencen sus pasiones y las sujetan a Dios, hombres se han de llamar, y los hombres que se dejan vencer de ellas, mujeres son. No consiste esto en la diversidad del cuerpo, sino en la fortaleza del alma.][15]

While Ribera suggests that the *fortaleza* shown by Teresa and other female saints like St Agatha and St Agnes was the result of both God's grace and personal effort, the biography published in 1606 under the name of Philip II's confessor Diego de Yepes, Bishop of Tarazona, presents her great undertakings and achievements as something purely miraculous:

> She was destined to be a wonder, a miraculous star of grace, and a spectacle of sanctity and perfection for the whole world. It is no small miracle that a weak woman has undertaken things which are more proper of men.

> [auia de ser vn prodigio de naturaleza, vna estrella milagrosa de la gracia, y vn espectaculo de santidad, y perfeccion al mundo. Que no lo es pequeño, que una muger flaca aya emprendido hazañas mas que de varones.][16]

The emphasis Yepes places on the miraculous stands in marked contrast with Teresa's own account of the intense fear she experienced when she felt misunderstood by her confessors, and her views on the importance of determination and endurance. This was a form of courage which could be cultivated by men and by women, as we shall now see.

Courage as Endurance

Among the models of courage prevailing in the sixteenth century we find Aristotle's account of moral virtue or excellence (*arête*) in the *Nicomachean Ethics* (1107a3–b4). In this text, the term *andreia* (literally, 'manliness') is used to refer to what we now translate as 'courage', and is defined as the mean condition between fear and overconfidence or rashness. In pointing out that some men exceed in fearlessness while other men exceed in confidence, Aristotle suggested that courage could be learnt. Nonetheless, the association between courage and masculinity underpinning the Greek term *andreia* was a dominant one in pre-modern culture, when courage was not only seen as a virtue particularly valued in men, but also perceived as a physiologically based manly attribute. For instance, the English edition of the *Nicomachean Ethics* (published in 1547) renders the Greek term *andreia* both as 'fortitude' and as 'strength', while in the first English edition of Juan Huarte de San Juan's *Examination of Men's Wits* (1594; *Examen de ingenios*, 1575), one of the most influential psychological treatises written in the sixteenth century, the Spanish term 'valentía' is translated sometimes as 'courage', sometimes as 'fortitude', and other times as 'manliness'.[17]

The term 'fortitude' in modern English evokes a less gendered kind of strength: an 'inner' kind of strength, which does not manifest externally in the visible physical manner in which muscular force may manifest. However, in the pre-Cartesian Aristotelian model promoted by Thomas Aquinas and by the early modern Christian writers who drew on him, there was no clear-cut distinction between inner and outer forms of courage or strength. We can see this, for instance, by turning back to the sermon on Teresa of Ávila preached by Ballester in Perpignan in 1614, which draws on Aquinas's claim in the *Summa* (II–II, quest. 123, art. 6) that endurance is more difficult than attacking [*sustinere est difficilius quam aggredi*].[18] Ballester rightly renders *sustinere* as 'to endure' [*sufrir*], but then takes Aquinas's argumentation outside the Aristotelian military context which still prevailed in the thirteenth-century scholastic author, by translating *aggredi* as 'to tackle' [*acometer*], and goes on to argue that Aquinas's point is that there is greater courage [*fortaleza*] in enduring than in tackling great things.[19]

As Ballester puts it in his free rendering of the *Summa* (II–II, quest. 123, art. 6), those who undertake great things are in a position of power because they trust that God will help them to overcome difficulties, while those who suffer are in a position of inferiority and therefore show greater courage:

> This confidence [i.e. trusting in God's help] makes him superior in tackling great things, since without this confidence, he would tackle nothing; but the one who suffers, endures the toils to which he is subjected by someone who is his superior and is more powerful, [...] it requires greater courage to contend with someone who is stronger than me than with someone I know to be weaker.
>
> [y essa confiança le haze superior para acometerlas, porque a no tener esta confiança no se acometeria ninguna cosa: pero el que sufre, padece los trabajos que otro superior y mas poderoso que el le da, (...) mas fortaleza es pelear con el que es mas fuerte que yo, que no con el que entiendo que es mas flaco.][20]

Aquinas's second argument, as rendered by Ballester, is that when people tackle something, they have not yet seen or experienced any difficulties, and therefore 'there is greater courage in enduring present difficulties than in anticipating future ones' [más fortaleza es sufrir los males presentes, que esperar los venideros].[21]

The third argument offered in the *Summa* was related to timescale. As we see from Ballester's free translation, Aquinas distinguished between the sudden actions required in the active type of courage he denoted by the term *aggredi* and the longer time-frame of *sustinere* [endure]:

tackling is a quick action, which I can stop at any time. By contrast, enduring that which is inflicted upon me by someone more powerful than me requires great courage since it is not up to me to stop the suffering.

> [el acometer es cosa que presto se haze, y está en mi mano desistir dello, mas el padecer lo que otro que puede mas que yo me da, esso es cosa muy fuerte y no tiene tiempo limitado a mi voluntad, sino a la que me da a padecer.][22]

Ballester applies the third argument to the distinction between the courage shown by those who patiently endure illnesses or pain sent to them by God and the courage shown by those who willingly engage in practices of mortification, such as self-flagellation:

> It cannot be denied that self-flagellation, if vigorous, is an act of courage, but it is up to us to stop it or to do it more gently. By contrast, with an illness or a pain on the side sent by God, it is up to God how long the suffering will go on for, and thus enduring the suffering with patience is the greater act of courage.

> [vna disciplina no se puede negar que si va bien tomada, y el braço va viuo, que es acto de fortaleza: pero está en nuestra mano dexarla o afloxar el braço: pero vna enfermedad que Dios embia, vn dolor de costado, vna hijada &c está a la disposición de Dios, que os la hara passar todo el tiempo que el fuere seruido: y estar todo este tiempo paciente, y sufriendo, esto es el mayor acto de fortaleza.][23]

As Ballester notes, Teresa did suffer many illnesses, and was also tormented by the devil on numerous occasions: 'the great bodily pain which the devil inflicted on her, battering her many times with God's permission, as he did to the holy Job' [grandes tormentos que el demonio le dio en su cuerpo, que la maltrato muchas vezes, dandole Dios licencia para esso, como al Santo Job].[24] Nonetheless, what made Teresa suffer the most (and is thus evidence of her great courage) was her having to deal with the conflicting opinions of her spiritual advisors about the origin of her visions and revelations: 'some told her that they were inspired by the devil, and that she should not believe him; others that they were inspired by God. This uncertainty made her suffer more than anything that we have recounted so far' [porque en ellas vnos le dezian que era espiritu del demonio, y que no le creyesse, otros que era espiritu de Dios, esta perplexidad era el mayor tormento de todos los que hasta aquí hemos referido].[25] Ballester stresses the intensity of Teresa's suffering by suggesting that the fear of condemnation is the worst possible kind of fear.[26] He also notes that, for twenty years, she experienced extraordinary dryness during prayer, 'without being able to see God and without receiving much divine consolation' [sin que todo ese tiempo viesse la cara a Dios sin recebir apenas vna consolacion de su mano].[27]

Citing Lactantius's view that the greatest form of courage does not involve being able to defeat a lion or a wild boar, but being able to dominate one's flesh, Ballester stresses how, 'despite her numerous illnesses' [estando enferma con tantos achaques], Teresa always wore a hair-shirt, which produced 'very sore wounds' [lastimosas llagas], and that she would sometimes throw herself over nettles and thorns, making her whole body bleed.[28] Teresa does mention in the *Life* that she was put under a severe programme of penance by her spiritual advisors in 1554; however, showing the spirit of humility expected in a spiritual autobiography, she does not make any specific reference to her methods of mortification. Ballester's references to the harsh penance endured by Teresa were probably inspired by the lurid account of her practices of mortification in the mid-1550s provided by Yepes:

> Since her grave illnesses and continuous ailments seemed to prevent her from doing, in a manly way, as much penance as she wanted, she received special light from Heaven and decided to ignore her ailments and do penance [...]. Thus determined, she placed her eyes on God, and her hands on punishing her body so harshly that she would demonstrate how detached she was from it. She then put on a hair-shirt made of tin, with holes, like a grater, with which she inflicted pain on her flesh, making it all sore. She would whip herself very frequently and harshly, sometimes with nettles, other times (most often) with keys, until she produced wounds from which much matter flowed. But the medicine with which she cured those wounds was to whip them again, using the cause of her wounds as a cure. Being thus hard on herself, moved by the pleasure she gave God through this bodily sacrifice, she sought a thousand ways of inflicting pain on her body. And, thus, she once put together a pile of brambles, took off her clothes and went inside it, tossing and turning, as if she were in a very comfortable bed, remembering Christ's bed on the cross.
>
> [Y porque las enfermedades grandes, y achaques continuos que padecía, parece la tenían atada, para hazer tanta penitencia como ella quisiera, varonilmente, y con particular luz del Cielo, se resolvió a no hazer caso dellas, y hazer penitencia: [...]. Con esta determinación puso los ojos en Dios, y las manos tan fuertemente en el castigo de su cuerpo, que mostraua bien, el grande aborrecimiento que le tenía. Porque luego se vistió de vn silicio de hoja de lata, hecho y agujereado a modo de rallo, con que affligia, y atormentaua la carne, dexandola toda llagada. Tomaua disciplinas muy ordinarias y muy rigurosas, vnas vezes con hortigas, otras (y esto era lo mas comun) con vnas llaues, hasta venirsele a hazer llagas, de las quales manaua, y corria mucha materia: pero la medicina con que las curaua, era renouarlas con nueuos golpes, y açotes, tomando por cura la causa de la herida. Y como la que estaua encarnizada en si mesma, y cebada con el gusto del que hazia a Dios con este sacrificio de su cuerpo: buscaua mil modos, como darle mas afflicion, y tormento. Y assi vna vez junto muchas zarças, y desnudando su cuerpo, començo a entrar, y rebouluerse entre ellas, como si fuera en alguna regalada cama, acordándose de la que Christo auia tenido enla Cruz.]²⁹

It is difficult to ascertain to what extent this account reflects Teresa's actual practices. She might have used brambles once, as noted by this biographer and by some of the witnesses who declared in favour of her canonization. She might well have used sharp metal objects as mortification tools in the mid-1550s, as a response to the fears of her spiritual advisors. All we can know is that when Teresa wrote about this time of her life ten years later, she emphasized that her first Jesuit confessor (Diego de Cetina) put her on a strict programme of penance: 'he willed me also, to doe certaine acts of Mortification, which were not very pleasing to me' [mandábame hacer algunas mortificaciones no muy sabrosas para mí].³⁰

Considering the evidence from Teresa's extant letters and from texts such as

El Cerro, written by Jerónimo de Gracián in 1582, Alison Weber is 'inclined to believe that the canonization witnesses exaggerated the severity of Teresa's penance, perhaps unconsciously, out of a desire to conform to the expectations of their interrogators'.[31] This is a plausible explanation, though we can perhaps make a more nuanced distinction between Teresa's practices in the 1550s, her views in 1562–65 (when she wrote the *Life* and the *Way*), and the attitude towards mortification which she shows in her extant letters (most of which were written in the 1570s) or with Gracián, who only knew her in the last seven years of her life (1575–82), when, despite her poor health, she had to deal with serious difficulties affecting her Discalced reform.

Yepes's account of Teresa's mortification is preceded by a quotation from her *Life*, in which she makes the following claim:

> My self, being so sicklie as I was, till I resolued to make no account at all, of my health, and of my bodie, was euer tyed vp, and was good for nothing; and euen now, it is very little, which I can doe. But yet, as soone as our Lord was pleased, that I should vnderstand this deceipt, and trick of the Diuel, if he obiected to me, my losse of health, I told him, it imported little, that I must dye; If he tempted me with loue of rest, and ease, I told him, that it was not ease which I needed now, but the sufferance of a Crosse.

> [Como soy tan enferma, hasta que me determiné en no hacer caso del cuerpo ni de la salud, siempre estuve atada, sin valer nada; y ahora hago bien poco. Mas como quiso Dios entendiese este ardid del demonio, y cómo me ponía delante el perder la salud, decía yo: 'poco va en que me muera'; si el descanso: 'no he ya menester descanso, sino cruz'.][32]

What was crucial, according to Yepes, is that Teresa would think of Christ on the Cross when dealing with pain and discomfort, and that this completely changed her experience: she felt as if the thorns were roses. Yepes thus suggests that thinking about Christ's voluntary suffering, as an act of love, could have a transformative power in people's ability to endure hunger, pain, and discomfort:

> When God's servants are afflicted by hunger or feel distressed when their food is unpleasant, their rough clothes are itchy and their hard beds make them feel shattered, or they are pained by any other form of penance or great hardship, they will find it all sweet and enjoyable if they visualize what Jesus Christ, their Lord, Father, and King, suffered for love.

> [quando a los sieruos de Dios les fatiga el hambre, y les da pena el majar desabrido, y les muerde la vistidura aspera, y les quebranta la cama dura, y les aflige qualquiera otra manera de penitencia, y aspereza, por muy graue que sea: todo se les haze dulce, y sabroso, viendo lo que voluntariamente Iesu Christo su Señor, su Padre, y su Rey padecio por su amor.][33]

This quotation summarizes both the life of hardship chosen by the nuns who joined Teresa's reformed convents, and the strategy which they were encouraged to follow so as to make their experience of hardship spiritually meaningful. Rather than fearing hunger or discomfort, they could endure them, and see their endurance as an act of love, in imitation of Christ.

Courage, like love, could be learned. It could be cultivated. One of the main messages which Teresa succeeded in conveying, through her writings and through her work as a foundress of reformed convents, is the idea that all individuals could learn to be courageous, just as they could learn to love. In this learning, it was essential not only to have access to appropriate models, but also to be in the right environment. Christians were expected to imitate Christ, who, according to well-known accounts such as the Letter to the Hebrews, displayed sadness (δάκρυα) and reverent fear (εὐλάβεια) as he anticipated his shameful death and the suffering that preceded it, and then showed courage by accepting his suffering and death as an act of obedience.[34] This seems a perfect example of the greater kind of courage discussed by Aquinas and Ballester, as we saw earlier: the courage which involves enduring toils to which one is subjected by someone who is more powerful than oneself. In Teresa's historical context, however, only a few people would find themselves in the extreme situation of dying a martyr's death. This would mean that the lives of the martyrs, whose stories were recounted in saints' lives and in sermons, would not be appropriate models of courage for most people. This is something Teresa learnt early on in her life, as we shall now see.

Teresa's Testimony in *The Book of her Life*

In the first chapter of the *Life*, Teresa recounts that she and her brother Rodrigo were in the habit of reading saints' lives and that they were 'so amazed' [espantávamos mucho] to find out about eternal suffering or eternal joy that they fantasized about imitating the martyrs by going to a Muslim land where they might be killed.[35] In Kavanaugh and Rodriguez's translation, 'espantávamos' is rendered as 'we were terrified', which might make sense in the case of eternal pain, but not in that of eternal glory.[36] It is worth noting here that, while, in modern Spanish, the term 'espantar' does mean 'to scare' or 'to frighten', in Teresa's day, it had a broader meaning, related to wonder and amazement.

In her account, Teresa does not mention running away. It was her early biographer Ribera who recounted how they did run away from home when Teresa was seven, presenting this as evidence of the great courage and determination which she already had: 'already at this age she was very courageous, and was keen on all things related to God, and put her wishes into action' [y aun desde entonces tenía mucho ánimo, y era muy determinada para las cosas de Dios, no se contentó con solos deseos].[37] In contrast with Ribera's hagiographic emphasis on how exceptional Teresa was from an early age, she simply notes that God was giving them courage: 'and it seemed, that he gaue vs courage enough, for this purpose, euen in that tender age of ours' [y paréceme, que nos dava el Señor ánimo, en tan tierna edad].[38] Her use of the imperfect tense, 'nos dava', suggests that she saw this as a slow learning process rather than as an exceptional or miraculous divine intervention.

Teresa's courage was shaped by the books she read, as well as by her circumstances. She was determined to lead a heroic life, but, unlike her brother Rodrigo, she would not be able to become a Conquistador in the new land of infidels, in America. Rodrigo's departure on 3 August 1535 on a ship heading to the American Río de la Plata, when Teresa was twenty years old, is usually seen by her biographers as having provided an incentive for her to leave her parental home to become a nun. By contrast, the explanation she offers in the *Life* is that she had been considering this idea for a while, had become ill, and had gathered strength from reading pious books such as St Jerome's letters, 'which holpe me to such hart, and courage, as to make me resolue' [que me animavan de suerte que me determiné].[39] It was through books, as she puts it, that God inspired her to force herself to take this difficult decision.[40] She also stresses how God gave her the courage to go against herself when she left her parental home in secret, at night, and walked towards the convent of the Incarnation in Ávila, feeling so sad that it seemed as if her bones were coming away from their joints. Unable to display courage by undertaking dangerous adventures as an army captain, like Rodrigo, she opted for the other form of courage included in Aquinas's notion of *fortitudo*: enduring illnesses and physical pain.

Almost two decades after entering the convent, Teresa began to have visions and to fear that she might be a victim of demonic delusion. This was indeed the opinion of Gaspar Daza, a canon in the Cathedral in Ávila, even though it was not shared by some of the young Jesuits who acted as her confessors and spiritual directors between 1554 and 1560.[41] Her Jesuit confessors placed her on a strict and structured programme of mortification, but Daza and four other men from his spiritual circle were so afraid that she might be deceived by the devil, that they suggested that she should try to prevent further visions by taking communion less frequently and by avoiding being on her own. Her confessors' fears, together with her weak heart [*mal de corazón*], made her so frightened that she did not even dare to be by herself in her own room: 'now, I was extreamly timorous in these cases, as I haue sayd; and the palpitation of my hart, helped me on, therein; so that I had not the courage, manie times, to be alone, in my roome, euen by day' [yo era temerosa en estremo, como he dicho. Ayudávame el mal de corazón, que aun en una pieza sola no osaba estar de día muchas veces].[42]

Teresa was well aware of the widespread view that women were weaker than men and thus were more prone to being deceived by the devil. However, she puts across a very different argument. Just because women are weak, priests should think twice before making them frightened and ashamed with their unfounded public claims about demonic delusion. Instead, they should protect women, advise them in private, and encourage them with patience and intelligence:

> I say therefore, that such as I was then, must be counsailed, with much discretion; and animated; and time must be expected; for our Blessed Lord will helpe them, as he did me; which if he had not done, the preiudice which I should haue suffered, would haue been extreame, by reason of my being so full of apprehensions, and feares; and especially, considering to how great palpitations of hart, I was subiect, I wonder, how this other accident, did me not more hurt.
>
> [Pues digo que se avise con mucha discreción, animándolas y aguardando tiempo, que el Señor las ayudará como ha hecho a mí; que si no, grandísimo

daño me hiciera, sigún era temerosa y medrosa. Con el gran mal de corazón que tenía, espántome cómo no me hizo mucho mal.]⁴³

Teresa's testimony of how God helped and sustained her during those difficult years is clearly intended to offer an encouraging example to other women.

One of the measures taken by Teresa's Jesuit confessors to ensure that she was on the right track was to ask her to avoid mystical flights and focus instead on meditation on Christ. When writing the *Life*, ten years later, at the age of fifty, she used this opportunity to give her readers some advice, based on her personal experience of meditation. She thus suggested that those who (like her) felt too sick or frail to think about the Passion did not need to visualize Christ being distressed and afflicted. Instead, they could meditate on the Risen Christ, and imagine him talking to his Apostles, 'giving strength of bodie to some, and courage of minde to others' [esforzando a los unos, animando a los otros].⁴⁴

Despite trying to prevent further visions by following her confessors' advice, Teresa began to experience mystical raptures. Her first such experience, produced a mixture of emotions, and left her feeling more courageous:

> This gaue me a great amazement; for, the commotion of the Soule was great; and those words were spoken to me, in the verie interiour part of the Spirit; so that they made me afrayd; though yet, on the other side, they gaue me also great consolation [...].
> From that day forward, I haue remained full of courage, and resolution, to leaue the whole world, for Almightie God [...].
>
> [A mí me hizo mucho espanto, porque el movimiento del ánima fue grande, y muy en el espíritu se me dijeron estas palabras, y así me hizo temor, aunque por otra parte gran consuelo (...).
> Desde aquel día yo quedé tan animosa para dejarlo todo por Dios (...).]⁴⁵

The term 'animosa' denotes a crucial concept in Teresa's writing. Tobie Matthew renders it here as 'full of courage, and resolution', and sometimes translates it simply as 'couragious'; for instance, when Teresa argues, in one of the chapters added in the second version (1565), that, contrary to the warnings she had received from her confessors, she did not see the need to be less spiritually ambitious because God 'is a very great friend, and fauourer of couragious Soules' [es amigo de ánimas animosas].⁴⁶

At times, however, Teresa lost courage. After she founded the Discalced convent of St Joseph in Ávila, overcoming serious difficulties, she started to have doubts about whether she would be able to endure the stricter life of penance and hardship expected of Discalced nuns. She feared that she might miss the friends she had made at the convent of the Incarnation, and that she might despair.⁴⁷ Such doubts and fears were dispelled when she began to see them as ideas put into her head by the devil.⁴⁸ As a way of counteracting her fears and apprehensions, she would reason to herself that if she had to endure afflictions, she might as well do this for God's sake, and thereby avoid having to spend time in Purgatory.⁴⁹ As we shall now see, she was able to draw on her experience of overcoming fear to give practical advice to her nuns.

Teaching Courage: *The Book of Perfection*

After three years in the Discalced convent of St Joseph, Teresa began to write the *Way* as guidance for her nuns. Reading between the lines of this text, we see that the nuns were hungry, or afraid of being hungry, and that she saw this as the reason why they continued to try to please people from outside the convent: to ensure that they made a donation. She warns them that this is incompatible with their life of prayer, and recommends that when they fear hunger, they could simply think that the worst thing that might happen is that they would die; they could then consider that if they were to die of hunger for God's sake, theirs would be a blissful death (like that of the martyr saints).[50] She thus seeks to persuade them that they have nothing to fear.

Teresa, furthermore, encourages the nuns to stop using endearing terms such as 'my life', 'my heart' or 'my dear' [mi vida, mi alma, mi bien y otras cosas semejantes], which were so common among women, and to cultivate moral strength:

> I would not have you, my Daughters, be, nor seem to be, Women, but stout Men: since, if ye do what in you lies, our Lord will make you so manly that even Men shall wonder at it. And how easy is this for his Majesty, since he of nothing created us!
>
> [y no querría yo, hijas mías, lo fuésedes en nada, ni lo pareciésedes, sino varones fuertes; que si ellas hacen lo que es en sí, el Señor las hará tan varoniles, que espanten a los hombres.][51]

In line with the Catholic Church's doctrine of free will, and its teaching on the importance of the individual's actions, and not just their faith, in guaranteeing their salvation, Teresa emphasized that strength and courage would be granted to those who did what was in their power to be strong.

Aware of the prohibitions on women's preaching, Teresa also questioned the prevailing assumptions about male superiority by comparing preachers to soldiers, while arguing that the nuns were rather like the chosen people, who would withdraw with the country's ruler into a fortified city: 'those in the Town, as persons purposely selected, being able to do more single, than many faint-hearted Souldiers all together can' [y ser tales los que están en la ciudad, como es gente escogida, que pueden más ellos a solas que con muchos soldados, si eran covardes].[52] While women could not take on public roles such as that of preacher or soldier, only open to men, Teresa's reference to cowardly soldiers made it clear that being a man did not guarantee having sufficient courage to perform such roles well.

One of the strategies which, as Teresa indicates, would help the nuns to become stronger and more courageous was to turn their thoughts away from time-limited sensations and to focus their 'affections' [afeciones] on permanent things.[53] In line with Platonic and Christian teaching, she encourages the nuns to see the body and material comfort as impermanent things, from which those seeking perfection should strive to detach themselves:

> Now, the first thing we are to endeavour after is the banishing from our selves the love of this; for, some of us are so delicate by our complexion, that there is

not a little pains [*sic*] to be taken herein; and such lovers of our health, that it is a wonder to see the war these two things raise, especially among Nunns, as also among such as are not.

[Ahora, pues, lo primero que hemos de procurar es quitar de nosotros el amor de este cuerpo; que somos algunas tan regaladas de nuestro natural, que no hay poco que hacer aquí, y tan amigas de nuestra salud, que es cosa para alabar a Dios la guerra que dan, a monjas en especial, y aun a los que no lo son.]⁵⁴

Ahlgren has suggested that Teresa's penitential practices, such as self-flagellation and wearing a hair-shirt, can be seen in the framework of 'heroic' or 'manly' activity, and that 'through such deprecation of the body one could become less embodied'.⁵⁵ Nonetheless, bearing in mind recent approaches to the notion of embodiment, it can also be argued that the practice of mortification promoted by Teresa in the *Way* was a fully embodied means of cultivating both endurance and love.⁵⁶ As we have seen, endurance was understood by some of her contemporaries as the greatest form of courage.

In the *Way*, Teresa exhorts the nuns to endure their mortifications, and not be afraid that they might be excessive or unreasonable: 'never fear that we shall want discretion in this point, that were a wonder: for, the Confessors presently suspect lest we should kill our selves with Penances' [No hayan miedo nos falte discreción en este caso, por maravilla; que luego temen los confesores nos hemos de matar con penitencias].⁵⁷ However, she also warns that some people have such an extreme desire to do penance that, as she puts it, they mortify themselves without moderation for a couple of days, only to come to fear the pain and give it up altogether:

> Sometimes a frenzy takes them of doing penances without moderation, or discretion, which last two day, as I may say: afterward the Devil suggests to their imagination, that these do them hurt, so that they never do Penance more, no, not that, which the Order enjoyns, having already found it hurtfull to them. Nay then, we observe not the meanest injunctions of the *Rule*, such as *Silence*, which can do us no harm; and no sooner have we a conceit, that our head akes, but we forbear going to the *Quire*, which is not likely to kill us neither: one day, because our head akes; the next day, because it did ake; and three more, lest it should ake: and we love to invent penances of our own heads, that we may be able to do neither the one, nor the other.

> [algunas veces dales un frenesí de hacer penitencias sin camino ni concierto, que duran dos días, a manera de decir; para después la imaginación que les pone el demonio que las hizo daño, que nunca más penitencia ni la que manda la Orden, que ya lo provaron. No guardan unas cosas muy bajas de la Regla — como el silencio, que no nos ha de hacer mal — y no nos ha venido la imaginación de que nos duele la cabeza, cuando dejamos de ir al coro — que tampoco nos mata — un día porque nos dolió, y otro porque nos ha dolido, y otros tres porque no nos duela.]⁵⁸

> [y queremos inventar penitencias de nuestra cabeza para que no podamos hacer lo uno ni lo otro.]⁵⁹

The strict life at the Discalced convent of St Joseph provided the nuns with ample opportunities to cultivate courage. Their courage would not involve fighting against others, as it had done in the context in which Aristotle wrote the *Nicomachean Ethics*. It would involve fighting against their fear of death and of bodily pain, and overcoming that fear:

> And, believe, Daughters, when once we begin to subdue these Bodies of ours, they do not so much molest us: there will be enow to observe what ye have need of; take no care of your selves, except there be a manifest necessity. Unless we resolve once for all to undervalue Death, and the want of Health, we shall never do any thing: endeavour not to fear it, and to resign your selves entirely up to God, come what will. What matter, though we dye? Since our Body so often hath mocked us, shall not we mock it once? Believe it, this resolution imports more than we can imagine. For, by our often practising it by little and little with God's assistance we shall come to master it.
>
> [Y creed, hijas, que, en comenzando a vencer estos corpezuelos, no nos cansan tanto. Hartas habrá que miren lo que es menester; descuidaos de vosotras, si no fuere a necesidad conocida. Si no nos determinamos a tragar de una vez la muerte y la falta de salud, nunca haremos nada. Procurad de no temerla y dejaros toda (*sic*) en Dios, venga lo que viniere. ¿Qué va en que muramos? De cuantas veces nos ha burlado el cuerpo, ¿no burlaríamos alguna de él? Y creed que esta determinación importa más de lo que podemos entender; porque de muchas veces que poco a poco lo vamos haciendo, con el favor del Señor, quedaremos señoras de él.][60]

Here, as throughout her writings, Teresa stresses the importance of both divine grace and personal effort. This has often been overlooked by scholars who, like Maria Berbara, have emphasized how she departed from her male predecessors:

> If, for the Platonist humanist Marsilio Ficino in the previous century, beatific vision was the ultimate degree of intellectual contemplation, achieved through the dominion of reason over the body, and through an effort to liberate oneself from its prison, for Teresa it was a divine gift solely bestowed by the will of God.[61]

Such interpretations take no account of the belief Teresa put forward in the *Life* (for example, *Vida* 13.2) that God would help those who showed courage. They also disregard her advice, in the *Way*, on how courage and strength could be cultivated by overcoming the fear of pain and the fear of dying.

As I hope to have demonstrated in this chapter, Teresa used the account of her life to offer a clear testimony of how she became courageous, little by little. In the *Way*, she drew on existing terms such as 'manly' [varonil], 'courageous and full of determination' [animosa], and 'to resolve' [determinarse], to promote the idea that courage and fortitude can be learnt. If, in the *Life*, she invites her readers to cultivate courage by claiming that God likes courageous people [es amigo de ánimas animosas (13.2)], in the *Way*, she offers practical advice to help her nuns lose their fear of bodily pain and their concern about their lack of food, and to see their practices of mortification not only as opportunities to become 'manlier' (in other words, more courageous), but also, more importantly, as ways of showing their commitment to God, and thus as acts of love.

The sermon delivered by Ballester in Perpignan, to mark Teresa's beatification in 1614, captures the essence of the great strength and courage [fortaleza] which she developed by enduring not only voluntary penance but also illnesses and difficulties with her spiritual advisors. The extant hagiographical accounts, such as that attributed to Yepes, of her practices of penance might seem exaggerated, but they need to be read in context. As I have shown, Yepes's description of her extreme mortifications served to illustrate the claim she made in the *Life* that she had felt 'good for nothing', restrained by her sickness and by her fear of dying, until she overcame that fear and decided not to worry too much about her health (*Vida* 13.7). Drawing on this experience, she was able to write with authority to tell the readers of the *Way* that, unless they lost their fear of illness and death, they would achieve nothing (CV 11.4).

The form of courage which Teresa teaches in her writings requires determination: the will to undertake difficult things and to persevere. It is the kind of courage which, as Aquinas had noted, and Ballester would explain again, involves being able to endure suffering, despite feeling weak. It is the kind of strength which, as Ribera pointed out, is not dependent on physiology. If Teresa felt encouraged as a result of her mystical prayer, this was not simply the effect of a divine gift, but also of her personal commitment. If she achieved the highest recognition the Catholic Church could offer by being beatified in 1614 and canonized in 1622, it was not because she had been a 'miraculous star' (Yepes), but because she was committed to spiritual perfection (Ribera). Today, Teresa can still be seen as a great model of courage, not because she was fearless but because she learnt to overcome her fears.

Notes to Chapter 10

1. *Relación de la solemnidad con que se han celebrado en la ciudad de Barcelona, las fiestas a la Beatificación de la Madre S. Teresa de Iesvs*, ed. by Joseph Dalmau (Barcelona: Sebastian Matevad, 1615), fols 29^r–37^v (35^r). All translations from Spanish sources are mine, unless otherwise stated. Ballester's sermon was published the following year in a collection containing other sermons preached in all main towns of Castile and Catalonia (including Barcelona, Mataró, Lerida, Tortosa, Tarragona, Girona and Perpignan), alongside poems entered in poetry contests, and reports of events such as parades in the streets and rivers, and children's performances inspired by Teresa's life and works.

2. In Spain, Judith had emerged as a positive model of female strength (based on her heroic chastity) in texts such as Álvaro de Luna's *Libro de las claras e virtuosas mugeres* and Martín de Córdoba's *Jardín de nobles doncellas*, written in the first half of the fifteenth century. Córdoba referred to Judith, Semiramis, and the Amazons to clarify that, despite their physical weakness, 'women have great courage within them, once they overcome their fear' [as mugeres an en si grand fortaleza, quitado el miedo]; see Córdoba, *Jardín de nobles doncellas, Fray Martín de Córdoba: A Critical Edition and Study*, ed. by Harriet Goldberg (Chapel Hill: Department of Romance Languages and Literatures, University of North Carolina, 1974), p. 249; cited in Robert Archer, *The Problem of Woman in Late Medieval Hispanic Literature* (Woodbridge: Tamesis, 2005), p. 31. Teresa de Cartagena used the example of Judith in *Arboleda de los enfermos* to validate her own authority as a writer; see Ronald Surtz, 'The New Judith: Teresa de Cartagena', in *Writing Women in Late Medieval and Early Modern Spain: The Mothers of Saint Teresa of Avila* (Philadelphia: University of Pennsylvania Press, 1995), pp. 21–40. For a brief discussion of textual representations of Judith as a 'manly woman' in seventeenth-century Spain, see Stephanie Fink de Backer, *Widowhood in Early Modern Spain: Protectors, Proprietors, and Patrons* (Leiden and Boston, MA: Brill, 2010), pp. 29–32. For the broader European context, see Kevin R. Brine, Elena Ciletti, and Henrike

Lähnemann, eds, *The Sword of Judith: Judith Studies across the Disciplines* (Cambridge: Open Book Publishers, 2010).
3. *Relación*, fol. 30^r.
4. Pedro Luis Sánchez, *Triangulo de las tres virtudes theologicas, fe, esperança, y caridad, y Cuadrangulo de las quatro cardinales, prudencia, templança, iusticia y fortaleza* (Toledo: Tomás de Guzmán, 1595).
5. Partida II.xxi.4, in Alfonso el Sabio, *Las siete partidas del Rey don Alfonso el Sabio, cotejadas con varios códices antiguos por la Real Academia de la Historia, II: Partida segunda y tercera* (Madrid: Imprenta Real, 1807), p. 200.
6. See Peter Dronke, *Women Writers of the Middle Ages: A Critical Study of Texts from Perpetua (d. 203) to Marguerite Porete (d. 1310)* (Cambridge: Cambridge University Press, 1984); Barbara Newman, 'Divine Power Perfect in Weakness: St Hildegard on the Frail Sex', in *Medieval Religious Women: Peaceweavers*, ed. by J. A. Nichols and Lillian Thomas Shank (Kalamazoo, MI: Cistercian Publications, 1987), pp. 103–22.
7. See, for instance, Abelard, *De auctoritate vel dignitate ordinis sanctimonialium (The Authority and Dignity of Nuns)*, ed. by J. T. Muckle, 'The Letter of Heloise on Religious Life and Abelard's First Reply', *Medieval Studies*, 17 (1995), 253–81.
8. See Rosemary Radford Ruether, 'Misogynism and Virginal Feminism in the Fathers of the Church', in her *Religion and Sexism: Images of Woman in the Jewish and Christian Traditions* (New York: Simon and Schuster, 1974), pp. 150–83; Barbara Newman, *From Virile Woman to WomanChrist: Studies in Medieval Religion and Literature* (Philadelphia: University of Pennsylvania Press, 1995).
9. The early modern English translations of Teresa's texts rendered the term *ánimo* either as 'courage of mind' or simply as 'courage'.
10. Sebastián de Covarrubias Horozco, *Tesoro de la lengua castellana*, ed. by Ignacio Arellano and Rafael Zafra, Biblioteca Áurea Hispánica, 21 (Madrid: Iberoamericana-Vervuert, 2006), p. 921.
11. Gillian T. W. Ahlgren, *Teresa of Avila and the Politics of Sanctity* (Ithaca, NY: Cornell University Press, 1996), pp. 154–66.
12. Domingo Báñez, Proceso de Salamanca, 1591, in *Procesos de beatificación y canonización de Santa Teresa de Jesús*, ed. by Silverio de Santa Teresa, 3 vols (Burgos: Monte Carmelo, 1935), I, 9. Báñez then adds that the Provincial was primarily 'drawing attention to the great steadiness and intelligence with which she governed herself and her nuns' ['dando a entender en esto su gran constancia y discreción en el gobierno de su persona y de sus monjas'], *Procesos*, I, 9.
13. Francisco de Ribera, *Vida de la madre Teresa de Jesús* (Salamanca: 1590), ed. by Jaime Pons (Barcelona: Gustavo Gilí, 1908), p. 88. The well-rooted view that men who do not control their passions behave like women has been promoted since antiquity (as we see in Plato's *Phaedo* 117d3–e5).
14. One of the most notable examples is Fray Íñigo de Mendoza's praise of the Queen: 'Oh what masculine renown of an astonishing lady, whom the female estate has endowed with manly strength and virtuous cunning' [¡O alta fama viril | de dueña maravillosa | que el estado feminil | hizo fuerza varonil | con cabtela virtuosa!]; *Dechado y regimiento de príncipes* (Zamora: Antonio de Centenera, 1493); the translation is from Roger Boase, *The Troubadour Revival: A Study of Social Change and Traditionalism in Late Medieval Spain* (London: Routledge and Kegan Paul, 1978), p. 112. Elizabeth Teresa Howe has noted that, even though Isabel's contemporaries compared her to warrior queens, her image was increasingly 'domesticated' and, by the seventeenth century, she had become an example of traditional feminine virtues: 'Zenobia or Penelope? Isabel la Católica as Literary Archetype', in *Isabel la Católica, Queen of Castile: Critical Essays*, ed. by David A. Boruchoff (New York: Palgrave Macmillan, 2003), pp. 91–102 (pp. 97–98).
15. Ribera, *Vida*, p. 88.
16. Diego de Yepes, *Vida, virtudes, y milagros de la bienaventurada virgen Teresa de Jesus* (Lisbon: Pedro Craesbeeck, 1614), p. 10. This biography is now believed to have been written by the Discalced Carmelite Tomás de Jesús (1563–1627), who had studied in Salamanca from 1583 to 1586, though the name 'Yepes' continues to be used for the sake of simplicity.
17. Juan Huarte de San Juan, *The Examination of Mens Wits*, trans. by Richard Carew (London:

Adam Islip, 1594), pp. 201, 207, and 253. Huarte draws on Aristotle to emphasize the physiological connection between courage and masculinity: 'hardinesse and naturall courage consist in heat', Huarte, *The Examination*, p. 311. The popularity of the *Examen* is demonstrated by the fact that, by 1675, it had had three editions in Latin, seven in Italian, six in English and six in Dutch. A revised, expurgated, version of the text appeared in Spanish in 1594, though the original 1575 text, which had been placed on the Index of Forbidden Books in 1584, continued to be published in Spanish in the Netherlands. For a modernized version of Carew's translations, see Richard Carew, *The Examination of Men's Wits*, ed. by Rocío G. Sumillera, MHRA Tudor and Stuart Translations, 17 (London: MHRA, 2014).
18. Thomas Aquinas, *Summa Theologicae*, XLII: *Courage*, trans. by Anthony Ross O.P. and P. G. Walsh (London: Blackfriars in conjunction with Eyre & Spottiswoode; New York: McGraw-Hill, 1966), pp. 20–21.
19. *Relación*, fol. 33^r.
20. *Relación*, fol. 33^v.
21. *Relación*, fol. 33^v.
22. *Relación*, fol. 33^v.
23. *Relación*, fol. 33^v.
24. *Relación*, fol. 33^r.
25. *Relación*, fol. 34^v. On the difficulties Teresa experienced with her confessors, see Elena Carrera, *Teresa of Avila's Autobiography: Authority, Power, and the Self in Mid-Sixteenth-Century Spain* (Oxford: Legenda, 2005), pp. 119–43.
26. *Relación*, fol. 34^v.
27. *Relación*, fol. 35^r.
28. *Relación*, fol. 35^r.
29. Yepes, *Vida*, pp. 75–76.
30. *The Flaming Hart, or, The Life of the Gloriovs S. Teresa*, trans. by Tobie Matthew (Antwerp: Meursius, 1642), p. 289; *Vida* 24.2, p. 132.
31. Alison Weber, 'Spiritual Administration: Gender and Discernment in the Carmelite Reform', *The Sixteenth Century Journal*, 31.1 (2000), 123–46 (p. 138).
32. *Flaming Hart*, p. 150; *Vida* 13.7, Santa Teresa de Jesús, *Obras completas: edición manual*, ed. by Efrén de la Madre de Dios and Otger Steggink, Biblioteca de Autores Cristianos, 212 (Madrid: Editorial Católica, 1986), p. 79.
33. Yepes, *Vida*, p. 76.
34. The tears of Christ in Gethsemane were the subject of much debate over the centuries. The wording in Hebrews (5.7) suggests that Christ receives God's help because he acknowledges his vulnerability (i.e. a consequence of his Incarnation) and the superiority of God as Father. For a discussion of this passage in its cultural context, see Patrick Gray, *Godly Fear: The Epistle to Hebrews and Greco-Roman Critiques of Superstition* (Atlanta, GA: Society of Biblical Literature, 2003), pp. 188–205.
35. *Flaming Hart*, p. 3; *Vida* 1.5, *Obras*, p. 35.
36. St Teresa of Ávila, *The Collected Works*, ed. and trans. by Kavanaugh, I, 5.
37. Ribera, *Vida*, p. 96.
38. *Flaming Hart*, p. 3; *Vida* 1.5, *Obras*, p. 35.
39. *Flaming Hart*, p. 21; *Vida* 3.7, *Obras*, p. 40.
40. *Flaming Hart*, p. 19; *Vida* 3.4, *Obras*, p. 40.
41. She notes, for instance, that her first Jesuit confessor (Cetina) was very supportive: '[he] encouraged me much, and told me, that it was euidently, the Spirit of Almightie God' [me animó mucho. Dijo ser espíritu de Dios muy conocidamente]; *Flaming Hart*, p. 325; *Vida* 13.16, *Obras*, p. 131.
42. *Flaming Hart*, p. 449; *Vida* 25.14, *Obras*, p. 138.
43. *Flaming Hart*, p. 321; *Vida* 23.13, *Obras*, p. 130.
44. *Flaming Hart*, pp. 295–96; *Vida* 22.6, *Obras*, p. 122.
45. *Flaming Hart*, pp. 34; *Vida* 24.57, *Obras*, p. 133.
46. *Flaming Hart*, pp. 145–46; *Vida* 13.2, *Obras*, p. 78.

47. *Flaming Hart*, p. 549; *Vida* 36.8, *Obras*, p. 196.
48. *Flaming Hart*, pp. 549–51; *Vida* 36.8–9, *Obras*, p. 197.
49. *Flaming Hart*, pp. 549–51; *Vida* 36.8–9, *Obras*, p. 197.
50. *The Way of Perfection*, in *The Second Part of the Works of the Holy Mother St. Teresa of Jesus*, trans. by Abraham Woodhead (London, 1675), p. 3; *Camino* (CV) 2.1, *Obras*, p. 241. Unless otherwise stated, all my references to this text are based on the Valladolid version, cited as CV.
51. *Way*, p. 25; CV 7.8, *Obras*, p. 271. The English translation shows greater grammatical coherence than the Valladolid version by maintaining the use of the second person. The Escorial manuscript (CE) uses 'ellas' throughout.
52. *Way*, p. 6; CV 3.1, *Obras*, p. 246.
53. *Way*, p. 31; CV 10.2, *Obras*, p. 277.
54. *Way*, p. 31. CV, 10.5; *Obras*, p. 278.
55. Ahlgren, *Teresa of Avila*, p. 155.
56. For a discussion of Aristotelian and recent notions of embodiment, see Elena Carrera, 'Embodied Cognition and Empathy in Cervantes's *El celoso extremeño* (1613)', *Hispania*, 97.1 (2014), 113–24.
57. *Way*, p. 32; CV 10.6, *Obras*, p. 279.
58. *Way*, pp. 32–33; CE 15.4, *Obras*, p. 279. The text on which Woodhead's translation is based uses here the more colourful wording of the Escorial Manuscript (CE).
59. CV 10.6, *Obras*, p. 279. The last phrase in Woodhead's translation does not appear in CE.
60. *Camino*, p. 35; CV 11.4, *Obras*, p. 282.
61. Maria Berbara, '"Esta pena tan sabrosa": Teresa of Avila and the Figurative Arts', in *The Sense of Suffering: Constructions of Physical Pain in Early Modern Culture*, ed. by Jan Frans van Dijkhuizen and Karl A. E. Enenkel, Intersections, 12 (Leiden: Brill, 2009), pp. 267–97 (pp. 269–70).

CHAPTER 11

The 'Library' of Santa Teresa: Teresa of Ávila's Sources and their Effect on her Writings

Hilary Pearson

The works of Teresa of Ávila, on first reading, seem disorganized, with an oral rather than a literary style, and with repeated self-depreciatory statements.[1] Of course, as shown by Alison Weber and others, including Christopher Pountain in this volume, this first impression of Teresa of Ávila's works is deceptive — and almost certainly deliberately so.[2] She was capable of using rhetorical devices, and, from occasional indiscreet statements, it seems that she did not really believe that women were inferior spiritually, but used the female humility tropes as a defence against the deeply embedded prejudice against women authors and the prying eyes of the Inquisition.[3] This essay examines how what she read could have influenced the way she wrote, and tests the conclusions by making a similar examination of the works of Teresa de Cartagena, who wrote in Spanish approximately a century earlier.

Teresa of Ávila and Books She Knew

Teresa's writings make it clear that she read, and loved, books, and she tells us how much she depended on them for her spiritual development. For many years, when she could not find a confessor who understood her path of prayer, only books gave her the guidance she needed. Speaking of Francisco de Osuna's *Third Spiritual Alphabet* [*Tercer abecedario espiritual*] in her first work, the *Life*, she says:

> Since the Lord had already given me the gift of tears and I enjoyed reading, I began to take time out for solitude, confess frequently, and to follow that path, taking the book as my master. For during the twenty years after this period of which I am speaking, I did not find a master, I mean a confessor, who understood me, even though I looked for one. (*Vida* 4.7)[4]

> [Y, como ya el Señor me havía dado don de lágrimas y guastava de leer, comencé a tener ratos de soledad, y a confesarme a menudo, y comenzar aquel camino teniendo aquel libro por maestro; porque yo no hallé maestro, digo confessor, que me entendiese, aunque le busqué, en veinte años después desto que digo.]

Education

Clearly, Teresa of Ávila could read and write Spanish, but she tells us very little about her education. It very likely took place at home, perhaps taught by her mother who, she tells us was very fond of 'books of chivalry' (*Vida* 2.1) [libros de caballerías], a fondness passed on to her daughter.[5] She also tells us that her father 'was fond of reading good books and thus he also had books in Spanish for his children to read' (*Vida* 1.1) [aficionado a leer buenos libros y ansí los tenía de romance para que leyesen sus hijos].[6] By 'good books', she means religious books. Teresa of Ávila did spend time with the Augustinian nuns of Our Lady of Grace in Ávila, but this was probably more like a finishing school, teaching skills required for married women, and some basic religious education, rather than giving an academic education.[7] It is clear, both from what she herself says and from other evidence reviewed by Delgado, that this education did not include the study of Latin.[8] This is not surprising, as very few women learned Latin at this time.

An inventory of her father's books at the time of the death of his first wife in 1507 shows a mixture of religious works, works by classical authors (probably translations), and various other works.[9] The religious works are *Retablo de la vida de Cristo* by Juan de Padilla and religious poems by Fernán Pérez de Guzmán. The classical works include Cicero's *De officiis* and Boethius's *Consolationes*. The former was translated into Spanish by Alonso de Cartagena in 1422, with a first printed edition in 1501.[10] The work by Boethius was very popular and widely translated in the medieval period; the 1457 inventory of the library of Alvar García de Santa María lists two vernacular versions.[11] It is probable that the listed copies of these works were Spanish translations,[12] and nothing else in the inventory appears to be in Latin.[13] It seems likely that he acquired many more books during his second marriage. Teresa was the third child of this marriage, born in 1515.

She tells us that, after her more frivolous teenage years reading romances, she was brought back to 'good' books by her uncle (*Vida* 3.3–5).[14] When she was recovering from the illness that made her leave the Augustinian convent, she went to visit her married half-sister María, the daughter by her father's first wife. During this visit she stayed a few days with her uncle, Don Pedro Sánchez de Cepeda, who lived close to her sister. By this time he was a widower and he later became a Hieronymite friar. He seems to have had an extensive library of spiritual works because Teresa tells us that 'He spent his time reading good books in the vernacular [...]. He asked me to read these books to him; and, although I did not like them, I pretended to' (*Vida* 3.4) [Su ejercicio era buenos libros de romance (...). Hacíame le leyese, y aunque no era amiga de ellos, mostraba que sí].[15] It is likely that these books included the *Letters of St Jerome*, because she says that her decision to become a nun, a process which began during this visit, was encouraged by reading this book.[16] It was the same uncle who later gave her the book which transformed her prayer life, *The Third Spiritual Alphabet*.[17]

Religious Literature in Spain during Teresa's Formative Years

Teresa grew up during a period of intense religious reform in Spain, mainly driven by Cardinal Francisco Jiménez de Cisneros (1436–1517), with the support of the Catholic Monarchs, Isabella and Ferdinand.[18] Under the leadership of Cisneros many spiritual works were translated into Spanish and printed, allowing access by literate laity to works that were previously only available to university-trained clergy. Among them would be the 'good books' that Teresa read from her father's and uncle's libraries.[19] The spiritual works in the vernacular that most influenced Teresa's thought and writing are discussed below.

Cisneros intended his reforms to work within the established Catholic Church and to avoid division. However, the more open atmosphere led to groups of lay Catholics meeting to read the Scriptures, discuss spiritual matters, and engage in meditative or contemplative prayer, called mental prayer, as opposed to the rote recitation of standard prayers such as the Lord's Prayer and the Hail Mary (vocal prayer). The members of such groups, which included and were sometimes led by women, became known as '*alumbrados*'.[20] This caused concern in the ecclesiastical hierarchy, as these activities were seen as being close to Lutheranism and other Protestant movements, and the movement was suppressed, ultimately by the Inquisition.[21]

This concern also led to the banning of books considered too dangerous for the laity and the Inquisition published Indexes of prohibited books. The Index of 1551 prohibited Protestant biblical translations, but the Index of 1559, promulgated under Inquisitor General Fernando de Valdés and generally referred to as the 'Valdés Index', comprehensively forbade the reading of Scripture in any vernacular translation (which led to the almost complete disappearance in Spain of Scripture in Spanish).[22] Religious works in Spanish, deemed to be Protestant, heterodox, mystical, or otherwise dangerous, met a similar fate.[23]

Teresa and the Bible

As might be expected for a religious writer, Teresa of Ávila's works contain extensive references to the Bible. A preliminary question must be how much access she had to the Bible.

We do know that vernacular translations of much of the New Testament and parts of the Old Testament had been made by the fifteenth century. The reading of the Bible in the vernacular was encouraged during the early sixteenth century under Cardinal Cisneros, who also encouraged serious academic study of the texts through the preparation and publication of the great Polyglot Bible of Alcalá de Henares.[24] Román Llamas says that an important work for spreading biblical knowledge among the literate laity was *Los evangelios y epístolas con sus exposiciones* by Gonzalo de Santa María, first published in 1485, then revised and improved at the request of King Ferdinand by Ambrosio de Montesinos. This version, first published in 1512, went into numerous editions between then and 1559.[25] Given its wide circulation, it is almost certain that either Teresa's father or uncle, if not both, would have had this in their collection of 'good books'.[26]

The 1559 prohibition by the Inquisition of all use of vernacular versions meant that Teresa of Ávila could not have access to any book of the Bible in Spanish while she was writing her works, the first of which was begun in the early 1560s. She did not know Latin. However, she does often quote the Bible, albeit, usually very briefly. Where could this have come from?

Teresa's Use of the Bible

It is first important to look at how she uses the Bible in her writings, and the parts of the Bible to which she either refers or, on occasion, directly quotes. The method used here was to read each of her works in the Kavanaugh and Rodriguez edition and translation, looking for anything which seemed to originate from the Bible. Where citations were given by these editors, they were checked against an English Bible (Revised Standard Version translation) for accuracy. Where no such citation was given, I used my own knowledge of the Bible and a concordance to look for the origin. If there seemed to be any ambiguity in the English translation, the reference was checked against the relevant Spanish edition listed in n. 1 above. Three broad categories were identified: word-for-word biblical quotations (either in Latin or Spanish); references (attribution by Teresa to a biblical source without a direct quotation); and allusions (which can be shown to originate from the Bible but without any such attribution by Teresa).[27]

Identifying biblical quotations, references and allusions in her works shows that they are unevenly spread. The fewest are found where she is describing her reforms, *Foundations* [Fundaciones] and the last ten chapters of her *Life*, as well as the *Constitutions* [Constituciones]. The work most densely studded with biblical references is *Soliloquies* [Exclamaciones]. The works on prayer, *Way, Interior Castle*, and Chapters 8–21 of the *Life*, contain many word-for-word quotations as well as numerous references and allusions.

To examine Teresa's use of the Bible, we will start with the *Life*. This contains rather more quotations than simple references or allusions, almost all from the Psalms and the New Testament. She does refer to reading the story of Job, but gives Gregory the Great's *Moralia* as the source.[28] New Testament quotations are from the Gospels (the most used being Matthew, the least used, Mark) and from particular Epistles by St Paul: Romans, I and II Corinthians, Galatians, and Philippians. She does not name the book of the New Testament when she quotes it, although she generally identifies St Paul as the origin of her references from his Epistles.

She does give a few quotations in Latin. Two of these, from Psalm 102.8 and Psalm 122.1, are written as pronounced in Castilian, rather than with Latin spelling.[29] Indeed, Delgado shows that throughout her writings she has spellings of Castilian words that vary from modern usage and that those variations also show up in many of the Latin quotations in her entire corpus.[30] Teresa also refers to 'the psalm *Quicumque vult*', but this is not a psalm but the opening words of the Athanasian Creed, also sometimes recited in the Office.[31] This indicates that she indeed did not understand Latin but knew phrases by heart from regular recitation.

In *Way*, there are only three verbatim quotations, none in Latin and all from the Gospels.[32] The references and allusions are mainly also from the Gospels. The next most common sources are the Song of Songs and the Psalms. There are two references to Paul's Epistles,[33] one reference to each of Peter's Epistles,[34] one to the First Epistle of John,[35] one to Proverbs,[36] and two to events in Exodus.[37]

In *Interior Castle*, again the majority of the references are to the Gospels, the Psalms, and the Song of Songs.[38] The title of the work comes from Christ's statement in John 14.2 that 'in my Father's house there are many dwelling places' (*Moradas* 1.1.1).[39] Psalm 112.1 is quoted in Latin.[40] She had earlier quoted this verse in Spanish, accompanied by the statement that God had given her an understanding of what this verse meant in the vernacular.[41] She also quotes Psalm 119.32 twice in Latin, on the second occasion giving a translation: '*Cun dilateste cor meun*' (*Moradas* 4.1.5) [*dilataste cor meun*, dice que se ensanchó el corazón].[42] She makes five references to what 'the bride says in the Song of Songs', the second reference giving a quotation 'He brought me into the wine cellar' (although she is not certain of the exact wording).[43]

There are many more Old Testament references to people in *Interior Castles* than in her other works. Examples include Lot's wife,[44] Jonah,[45] Jacob and his ladder,[46] Moses and the burning bush,[47] and Elijah calling down fire from heaven.[48] There are references to New Testament people (besides numerous references to Jesus Christ and the Virgin Mary), the most frequently referenced being St Paul (five references),[49] Mary Magdalene (four references),[50] and St Peter (three references).[51] Martha and Mary, representing the relationship between the active and contemplative life, are discussed in the Seventh Mansion.[52] As well as the references to St Paul himself, Teresa refers to several of his Epistles,[53] including a quotation in very idiosyncratic Latin from Philippians 1.21.[54] She also advises her sisters to 'consider yourselves useless servants', giving 'St Paul or Christ' as the origin of this saying.[55]

As mentioned above, there are not many biblical references in *Foundations*, and these are found in Chapters 5 to 8 (which deal with general spiritual matters rather than the details of a particular foundation) and Chapters 20 to 29. There is one citation in Latin and two quotations in Spanish, both, according to Teresa, spoken by Christ.[56] All three quotations occur in Chapter 5. From the Old Testament, there are two references to the story of Jonah,[57] three to Elijah,[58] one to David dancing before the Ark of the Covenant,[59] and one to the story of Saul.[60] New Testament references include Peter's denial of Christ and references to the miracle of healing of a blind man found in John 9.[61] As might be expected from its intensely practical nature, there are very few biblical references in *Constituciones*. There are, however, three: two of those are references to Paul supporting himself by manual work and one is to Christ's commandment to his disciples to love one another.[62]

There are also relatively few scriptural references in the *Spiritual Testimonies* [*Cuentas de conciencia*], although there are many quotations of words God speaks directly to Teresa. There are biblical quotations in Latin; one from the Song of Songs (used twice),[63] one from the opening of the Magnificat (also used twice),[64] and one from the Psalter.[65] St Peter's acknowledgment of Jesus as Christ is quoted in Spanish.[66] Most of the indirect references are to the New Testament, although she does refer to Job.[67] She also refers to the crossing of the Red Sea.[68]

In the *Soliloquies*, there are no Latin quotations and five quotations in Spanish: two of these are words of Christ,[69] two are from Song of Songs,[70] and one from the Psalms.[71] Of the many biblical references and allusions, her more extended discussions are on Martha's complaint about her sister,[72] the man born blind,[73] and the living water.[74]

In those of Teresa's poems that have been preserved,[75] the only quotation is the title of the poem 'On the words "My beloved is mine"' [Sobre aquellas palabras 'Dilectus meus mihi'],[76] the Latin being a quotation from the Song of Songs 'my beloved is mine'.[77] The poem 'In God's hands' [En las manos de Dios] contains a number of biblical references, contrasting examples of suffering and joy: Calvary or Tabor, Job suffering or John resting on Christ's breast; Joseph in chains or governor of Egypt; David pained or exalted; Jonah drowned or freed.[78] Several of the poems, written to mark the profession of her nuns, contain marital imagery deriving from the Song of Songs, and, in one, there is reference to the parable of the wise and foolish virgins.[79] There are a number of poems written for the various feasts of the Christmas season that allude to the relevant stories in the Gospels.

Her only work expressly based on Scripture is the *Meditations*. Even here, she bases the work on only a few verses from the Song of Songs (1.2–3; 2.4–5). However, it must be understood that Teresa is not attempting an exegesis of this book of the Bible, something anyway forbidden to women and those without a theological training, but instead uses these verses as an opening to teaching her sisters about prayer and union with God. Besides these verses, and a quotation from Song of Songs 6.10,[80] there are quotations from St Paul,[81] Christ in the garden of Gethsemane,[82] and the Annunciation.[83] There is reference again to the parable of the wise and foolish virgins,[84] and Peter walking on the water.[85] When her works are examined as a whole, it is clear that the major biblical influences on Teresa's writings are the Psalms, the Song of Songs, Job, the Gospels, and the Epistles.[86]

Teresa's Biblical Sources

Teresa's use of Scripture, mainly allusions or indirect quotations, very few verbatim quotations or with attribution, gives clues about her sources. First, there is good reason to think that she read some of the Bible in the vernacular before it was banned in 1559. As mentioned above, between 1521 and that date, Montesinos's *Evangelios y epístolas* was very widely available and it is difficult to imagine that she never had access to a copy, either when she was with her family or when she was in the wealthy Encarnación convent in Ávila.[87]

Even if she did not deliberately memorize verses, the scriptural events she refers to, sometimes with a brief quotation, are those likely to remain in the memory. She seems to have been particularly attached to the story in John's Gospel of Christ's encounter with the Samaritan woman at the well.[88] In the *Life* she refers to the story and says that she always carried with her a painting of it, quoting the Latin words inscribed on the picture '*Domine, da mihi aquam*' (*Vida* 30.19).[89] She also refers to this biblical story in *Way*, *Meditations*, and *Interior Castle*.[90]

The supposition that she was using memories of Scripture that she had read is supported by the fact that she is wrong about the details of how long the man cured at the Pool of Siloam had been there. She says thirty years but the verse says thirty-eight years.[91] Another example is where, after referring to the soldiers who knelt down to drink before going into battle, a reference to the story of Gideon (Judges 7.5), she says that she cannot remember with whom the battle was to be fought.[92] In the Seventh Mansion of the *Interior Castle* she says that the Lord makes the soul 'blind and deaf, as was St. Paul in his conversion' (*Moradas* 7.1.5) [mas es haciéndola ciega y muda, como lo quedó San Pablo en su conversión].[93] However, Acts 9 says only that he became blind, which again points to reliance on memory rather than written text. Further, all the verbatim quotations, apart from those from the Psalms, which could come from the liturgy (see below), are from the Gospels and Epistles. This supports the thesis that she was familiar with the translation by Montesinos, rather than a full translation of the Bible. Indeed, Llamas argues that Teresa's complaint in the *Life* about the prohibition of reading many books in the vernacular must have primarily been about the removal of the translations of Scripture, because most of the Spanish versions of the books that she mentions by name in the *Life* were not prohibited by the 1559 Index.[94]

Another possible source is quotations in books in the vernacular which had not been banned. For example, in *Life* she writes of a time when she was being told that her experiences came from the devil: 'I read in a book — which it seems that the Lord placed in my hands — what St Paul said, that God was very faithful, that He would never let those who love Him be deceived by the devil' (*Vida* 23.15) [lei en un libro — que parece el Señor me lo puso en las manos — que decía San Pablo que era Dios muy fiel, que nunca a los que le amaban consentía ser del demonio engañados].[95] The Church authorities did not ban scriptural passages quoted in Spanish in approved vernacular spiritual works.[96] Their reason for banning the reading of the Bible itself in the vernacular was fear, spurred on by the Protestant Reformation, that people who had not had the necessary education and training would fall into error. They considered, however, that this danger might be avoided if an orthodox explanation was attached to the passage. Certainly, some of the books we know that she read and that she wanted the sisters in her reformed convents to have contained extensive quotations from Scripture.[97] For example, the *Imitation of Christ* is expressly based on the Bible and contains many biblical quotations. Indeed, early in the first book there is a chapter headed 'On reading the Holy Scriptures'. Another, the *Life of Christ* by Ludolph of Saxony, contains extended passages from the Gospels with commentaries from patristic literature.

Another likely source is the liturgy. In particular, most of the quotations in Latin that she does give come from the Psalms, which as a choir nun she would recite in Latin every day, working through the entire Psalter every four weeks.[98] In connection with her quotation of Psalm 119.32 in *Moradas*, she says that she remembers 'a line that we say at prime, in the latter part of the verse at the end of the last psalm' (*Moradas* 4.1.5) [ahora me acuerdo en un verso que decimos a Prima, al fin del postrer Salmo].[99] The other Latin quotations which would form part of the liturgy are the beginning of the Athanasian Creed, cited in her *Life*.[100] She also cites from the Magnificat.[101] Teresa gives two quotations in Latin from the Song of Songs and one from Paul's Epistle to the Philippians, which might also have come from the liturgy.[102] Certainly, she refers to reciting the Office of our Lady weekly, which she says contained quotations from the Song of Songs.[103] There is one Latin quotation from John's Gospel, but, in this case, Teresa gives her source.[104] The text in question is from the story of the Samaritan woman and she says, as noted earlier, these words were written on a picture she kept with her.

Other texts may have come from sermons she heard. She speaks of her love of hearing sermons and their effects on her in her *Life*.[105] Another possible source is her frequent contacts with *letrados*. She had wide connections: those she had consulted up to 1576 are listed in the account of her spiritual life that she wrote for the Inquisitor of Seville in that year.[106] She believed these men called by God to explain the Scriptures and says she asked learned men to explain to her the meaning of verses from the Song of Songs.[107]

The Ban on Vernacular Scriptures and its Effect on Teresa's Writing

Her inability to consult original scriptural texts manifests itself in her writing. It is interesting to note that most of the direct quotations from Scripture, especially those in Latin, are in works intended to be read by her confessors and other 'learned men', namely the *Life*, *Interior Castle*, *Foundations*, and *Spiritual Testimonies*. As noted above, some of these quotations are inaccurate and she does not always get the details right. She uses Scripture generally to illustrate a point she is making, rather than to act as an authority for it.

A related factor is the effect of having the Inquisition 'looking over her shoulder', the reason for some statements made about her use of Scripture. For example, in respect to quotations from the Psalms, she makes a curious statement that, when in the prayer of quiet, she could comprehend the Latin Psalms and 'understand the Latin verse in the vernacular' (*Vida* 15.8) [entender el verso en romance].[108] Perhaps this was because she had read and memorized at least some of the Psalms in the vernacular, before the reading of vernacular translations was banned, and was wary of the Inquisition investigating her reading practices. This would also explain the passage in the *Life*, where she refers to what 'the Bridegroom says to the Bride in the *Song of Songs*' — then hastily adds 'I think I heard that it is there' (*Vida* 27.10) [a lo que creo helo oído, que es aquí].[109]

The work that most clearly shows the effect of the Inquisition on her and the general religious climate in Spain in the second half of the sixteenth century is *Meditations on the Song of Songs* [Meditaciones]. This is not surprising, given the Church's prohibition on women teaching and the banning of vernacular Scriptures. The dangers of writing in the vernacular on this text are clear from the experience of Luis de León, who, despite being an Augustinian friar, a *letrado*, and professor at Salamanca, was imprisoned by the Inquisition in 1572.[110] The two main charges against him were challenging the accuracy of the Vulgate Latin Bible and translating the Song of Songs into the vernacular.[111] The first chapter of *Meditations* stresses how difficult it was for women to understand Scripture, in particular this book. She makes it clear that she is not offering an interpretation of the verses but some insights from her experience: 'It matters little if what I say is not what the passage says, provided [...] we benefit from the thoughts' (*Meditaciones* 2.16) [poco va que no sea a este proposito (...) si de ello nos aprovechamos].[112]

It is interesting to compare Teresa's use of Scripture with that of John of the Cross. John quotes extensively, sometimes in Latin, with a translation, and sometimes in Spanish. The scriptural index given by Kavanaugh and Rodríguez shows a wide coverage of both Old and New Testaments, although, unsurprisingly, the books most used are the Psalms, Song of Songs, and the Gospels of Matthew, Luke, and John.[113]

Books Read by Teresa of Ávila

Knowledge of books Teresa read may be based on her mentioning them in her writings, mainly in the *Life*.[114] We also have her list of the 'good books' that she particularly required the prioress of each of her reformed convents to have available for the sisters.[115] This list appears in the early versions of her constitutions for houses she founded, showing the importance she placed on reading such books.[116]

Chivalry novels

Although Teresa later viewed her reading of these popular novels about the adventures of knights and noble ladies as detrimental, it is clear that, following her mother's example, she was addicted to these in her early adolescence.[117] One of the best-known novels in Spanish was *Amadís de Gaula*, frequently mentioned as a model by Don Quixote in the famous novel satirizing these chivalric stories by Cervantes.

While these works were unlikely to have been a conscious influence on Teresa, apart from contributing to her view of her teenage self as frivolous and far from God, they could well have had an unconscious influence.[118] Although Etchegoyen warns against exaggerating the influence of such works, he points out a number of aspects of Teresa's writings which could have been influenced by reading chivalry novels, including her approach to the love of God which has elements of the concept of 'courtly love'.[119] García de la Concha also finds some chivalric influences on Teresa's writings.[120]

Lives of the Saints

Teresa tells us that some of her earliest reading was lives of the saints, which she read with the brother closest to her in age, Rodrigo de Cepeda.[121] Presumably, these were among her father's 'good books' in Spanish for his children to read (*Vida* 1.1).[122]

The lives of saints continued to form part of her reading. She talks in the *Life* of testing her path of walking close to Christ against the lives of contemplative saints, listing Francis of Assisi, Anthony of Padua, St Bernard, and St Catherine of Siena (22.7).[123] The list of 'good books' required in the *Constitutiones* includes the *Flos Sanctorum* [Lives of the saints].[124] There were various works which went under this generic title; the best known is the *Legenda Aurea* or *Golden Legend*, but Teresa was more likely to be referring to a work entitled *Flos Sanctorum* by Pedro de la Vega.[125]

Letters of St Jerome

The first book she specifically mentions as affecting her spiritual life is the *Letters of St Jerome*.[126] She says that it was this book that encouraged her to decide to become a nun and tell her father of this decision.[127] Jerome's letters were first translated into Spanish by Juan de Molina and published in 1520.[128] His second letter, addressed to Theodosius and the rest of the Anchorites living in the Syrian desert, might well have affected her deeply, because it is about Jerome's struggle with a decision to enter the monastic life and his concern for his sins. Jerome's statement that the devil continuously ensnares him and puts obstacles in the path is matched by Teresa's statement, immediately before she refers to reading the *Letters*, that the 'devil was suggesting that I would not be able to suffer the trials of religious life because I was too pampered.'[129] She refers to Jerome's tempting thoughts in the desert, although she takes a kinder approach to such thoughts than Jerome's self-laceration.[130]

Moralia in Job

She also refers to reading the story of Job from Gregory the Great's *Moralia*.[131] Parts of this had been translated from Latin into Castilian in the fourteenth century and compiled into a florilegium, known as *De Flores*, by Pero López de Ayala, of which many manuscript copies were known.[132] A printed edition in two volumes of the whole work translated by Alonso Álvarez was published in 1527. This latter is the most likely source for Teresa's knowledge of this work, as there is a copy of the second volume kept in St Joseph's convent in Ávila.[133]

Confessions of St Augustine

Perhaps the most important classical religious work for Teresa's spiritual development was Augustine's *Confessions*, translated into Spanish by Sebastián Toscano and published in 1554. It seems likely that this is the version to which she is referring.[134] She says that she was given a copy and that 'As I began to read the *Confessions*, it seemed to me that I saw myself in them' (*Vida* 9.7–8) [Como comencé a leer las *Confesiones* paréceme me vía yo allí].[135] She goes on to say that she commended herself to him and found the passage about his conversion on hearing the voice in the garden to speak directly to her.[136] There are certainly similarities between the experience that she describes in Chapter 9 of the *Life* and Augustine's (Book 8, 8–12). Both involve great distress and weeping, leading to a profound change of relationship with God.

The *Life* is certainly in the same genre as the *Confessions*, and has a similar structure: misspent youth (although Teresa's seems to have been considerably less misspent than Augustine's), followed by a turning to God and a religious life, then a transcendental second conversion experience. There are other similarities; for example, Teresa's view that her early addiction to fiction, particularly books of chivalry, was dangerous has echoes of Augustine's complaint that the fiction of the Greek classics that he studied as a boy led him astray spiritually.[137]

Meditations of St Augustine

Teresa quotes St Augustine in *Moradas*, referring to his *'Meditations or Confessions'*.[138] The *Meditations* were first translated into Spanish by Ambrosio de Montesinos under the title *Meditaciones, soliloquios, manual y suspiros*, a translation first published in 1511.[139] The existence of another translation in Teresa's lifetime (made in 1553), and many editions of both, is evidence of the widespread popularity of this work. The *Soliloquies* is a genuine work of Augustine, written about the time he converted to Catholic Christianity after several years following the teachings of the Manichee sect.[140] The *Meditations*, very popular in the Middle Ages, are not by Augustine himself, although they are written in the style of his *Confessions*.[141]

Teresa's writings are often regarded as stylistically spontaneous, if naïve, with frequent cries addressed directly to God. For example, at the beginning of the *Life*, in the middle of talking about her upbringing, she cries: 'Oh my Lord, since it seems You have determined to save me, I beseech Your Majesty that it might be so' [¡Oh, Señor mío!, pues parece tenéis determinado que me salve, plega a vuestra Majestad sea ansí].[142] This style may well have been genuine, but Teresa would have been encouraged to write in this way by her reading of these particular works, the *Confessions* and the *Meditations and Soliloquies*, which are essentially spiritual autobiography in the form of confessions, thanksgiving, and prayers addressed directly to God. Teresa's style has many parallels to Augustine's in these works. She makes no reference to any of Augustine's more theological works, and indeed most of these were not available in Spanish.

Franciscan devotional writings

There can be no question but that a major influence on Teresa was the devotional writings which came out of the Franciscan reform in the early sixteenth century under Cardinal Cisneros.[143] Teresa read Franciscan authors, such as Francisco de Osuna, Bernardino de Laredo, Alonso de Madrid, Antonio de Guevara, and St Peter of Alcántara.

Francisco de Osuna's Third Spiritual Alphabet

It is clear from the *Life* that an important turning point in Teresa's spiritual life was when her uncle gave her a copy of the *Third Spiritual Alphabet* by Francisco de Osuna.[144] Osuna, an Observant Franciscan, lived a life of prayer and contemplation, and wrote several books called spiritual alphabets, given that name because the title of each chapter begins with a letter of the alphabet in turn.[145] The works were intended to teach Christians the 'prayer of recollection', as he called his method of contemplative prayer. They were extremely popular in the first half of the sixteenth century.[146]

As Osuna was writing for lay Christians, he adopted a plain style, avoiding Latinisms and technical theological vocabulary.[147] He mainly uses short sentences without many subordinate clauses. He frequently uses everyday images to explain his points; the heart as a broken pot that has to be glued together before it can hold God,[148] pigs eating acorns while ignoring the source of their meal,[149] the effect of mystical theology on the soul being like boiling a pot of water.[150] He also uses images as extended metaphors; the importance of eyes and the use of spectacles to improve sight when teaching about spiritual blindness,[151] sailing a ship to demonstrate the need to balance caution with openness to the wind of the Holy Spirit.[152] Teresa also makes use of everyday images to illustrate her teaching on prayer, such as watering a garden and the life-cycle of a silkworm.

However, Osuna also has convoluted passages, which are not easy to follow; these are mainly places where he is giving an elaborate, highly allegorical, interpretation of Scripture. For example, in saying that reason and will must work in harmony like brothers, he refers allegorically to David, Jacob and Esau, Abraham and Lot, Saints Peter and Andrew, St Stephen, the parable of the Good Samaritan, and Adam and Eve; as a result, the argument is not easy to follow.[153] In this approach to Scripture he is following the, by then, long-established traditional method of exegesis, the 'four senses of Scripture': literal, allegorical, moral, and analogical, of which the first, though foundational, was less open to more imaginative forms of exegesis.[154] Teresa does not follow his example; she left explanation of Scripture to *letrados*.[155] He is also less clear when dealing with more philosophical topics, for example, as in the Eleventh Treatise which deals with different kinds of memory.[156]

At a time when Teresa could not find a confessor to help her, Osuna's teaching, given in simple language, started her on her spiritual path.[157] She must have been particularly encouraged by his description of spiritual directors and 'learned men' who, from fear, tried to discourage him from the path of contemplative prayer,[158] as this was what she experienced.[159] She went on to use some of his theological terms in her writings. Tyler demonstrates how central to Teresa's teaching on prayer are the themes developed by Osuna in the *Third Spiritual Alphabet*.[160] She would also have been encouraged by Osuna's insistence that those who had received special gifts from God should share them to help others.[161] He comments that 'it is a very foolish and great defect in spiritual people that they think God comes to dwell only in them, when in truth he might have been on his way elsewhere and decided it was worthwhile to visit them for a moment'.[162] This tart comment could equally have come from Teresa's pen.

Despite its importance to Teresa's thinking, the *Third Spiritual Alphabet* is not in the list of books Teresa required to be in her convents.[163] This omission is difficult to explain, as the book was not one banned by the Valdés Index.[164] One possibility is that, as the original constitution was written for her first foundation of St Joseph's and that her other foundations were headed by nuns who knew Teresa well, she would assume that these close companions knew of the importance of Osuna to her and would automatically include a copy of *Third Spiritual Alphabet* in the collection of 'good books'. A contrary possibility is that, as Osuna's teaching on the prayer of recollection could be misunderstood by theologically unsophisticated readers as being heretical *alumbradismo*, Teresa could have been concerned about recommending something to her nuns, of necessity 'unlearned', as it might attract the attention of the Inquisition.[165]

Laredo and The Ascent of Mount Zion

A very popular book in the vernacular in the sixteenth century was *The Ascent of Mount Zion* by Bernardino de Laredo, a Franciscan lay brother who was a physician. It was first published in Seville in 1535.[166]

Teresa first refers to it in the section of the *Life* where she is explaining how beginners in the first stage of prayer can use their intellect to develop devotion, the equivalent of using the well to water the garden. She says it is a 'very good and appropriate book for those who are in this state in which the intellect is at work' (*Vida* 12.2) [que es muy bueno y apropiado para los que están en esto estado, porque obra el entendimiento].[167] Then, when she was trying to explain her experiences in prayer at a crucial time in her spiritual development, she says that this book helped her to understand what she was experiencing.[168] Indeed, to try to explain to her confessors what was happening, she says she marked the relevant passages in this book and gave it to them.[169]

Laredo's style is not as clear as Osuna's. He has a liking for very long sentences with many subordinate clauses, and has some convoluted interpretations of Scripture.[170] However, he does give a definition of mystical theology as:

> [...] a sudden and momentary uplifting of the mind, wherein, by Divine instruction, the soul is raised up suddenly, through pure love, by the affective way alone, to union with its most loving God, without the intervention of any thought, or operation of the intellect, or understanding, or natural reasoning.[171]

> [un súbito y momentáneo levantamiento mental, en el cual el anima por divino enseñamiento es alzada súbitamente a se ayuntar por puro amor, por vía de sola afectiva, a su amantísimo Dios, sin que antevenga medio de algún pensamiento, ni de obra intelectual o del entendimiento, ni de natural razón.]

This definition must have been very helpful to Teresa, as it corresponds to the experiences she describes in the *Life* as the fourth degree of prayer.[172]

Peers says of Laredo that: 'For all his repetitions, the occasional obscurity of his style, the frequency of his digressions [...] he speaks with his own voice and with the quiet authority of experience.'[173] That 'quiet authority' must have been very encouraging to Teresa when she was struggling to explain to her confessors what she was experiencing, and her writings show the same quiet authority, despite the self-depreciatory statements which she probably intended to protect herself from ecclesiastical scrutiny. She was probably also encouraged by his statement that:

> [...] a soul without scholastic learning but versed in mystical theology can more readily understand certain difficulties in Holy Scripture, and more profitably expound them, than a scholastic theologian, however notable he be, if he lack spiritual wisdom.[174]

> [más pronto y mas provechosamente pueda sentir y dar a entender algunas dificultades de la Escritura santa una ánima cebada en mística teología sin saber letra escolástica, que algún teólogo escolástico, cuanto quiera sea notable, si le falta espiritual sabiduría.]

Like *Third Spiritual Alphabet*, this book is not on Teresa's list for her convents, although it was not prohibited by the Valdés Index. Again, the reason for this omission can only be surmised.

Alonso de Madrid

Alonso de Madrid was a Franciscan active in the early sixteenth century. He wrote several books, the best known being *The Art of Serving God* [*Arte para servir a Dios*], first published in Seville in 1521.[175]

In her discussion of the first stage of prayer in the *Life*, Teresa recommends *The Art of Serving God* as 'a very good and appropriate book' [que es muy bueno y apropriado] for those at the stage of prayer when the intellect is still active.[176] She says that this book encourages acts to awaken love for God, resolutions to serve God, and other acts that make the virtues grow.

Antonio de Guevara

One of the books Teresa required to be available for nuns in her reformed houses was *The Oratory of Religious* [*Oratorio de religiosos*] by the Franciscan Antonio de Guevara, published in Valladolid in 1542.[177] It was a very detailed manual of monastic discipline, aspects of which are mirrored in Teresa's writings on rules for her reform, including *Foundations* and *Constitutions*.[178]

St Peter of Alcántara

Peter of Alcántara, an Observant Franciscan, recognized during his lifetime as a holy man and later canonized in 1699, was an important influence on Teresa. For over two years, she had been experiencing visions and having similar experiences in prayer, while being told that these were diabolical in origin and to be resisted at all costs.[179] In Chapter 30 of the *Life*, she tells how Fray Peter visited Ávila and how a friend arranged for her to meet him. When she tried to explain to him what had been happening to her, he immediately understood and told her that, because of his own experiences, he knew that what was happening to her was from God. He also reassured her spiritual advisers, agreeing she could write to him about her experiences.[180] When she was first planning her reform, and receiving considerable opposition to her desire for the houses to be founded in poverty, that is without property and an income, he supported her in this desire for poverty.[181] Indeed, she says that he continued to encourage her, even after his death; when she was under great pressure to accept an income for her first reformed foundation and ready to give in, she had vision of him as she was praying. He looked sternly at her and told her that she should not accept an income, then disappeared.[182]

Given his encouragement of both her prayer life and her reform, it is not surprising that she wanted works by him in her reformed convents.[183] She does not name these works, but there are two works on prayer at that time attributed to him, *Book of prayer* [Libro de la oración] and *Treatise on prayer and meditation* [Tratado de la oración y meditación].[184]

Other Works Teresa Read

In the list of books that Teresa requires the prioress to make available to the sisters, in addition to those discussed above, she includes the translation of the *Life of Christ* [*Vita Christi*] by the Franciscan Ambrosio de Montesinos, written by Ludolph of Saxony, known as 'El Cartujano'. She also includes *The Imitation of Christ*, referring to it as *Contentus* [*Contemptus*] *Mundi*, the title under which it was published in Seville in 1536, and 'good books, in particular those by Fray Luis de Granada' [buenos libros, en especial (...) los de fray Luis de Granada].[185]

The Life of Christ

This extremely popular work was translated into Spanish at the request of Isabella and Ferdinand and first published in 1503 as part of Cardinal Cisneros's reform project.[186] The author, 'the Carthusian', was Ludolph of Saxony who lived in the fourteenth century, originally a Dominican who later became a Carthusian. This book not only had a direct influence upon Ignatius Loyola and the Jesuits, but also influenced the *devotio moderna* movement and the Carmelites.[187]

A lengthy work, it is an extended meditation on the life of Christ, emphasizing the Passion, based on passages from all four Gospels. This work influenced Teresa's writings by providing her with access to Gospel texts in the vernacular. It was not banned by the Inquisition because Gospel texts were accompanied by extensive commentary from orthodox sources, patristic literature. It also provided her with clear information about how to recognize the work of the Holy Spirit in the various stages of mystical prayer.[188]

The Imitation of Christ

This book originated from various spiritual pamphlets by a member of the Brethren of the Common Life, the lay community formed in the Low Countries in the late fourteenth century, from which came the *devotio moderna* movement.[189] There is controversy as to the identity of the author, usually identified as Thomas à Kempis, an Augustinian canon.[190] This was an enormously popular and influential book. There are nearly nine hundred surviving manuscripts and hundreds of printed editions, with many translations. Among those influenced by *The Imitation of Christ* were Ignatius Loyola, Erasmus, and John Calvin.[191] Teresa refers to the book as *Contentus* [*Contemptus*] *Mundi*. It was first translated into Spanish in 1491.[192]

Luis de Granada

Luis de Granada was a Dominican who shared similar spiritual concerns to his contemporary Franciscan authors. His best-known work was *Of Prayer and Meditation* [Libro de la oración y meditación], first published in 1554.[193] His other works include *The Sinners' Guide* [Guía de pecadores] and *Manual of Diverse Prayers* [Manual de diversas oraciones].[194] All of them were banned by the 1559 Index, but Granada appealed to the Council of Trent and was allowed to republish the books with some modifications.[195] These are likely to be the works Teresa mentions in *Constitutions*.

The Reader Shapes the Writer

A compelling and attractive characteristic of Teresa of Ávila's writings is the use of common, practical images and extended metaphors to illustrate her teachings. One of the reasons why she is still read and relevant today is that she explains her experience of prayer, by definition almost inexplicable, in images that, even five hundred years later, prove attractive — in particular, watering a garden and the life cycle of a butterfly.

As discussed above, both Osuna and Laredo also use images and extended metaphors. However, many of their images no longer speak to us. For example, Osuna uses royal visits to hunting lodges[196] and baptizing a two-headed man.[197] Laredo has an extended passage about eagles teaching their chicks to fly and making them look directly at the sun (believed at the time, but not true, as this would blind the chicks).[198] Teresa, perhaps because she did not have an academic education, sticks to everyday images, still relevant. So, even though her reading of the Franciscans must have encouraged her to use images to teach about prayer, she had her own distinct style and approach. Although she uses simple images, these are not always used simply. The outstanding example is the castle in *Moradas*. This is not a real building with a set number of rooms leading off each other, but an almost four-dimensional space with innumerable rooms.[199]

While her adult spiritual reading affected her writing, there must also be a suspicion that those chivalric tales that she had eagerly absorbed in the past played a role in her use of imagery, even if the actual images (the butterfly, watering a garden) were not found in those books. As the subject of this essay is writing style rather than content, I will not deal in detail with the arguments and extensive commentary on where Teresa found the image of a castle as a metaphor for the soul. Living in a country full of castles, which she must have seen wherever she travelled in making her reforms must be at least part of the explanation and more influential than the chivalric romances she read in her youth. As discussed above, how she wrote about her love relationship with Christ was doubtless influenced by the emphasis on courtly love in these romances.[200]

Teresa of Ávila's simple language and informal style may have been at least in part inspired by the similar language and styles of Osuna and Laredo (and, perhaps, also her recourse to frequent digressions). While this may have been her instinctive approach to writing, given her education and character, she would have been encouraged to use this natural style by her reading of these established, educated male authors.

Given the parallels discussed above, it seems very likely that the structure of the *Life*, in which St Teresa gives us an extensive account of her spiritual development, is based on, or at least strongly influenced by, Augustine's *Confessions*. Similarly, the structure of the *Meditaciones*, spiritual thoughts inspired by the Song of Songs rather than an exegesis of these verses, is the approach to Scripture of much of her reading, from Gregory the Great's *Moralia* to Ludolph of Saxony's *Life of Christ*.

Before concluding on the effect Teresa's reading and access to book might have had on her writing style, it is instructive to briefly outline a similar analysis of the works of another Spanish nun, Teresa de Cartagena.

Teresa de Cartagena

Teresa de Cartagena lived in the fifteenth century, approximately a century before her more famous namesake. She was born in about 1425. She was a nun for all her adult life, first as a Poor Clare in Burgos where her prominent *converso* family was based and then, having obtained papal permission in 1449 to move from the Franciscans, she became a Cistercian in the convent of Las Huelgas, also in Burgos, a royal foundation. She did not have good health, and became deaf as a result of illness, most probably in her late twenties. Some twenty years later she wrote *Grove of the Infirm* [Arboleda de los enfermos] which told of her sufferings and the spiritual lessons she had learned from them. Later, when she had been criticized for having the temerity to write a book circulated beyond her own convent, she wrote a work called *Admiration of the Works of God* [Admiraçión operum Dey], defending her authorial authority.[201]

The works of the two Teresas show a marked difference in style. Teresa de Cartagena writes in a much more 'masculine' style, showing clear use of rhetorical methods and logical argument based on traditional 'authorities', namely Scripture and the Fathers of the Church. Apart from the opening of *Arboleda*, when she talks of the loneliness her deafness engendered, there is very little autobiographical or affective writing. There is no mention of any 'mystical' spiritual experience. Can Teresa de Cartagena's writing style be connected to what she read?

Like Santa Teresa, Teresa de Cartagena depended on books for her spiritual development. In describing her suffering caused by her deafness at the beginning of her first book, *Grove*, says that:

> And since my suffering is of such treacherous nature that it prevents me from hearing good as well as bad counsel, it is necessary that my consoling counsels be able to bring me to the cloister of their gracious and holy wisdom without shouting into my deaf ears: for this, I must recur to my books which have wondrous graftings from healthful groves.[202]

> [E porque mi pasyónes de tal calidat e tan porfiosa que tan poco me dexa oýr los buenos consejos como los malos, conviene sean tales los consejos consoladores que syn dar bozes a mi sorda oreja, me pued[a]n poner en la claustra de sus graçiosos e santos consejos; para lo qual es neçesario de recorrer a los libros, los quales de arboledas saludables tienen en sý marauillos enxertos.]

It is clear from Teresa de Cartagena's writings that she could read and write Spanish. Further, her extensive use of and quotations from the Bible and the Church Fathers gives a strong indication that she could read Latin. All of this would indicate that she was well educated, perhaps unusually so for a late-medieval Spanish woman.

This education very likely came from her family. The fact that amongst its male members there were some of fifteenth-century Spain's leading authors and intellectuals means that it is possible, indeed likely, that she would have received a good education, even before entering the convent. There is circumstantial evidence that she may have had access to the extensive library of her great uncle, the famous chronicler, Alvar García de Santa María.[203] Teresa's grandfather, Pablo de Santa María, and her uncle, Alonso de Cartagena, also had considerable libraries. She also makes an intriguing reference to 'the few years that I was at the University of Salamanca'.[204] This reference, close to the end of *Grove*, is a statement of authorial humility, clearly set in the context of claiming to be educated. This does raise a question as to what Teresa was doing at the University of Salamanca, because in none of the universities of Europe could women officially enrol as students until many years later, although there is some evidence that women, generally those in religious orders, were sometimes permitted to attend lectures. Another question is what she would have studied at Salamanca. The main field of study at Salamanca in her time was law, and traditional arts subjects. As law and theology were advanced courses, it is unlikely that Teresa studied them. Probably, she took the introductory courses of grammar, logic, and rhetoric.

Unlike Teresa of Ávila, Teresa de Cartagena, as she wrote, could have had access to part, at least, of the Bible in Spanish. She seems to have been able to read the Scriptures in Latin, since her quotations are widely taken from both Old and New Testaments, whereas available Spanish translations were mainly limited to the New Testament and Psalms. Further, comparison of her biblical quotations in Spanish with the Vulgate show that they are, mostly, accurate. She employs biblical quotations extensively, deliberately, and purposefully, often to provide authority for a statement or proposition. She does not, in general, specify the book of the Bible she is quoting but that was general practice at the time. Highly educated male writers, fluent in Latin, used similarly vague references.[205]

Teresa de Cartagena does not give any indication of the titles of the books mentioned at the beginning of her *Grove*.[206] However, a study of the sources used in her two books shows that these are mainly the writings of patristic theologians. Teresa most frequently quotes from Augustine (seven references), Gregory the Great (four references), Jerome (two authentic references plus one attributed in her time to Jerome but now regarded as non-authentic), and Ambrose (one).[207] She also quotes once from Boethius and once from Bernard of Clairvaux, and from the Missal.

It is interesting to note which works by the above patristic authors she quotes. In the case of Augustine, she quotes from only a small number of his numerous works. For example, she makes no reference to his most popular work, the *Confessions*, although *Grove* belongs to the same genus of works, the history of salvation of an individual. All the quotations from Gregory the Great are taken from his homilies on the Gospels.[208] Again, it is surprising that she makes no mention of Gregory's best-known work, the *Moralia in Job*, although she includes an extensive discussion of Job in her *Grove*. A detailed analysis of this discussion shows that she may have been familiar with the *Moralia* but she has clearly not just copied Gregory's exegesis but interprets the cited verses to fit with her overall theme.

In contrast to Teresa of Ávila's early reading habits, it is likely that Teresa de Cartagena was raised on more serious literature, as evidenced by the contents of her great-uncle Alvar García de Santa María's library. She was unlikely in any event to have had access to the same type of chivalric fiction. The rise of the novel coincided with the advent of printing, making such works economically viable to produce. However, printed books only became widely available in Spain after the time she was writing.

Teresa de Cartagena's writings must have been influenced by the formal, academic style of many of the works she references, mainly written by theologians. Her education at Salamanca, if it included the standard courses on grammar and rhetoric, could also be, at least in part, an explanation of her apparently masculine writing style. Certainly, the access she had to very different sources from those of Teresa of Ávila would seem to provide a partial explanation of their very different styles of writing.

Conclusion

From an analysis of what we know Teresa of Ávila read, and by comparing this to the known sources used by Teresa de Cartagena, there are grounds for saying that what Teresa of Ávila read affected the way she wrote. However, this is far from being a full explanation. Teresa of Ávila brought considerable creativity to her writing, and was not merely imitating what she had read. Further, the two Teresas led different lives and had very different experiences, which clearly resulted in differences in the content and style of their writings. Above all, Teresa of Ávila brought to her writings her unique personality, which still shines through five hundred years later.

Notes to Chapter 11

1. All English translations of Teresa of Ávila's works are from *The Collected Works of St Teresa of Ávila*, ed. and trans. by Kieran Kavanaugh and Otilio Rodriguez, 3 vols (Washington, DC: Institute of Carmelite Studies, 1976–85). Spanish quotations and page references in this chapter are from the following editions: Teresa de Jesús, *Libro de la vida* (*Vida*), ed. by Dámaso Chicharro, 16th edn, Letras Hispánicas, 98 (Madrid: Cátedra, 2011); *Las moradas del castillo interior*, ed. by Dámaso Chicharro (Madrid: Biblioteca Nueva, 2015); all others are from *Obras completas: edición manual*, ed. by Efrén de la Madre de Dios and Otger Steggink, Biblioteca de Autores Cristianos, 212 (Madrid: La Editorial Católica, 1967).
2. Alison Weber, *Teresa of Ávila and the Rhetoric of Femininity* (Princeton, NJ: Princeton University Press, 1990).
3. The most outspoken is in *Camino* 3.7, p. 205, n. 1. These words were in the first redaction, but deleted by García de Toledo, and omitted by Teresa from the second redaction; see *The Complete Works*, ed. by Kavanaugh and Rodríguez, II, 459.
4. *Vida*, p. 137.
5. *Vida*, p. 123.
6. *Vida*, p. 123.
7. *The Complete Works*, ed. and trans. by Kavanaugh and Rodriguez, I, 17–18.

8. José Jiménez Delgado, 'Las citas latinas de santa Teresa', in *Revista Helmántica*, 24 (1983), 339–49.
9. Victor García de la Concha, *El arte literario de Santa Teresa* (Barcelona: Ariel, 1978), p. 17.
10. R. P. L. Serrano, *Los conversos D. Pablo de Santa María y D. Alfonso de Cartagena* (Madrid: Instituto Arias Montano, 1942), p. 459; Alonso de Cartagena, *Libro de los oficios. Texto y concordancias del 'De officiis' de Cicerón: traducción castellana por Alonso de Cartagena. MS 7815, Biblioteca Nacional de Madrid*, ed. by María Morrás (Madison, WI: HSMS, 1989).
11. Serrano, *Los conversos*, pp. 199–200. These are probably the two translations listed by Julian Weiss in 'Vernacular Commentaries and Glosses in Late Medieval Castile, II: A Checklist of Classical Texts in Translation', in *Medieval Hispanic Studies in Memory of Alan Deyermond*, ed. by Andrew M. Beresford, Louise M. Haywood, and Julian Weiss, Colección Támesis Série A: Monografías, 315 (Woodbridge: Boydell & Brewer, 2013), pp. 237–71 (pp. 244–45).
12. García de la Concha (p. 17) believes that the Cicero listed here was the Alonso de Cartagena translation, and for the Boethius he refers to a translation made from the Catalan version by Pere Saplana. See Weiss, 'Vernacular', p. 244.
13. We do not have any information about the education of Teresa's father or whether he could read Latin. Teresa tells us that his brother, her uncle Don Pedro, liked reading spiritual books in the vernacular [buenos libros de romance] (*Vida* 3.4, p. 131), which suggests he was not familiar with Latin.
14. *Vida*, pp. 130–31.
15. *Vida*, p. 131.
16. *Vida* 3.7, p. 132.
17. *Vida* 4.7, p. 137.
18. J. N. Hillgarth, *The Spanish Kingdoms, 1250–1516* (Oxford: Clarendon Press, 1978), II: *1410–1516, Castilian Hegemony*, pp. 400–10.
19. Peter Tyler, *Teresa of Ávila: Doctor of the Soul* (London: Bloomsbury, 2013), p. 40, n. 16.
20. Gillian T. W. Ahlgren, *Teresa of Avila and the Politics of Sanctity* (Ithaca, NY: Cornell University Press, 1996), pp. 9–13.
21. Elena Carrera, *Teresa of Avila's Autobiography: Authority, Power, and Self in Mid-Sixteenth-Century Spain* (London: Legenda, 2005), p. 84. On the Inquisition, see John Edwards, *Inquisition* (Stroud: Tempus, 1999), pp. 121–24. Teresa was suspected by the Inquisition of heresy akin to that of the *alumbrados*; Enrique Llamas Martínez, *Santa Teresa de Jesús y la Inquisición española* (Madrid: CSIC, 1971), p. 3.
22. Román Llamas, *Biblia en Santa Teresa* (Madrid: Editorial de Espiritualidad, 2007), p. 30.
23. Carrera, *Teresa of Avila's Autobiography*, pp. 80–81.
24. Llamas, *Biblia*, p. 21.
25. Llamas, *Biblia*, pp. 21–22.
26. This was first published five years after the date of the inventory of Teresa's father's books, mentioned above. It seems inconceivable that he did not continue buying books during his second marriage, particularly as Teresa tells us in the second sentence of the *Vida* that he 'was fond of reading good books' (*Vida* 1.1) [muy aficionado a leer buenos libros], as noted earlier.
27. Similar categories were identified by Alan Deyermond in relation to the works of Encina; 'la presencia de citas textuales, tanto en latín como en castellano; las alusiones no explícitas; la influencia bíblica en el estilo; los exempla bíblicos; los breves resúmenes de la narrativa bíblica y la escenificación de dicha narrative [...]'. See his 'La Biblia en la poesía de Juan del Encina', in *Poética figural: usos de la Biblia en la literatura medieval española* (Salamanca and Oxford: Sociedad de Estudios Medievales y Renacentistas, 2015), pp. 155–73 (p. 156).
28. *Vida* 5.8, p. 146. There were a number of translations of the *Moralia* into Spanish, of which the first was probably that made in the fourteenth century by Pero López de Ayala as *Flores de los Morales de Job*. A translation by Alfonso Álvarez de Toledo was published in 1527; see Richard P. Kinkade, and John A. Zahner, 'Pero López de Ayala's Translation of the *Magna moralia*', in *Homenaje a Don Agapito Rey: trabajos publicados en su honor*, ed. by Josep Roca-Pons (Bloomington: Indiana University, 1980), pp. 131–48 (pp. 145–46).
29. *Vida* 20.10, p. 267 (this is Psalm 101 in the Vulgate); *Vida* 27.18, p. 333 (Psalm 121 in the Vulgate).

For Psalm 102.8, Teresa gives '*vigilavi ed fatus sun sicud passer solitarius yn tecto*', instead of '*Vigilavi, et factus sum sicut passer solitarius in tecto*'; for Psalm 122.1, her version is '*letatum sun yn is que dita sun miqui*', instead of '*Laetatus sum in his quae dicta sunt mihi*'. Kavanaugh and Rodriguez comment on her knowledge of Latin in *The Complete Works*, I, 476, n. 8; 481, n. 16).

30. Jiménez Delgado, 'Las citas latinas', pp. 34–36.
31. *Vida* 39.25, p. 469. *The Complete Works*, ed. by Kavanaugh and Rodríguez, I, 490, n. 21. Chicharro gives this quotation as '*Quicunque vul*'. *Vida*, ed. by Chicharro, p. 469.
32. John 4.14 (*Camino* 19.2, p. 252); Matthew 17.4 (*Camino* 31.3, p. 291); Luke 2.15 (*Camino* 42.1, p. 239).
33. Ephesians 3.15 (*Camino* 27.4, p. 278); Philippians 4.13 (*Camino* 42.2, p. 329).
34. I Peter 1.8–19 (*Camino* 4.8, p. 209); II Peter 1.4 (*Camino* 27.2, p. 277).
35. I John 1.10 (*Camino* 42.2, pp. 329–30).
36. Proverbs 1.20 (*Camino* 20.2, p. 258).
37. The escape from Egypt (*Camino* 10.4, p. 226) and the provision of manna (*Camino* 34.2, p. 304).
38. The Song of Songs was evidently an important book for Teresa, as she wrote specifically on it in *Meditaciones*. Bernard of Clairvaux, the founder of the Cistercian Order, left eighty-six written sermons on this book. Pauline Matarasso (ed.), *The Cistercian World: Monastic Writings of the Twelfth Century* (London: Penguin Books, 1993), p. 65.
39. *Moradas* 1.1.1, p. 211.
40. *Moradas* 1.1.4, p. 252.
41. *Moradas* 3.1.1, p. 249: '¿qué les diremos sino bienavanturado el varón que tema el Señor?'
42. *Moradas* 4.1.5; 2.5, pp. 272, 281.
43. Song of Songs 8.12 (*Moradas* 4.1.12, p. 276); Song of Songs 2.4 and 3.2 (*Moradas* 5.1.12, pp. 307–08); Song of Songs 2.4 (*Moradas* 5.2.12, p. 314); Song of Songs 3.2 (*Moradas* 6.4.10, p. 365 and 7.9, p. 389); Song of Songs 1.2 (*Moradas* 7.1.2, p. 428).
44. Genesis 19.26 (*Moradas* 1.1.6, p. 217).
45. Jonah 4.67 (*Moradas* 5.3.6, p. 320); Jonah 4.1–3 (*Moradas* 6.3.9, p. 355).
46. Genesis 28.12 (*Moradas* 6.4.6, p. 362).
47. Exodus 3.1–6 (*Moradas* 6.4.7, p. 362–63).
48. I Kings 18.30–39 (*Moradas* 6.7.8, p. 389). Teresa refers to him as 'our Father Elijah' [nuestro padre Elías, p. 389], referring to the belief at the time that the Carmelite Order was founded by Elijah. For a fuller treatment of Elijah in the Carmelite tradition, see the essay by Patrick Mullins in this volume.
49. *Moradas* 1.1.3, p. 215; 6, 9.10, p. 406; 7.1.5, p. 430; 3.9, p. 446; 4.5, p. 452.
50. *Moradas* 1.1.3, p. 215; 6.7.4, pp. 386–87; 11.12, p. 424; 7.2.7, p. 439.
51. *Moradas* 3.1.8, p. 254; 6.7.4, pp. 386–87; 7.4.5, p. 453 — the last is not from the Bible but is the apocryphal story of Peter fleeing from prison and impending death in Rome and meeting Christ on the way.
52. *Moradas* 7.1.10, p. 432; 4.12–13, pp. 456–57.
53. II Corinthians 11.14 (*Moradas* 1.2.15, 5.1.1), pp. 231, 303; Philippians 4.13 (*Moradas* 4.3.9, p. 294); Colossians 3.3–4 (*Moradas* 5.2.4, p. 231); I John 4.20 (*Moradas* 5.3.8, p. 320–21); I Corinthians 10.13 (*Moradas* 6.1.6, 3.17, pp. 339); II Corinthians 12.2–4 (*Moradas* 6.5.8, p. 373); I Corinthians 6.17 (*Moradas* 7.2.5, p. 437); I Thessalonians 2.9 (*Moradas* 7.4.5, pp. 452–53). On II Corinthians 11.14, see Chicharro pp. 231, n. 44; 303, n. 15.
54. *Moradas* 7.2.5, p. 438: '*miqi bibere cristus est, mori lucrum*'; *The Complete Works*, ed. and trans. by Kavanaugh and Rodriguez, II, 497, n. 10.
55. *Moradas* 3.1.8, p. 255. The reference is to Luke 17.10, and Gracián, correcting the manuscript, crossed these words out and instead referred to Luke, with the details in the margin, *Moradas*, ed. by Chicharro, p. 255, n. 26.
56. Philippians 2.8 (*Fundaciones* 5.3, p. 527); Matthew 25.40 (*Fundaciones* 5.3, p. 527); Luke 10.16 (*Fundaciones* 5.12, p. 529).
57. *Fundaciones* 20.12, p. 572; 28.5, p. 599.
58. I Kings 18.38 (*Fundaciones* 5.12, p. 529); I Kings 19.2–5 (*Fundaciones* 27.17, p. 596); I Kings 19.9–13 (*Fundaciones* 28.20, p. 602).

59. II Samuel 6.3–5, 14–15 (*Fundaciones* 27.20, p. 597).
60. I Samuel 15.22 (*Fundaciones* 6.22, p. 535).
61. Matthew 26.31–35, 67–75 (*Fundaciones* 5.12, p. 259). *Fundaciones* 22.7, p. 576; 29.24, p. 611.
62. Acts 20.24 (*Constituciones* 9, p. 633); John 15.12, 17 (*Constituciones* 28, p. 638).
63. Song of Songs 4.16 (*Cuentas* 20, p. 464; 39, p. 468). The numbering of the *Spiritual Testimonies* is that used by Kavanaugh and Rodriguez.
64. Luke 1.47 (*Cuentas* 25, p. 483; 56, p. 472).
65. Psalm 147.14 (*Cuentas* 36.4, p. 466).
66. Matthew 16.16 (*Cuentas* 49, p. 470).
67. Job 16.1 (*Cuentas* 6, p. 459).
68. Exodus 14.5–31 (*Cuentas* 33, p. 465).
69. Matthew 11.28 (*Exclamaciones* 8.2, p. 491); John 7.7 (*Exclamaciones* 9.1, p. 492).
70. Song of Songs 2.16 (twice) (*Exclamaciones* 16.2, 3, p. 497); Song of Songs 8.6 (*Exclamaciones* 17.3, p. 498).
71. Psalm 18.5 (*Exclamaciones* 10.1, p. 492).
72. Luke 10.38–42 (*Exclamaciones* 5.2, p. 489).
73. John 9 (*Exclamaciones* 8.2–3, p. 491).
74. John 7.37 (*Exclamaciones* 9, p. 492).
75. Kavanaugh, in his introduction to the poems, points out that probably a majority of her poems have not been preserved, from the evidence of those close to Teresa. See *The Complete Works*, ed. and trans. by Kavanaugh and Rodriguez, III, 372–73. See also Enrique Llamas Martínez, 'Poesías', in *Introducción a la lectura de Santa Teresa* (Madrid: Editorial de Espiritualidad, 2002), pp. 607–10.
76. *The Complete Works*, ed. and trans. by Kavanaugh and Rodriguez, III, 379–80; *Obras completas*, ed. by Madre de Dios and Steggink, p. 499.
77. Song of Songs 2.16.
78. *The Complete Works*, ed. and trans. by Kavanaugh and Rodriguez, III, 377–79, *Obras completas*, ed. by Madre de Dios & Steggink, pp. 501–02.
79. Matthew 25.1–13. 'Al velo de la hermana Isabel de los Ángeles'. *The Complete Works*, ed. by Kavanaugh & Rodriguez III, 401–02; *Obras completas*, ed. by Madre de Dios and Steggink, pp. 507–08.
80. *Meditaciones* 6.11, p. 357.
81. Romans 8.18 (*Meditaciones* 4.7, p. 350).
82. Matthew 26.36–41 (*Meditaciones* 3.10, 11, p. 347).
83. Luke 1.34–35 (*Meditaciones* 5.2, p. 352; 6.7, p. 356).
84. Matthew 25.1–13 (*Meditaciones* 2.5, p. 338).
85. Matthew 14.27–31 (*Meditaciones* 2.29, p. 343).
86. See Gregorio de Olmo Lete, 'La Biblia en la literatura spiritual del Siglo de Oro', in *La Biblia en la literatura Española*, II: *Siglo de Oro*, ed. by Rosa Navarro Durán (Madrid: Editorial Trotta, 2008), pp. 101–79 (p. 104). Olmo Lete, in his study of the Bible in spiritual literature of the Golden Age, finds that the preponderance of influences are the Psalms, prophetic books, Wisdom literature, the Gospels, and the Epistles.
87. Román Llamas is of the same opinion; see *Biblia*, pp. 31, 33.
88. John 4.1–42; *Vida* 30.19, p. 364.
89. John 4.15; *Vida*, p. 364.
90. *Camino* 19.2, p. 252; 21.2, p. 260; 23.5, p. 269; 32.9, p. 298; *Meditaciones* 7.6, p. 360; *Moradas* 6.11.5, p. 420. Chicharro comments on this allusion, linking it to the repeated references to 'agua viva' [living water], throughout Teresa's writing; *Moradas*, ed. by Chicharro, pp. 419–20, n. 20.
91. John 5.5 (*Moradas* 1.1.8, p. 218). At n. 29 in *Moradas*, Chicharro notes how Gracián corrected the error, adding 'y ocho' [thirty-eight] in the margin.
92. *Moradas* 2.1.6, p. 241: 'cuando iban a la batalla, no me acuerdo con quien'. Chicharro notes how Gracián added in the margin 'Con Gedeón en los Jueces, cap. 7'; *Moradas*, ed. by Chicharro, p. 241, n. 21.
93. *Moradas*, p. 430. Chicharro comments on this verse in *Moradas*, ed. by Chicharro, p. 430, n. 12.
94. Llamas, *Biblia*, pp. 36–39; *Vida* 26.5, pp. 322–23.

95. *Vida*, p. 301. Chicharro considers that this reference is to 1 Cor. 10.13: 'God is faithful; he will not let you be tempted beyond what you can bear'; *Vida*, ed. by Chicharro, p. 301, n. 21.
96. *The Complete Works*, ed. and trans. by Kavanaugh and Rodriguez, II, 208.
97. *Constitutiones* 8, p. 632.
98. In the *Life*, these are Psalm 119.137 (*Vida* 19.9, p. 258), Psalm 102.8 (*Vida* 20.10, p. 267), Psalm 122.1 (*Vida* 27.18, p. 333), Psalm 42.2 (*Vida* 29.11, p. 352); in *Spiritual Testimonies*, Psalm 147.14 (*Cuentas* 36.4), p. 466; in *Interior Castle* Psalm 112.1 (*Moradas* 3.1.4, p. 272), Psalm 119.32 (*Moradas* 4.1.5 and 2.5, pp. 307–08, 314).
99. *Moradas*, p. 272.
100. *Vida* 39.25, p. 469. However, Teresa thinks this was from one of the psalms.
101. *Cuentas* 25.1, p. 483; 56, p. 472.
102. Song of Songs 4.6 (*Cuentas* 20, p. 464); Song of Songs 5.1 (*Cuentas* 39:2, p. 468); in *Fundaciones* 5.3, p. 527, citing Philippians 2.8.
103. *Meditaciones* 6.8, p. 356.
104. *Vida* 30.19, p. 364; John 4.15.
105. *Vida* 8.12, p. 176.
106. *Cuentas* 58.3, 4, 6, 8, 12, pp. 473–75.
107. *Meditaciones* 1.2, 8, pp. 334–36. This was not always a satisfactory experience. She complains that such men 'want to be so rational about things and so precise in their understanding that it doesn't seem anyone else but they with their learning can understand the grandeurs of God' [que quieren llevar las cosas por tanta razón y tan medidas por sus entendimentos, que no parece sino que han ellos con sus letras de comprender todas las grandezas de Dios] (*Meditaciones* 6.7, p. 356).
108. *Vida*, p. 243.
109. *Vida*, p. 344. She makes this reference in connection with the statement 'these two lovers gaze directly at each other'. This is not a direct quotation from the Song of Songs but may derive from 4.9 and 7.6. She makes a similar reference in *Meditaciones* 4.8, p. 350, although she does not give a source: 'I look at my Beloved and my Beloved at me'.
110. Teresa probably wrote *Meditations* sometime between 1566 and 1575. See *The Complete Works*, ed. by Kavanaugh and Rodríguez, II, 213.
111. Luis de León, *The Names of Christ*, trans. by Manuel Durán and William Kluback (London: SPCK, 1984), pp. 4–5.
112. *Meditaciones*, p. 343.
113. *The Collected Works of St John of the Cross*, trans. by Kieran Kavanaugh and Otilio Rodriguez (Washington, DC: Institute of Carmelite Studies, 1994), pp. 806–14.
114. Carmen Conde argues that Teresa must have been influenced by the writings of Ramon Llull, in particular *Arte amativa* and *Libro del amigo y del amado*, but admits there is no direct evidence that she knew of Llull's writings; Conde, 'La escritura de santa Teresa y su amor a los libros', *Boletín del Museo e Instituto 'Camón Aznar': obra social de la Caja de Ahorros de Zaragoza, Aragón y Rioja*, 10 (1983), 5–14.
115. *Constituciones* 8, p. 632.
116. The history of these constitutions is given by Kavanaugh and Rodriguez in their edition of *The Complete Works*, III, 311–14.
117. *Vida* 2.1, pp. 123–24.
118. *Vida* 2.1–2, pp. 123–25.
119. Gaston Etchegoyen, *L'Amour divin* (Bordeaux: Bibliothèque de l'École des Hautes Études Hispaniques, 1923), pp. 44–46.
120. García de la Concha, *El arte literario*, pp. 50–52.
121. *Vida* 1.4, p. 121. The name of the brother, whom Teresa does not identify, was given in a note by Father Gracián. See *The Complete Works*, ed. by Kavanaugh and Rodriguez, I, 467, n. 4.
122. *Vida* 1.1, p. 119.
123. *Vida*, p. 287.
124. *Constituciones* 8, p. 632.
125. García de la Concha, *El arte literario*, pp. 52–54. The reason includes the presence of copies of two early printed editions in the Valladolid convent.

126. St Jerome, *Letters*, trans. by W. H. Fremantle, G. Lewis, and W. G. Martley (1893). <http://www.newadvent.org/fathers/3001.htm> [accessed 15 September 2016]; *Epístolas de San Hierónimo traduzidas en lengua castellana por Juan de Molina* (Valencia: Juan Jofre, 1520).
127. *Vida* 3.7, p. 132.
128. St Teresa, *Collected Works*, I, 468.
129. *Vida* 3.6, p. 132: 'Poníame el demonio que no podría sufrir los trabajos de la relisión, por ser tan regalada'.
130. *Vida* 11.10, pp. 195–96; *Letters of Jerome*, 22.7.
131. *Vida* 5.8, p. 146.
132. López de Ayala was a leading statesman, poet, and chronicler. See Joseph F. O'Callaghan, *A History of Medieval Spain* (Ithaca, NY: Cornell University Press, London, 1975), pp. 645–46.
133. Etchegoyen, *L'Amour* , pp. 13–14.
134. Kavanaugh and Rodriguez, *The Complete Works*, I, 471.
135. *Vida* 9.7, pp. 180–81.
136. *Vida* 9.7–9, pp. 180–82.
137. *Vida* 2.1, pp. 123–24; St Augustine, *Confessions*, trans. by J. G. Pilkington (Edinburgh: T. & T. Clark, 1876), I, chapter 13.
138. *Moradas* 6.7.9, p. 390.
139. Llamas, *Biblia*, p. 41, n. 24. St Augustine, *Meditaciones, Soliloquios, Manual, Suspiros*, trans. by Ambrosio Montesino (Mexico: Aguilar, 1977).
140. Mary T. Clark, *Augustine* (London and New York: Continuum, 1994), pp. 6–8.
141. Llamas, *Biblia*, p. 41, n. 24.
142. *Vida* 1.8, p. 122.
143. Kieran Kavanaugh, 'Introduction', in Francisco de Osuna, *The Third Spiritual Alphabet*, trans. by Mary E. Giles (Mahwah, NY: Paulist Press, 1981), pp. 1–4.
144. *Vida* 4.7, pp. 137–38.
145. E. Allison Peers, *Spanish Mysticism: A Preliminary Survey* (London: Methuen, 1924), p. 18, n. 3.
146. Francisco de Osuna, *Tercer Abecedario spiritual: estudio histórico y edición crítica por Melquíades Andrés* (Madrid: Biblioteca de Autores Cristianos, 1972), p. xiii.
147. Kavanaugh, 'Introduction', *The Third Spiritual Alphabet*, p. 30.
148. Osuna, *The Third Spiritual Alphabet*, pp. 51–52 (First Treatise, Chap. II).
149. Osuna, *The Third Spiritual Alphabet*, p. 69 (Second Treatise, Chap. I).
150. Osuna, *The Third Spiritual Alphabet*, p. 163 (Sixth Treatise, Chap. II).
151. Osuna, *The Third Spiritual Alphabet*, pp. 84–86, 97–101 (Second Treatise, Chap. VI, Third Treatise, Chap. I).
152. Osuna, *The Third Spiritual Alphabet*, pp. 139–42 (Fifth Treatise, Chap. II).
153. Osuna, *The Third Spiritual Alphabet*, pp. 61–67 (First Treatise, Chap. V).
154. Henri de Lubac, *Medieval Exegesis, I: The Four Senses of Scripture*, trans. by Mark Sebanc (Grand Rapids, MI: Eerdmans, 1998), pp. 1–3.
155. *Meditaciones* 1.2, p. 334.
156. Osuna, *The Third Spiritual Alphabet*, pp. 292–314.
157. Her first foundation, San José in Ávila, retains a copy of the work, marked in the margins by Teresa herself. See García de la Concha, *El arte literario*, p. 66.
158. Osuna, *The Third Spiritual Alphabet*, pp. 142–45 (Fifth Treatise, Chap. II).
159. *Vida* 5.3, pp. 142–43; 28.4 and 28.17–18, pp. 336–37, 344–45; 29.5–7, pp. 348–50.
160. Tyler, *Teresa*, pp. 48–51.
161. Osuna, *The Third Spiritual Alphabet*, pp. 209–10, 212–17 (Eighth Treatise, Chap. I, Chap. II).
162. Osuna, p. 213 (Eighth Treatise, Chap. II); Osuna, *Tercer Abecedario espiritual*, p. 283: 'Cortedad es muy grande y defecto no pequeño en los varones espirituales pensor que vino Dios para solamente morar con ellos, como de verdad no sea sino un pasar por ellos a otra parte, lo qual quiso El hacer porque le tuvo por bien [...]'.
163. Ahlgren, *Teresa of Ávila*, p. 38, n.18.
164. Kavanaugh, 'Introduction', *The Third Spiritual Alphabet*, p. 8.
165. Carrera, *Teresa of Ávila's Autobiography*, p. 69.

166. E. Allison Peers, 'Introduction', in Bernardino de Laredo, *The Ascent of Mount Sion: Being the Third Book of the Treatise of that Name*, trans. by E. Allison Peers (London: Faber and Faber, 1952), pp. 12–13.
167. *Vida*, p. 201.
168. This is the period described in Chapters 23–29 of the *Vida* when she was regularly having spiritual experiences (visions, locutions), which those advising her regarded as dangerous, even diabolical.
169. *Vida* 23.12, pp. 299–300.
170. A good example of this is Chapter 19 of *The Ascent*, which has an almost incomprehensible interpretation of Psalm 68.13.
171. Laredo, *Ascent of Mount Sion*, p. 100 (Part 3, Chap. 9); Bernardino de Laredo, *Subida del Monte Sión*, in *Místicos franciscanos españoles*, ed. by Los redactores de 'Verdad y vida' (Madrid: Biblioteca de Autores Cristianos, 1968), II, 324–25.
172. *Vida* 18, pp. 246–53.
173. Peers, *Spanish Mysticism*, p. 17.
174. Laredo, *Ascent of Mount Sion*, p. 139 (Part 3, Chap. 20); Laredo, *Subida del Monte Sión*, p. 350.
175. Etchegoyen, *L'Amour*, p. 43. *Arte para servir a Dios* (Palma: En la Emprenta de la Vidua Guasp, 1685).
176. *Vida* 12.2, p. 201.
177. *Constituciones* 8, p. 632. *The Complete Works*, ed. and trans. by Kavanaugh and Rodriguez, III, 445, n. 7; Guevara's *Oratorio* was rendered in English and published in *c.* 1550 in Anvers, *Oratorio de religiosos y exercicio de virtuosos* (Anvers: Martin Nucio, *c.* 1550).
178. Etchegoyen, *L'Amour*, p. 43.
179. *Vida* 29.2–6, pp. 346–49.
180. *Vida* 30.2–7, pp. 354–58.
181. *Vida* 35.3–5, pp. 414–15.
182. *Vida* 36.20–21, p. 431–32.
183. *Constitutiones* 8, p. 632.
184. See García de la Concha, *El arte literario*, p. 64. The latter is now believed to be by Luís de Granada.
185. *The Complete Works*, ed. and trans. by Kavanaugh and Rodriguez, III, 445 n. 7; *Constituciones* 8, p. 632.
186. Carrera, *Teresa of Ávila's Autobiography*, pp. 28–29.
187. Paul Shore, 'The *Vita Christi* of Ludoph of Saxony and its Influence on the *Spiritual Exercises* of Ignatius of Loyola', *Studies in the Spirituality of Jesuits*, 30 (1998) <https://ejournals.bc.edu/ojs/index.php/jesuit/article/viewFile/3970/3534> [accessed 9 September 2015], p. 2.
188. *Vida* 38.9, pp. 448–49.
189. John van Engen, *Sisters and Brothers of the Common Life: The Devotio Moderna and the World of the Late Middle Ages* (Philadelphia: University of Pennsylvania Press, 2008), pp. 1–5, 80–81.
190. Max von Hapsburg, 'Introduction', in Thomas à Kempis, *The Imitation of Christ*, trans. by Robert Jeffery (London: Penguin Books, 2013), pp. 3–4.
191. Engen, *Sisters and Brothers*, pp. 118–20.
192. García de la Concha, *El arte literario*, p. 57 n. 19; *The Complete Works*, ed. and trans. by Kavanaugh and Rodriguez, III, 445, n. 7.
193. Carrera, *Teresa of Ávila's Autobiography*, pp. 32, 41, n. 33; Luis de Granada, *Libro de oración y meditación en la cual se trata de la consideración de los principales misterios de nuestra fe* (Zaragoza: en la oficina de Medardo Heras, n.d.).
194. Luis de Granada, *Manual de diuersas oraciones y spirituales exercicios* (Anvers: Juan Bellero, 1558); *Guía de pecadores*, ed. by Ignacio Arellano (Madrid: Homo Legens, 2012). *The Sinners' Guide* was translated into English in the seventeenth century, *The Sinners' Guide: A Worke Contayning the Whole Regiment of a Christian Life, Devided into Two Books*, trans. by Francis Meres (London: Richard Field in St Paule's Church-yard at the Sign of the Beare, 1614).
195. Carrera, *Teresa of Ávila's Autobiography*, pp. 80–81.
196. Osuna, *The Third Spiritual Alphabet*, p. 124.

197. Osuna, *The Third Spiritual Alphabet*, pp. 115–16
198. Laredo, *Ascent of Mount Sion*, pp. 126–30.
199. As noted above, she refers to her love of novels (*Vida* 2.1), pp. 123–24). It may be to the same novels she mentions in *Moradas* 1.1.3, p. 270.
200. García de la Concha, *El arte literario*, p. 52.
201. Hilary E. Pearson, 'Teresa de Cartagena: a late medieval woman's theological approach to disability' (DPhil, University of Oxford, 2011), <http://ora.ox.ac.uk/objects/uuid:c416992a-09f6-4516-b7cc-59bd88ff4717>, pp. 78–80. All English quotations from Teresa de Cartagena's works are from Dayle Seidenspinner-Núñez, ed. and trans., *The Writings of Teresa de Cartagena* (Cambridge: D. S. Brewer, 1998). Spanish quotations are from Teresa de Cartagena, *Arboleda de los enfermos y Admiraçion Operum Dey*, ed. by Lewis J. Hutton (Madrid: Biblioteca de la Real Academia Española, 1967).
202. Seidenspinner-Núñez, *The Writings*, p. 24; Hutton, p. 38.
203. The inventory of the library of Alvar García de Santa María lists a copy of Boethius in Castilian and Latin which had been borrowed by Teresa's sister and not returned; Francisco Cantera Burgos, *Alvar García de Santa Maria: historia de la judería de Burgos y de sus conversos más egregios* (Madrid: Instituto Arias Montano, 1952), p. 200.
204. Seidenspinner-Núñez, *The Writings*, p. 80; Hutton, ed., *Arboleda*, p. 103: 'y los pocos años que yo estudié en el estudio de Salamanca'. Hutton's reading, p. 103: 23–24. Cantera Burgos, *Alvar García*, p. 539 gives the original as '*estude*', suggesting '*estuve*' [was] and '*estudié*' [studied] as alternative readings. However, the penultimate letter is clearly a 'd' and there is a mark over the final 'e' which seems to indicate an abbreviation (personal observation).
205. For example, her uncle, Alonso de Cartagena, when quoting Scripture in his *Oracional*, uses phrases such as 'as the Apostle said' (St Paul) [commo dixo el Apostol], 'where Our Lord said' [onde dize nuestro Redemptor], 'according to the words of the Prophet' [segund aquella palabra del Profecta que dize], or 'the Prophet says in the Psalm' [el Profeta dize en el Salmo]. See Alonso de Cartagena, *El oracional*, ed. by Silvia González-Quevedo Alonso (Valencia: Albatros, 1983), pp. 52, 61, 75, 115.
206. Seidenspinner-Núñez, *The Writings*, p. 24; Hutton, p. 38.
207. These were main sources of patristic authority for medieval theologians, John W. Baldwin, *The Scholastic Culture of the Middle Ages, 1000–1300* (Lexington, MA: Heath, 1971), p. 82.
208. Gregory the Great, *Forty Gospel Homilies*, trans. by David Hurst (Kalamazoo, MI: Cistercian Publications, 1990).

CHAPTER 12

Seeing and Knowing God

Reinterpreting Vision in the Writing of Teresa of Ávila and Other Cloistered Women Writers

Lesley K. Twomey

This study aims to re-evaluate how St Teresa of Ávila understood vision, using the prism of medieval optics. I examine vision using the context defined by theologians or proto-scientists who developed Neoplatonic ideas about sight. The question for this essay is to determine whether optics, disseminated by the Franciscans, could have influenced those who had never studied it and I select the writings of a number of cloistered women from 1400 to the time of St Teresa in order to show how widely disseminated scientific ideas could have been imbibed by them.[1]

Scholars coincide in asserting that, in the West, there was a tendency to equate knowledge with seeing, fostering 'an intellectual tradition for the eternal over the temporal, being over becoming'.[2] Vision remained the pre-eminent sense up to the time of René Descartes (1596–1650) and Mark A. Smith considers this is why, for historians, observation has continued to be the prime mode of examining the past.[3] Even today, intellectual knowledge continues to be expressed in terms of sight. Words such as perceptive (for someone who discerns knowledge), seeing the point (for grasping an argument), and point of view (for expressing the way an argument is focused) reflect past influence of sight on knowledge.[4] Seeing and the gaze have been the subject of numerous recent studies, as scholars have sought to engage with the range of visual metaphors and their increasing potency after the 1200s.[5] The medieval gaze has been discussed by Michael Camille, who points out how the gaze has often been characterized as a Renaissance invention, despite evidence to the contrary.[6]

Vision is often set in the wider context of the five senses. In the Middle Ages, preoccupation with the senses bordered on the 'obsessive'.[7] Several studies are dedicated to a wider view of the senses, for example, Constance Classen's anthropological approach and C. M. Woolgar's study of medieval senses in an English context offers a chapter for each sense.[8] Suzanne Biernoff combines seeing and feeling,[9] whilst Jeffrey F. Hamburger sets vision in the context of affective piety, examining protocols of vision, vision and devotion, and wounding and vision.[10] Both Pedro Gómez and Peter Dronke examine theological approaches to the five senses.[11] For a now classic study of the spiritual senses, see Karl Rahner, who traces how theologians gradually developed a Christian understanding of the inner, spiritual senses.[12] The senses and how they were understood by Plato and Aristotle (b. 384 BC) are addressed by Simon Kemp and Garth J. O. Fletcher, together with a brief overview of the role they played in the Middle Ages.[13] The impact of vision on piety has been studied by Cynthia Hahn, among others.[14] Caroline Walker Bynum approaches vision from the perspective of medieval material culture.[15]

For medieval theologians, the faculty of seeing was the principal means of coming to *sapientia*, or fullness of knowledge.[16] Aristotle voices the tradition of the pre-eminence of sight, emphasizing how seeing channels knowledge. At the start of his *Metaphysics*, he states: 'All men desire to know. An indication of this is the delight we take in our senses; [...] and above all others the sense of sight'.[17] Accepting that vision was primordial in the Middle Ages does not sit entirely comfortably, however, with thinking about the period as a spoken and aural world.[18] Walter Ong and others believe the influence of the spoken word waned towards the end of the Middle Ages and they associate this with how the written word — a word seen rather than heard — came to prominence with the invention of the printing press, transformation in the University curriculum, and the rise of humanism. St Teresa lived in the aftermath of these momentous changes. The landscape of knowledge experienced by a woman like St Teresa might therefore be a tangible, visible one, very different to the one experienced by women some fifty or sixty years earlier, because of the invention of print. Such thinking reveals a tendency to divide the world into a binary before and after scenario. Smith critiques Ong's premise, for this reason.[19] He, like other scholars, rejects its emphasis on ear as opposed to eye and its focus on the aural or oral, as opposed to print. Some place the rise of visuality much earlier (at the start of the thirteenth century), taking account of the new work on optics in the Universities.[20]

From the early thirteenth century, the science of optics began to spread through the West, mediated by the writings and teachings of the Franciscans, in particular Robert Grosseteste (1175–1253), Roger Bacon (born c. 1210), and John Pecham (c. 1230–1292).[21] Knowledge of optics transferred from Aristotle to the Islamic world and, later, to medieval France and England. Grosseteste, in Oxford, then Bacon, in Paris, further developed its study.[22] Franciscan-led optics has been shown to spread from convent to convent, as friars moved across provinces.[23] More important than these direct influences however, is the pervasive influence of medieval optics, discerned by Stephen G. Nichols in his essay on the *Roman de la Rose*.[24] Scholars have examined how understanding of vision might reveal itself through literary texts, albeit too few.[25]

The approach of women writers to this scientific subject has never been addressed. I compare St Teresa's writing with that of cloistered women from the previous century, Constanza de Castilla (1354–1478), Teresa de Cartagena (born c. 1425), and Isabel de Villena (1430–1490).[26] Medieval theories about vision did not decline until after 1600 and have the possibility of increasing understanding of seeing in St Teresa's works, particularly affecting her treatment of her visions, of the role of the soul in seeing, of the imagination and of darkness, of the connection between light and revelation.[27]

Teresa of Ávila's Visions and the Nature of Seeing

St Teresa's visions have previously drawn critical attention because they are essential to her mystical experience. In a brief study of the *Interior Castle*, Helmut Hatzfeld discusses the different perspectives presented by St Teresa, interpreting them as an example of the mirror technique: 'It is as though at the beginning of the Baroque age, Santa Teresa is attempting something like a mirror technique, something like a theatre within a theatre, a picture within a picture'.[28]

Other scholars discuss how St Teresa's visions can be interpreted in terms of an artist's eye view.[29] It has been noted that St Teresa's account in the *Book of her Life* 'offer the closest [...] parallels between artistic and literary representation of visions' and this brings into focus the question of perspective.[30]

Because St Teresa's *Life* enables insight into the 'world of her experience' and into the communications she receives, they reveal an unseen, heavenly world, offering 'a different kind of "seeing"'.[31] St Teresa, when discussing her visions, seeks to make it clear that seeing can be with the 'eyes of the body', or 'with the imagination', or, finally, in another way, the clearest of all, for it 'comes with greater clarity than either of these, can only be grasped through inadequate comparisons and paradox'.[32]

> I was at prayer on a festival of the glorious Saint Peter, when I saw Christ at my side — or to put it better, I was conscious of him for neither with the eyes of the body nor with those of the soul did I see anything. I thought He was quite close to me and I saw it was He Who, as I thought, was speaking to me. (*Vida* 27.2)[33]
>
> [Estando un día del gloriosa San Pedro en oración, vi cabe mi, u sentí, por mijor decir, que con los ojos del cuerpo ni del alma no vi nada, más pareciome que estaba junto cabe mí Cristo y vía ser Él que me hablaba, a mi parecer.]

The third kind of vision, according to Thompson, is a type of intellectual vision. Although Thompson does not mention it, these types of seeing map onto theories of vision developed in the Middle Ages. The first level of vision, identified by St Teresa as 'with the eyes of the body', is concerned with the physical perception of 'species', which are 'images', 'similitudes', 'phantasms', or 'forms' conveyed to the eye by light.[34] Such images are multiplied along the rays proceeding from all points on the object, enter the eye and are multiplied again. This information is gathered in the 'sensus communis vel sensatio' or common sense. It is then stored in the second of the inner senses, the imagination, which receives the impressions and inscriptions.[35] The common sense is, thus, the bridge between the corporeal and the spiritual senses.[36] This second-level sense 'preserves what the "*sensus communis*" has received from the individual five senses', including the eye.[37] Within the imagination, images are retained, 'even in the absence of the perceived object'.[38]

In depictions of the medieval brain, two linked cells lie above the imagination. The first of these is the 'cogitativa vel formalis', the 'cogitative imagination'. This is the faculty which reflects on the images stored and separates one from another. It also fantasizes.[39] The second is the 'estimativa', or estimative. This function is the highest. It is the 'iudicium intellectuale' [intellectual judgement] that is able to 'perceive the non-sensible intentions', in other words things which are not physically present.[40] The intellectual vision, correlating with Teresa's highest level of seeing, is neither with the eye of the body nor that of the soul. 'Aestimatio' [judgement] has also been interpreted by some medieval theologians as pertaining to faith and this provides an additional insight into the grades of seeing, outlined here by St Teresa. William of Auxerre (1140/50–1231?), for example, accords it the 'highest degree of certitude and confidence' and his idea seems to point the way to St Teresa's view that the inner eye perceives with greater clarity than the eyes of the body, which may be deceived.[41]

Immediately after mentioning the eyes of the body and soul, St Teresa recounts how, at the time, she did not know about the eyes of the soul (*Vida* 27.2).[42] She proclaims herself 'inorantísima', unaware that there was any way of seeing other than with the eyes of the body:

> Being completely ignorant that visions of this kind could occur, I was at first much afraid, and did nothing but weep, though as soon as He addressed a single word to me to reassure me I became quiet again, as I had been before, and was quite happy and free from fear. (*Vida* 27.2)[43]
>
> [Yo, como estaba inorantísima de que podía haber semejante visión, dióme gran temor a el principio, y no hacía sino llorar, aunque, en diciéndome una sola palabra, quedaba como solía, quieta y con regalo y sin ningún temor.]

In this commentary on her vision, St Teresa is at pains to show herself as a simple recipient of visions, unschooled in vision theory, and dependent on God's purpose for her.[44]

Exterior and Interior Vision in St Teresa's *Life*

St Teresa claims she was ignorant of theories of vision. At her first vision of Christ, Teresa even attributes her lack of knowledge to the action of the devil leading her astray: 'It did me great harm not to know it was possible to see something otherwise than with the eyes of the body. It was the devil who encouraged me in this ignorance [...]' (*Vida* 7.7) [Hízome mucho daño no saber yo que era posible ver nada si no era con los ojos de el cuerpo, y el demonio, que me ayudó a que lo creyese ansí y hacerme entender que era imposible].[45]

When St Teresa's recounts what she saw and how she saw it, she distinguishes three superimposed time-frames. The first of these is the time of the vision, when she did not understand the way she saw Christ. Then there is another time-frame, when someone, presumably her confessor, explained to her the nature of seeing in her vision. That commentary by her confessor is likely to have drawn on the doctrine on optics prevalent at the time, because St Teresa mentions she now knows about types of seeing which do not involve the eyes of the body. In the third time-frame, St Teresa finally narrates how she remembers her vision. She reflects, now aware of her previous lack of understanding, upon it from the perspective of having learned about possible modes of seeing.

Is it possible that St Teresa knew nothing about seeing with the eyes of the soul or of the heart, as she declares? This might be questioned for two reasons. First, she demonstrates knowledge of St Augustine's *Confessions* and, there, Augustine gives an account of inner and bodily vision: 'Augustine also tells in the *Confessions* how, after his conversion, his soul *and* his body could rejoice simultaneously in their spiritual pleasure at God's presence as it flooded the five senses, both outer and inner, of his being'.[46] St Augustine was the first theologian to distinguish bodily from interior senses.[47] He assigned to the latter all the powers Aristotle before him assigned to the 'common sense'.[48] In the triple time-frame Teresa establishes she knew nothing about the eyes of the body in the earlier one, emphasizing that this was the case before she read the *Confessions*.[49]

Although St Teresa claims ignorance of interior vision, evidence from other women writers suggests that the concepts of how vision could take place in both corporeal and spiritual form were widespread. Isabel de Villena, writing about Adam's sin, distinguishes two kinds of seeing, one with the eyes of the body, 'ulls corporals' and another with those of the soul, 'ulls de l'ànima'.[50] Villena has Adam confess that sin has caused the eyes of his soul to be clouded and that he is deliberately 'consenting to temptation' [consentint a la tentació]:

> I, Lord, consenting to temptation, closed the eyes of my soul and lost the clear light of wisdom which was given me through you; and you, merciful Lord, ending your life on the cross, closed your eyes in death to recover my sight, bringing me to know and look at you my God and Creator![51]
>
> [Yo, Senyor, consentint a la tentació, tanquí los ulls de la mia ànima e perdí la lum de saviesa molt clar que per vós me era donat; e vós, clement Senyor, finint la vida en la creu haveu per mort los ulls vostres tancats per recobrar a mi la vista, fent-me conéxer e mirar a vós mon Déu e creador!]

Through these words, spoken by Adam, Villena reveals she is aware that the eyes of the soul can be deliberately closed and that sin has an impact in clouding, distorting, or impeding spiritual vision. She also shows that the eyes of the soul bring clearer and better vision than the eyes of the body because they facilitate seeing God.

Teresa de Cartagena shows similar awareness of how spiritual vision is clouded by sinfulness.[52] She refers to her 'eyes of the spirit or understanding' [ojos espirituales], rather than St Teresa's 'eyes of the soul' [ojos del alma].[53] In Teresa de Cartagena's opinion, suffering is capable of dispelling the fog induced by temporal possessions.[54] Suffering enables the eyes to perceive the truth: 'Suffering readies our will for spiritual matters and removes the cloud of vain temporal [possessions] from the eyes of our understanding and makes the light of true knowledge [shine through]' [y avn la dolençia dispone la voluntad a las cosas espirituales e quita delante los ojos espirituales la niebla de los bienes caedizos y vanos y haze trasluzir el rayo del verdadera entendimiento].[55]

Teresa de Cartagena turns to the topic of how the eyes of the soul can be blinded, already discussed in her *Arboleda de los enfermos* (*Arboleda*) [Grove of the Infirm]. Her authoritative approach to theological issues is defended in her *Admiraçión operum Dey* (*Admiraçión*) [Admiration of the Works of God].[56] In the *Arboleda*, she wrote of a barrier to clear vision: possessions. She makes explicit the role of earthly covetousness, with its desire to seek out wrong things, in her *Admiraçión*. Covetousness is a sin dependent on seeing and the very grasping for things of the material world is the 'poluo', or dust, which blinds: 'And if these [intellectual] eyes [of our soul] are obscured by our sins and blinded with the dust of earthly covetousness, we are in darkness and cannot see the road to our country and city of Jerusalem' [E sy estos (ynteletuales del ánima) por nuestros pecados se oscuresçen e çiegan con el poluo de las terrenales cobdiçias, en tinieblas estamos e non podemos ver el camino de la nuestra tierra e çibdad de Iherusalem].[57] In her comment on how bodily sight is clouded so that it cannot perceive the rays of true understanding, she adopts the lexis and theories of optics. She speaks of the 'ojos del ánima' but at the same time refers to them as 'intellectual' [ynteletuales]. Further truth is represented by 'rays'. The clouds, caused by the myriad of vain things, part and the rays of truth pierce or shine through them. Teresa de Cartagena refers to the rays emitted by the object and perceived by the eye. She here follows well-accepted theories of intromission. Both Bacon and, following him, Pecham, thought 'intromitted rays are the immediate cause of vision', and in this brief allusion to seeing, Teresa de Cartagena shows that she knew something about such theories of vision, emitted rays, and the part medieval thinkers believed they played in seeing.[58] Pecham rejects extramission (that the eye issues a ray which falls on the object seen): 'Rays issuing from the eye and falling on the object seen cannot suffice for vision'.[59]

When St Teresa speaks of her vision, she uses 'eyes of the soul' [ojos del alma] to distinguish how she sees Christ. She considers the eyes of the soul are different from the bodily type, because they see 'more clearly': 'I saw Him with the eyes of the soul more clearly than I could ever have seen Him with those of the body (*Vida* 7.6) [vile con los ojos del alma más claramente que le pudiera ver con los del cuerpo].[60]

Grosseteste's view of *oculus mentis* or the mind's eye, however, casts light on the nature of St Teresa's commentary on her experience of seeing Christ:

> I [Grosseteste] therefore say that there is a spiritual light [*lux spiritualis*] that floods over intelligible objects and over the mind's eye [*oculus mentis*] — [this is a light] that is related to the interior eye and to intelligible objects just as the corporeal sun relates to the bodily eye and to corporeal visible objects. Therefore the intelligible objects that are more receptive of this spiritual light are more visible to the interior eye [...]. And so things that are more receptive of this light are more perfectly penetrated by the mind's gaze [*acies mentis*] that is likewise a spiritual irradiation, and this more perfect penetration is greater certitude.[61]

In presenting his view of interior vision, Grosseteste writes of both the 'interior eye' and of the 'mind's eye', using two different terms to refer to spiritual vision.[62] Grosseteste distinguishes between what is physically seen and what is present only to the intellect. He describes this as an object bathed in 'spiritual light'. As Teresa did when describing her vision, Grosseteste shows how a divine revelation is more perfectly penetrated by the 'mind's gaze'. What he refers to as the 'mind's gaze' is akin to what Teresa calls the 'ojos del alma'. St Teresa, like Grosseteste, considers that seeing with the eyes of the soul is the more perfect kind, certainly bathed in a similar 'spiritual light' to Grosseteste's.

To return to Teresa of Jesús's 'lack of knowledge' [inorancia], mentioned in her *Life*, with which I began this section, it seems unlikely, given the way in which women writers like Villena and Teresa de Cartagena refer to seeing with the inner eyes and those of the body, that St Teresa should have been ignorant of the more perfect type of vision, seeing with the eyes of the soul. Yet perhaps this is the case. The power of the Inquisition reached into the interior of convents in a way it did not in the late fifteenth century in a desire to control and prevent nuns from gaining access to any religious literature deemed unsuited to their weaker minds and intellects, since they might otherwise be led astray.[63] As Gillian Ahlgren notes, 'the Inquisition opened cases against Teresa at least five times' and caution had to be Teresa's watchword.[64] There was a desire to control women and keep them behind convent walls. Convent reform had already taken hold under the rule of Isabella and Ferdinand, the Catholic Monarchs, necessary in order to set the 'proper moral and spiritual example for Spanish society at large'. Such reform was particularly concerned with nuns' enclosure.[65] At the same time, science was being carefully scrutinized by the Inquisition for possible heresy.[66] In 1616, scientific thinking in the shape of Galileo's ideas about the sun and the earth came under scrutiny and was roundly rejected as heretical by the Inquisition. Galileo was forced to retract.[67] Knowledge of optics, though it was found in the writings of staunch churchman, ultimately derived from Islamic thinkers such as Al-Kindi, and as such must have been suspect.

St Teresa is keen to separate herself from any taint of such knowledge when she uses 'lack of knowledge' [inorancia]. Her 'inoracia' also reveals she had no experience of such seeing and that, at the time, she did not connect the words with the nature of the experience she had. Seeing, nevertheless, led her to knowledge.

The close relationship between seeing and knowledge can be discerned, for example, in Ockham's prologue to his collected works on theology:

> It is clear that, even in this life (of which the Philosopher speaks), some simple cognition of a sensible [object] is possible, by virtue of which one can know evidently if the object is or not. And nevertheless it is certain that concerning [what is] sensible and is able to be otherwise (*contingenter aliter se habere*), when it is outside the sense and **beyond the gaze**, some simple cognition is possible for the intellect, by virtue of which [cognition] whether [the thing] is or not cannot be evidently known.[68]

Ockham's thinking on how the invisible can be perceived is relevant to Teresa's vision of Christ cited earlier. St Teresa indicates: 'I saw Christ at my side — or, to put it better, I was conscious of Him, for neither with the eyes of the body, nor with those of the soul, did I see anything' (*Vida* 27.2) [vi cabe mí u sentí, por mijor decir, que con los ojos del cuerpo ni del alma no vi nada, más parecióme que estaba junto cabe mí Cristo].⁶⁹ It is apparent here that St Teresa is describing seeing something 'beyond the gaze', to use Ockham's term. The consciousness she describes is also outside ordinary cognition, relying on the corporeal senses. St Teresa states her faith in the truth of what she saw.

Optical Theory and Curiosity

Seeing can lead to sin, through curiosity, because it may lead to ocular over-indulgence or covetousness, as Teresa de Cartagena believed. St Augustine had already indicated that careless or 'aimless' use of the senses should be avoided, triggering a 'history of curiosity as a sin'.⁷⁰ Anselm of Canterbury lists twenty-eight types of sinful curiosity or careless use of the senses, holding that sin occurs when the sensation of seeing becomes an end in itself.⁷¹ St Teresa writes frequently about curiosity, considering that it contains the potential for sin and emphasizing how it could lead her away from God. She considers she 'sinned with her eyes' in her early life: 'I began to deck myself out and to try to attract others by my appearance, taking great trouble with my hands and hair, using perfumes and all the vanities I could get — and there were a good many of them, for I wanted all I set eyes on' (*Vida* 2.2) [Comencé a traer galas y a desear contentar en parecer bien, con mucho cuidado de manos y cabellos y olores, y todas las vanidades que en esto podía tener, que eran hartas por ser muy curiosa].⁷²

Being 'curiosa' leads to sin through a focus not only on things of the world but also on outward appearances. It seems not unlike the dust of covetousness Teresa de Cartagena describes. St Teresa's early life brought her to desire pretty things for her hands and her hair. She also sought after scents. During her noviciate, St Teresa still indicates how she was 'curiosa', now wanting things which looked 'religious'. Her covetousness is still connected to outward appearances, although now with a religious bent: 'I was fond of everything to do with the religious life but I could not bear anything which made me seem ridiculous. I delighted in being thought well of; I fussed over everything I did and all this I thought was a virtue [...]' (*Vida* 5.1) [Era aficionada a todas las cosas de religión, más no a sufrir ninguna que pareciese menosprecio. Holgábame de ser estimada. Era curiosa en cuanto hacía. Todo me parecía virtud].⁷³

Teresa now demonstrates how her love of outward show transfers itself to the religious sphere. She condemns herself for this show of religion and a love of external appearance, far from the reality of knowing God. When St Teresa writes that she was 'curiosa', she therefore intends the reader to understand that she sinned by seeing and coveting things with her eyes and she intends the reader to acknowledge and be aware of how her model, St Augustine, also rejected curiosity.

In this passage, St Teresa acknowledges she remains on the level of things, rather than raising her sights beyond them to a higher plane. Peter of Limoges sets out the connection of the senses and volition for it is the 'well-educated will' which directs how the eye perceives and chooses on what to concentrate. Without that governance, as elsewhere in medieval texts, the body is the site of anxiety, the pleasures, and the moral dangers of sensory experience unchecked.[74] In this case, St Teresa confesses that her will is fixed on the worldly rather than the spiritual.

Later, as Superior of the Order, she must be vigilant in case interiority is pursued for its own sake, a 'false spirituality', to do with absorption with self, which she discerns in the sisters under her tutelage, although she does not mention curiosity in their regard.[75] These are nuns who may have arrived at the Fifth Mansions but who cannot progress any further:

> When I see people very diligently trying to discover what kind of prayer they are experiencing and so completely wrapped up in their prayers that they seem afraid to stir or indulge in a moment's thought lest they should lose the slightest degree of the tenderness or devotion they have been feeling, I realize how little they understand of the road to attainment of union. (*Moradas* 5.3)[76]
>
> [Cuando yo veo almas muy diligentes a entender la oración que tienen y muy encapotadas cuando están en ella (que se parece no osan bullir ni menear el pensamiento, porque no se les vaya u n poquito de gusto y devoción que hayan tenido), háceme ver cuán poco entienden del camino por donde se alcanza la unión.]

This stage of union with its desire to cling to something enjoyable has much in common with St Teresa's own early displays of curiosity and being bound up in experience.

Images and Imagination

St Teresa uses different images of Christ in her *Life* and writes of how she keeps images of Christ in many places. She declares 'liking to have pictures of him in a great many places, wanting an oratory of my own, trying to get objects of devotion for it' (*Vida* 7.2) [amiga de hacer pintar la imagen en muchas partes y de tener oratorio y procurar en él cosas que hiciesen devoción].[77] The physical nature of her devotion enables her to turn from the material presence of the canvas she sees before her. As she engages in this activity, God calls forth a spiritual response.

Her relationship with the painted Christ which she uses to spur inner vision is made clear in one of her poems, 'Soul, Thou must seek thyself in Me' [Búscate en mí].[78] In this poem, with its complexity of relationship between the soul and God, Teresa writes of the impression made on her heart by the image of God

> Such is the power of Love's impress,
> O soul, to grave thee on my heart
> That any craftsman must confess
> He ne'er could have the like success
> Howe'er superlative his art.[79]
>
> [De tal suerte pudo amor,
> alma, en Mí te retratar,
> que ningún sabio pintor
> supiera con tal primor
> tal imagen estampar.]

Peers introduces 'graved on the heart' in his translation. However, Teresa's words may be rendered differently: 'So could Love, o Soul, depict you in me, so clearly that no artist could catch [impress] such an image'.

Ángel Custodio Vega considers St Teresa's use of the topos of love as an image imprinted on the heart as 'almost too common' [casi vulgar].[80] He considers that, because Petrarch had used it, love and engraving had become something akin to a literary motif, used and abused by later poets. St Teresa may have adopted the image because she thought it was a fitting expression of how the lover and the beloved related to each other. She may have followed love poets in doing so. It is far more likely, however, that the love poets were responding to optical theories prevalent in their day and that St Teresa saw the imprint of God on her heart as equivalent to the imprint of his likeness on her soul.

St Teresa returns to the imprinted image on several occasions in her writing. In her Fifth Mansions in the *Interior Castle*, for example, she writes of how a vision of God enraptures the soul, leaving it so completely stupid or stupefied [boba] 'in order the better to impress upon it true wisdom' (*Moradas* 6.1) [Para imprimir mejor en ella la verdadera sabiduría].[81] Since wisdom is to be reached through seeing, St Teresa's meaning is wrapped in the language of vision and the way that images, once seen, are impressed upon the soul, leading it to perfect knowledge. In the Sixth Mansions, St Teresa returns to the language of vision, this time indicating that the vision she had was fixed in her memory so completely that it is indelible:

> When the soul is in this state of suspension and the Lord sees fit to reveal some mysteries to it, such as heavenly things and imaginary visions, it is able subsequently to describe these, for they are so deeply impressed upon the memory that they can never again be forgotten. (*Moradas* 6.4)[82]
>
> [Cuando, estando el alma en esta suspensión, el Señor tiene por bien demostrarle algunos secretos, como de cosas del cielo y visiones imaginarias, esto sábelo después decir, y de tal manera queda imprimido en la memoria, que nunca jamás se olvida.]

What Peers translates as 'imaginary visions' is, in fact, the image storehouse described in optics. St Teresa is writing about an ability to record and retrieve images from that store. Again, optical terminology infuses St Teresa's words for the images are 'impressed upon memory'.

St Teresa is also eager to demonstrate that she did not possess a good 'imagination' or store of images. In her *Life*, she refers to her imagination as slow or poor [torpe]:

> God had not given me talent to reason with my understanding or for making good use of my imagination; my imagination is so poor that, even when I thought about the Lord's Humanity, or tried to imagine it to myself, as I was the habit of doing, I never succeeded. (*Vida* 4.7)[83]
>
> [No me dio Dios talento de discurrir con el entendimiento ni de aprovecharme con la imaginación, que la tengo tan torpe, que aun para pensar y representar en mí, como lo procuraba traer, la humanidad de Cristo, nunca acababa.]

In medieval vision, the imagination, as noted above, acts as the storehouse. Its main function is to enable understanding, because it can retain images of what has been seen and ultimately prompts decision. In this passage, Teresa is referring to imagination, not in the modern sense of an unreal or fantastic vision, but in the optical sense of something seen and stored for later reference. This is again apparent in her comment about bringing to mind a 'paso' or religious sculpture, used for part of an altarpiece or taken out in procession: 'if I thought of sculpture representing Him; I would imagine it inwardly' (*Vida* 4.7) [Si pensaba en algún paso; le representaba en el interior].[84] Later in her *Life*, she refers to how she began to pray using such 'representation': 'My method of prayer was this. As I could not reason with my mind, I would try to make pictures of Christ inwardly; and I used to think I felt better when I dwelt on those parts of His life when He was most often alone' (*Vida* 9.4) [tenía este modo de oración: que como no podia discurrir con el entendimiento, procuraba representar a Cristo dentro de mí y me hallaba mijor].[85]

St Teresa is asked by her confessor in her *Life* how she can be sure that her vision is of Christ. She replies, relying on the same concept that what is seen with the inner eye, but also, on this occasion, heard with the inner ear, becomes impressed upon the soul:

> 'He often tells me so Himself', I replied, 'but, before ever He told me so, it was impressed upon my understanding that it was He and, before that, He used to tell me He was there, when I could not see Him. (*Vida* 27.5)[86]
>
> [Él me lo dice muchas veces, respondí yo; mas antes de que me lo dijese se emprimió en mi entendimiento que era Él y antes de esto me lo decía y no lo veía.]
>
> I saw Him with the eyes of the soul more clearly than I could ever have seen Him with those of the body; and it made such an impression on me that, although it is more than twenty-six years ago, I seem to have Him present with me still. (*Vida* 7.6)[87]
>
> [Representóseme Cristo delante con mucho rigor dándome a entender lo que de ello le pesaba: víle con los ojos del alma más claramente que le pudiera ver con los del cuerpo y quedóme más imprimido que ha esto más de veinte y seis años y me parece lo tengo presente.]

She also mentions the lasting 'impression' made by seeing Christ, retained after twenty-six years. Peers's translation seems almost too easy to pass over: 'it made such an impression on me'.

Indeed, St Teresa's words in her *Life*, 'it made such an impression on me' [se me emprimió] and 'it made a greater impression on me' (7.6) [quedóme más imprimido] are an indicator of her seeming familiarity, albeit untutored, with vestiges of the medieval theory of perception.[88] Even today, an echo of perception theory is retained when we speak of seeing something which makes an 'impression'. In St Teresa's time, the connection between impression and the mechanics of optics was more closely intertwined. Taking Aristotle's example of the wax and seal, perspectivists, like Robert Kilwardby (1215–1279), Dominican Provincial and, later, Archbishop of Canterbury, argue:

> If you place a seal before wax so that it touches it, and you assure the wax has a life by which it turns itself towards the seal and by striking against it comes to be like it, by turning its eye upon itself, it sees in itself the image of the seal.[89]

Like St Augustine, Kilwardby believes that the inner eye turns toward the seal and strikes against it. In a similar way, as discussed earlier, he believes that the soul takes an active role in selecting what to see and in seeking out the impression. The medieval optical theories about the active role of the soul in achieving the image imprinted on the soul as the seal on wax, underpin St Teresa's concept of the impression made by an image on her soul.

St Teresa in this passage refers to another aspect of perception, accepted by medieval theologians, the soul's relationship to what has been seen. According to these medieval theories, based on St Augustine's thinking, the soul is active in seeing rather than being a passive receptor, according to the Aristotelian view, of what it sees.[90] St Augustine argued that the soul must be active in perceiving rather than passive, because it is an entity superior to the bodily senses.[91] His logic was that the capacity to act on something was a sign of superiority and being acted upon, a sign of inferiority. According to Augustine, *intentio* is the act of the soul, directing the sense to perceive the object of vision.[92] An external object does not impress its image on the soul. Instead the soul makes the images of external objects from itself [*de semetipsa*] and in itself [*in semetipsa*]. Intention should be defined as that which can be grasped by the interior senses.[93] In other words, behind the appearance of Christ in the vision to the saint, lies her understanding, drawn from optical theory, that her soul has a part to play in choosing to direct the gaze at the vision before her.

She returns to the soft wax in her *Interior Castle*, describing how the soul must be ready for the vision it is to receive:

> His will is that, without knowing how, the soul goes thence sealed with his seal. In reality a soul in that state does no more than the wax when a seal is impressed upon it — the wax does not impress itself, it is only prepared for the impress: that is, it is soft [...]. (*Moradas* 5.2)[94]
>
> [quiere que, sin que ella entienda cómo salga de allí sellada con su sello, porque verdaderamente el alma allí no hace más que la cera cuando imprime otro sello, que la cera no imprime a sí, sólo está dispuesta, digo blanda.]

Whilst St Teresa here echoes the biblical verse about union between God and his people: 'I have set my seal upon your heart' (Song of Songs 8.6), her words are also close to those of theologians and scientists, who express vision in the same way, often describing the action of the eyes of the soul as like an impression on wax. Although the wax Teresa describes seems passive, for the soul does nothing and the imprint is simply made upon it, it is not passive. It is ready and chooses to be soft for the moment when Christ comes.

Darkness, Illumination of the Soul, and God

Light and dark have been identified as one of the key themes in Golden Age mystical writing.[95] Light and darkness have been a frequent topic discussed in exploring the writing of St Teresa, particularly when she is compared with other mystics.[96] Light is also at the heart of theological thinking about optics in the medieval period. Optics places emphasis on both light and darkness in determining how seeing occurs. For Bacon, light is one of the principal pre-conditions for vision to occur and seeing involves rays of light emanating from the object seen.[97]

St Teresa writes that the darkness of sin is represented by the place of the greatest deprivation of light: 'No thicker darkness exists, and there is nothing dark and black which is not much less so than this' [No hay tinieblas tan oscuras ni cosa tan oscura y negra, que no lo esté mucho más].[98] It has been suggested that the darkness of the soul, different in St John of the Cross's and St Teresa's writing, derives from Islamic symbolism.[99] This intriguing suggestion may not sift all the information about the subject. The play of light and dark is deeply embedded in Christian symbolism too. Since the earliest mystical writing, such as Pseudo-Dionysius, 'mystical writers have used darkness for its symbolic possibilities'.[100] Darkness reaches deep into Christian and Jewish understanding of God's purposes. Darkness covering the face of the earth is closely allied both to creation, Genesis 1, and to Christ as the new creation who is the Light of the world (John 1). Elizabeth Teresa Howe notes how darkness operates in two different ways. First it 'evokes a mental impression formed through sense impressions. Second it stands for the divine darkness in which the mystic is illuminated'.[101]

Light and dark featured, as might be expected in medieval women's works. Writing about Pentecost and the descent of the Holy Spirit, Constanza de Castilla contrasts the light of the Holy Spirit with the darkness of her soul: 'I beg of you, God the Holy Spirit, who are supreme light, to cleanse my understanding of the darkness where I am and inflame my heart with longing for you' [Te suplico Dios Spíritu Santo que eres lux soberana, que alinpies mi entendimiento de la tiniebra en que estó e inflames mi coraçón de tu deseo].[102] The divine light about which Constanza writes has a number of functions. It casts light on what was darkness. It changes her understanding. It cleanses. It purifies through fire (it inflames). It has an effect on the inner being causing it to long for God.

The perspectivist understanding of how light penetrates even the darkest of places may also refresh St Teresa's topos of the sin-darkened soul. Pecham explains dark as the absence of light: 'darkness, however, exists in a place totally deprived of light' [Tenebra vero est si tamen alicubi est ubi nichil est de lumine].[103] He continues by adding that nothing can be so dark that light cannot penetrate it: 'I do not know, in fact, if any earthly bodies are capable of altogether impeding the propagation of light, for nothing is totally deprived of transparency and cannot, at any rate, impede the circumfusion of secondary light' [Nescio enim si aliquod corporum mundanorum potest omnino lucis transitum impedire, cum nullum penitus natura perspicui sit privatum et ad minus circumfulgentiam impedire non potest lucis secundarie].[104] Pecham's understanding of how some 'secondary' light penetrates into even the darkest spaces adds to appreciation of how St Teresa understands darkness. Whilst Teresa considers that the darkness the soul in mortal sin experiences is more profound than any other, she also believes there is nothing impenetrable to God's light: 'the Sun Himself, Who has given it all its splendour and beauty, is still there in the centre of the soul' (*Moradas* 1.2) [con estarse el mesmo Sol, que le daba tanto resplandor y hermosura todavía en el centro de su alma].[105] Thus, when she discusses God's presence in sinful souls in the *Interior Castle*, she is at pains to emphasize how God never departs, even though he cannot be seen: 'the poor soul becomes darkness itself likewise' (*Moradas* 1.2) [ansí el pobre ánima queda hecha una mesma tiniebla].[106] Darkness can, however, be left behind, as she outlines in her *Life*, if the soul awakens: 'by which means the Lord began to awaken her soul and give her light amid such great darkness' (*Vida* 9.1) [por qué término empezó el Señor a despertar el alma y darle luz en grandes tinieblas].[107]

Conclusion

In this chapter, I have re-examined aspects of St Teresa's explanation of her visions, allying it to contemporary thinking about optics. I have examined St Teresa's views on different gradations of seeing and have been able to point to women's awareness of some of the theories of vision, such as Teresa de Cartagena's awareness of the mind's eye and Isabel de Villena's contrast of eyes of the body and soul. I have turned to optics to deepen awareness of St Teresa's references to imagination and impressions made by images, also using this to re-position the metaphor of love and impression. I have finally explored how optics provides insight into the principal metaphors of Golden Age mysticism, darkness and light.

Notes to Chapter 12

1. In a series of recent articles on related themes, I considered aspects of seeing and vision and how women approach the senses more generally in their writing, whether courtly or religious. See, for example, Lesley K. Twomey. 'Court and Convent: Senses and Spiituality in Hispanic Medieval Women's Writing', in *The Routledge Companion to Iberian Studies*, ed. by Javier Muñoz-Basols, Laura Lonsdale, and Manuel Delgado (Abingdon: Routledge, 2017), pp. 65-78, at pp. 65-67. This chapter is part of the project 'Emergencia de la autoridad femenina en la corte y el convento', MINECO EXCELENCIA FFI2015–63625-C2–1P.
2. Dallas G. Denery, *Seeing and Being Seen in the Later Medieval World: Optics, Theology, and Religious Life* (Cambridge: Cambridge University Press, 2005), p. 8.
3. Mark A. Smith, *Sensing the Past: Seeing, Hearing, Smelling, Touching, Tasting in History* (Berkeley: University of California Press, 2008), p. 13.
4. This intellectual tradition led to the so-called 'spectator theory of knowledge'. John Dewey, *The Quest for Certainty* (New York: Putnam, 1960), p. 23, cited in Denery, *Seeing and Being Seen*, p. 8.
5. Elizabeth Edwards and Kausik Bhaumik begin their reader on visual sense by determining that 'visual culture' began to emerge as a discipline in the new millennium, influencing other disciplines: in their *Visual Sense: A Cultural Reader* (Oxford: Berg, 2008), p. 5. Although they include one essay on medieval vision, there is no real sense of how vision in a medieval context might be different from that of the nineteenth or twentieth century. It is not my purpose to give a full bibliography of visual culture.
6. Michael Camille, 'Before the Gaze: The Internal Senses and Late-Medieval Practices of Seeing', in *Visuality Before and Beyond the Renaissance: Seeing as Others Saw*, ed. by Robert S. Nelson

(Cambridge: Cambridge University Press, 2000). The medieval gaze is addressed by Thomas Lentes, '"As Far as the Eye Can See": Rituals of Gazing in the Late Middle Ages', in *The Mind's Eye: Art and Theological Argument in the Middle Ages*, ed. by Jeffrey E. Hamburger and Anne-Marie Bouché (Princeton, NJ: Princeton University Press and the Department of Art and Archeology, 2006), pp. 360–73.

7. Denery, *Seeing and Being Seen*, p. 8. Smith, *Sensing the Past*, p. 5, refers to an upsurge of critical attention on the senses, particularly seeing. See also Suzannah Biernoff, *Sight and Embodiment in the Middle Ages* (Basingstoke: Palgrave Macmillan, 2002).
8. Classen, *Worlds of Sense: Exploring the Senses in History and Across Cultures* (London: Routledge, 1993); Woolgar, *The Senses in Late Medieval England* (New Haven, CT: Yale University Press, 2006), particularly Chapter 8, 'Vision', pp. 147–89. See also Smith, *Sensing the Past*. Smith dedicates the first chapter to 'Seeing', pp. 19–31. For several chapters on seeing as well as the other senses, see Stephen G. Nichols, Andreas Kablitz, and Alison Calhoun, eds, *Rethinking the Medieval Senses: Heritage/Fascinations/Frames* (Baltimore, MD: Johns Hopkins University Press, 2008).
9. Suzanne Biernoff, 'Seeing and Feeling in the Middle Ages', in *Visual Sense: A Cultural Reader*, ed. by Elizabeth Edwards and Kausik Bhaumik (Oxford: Berg, 2008), pp. 51–57.
10. Jeffrey F. Hamburger, *Nuns as Artists: The Visual Culture of a Medieval Convent* (Berkeley: University of California Press, 1997).
11. For example, Dronke, 'Les Cinq Sens chez Bernard Sylvestre et Alain de Lille', *Micrologus*, 10 (2002), 1–14; Gómez, '"Accende lumen sensibus": una aproximación filosófico-teológica a la doctrina de los sentidos en la teología monástica medieval', *Teología y vida*, 49.4 (2008), 749–69. See also various chapters in *The Mind's Eye: Art and Theological Argument in the Middle Ages*, ed. by Jeffrey F. Hamburger and Anne-Marie Bouché (Princeton, NJ: Princeton University Press and the Department of Art and Archeology, 2006). On seeing God, see Bernard McGinn, '*Visio Dei*: Seeing God in Medieval Theology and Mysticism', in *Envisaging Heaven in the Middle Ages*, ed. by Carolyn Muessig and Ad Putter (London: Routledge, 2007), pp. 15–33; see also various chapters in *The Spiritual Senses: Perceiving God in Western Christianity*, ed. by Paul L. Gavrilyuk and Sarah Coakley (Baltimore, MD: Johns Hopkins University Press, 2011).
12. Rahner, 'La Doctrine des "sens spirituels" au Moyen Âge: en particulier chez Saint Bonaventure', *Revue d'Ascétique et de Mystique*, 14 (1933), 263–99.
13. Kemp and Fletcher, 'History of Psychology: The Medieval Theory of the Inner Senses', *The American Journal of Psychology*, 106.4 (1993), 559–76.
14. Cynthia Hahn, '*Visio Dei*: Changes in Medieval Visuality', in *Visuality Before and Beyond the Renaissance: Seeing as Others Saw*, ed. by Robert S. Nelson (Cambridge: Cambridge University Press, 2000), pp. 169–96. See also Robert W. Schribner, 'Popular Piety and Modes of Visual Perception in Late-Medieval and Reformation Germany', *Journal of Religious History*, 15 (1989), 448–69.
15. Bynum, *Christian Materiality: An Essay on Religion in Late Medieval Europe* (New York: Zone, 2011), especially 'Visual Matter', pp. 37–122.
16. Woolgar, *The Senses in Late Medieval England*, pp. 23 and 147; see also Jan-Dirk Müller, 'Blinding Sight: Some Observations on German Epics of the Thirteenth Century', in *Rethinking the Medieval Senses*, ed. by Stephen G. Nichols, Andreas Kablitz and Alison Calhoun, pp. 206–17; Denery, *Seeing and Being Seen*, p. 8.
17. Aristotle, *Metaphysics*, I.1, trans. by W. D. Rose, in *The Complete Works of Aristotle: The Revised Oxford Translation*, ed. by Jonathan Barnes, 2 vols (Princeton, NJ: Princeton University Press), II, 1552, cited in Denery, *Seeing and Being Seen*, p. 8.
18. Walter Ong, *Ramus, Method and the Decay of Dialogue* (Cambridge, MA: Harvard University Press, 1958), pp. 306–15.
19. Smith, *Sensing the Past*, p. 11.
20. Studies on optics include David C. Lindberg, *Theories of Vision from Al-Kindi to Kepler* (Chicago, IL: University of Chicago Press, 1976); on visuality and the gaze, various essays in Robert S. Nelson's collection, *Visuality Before and Beyond the Renaissance: Seeing as Others Saw* (Cambridge: Cambridge University Press, 2000); Smith, *Sensing the Past*; Denery, *Seeing and Being Seen*; essays on Christ's infancy, on active and passive vision, on the Mass of St Gregory, on contemplation,

on rituals of gazing in Hamburger and Bouché's collection; various essays in *Rethinking the Medieval Senses*, ed. by Stephen G. Nichols, Andreas Kablitz and Alison Calhoun, particularly, Stephen G. Nichols, '"The Pupil of Your Eye": Vision, Language and Poetry in Thirteenth-century Paris', in *Rethinking the Medieval Senses: Heritage/Fascinations/Frames*, ed. by Nichols, Andreas Kablitz and Alison Calhoun (Baltimore, MD: Johns Hopkins University Press, 2008), pp. 286–307. Hamburger has written several essays on seeing, including 'Speculations on Speculation: Vision and Perception in the Theory and Practice of Mystical Devotion', in *Deutsche Mystik im abendländischen Zusammenhang: Neu erschlossene Texte, neue methodische Ansätze, neue theoretische Konzepte, Kolloquium Kloster Fischingen 1998*, ed. by Walter Haug and Wolfram Scheider-Lastin (Tübingen: Niemayer, 2000), pp. 353–408. For further bibliography on occularity, see Bynum, *Christian Materiality*, pp. 298–99, n. 1. David C. Lindberg and Katherine H. Tachau, 'The Science of Light and Colour', in *The Cambridge History of Science*, ed. by David C. Lindberg and Michael H. Shank (Cambridge: Cambridge University Press, 2013), II: *Medieval Science*, pp. 486–511 (p. 487), also provide an overview of the history of the study of optics, beginning with the ancient Greeks, summarizing much of their previous work.

21. Dominique Raynaud in her 'Effets de réseau dans la science pré-institutionnelle: le cas de l'optique médiévale', *European Journal of Sociology*, 42.3 (2007), 483–505. Raynaud demonstrates this in her analysis of the diffusion of optics treatises throughout the West (p. 487). She shows convincingly how the spread of the ideas of these writers took place through the social networks of the Franciscan friaries, both of teachers and students, rather than through University teaching.
22. For a study of the influence of Bacon, Witelo, and Pecham on each other, see David C. Lindberg, 'Lines of Influence in Thirteenth-Century Optics: Bacon, Witelo and Pecham', *Speculum*, 46.1 (1971), 66–83. Because the Franciscans were barred from teaching the new thinking on optics, Bacon was required to pass his treatises to the papal court at Viterbo, where they had far greater influence on other theologians, including Witelo. There is little acknowledgement of other philosophers, such as the Majorcan philosopher, Ramon Llull. Llull also wrote a treatise on optics, his *Liber de Lumine*, disseminated in six manuscripts, although his influence outside his immediate circle was smaller than Bacon or Pecham's, whose works were disseminated in seventy-five and seventy-two manuscripts respectively, according to Raynaud, 'Effets de réseau', p. 487.
23. Raynaud, 'Effets de réseau', pp. 493–94.
24. Nichols, '"The Pupil"', p. 289. Nichols's study is insightful. Too few studies have approached literature and optics with similar interdisciplinary rigour. For example Joachim Küpper, 'Perception, Cognition, and Volition in the Arcipreste de Talavera', in *Rethinking the Medieval Senses*, ed. by Nichols, Kablitz and Calhoun, pp. 119–53, despite a promising title, does not address the influence of optics on the *Corbacho* to any great degree. On seeing, the gaze, and dream vision in Hispanic medieval texts, see 'Visions of Hagiography', ed. by Andrew M. Beresford and Lesley K. Twomey, *La corónica*, 43 (2013).
25. Woolgar, *The Senses*, pp. 23 and 147; see also Jan-Dirk Müller, 'Blinding Sight: Some Observations on German Epics of the Thirteenth Century', in *Rethinking the Medieval Senses*, ed. by Nichols, Kablitz and Calhoun, pp. 206–17; Hildegard Elisabeth Keller, 'Blinded Avengers: Making Sense of Invisibility in Courtly Epic and Legal Ritual', pp. 218–262, in the same volume; on Petrarch and other poets, see Rainer Warning, 'Seeing and Hearing in Ancient and Medieval Epiphany', pp. 102–116, in the same volume.
26. Constanza de Castilla, *Book of Devotions: Libro de devociones y oficios*, ed. by Constance L. Wilkins, Exeter Hispanic Texts, 52 (Exeter: Exeter University Press, 1998); Teresa de Cartagena, *Arboleda de los enfermos. Admiraçión operum Dey*, ed. by Lewis Joseph Hutton, Boletín de la Real Academia Española, Anejo 16 (Madrid: RAE, 1967); Sor Isabel de Villena, *'Vita Christi', compost per Isabel de Villena, abadessa de la Trinitat de Valencia, ara novament publicat segons l'edició de l'any 1497*, ed. by Ramón Miquel y Planas, 2nd edn, 3 vols (Barcelona: Casa Miquel-Rius, 1916).
27. Medieval theories of vision and their decline are discussed by Gareth B. Matthews, 'Medieval Theory of Vision', in *Studies in Perception in the History of Philosophy and Science*, ed. by Peter K. Machamer and Robert G. Turnbull (Columbus: Ohio State University Press), pp. 87–99.

28. Helmut Hatzfeld, *Santa Teresa de Ávila*, TWAS, 79 (New York: Twayne, 1969), p. 61.
29. Colin P. Thompson discusses aspects of vision in a perceptive article in which he compares Teresa of Ávila with Golden Age artists, including Estebán Murillo and Alonso Cano. His purpose is, however, different from that of this essay. Thompson, 'Seeing the Unseen: The Representation of Visions in Golden Age Painting and Writing', *Bulletin of Hispanic Studies*, 86.6 (2009), 797–809. Much earlier, Helmut Hatzfeld had compared Teresa of Ávila's approach to that of El Greco. Hatzfeld, *Estudios literarios sobre la mística española*, 2nd edn, Biblioteca Románica Hispánica, II: Estudios y Ensayos, 16 (Madrid: Gredos, 1968), pp. 246–73.
30. Thompson, 'Seeing the Unseen', p. 797.
31. Thompson, 'Seeing the Unseen', p. 806.
32. Thompson, 'Seeing the Unseen', p. 806.
33. Teresa of Ávila, *Libro de la vida*, ed. by Dámaso Chicharro, Letras Hispánicas, 98, 17th edn (Madrid: Cátedra, 2014), p. 340, henceforth *Vida*; *The Complete Works of St Teresa of Jesus*, ed. and trans. by E. Allison Peers, 3 vols (London: Sheed and Ward, 1946), I, 170. Cited also by Thompson, 'Seeing the Unseen', p. 805.
34. Katherine H. Tachau, *Vision and Certitude in the Age of Ockham: Optics, Epistemology, and the Foundations of Semantics, 1250–1325*, Studien und Texte zur Geistesgeschichte des Mittelalters, 22 (Leiden: Brill, 1988), p. 8; Teresa of Ávila, *Vida* 27.2, p. 340; Peers, *The Complete Works*, I, 170.
35. According to Camille, this is the 'common center for relating all the *sensibilia* from all the sensory organs that provides a compound image of the external sensed object'. See Camille, 'Before the Gaze', p. 200.
36. Daniel Heller-Roazen, 'Common Sense: Greek, Arabic, Latin', in *Rethinking the Medieval Senses*, ed. by Nichols, Kablitz, and Calhoun, pp. 30–50 (p. 38): 'The common sense is intermediate between the corporal sense of sight and the imaginative faculty'. See Salomon Freud, *Sefer ha-Yesodot. Buch der Elemente: Ein Beitrag zur jüdischen Religionsphilosophie des Mittelalters* (Frankfurt: J. Kaufmann, 1900), p. 53, cited in Heller-Roazen, 'Common Sense', p. 38.
37. Camille, 'Before the Gaze', p. 200.
38. Camille, 'Before the Gaze', p. 200.
39. Camille, 'Before the Gaze', p. 200.
40. Camille, 'Before the Gaze', pp. 200–01; see also Boyd Taylor Coolman on William of Auxerre, *Knowing God by Experience: The Spiritual Senses in the Theology of William of Auxerre* (Washington, DC: Catholic University of America Press, 2004), p. 126.
41. Coolman, *Knowing God by Experience*, p. 127.
42. Teresa of Ávila, *Vida*, p. 340, translated in Peers, *The Complete Works*, I, 170.
43. Teresa of Ávila, *Vida*, p. 340, translated in Peers, *The Complete Works*, I, 170.
44. On Teresa's lack of knowledge of book learning, see Elena Carrera, *Teresa of Avila's Autobiography: Authority, Power, and the Self in Mid-Sixteenth Century Spain* (Oxford: Legenda, 2005), p. 19.
45. Teresa of Ávila, *Vida*, p. 176, Peers, *The Complete Works*, I, 40. On the devil in St Teresa's thinking, see María Jesús Zamora Calvo, 'Demonología y misticismo: Teresa de Ávila', *Alpha*, 31 (2010), 147–61.\
46. Eugene Vance, 'Seeing God: Augustine, Sensation, and the Mind's Eye', in *Rethinking the Medieval Senses*, ed. by Nichols, Kablitz, and Calhoun, pp. 13–29 (p. 21).
47. Matthew Lootens gives a much-needed overview of the spiritual senses in the writings of St Augustine. Lootens, 'Augustine', in *The Spiritual Senses: Perceiving God in Western Christianity*, ed. by Paul L. Gavrilyuk and Sarah Coakley (Baltimore, MD: Johns Hopkins University Press, 2011), pp. 56–70.
48. Heller-Roazen, 'Common Sense', p. 37.
49. Teresa declares that the *Confessions* were placed in her hands in *Vida* 9.7. See also O'Reilly's essay in this volume, p. 112. She sees God's action in this. See Carrera, *Teresa of Ávila's Autobiography*, p. 180.
50. For a study of the life and work of Isabel de Villena, see Twomey, *The Fabric of Marian Devotion in Isabel de Villena's Vita Christi*, Colección Támesis, Série A: Monografías, 313 (Woodbridge: Boydell & Brewer, 2013). Twomey, 'The Aesthetics of Beauty in the Writings of Cloistered Women in Late Medieval and Golden Age Spain (Constanza de Castilla, Teresa de Cartagena,

Isabel de Villena, and Teresa de Ávila)', *e-Humanista*, 43 (2016), 50–68, examines women's relationship with Christ and the redemptive beauty of his shattered body.

51. '*Vita Christi*', *compost per Isabel de Villena*, ed. by Ramón Miquel y Planas, III, 51. All translations from the *Vita Christi* are the author's own.
52. For the life of Teresa de Cartagena, particularly for new historical details, see Dayle Seidenspinner-Núñez and Yonsoo Kim, 'Historicizing Teresa: Reflections on New Documents Regarding Sor Teresa de Cartagena', *La corónica*, 32.2 (2004), 121–50. For an overview in English of Teresa de Cartagena's two treatises, see Ronald E. Surtz, *Writing Women in Late Medieval and Early Modern Spain: The Mothers of St Teresa of Ávila* (Philadelphia: University of Pennsylvania Press, 1995). For an early study of Spain's women writers, including Teresa de Cartagena but not Isabel de Villena, a subject previously ignored by scholars, see Alan D. Deyermond, 'Spain's First Women Writers', in *Women in Hispanic Literature: Icons and Fallen Idols*, ed. by Beth Miller (Berkeley: University of California Press, 1983), pp. 27–52. See also the introductory study by Dayle Seidenspinner-Núñez in her edition of *The Writings of Teresa de Cartagena* (Cambridge: Brewer, 1998), pp. 1–21; Yonsoo Kim, *El saber femenino y el sufrimiento corporal de la temprana Edad Moderna: Arboleda de los enfermos y Admiraçión Operum Dey de Teresa de Cartagena* (Córdoba: Universidad de Córdoba, Servicio de Publicaciones, 2008).
53. Teresa de Cartagena, *Arboleda*, p. 80; Seidenspinner-Núñez, ed., *The Writings*, p. 62. Seidenspinner-Núñez chooses 'eyes of the understanding' but she might have used the 'eyes of the spirit'.
54. For an overview of deafness and the legal status of the deaf, see Yonsoo Kim, 'Writing to Survive and Heal: Teresa de Cartagena's Life and Works', in her *Between Desire and Passion: Teresa de Cartagena* (Leiden: Brill, 2012), pp. 11–34 (pp. 32–33); Hilary E. Pearson dedicates her thesis to exploration of Teresa's theology of disability, Pearson, 'Teresa de Cartagena: A Late Medieval Woman's Theological Approach to Disability' (unpublished DPhil, University of Oxford, 2011). Teresa de Cartagena's translation of deafness into the physical and spatial is discussed by Ronald E. Surtz, 'Image Patterns in Teresa de Cartagena's *Arboleda de los enfermos*', in *La Chispa 87: Selected Proceedings. The Eighth Louisiana Conference on Hispanic Languages and Literatures, Tulane University, Louisiana, 1987*, ed. by Gilbert Paolini (New Orleans, LA: Tulane University Press, 1987), pp. 297–304 (p. 300); Victoria Rivera-Cordero, 'Spatializing Illness: Embodied Deafness in Teresa de Cartagena's *Arboleda de los enfermos*', *La corónica*, 37.2 (2009), 61–77.
55. Adaptations to the Seidenspinner-Núñez's translation are indicated in square brackets. Teresa de Cartagena, *Arboleda*, p. 80. Translation adapted from Seidenspinner-Núñez, ed., *The Writings*, p. 62. Seidenspinner-Núñez translates 'bienes' as 'blessings', rather than 'chattels' or 'possessions'. Either alternative, because of its negative connotations, is to be preferred to 'blessings'. Teresa de Cartagena's approach to suffering has been much studied by, among others, Alan D. Deyermond, '"El convento de dolençias": The Works of Teresa de Cartagena', *Journal of Hispanic Philology*, 1 (1976–77), 19–29; Surtz, 'Writing Women', pp. 23–24; Raquel Trillia, 'Teresa de Cartagena: Agent of Her Own Salvation', *Revista canadiense de estudios hispánicos*, 32 (2007), 51–70 (p. 63); Kim, *El saber femenino*.
56. For women's authority to write, see also Dayle Seidenspinner-Núñez, '"But I Suffer not Woman to Teach": Two Women Writers in Late Medieval Spain', in *Hers Ancient and Modern: Women's Writing in Spain and Brazil*, ed. by Catherine Davies and Jane Whetnall, Manchester Spanish and Portuguese Studies, 6 (Manchester: University of Manchester, Department of Spanish and Portuguese, 1997), pp. 1–14; for Teresa de Cartagena and how she considers 'understanding', see Teresa Elizabeth Howe, 'Sor Teresa de Cartagena and *entendimiento*', *Romanische Forschungen*, 108 (1996), 133–45.
57. Teresa de Cartagena, *Arboleda* [*Admiraçión*], p. 136. Translation Seidenspinner-Núñez, ed., *The Writings*, p. 108.
58. Tachau, 'Seeing as Action', p. 351. The two main theories, intromission and extramission, are explored by David C. Lindberg, 'The Intromission-Extramission Controversy in Islamic Visual Theory: Alkindi versus Avicenna', in *Studies in Perception in the History of Philosophy and Science*, ed. by Peter K. Machamer and Robert G. Turnbull (Columbus: Ohio State University Press, 1978), pp. 137–159.

59. John Pecham, 'Proposition', I, 48, cited in Lindberg, ed. and trans., *John Pecham and the Science of Optics: Perspectiva communis* (Madison: University of Wisconsin Press, 1970), p. 34.
60. Teresa of Ávila, *Vida*, p. 176. Translated in Peers, *The Complete Works*, I, 40.
61. Grosseteste, *Commentarius in posteriorum analyticorum Aristotelis*, Lib. 1, cap. 17, pp. 240–41: Dico ergo quod est lux spiritualis, que superfunditur rebus intelligibilibus et oculo mentis, que se habet ad oculum interiorum et ad res intelligibiles sicut se habet sol corporalis ad oculum corporalem et ad res corporales visibiles. Res igitur intelligibiles magis receptibiles huius lucis spiritualis magis visibiles sunt oculo interiori, et magis sunt huius lucis receptibiles que nature huius lucis magis assimilantur. Res itaque huius lucis magis receptibiles ab acie mentis, que similiter est irradiatio spiritualis, perfectius penetrantur, et hec penetratio perfectior est certitudo maior. Cited in Tachau, 'Seeing as Action', pp. 343–44. Grosseteste returns to spiritual light in Liber 2, cap. 6.
62. Gavrilyuk and Coakley, *The Spiritual Senses*, p. 1, refer to various expressions to express the spiritual senses. For vision this includes 'eyes of the spirit', 'eyes of the soul', 'mind's eye', 'inner eyes', 'eyes of faith'.
63. Teresa needed to 'be particularly careful' because her activities, writing and reforming convents were not the type of good works expected of a woman. Carrera, 'Teresa of Avila's Autobiography', p. 182.
64. Ahlgren, 'Negotiating Sanctity: Holy Women in Sixteenth-century Spain', *Church History*, 64 (1995), 373–88.
65. Elizabeth Lehfeldt, *Religious Women in Golden Age Spain: The Permeable Cloister* (Aldershot: Ashgate, 2005), p. 139.
66. Paula Findlen and Hannah Marcus, 'Science under Inquisition: Heresy and Knowledge in Catholic Reformation Rome', *Isis*, 103 (2012), 376–82.
67. See Thomas F. Mayer, *The Roman Inquisition: A Papal Bureaucracy and its Laws in the Age of Galileo* (Philadelphia: University of Pennsylvania Press, 2013).
68. William of Ockham, *Opera Theologica*, ed. by G. Gál, S. Brown, G. Etzkorn, and F. Kelley, 4 vols (St Bonaventure, NY: St Bonaventure University, 1980), I, 23, lines 14–21, cited in Tachau, *Vision and Certitude*, p. 125. Author's emphasis.
69. Teresa of Ávila, *Vida*, p. 340; translated by Peers, *The Complete Works*, I, 170.
70. Richard G. Newhauser, 'Optics and the Science of the Senses', *The Senses and Society*, 5 (2010), 28–44 (p. 28).
71. Newhauser, 'Optics', p. 29.
72. Teresa of Ávila, *Vida*, p. 140. Peers translates 'curiosa' by 'fastidious' but it has within in the sense of paying too much attention to seeing and of sinning through that attention paid to objects, possessions, or things of the world. Peers, adapted, *The Complete Works*, I, 13.
73. Teresa of Ávila, *Vida*, p. 157. In this case, Peers translates 'curiosa' by 'particular'. Peers, adapted, *The Complete Works*, I, 26.
74. Newhauser, 'Optics', p. 37.
75. Rowan Williams, *Teresa of Avila* (London: Continuum, 1991), pp. 109, 126.
76. Teresa of Ávila, *Las moradas del castillo interior*, ed. by Dámaso Chicharro, 2nd edn, Clásicos de Biblioteca Nueva, 11 (Madrid: Biblioteca Nueva, 2015), p. 322, henceforth *Moradas*. Translated by Peers, *The Complete Works*, II, 262–63.
77. Teresa of Ávila, *Vida*, p. 173, translated by Peers, *The Complete Works*, I, 38.
78. Ángel Custodio Vega, ed., *La poesía de Santa Teresa* (Madrid: Biblioteca de Autores Cristianos, 1972), pp. 244–45.
79. Vega, ed., *La poesía de Santa Teresa*, p. 244, translated by Peers, *The Complete Works*, II, 287.
80. Vega, 'La producción poética de Santa Teresa', in Vega, ed., *La poesía de Santa Teresa*, p. 95.
81. Teresa of Ávila, *Moradas*, p. 306, translated by Peers, *The Complete Works*, II, 251.
82. Teresa of Ávila, *Moradas*, p. 361, translated by Peers, *The Complete Works*, II, 288. Peers translates 'visiones imaginarias' as 'visions of the imaginary type'.
83. Teresa of Ávila, *Vida*, p. 154, translated by Peers, *The Complete Works*, I, 24.
84. Teresa of Ávila, *Vida*, p. 154, translated by Peers, *The Complete Works*, I, 23 (adapted).
85. Teresa of Ávila, *Vida*, p. 194, translated by Peers, *The Complete Works*, I, 52.

86. Teresa of Ávila, *Vida*, p. 342, translated by Peers, *The Complete Works*, I, 171–72.
87. Teresa of Ávila, *Vida*, p. 176, translated in Peers, *The Complete Works*, I, 40.
88. Teresa of Ávila, *Vida*, p. 176; Peers, *The Complete Works*, I, 40.
89. José Filipe Silva and Juhana Toivanen, 'The Active Nature of the Soul in Sense Perception: Robert Kilwardby and Peter Olivi', *Vivarium*, 48 (2010), 245–78 (pp. 257–58).
90. Silva and Toivanen, 'The Active Nature of the Soul', p. 248.
91. Silva and Toivanen, 'The Active Nature of the Soul', p. 248; Mary Ann Ida Gannon, 'The Active Memory of Sensation in St Augustine', *The New Scholastic*, 30 (1956), 154–80. Gannon writes: 'Intentio is the act of the soul which directs the sense to the object' (p. 161). See also Katherine H. Tachau, 'Seeing as Action and Passion in the Thirteenth and Fourteenth Centuries', in *The Mind's Eye*, ed. by Hamburger and Bouché, pp. 336–59.
92. Gannon, 'The Active Theory', p. 160.
93. *John Pecham and the Science of Optics*, ed. by Lindberg, p. 253, n. 141.
94. Teresa of Ávila, *Moradas*, p. 315, translated by Peers, *The Complete Works*, II, 257.
95. See for example Colin P. Thompson's interpretation of darkness and beyond in the poetry of St John of the Cross: *The Poet and the Mystic: A Study of the Cántico Espiritual of San Juan de la Cruz* (Oxford: Oxford University Press, 1977), p. 160; see also Dámaso Chicharro, 'Introducción', in Teresa of Ávila, *Moradas*, p. 130.
96. See Américo Castro, 'Teresa la Santa', in his *Santa Teresa y otros ensayos*, Hombres, hechos, e ideas, 23 (Madrid: Alfaguera, 1972), pp. 59–66.
97. Matthews, 'A Medieval Theory', p. 190.
98. Teresa of Ávila, *Moradas*, pp. 221–22. Translated by Peers, *The Complete Works*, II, 205.
99. Luce López Baralt, 'Símbología mística musulmana en San Juan de la Cruz y Santa Teresa de Jesús', *Nueva Revista de Filología Hispánica*, 30.1 (1981), 21–91 (pp. 30–41).
100. Elizabeth Teresa Howe, *Mystical Imagery: Santa Teresa de Jesús and San Juan de la Cruz*, Series II: Romance Languages and Literatures, 76 (New York: Peter Lang, 1988), p. 48. For a detailed study of Pseudo-Dionysius, see Peter Tyler's chapter in this volume.
101. Howe, *Mystical Imagery*, p. 48.
102. Constanza de Castilla, *Book of Devotions*, p. 35. For study of Constanza, her life and works, see Constance L. Wilkins's preliminary study to her edition: 'Introduction', in Constanza de Castilla, *Book of Devotions*, pp. vii–xxiv.
103. *John Pecham and the Science of Optics*, ed. and trans. by Lindberg, pp. 102–03.
104. *John Pecham and the Science of Optics*, ed. and trans. by Lindberg, pp. 102–03.
105. *Moradas* 1.2, p. 222, translated by Peers, *The Complete Works*, II, 205.
106. *Moradas* 1.2, p. 222, translated by Peers, *The Complete Works*, II, 205.
107. *Vida* 9.1, p. 193, translated by Peers, *The Complete Works*, I, 54.

CHAPTER 13

Traditions of Discourse and Santa Teresa

Christopher J. Pountain

1. Introduction

Santa Teresa's writings long held a fascination for historians of Spanish because they appeared to offer the prospect of supplying data which is close to the spontaneous speech of the sixteenth century. The powerful tradition which indeed sees her language as a spontaneous form of Spanish corresponding to her everyday speech can be traced back to A. Sánchez Moguel and is essentially the position taken by Ramón Menéndez Pidal.[1] But this sits uncomfortably with the thought that Teresa, as a self-confessed avid reader and enviably fluent writer, was not at all illiterate. Menéndez Pidal's view is therefore that Teresa's manner of writing is a conscious rejection of the literary styles with which she was familiar, in a deliberate demonstration that she had forgotten the books which had fallen victim to the proscriptions of Valdés three years before she began writing the *Libro de la vida*. Fernando Lázaro Carreter, on the other hand, rejected the view that Teresa wrote as she spoke, pointing to cultured and literary aspects of her style which, he suggested, derived from her own wide reading, a view which had been forcefully expressed on the basis of an apparently more systematic syntactic comparison by Hans Flasche.[2] It is now generally accepted that Teresa was very conscious of the style of her writing:[3] the evidence of the two revisions of the *Camino de perfección* made by her is often cited in support of this view, recently the subject of a systematic syntactic study by Álvaro S. Octavio de Toledo y Huerta.[4] Such debate is crucial from the point of view of philological interpretation, but close comparative studies of the actual linguistic (as distinct from rhetorical) features of Teresa's writings are relatively few.[5]

What can philological methods bring to this complex issue on the quincentenary of the Saint's birth? Three strands of important developments in Spanish historical linguistics over the last quarter of a century make a reassessment of this question timely.

The first is the recognition of the significance of **text-types** and **traditions of discourse** for the historical development of a language. In simple terms, no text exists in isolation, but is written by an author who has knowledge of other texts. The consequent hypothesis is that any document is subject to a 'double filter' of conformity, not only to the grammatical rules of the language but also to a discourse tradition; such an approach redefines the question in hand as that of how such a double filter could have acted in the case of Santa Teresa.[6] Closely associated with this, and most germane to a study of Teresa's style, has been the study of the nature of **the representation of the spoken language in the written**. This has led to a more critical evaluation of the traditional rather simplistic dichotomy between 'written' and 'spoken' language and the suggestion of a cline between 'inmediatez' [closeness] and 'distancia comunicativas' [distance between speakers].[7] Wulf Oesterreicher comments apropos of Teresa's *estilo llano* [plain style]: 'este estilo se concibe esencialmente con finalidades estéticas y no con el interés de imitar la lengua hablada' [this style is conceived for aesthetic purposes rather than for imitating spoken language].[8] But it is in fact very difficult to establish any plausible reference for the spoken language of the sixteenth century, since even texts which purport to represent the spoken language may do so only in a rather indirect way which requires a good deal of philological mediation. My own investigations of register in the prose dramas of Lope de Rueda, for example, have revealed significant variation in styles of speech by his characters, not only in terms of what might be regarded as their 'default' styles, but also in terms of style-shifting and accommodation within the same character.[9]

The second strand of recent developments, which has been to a large extent inspired by the first, is the philological interest in and editing of **texts of a non-literary nature**:[10] legal documents, reports, travelogues and official and personal correspondence.

Lastly, of immense practical and methodological significance, is the availability of **texts in electronic format** and **large reference historical corpora** (CORDE and the Corpus del español) which permit quantitative analysis of some linguistic features and comparison across texts with relative ease.[11]

As an example, we can re-examine an interesting claim made by Flasche, who analyses the insertion of the clause beginning with *como*, shown in bold in (1), in the first sentence of the prologue to the *Book of her Life* [*Libro de la vida*].[12] He asks whether, although we might be tempted to think of this rather awkward construction as a feature of spoken language, it might not also represent in its complexity a sophisticated style of writing.

> (1) Quisiera yo <u>que como</u> **me han mandado y dado larga licencia para que escriba el modo de oración y las mercedes que el Señor me ha hecho**, me la dieran para que muy por menudo y con claridad dijera mis grandes pecados y ruin vida.[13]

The sequential combination of conjunctions such as *que si*, *que como*, etc. is for Flasche a symptom of Teresa's debt to cultured sources (*que como* is exemplified in [1] and *que si* in [2] [underlined]).

> (2) [...] y había algunas de las más mozas que me ayudaban en esto, <u>que si</u> todas fueran de un parecer, mucho me aprovechara. (*Vida* 3.2)[14]

Running a check on these sequences (*que si* and *que como*) in the CORDE corpus yields interestingly significant results (Table A). CORDE has the advantage of permitting retrieval of examples by date range and textual genre, and so we can compare these sequences for the Golden Age section of the corpus (1493–1713) according to genre.

	Prosa narrative	Prosa/verso dramatic	Prosa didáctica	Prosa científica	Sociedad	Religión	Historia y documentos	Derecho
que si	7,826	470	1,873	4,002	1,976	5,200	8,869	3,354
no. texts	203	48	62	206	157	119	589	815
frequency ptw[15]	0.89‰	0.12‰	0.71‰	0.86‰	0.69‰	2.31‰	1.92‰	1.92‰
que como	3,491	121	806	1,950	660	3,200	4,508	1,035
no. texts	184	29	60	151	93	102	429	422
frequency ptw	0.40‰	0.03‰	0.31‰	0.42‰	0.23‰	1.42‰	0.97‰	0.59‰
sample	8,750,000	4,062,000	2,625,000	4,637,500	2,875,000	2,250,000	4,625,000	1,750,000

TABLE A. *que si* and *que como* sequences in CORDE (1493–1713)

A random inspection of the results (I have not for practical reasons analysed all 49,341 instances) suggests that most are comparable to the Teresian examples and represent the insertion of a subordinate clause immediately after the *que*, which can be a complementizer or a relative. The sequences are most favoured in the three right-hand genres (religious, historical/documentary, and legal texts) whilst being less favoured in literature (especially drama). The likely conclusion, and an important refinement of Flasche's view, is therefore that Teresa's stylistic debt is to 'practical literacy' models rather than what have traditionally been regarded as cultured sources.

2 The parameters of Teresa's style

I want to begin by evaluating the language of the *Libro de la vida* in terms of discourse parameters which date back to M. A. K. Halliday's approach to the analysis of the notion of the register of texts.[16] Curiously, I have never seen these applied as such to Teresa's writings, and yet they seem to me to be a fundamental starting point, since they can be seen to determine a number of features of her writing which may set it apart from other traditions of discourse altogether.

2.1 Mode

First, the parameter of **mode**, which is crucial in situating texts on Koch and Oesterreicher's immediacy/distance scale. If we are to take Teresa literally, we will know that she wrote the *Life* quickly and without subsequent revision:

> Yo he hecho lo que vuestra merced me mandó en alargarme, a condición que vuestra merced haga lo que me prometió en romper lo que mal le pareciere. No había acabado de leerlo después de escrito, cuando vuestra merced envía por él. Puede ser vayan algunas cosas mal declaradas y otras puestas dos veces; porque ha sido tan poco el tiempo que he tenido, que <u>no podía tornar a ver lo que escribía</u>. (*Vida*, Epílogo) [my underlining][17]

This is not the same thing as transcribing speech, since even fast writing is of necessity slower than speech. But such a mode of text production is *a priori* likely to have resulted in what linguists since Chomsky have called 'performance errors', i.e. features which in retrospect might have been recognized as unacceptable by the writer and amended ('cosas mal declaradas'). Thus when Teresa writes (3):

> (3) [...] si no usamos bien del tesoro y del gran estado en que [~~nos~~] pone, nos lo tornará a tomar [...]. (*Vida* 10.6) [my strike-through][18]

can we be sure that she would not have added *nos* before *pone* if she had had the opportunity to revise the text herself, or that, as it stands, it is something she would have said? Perhaps it was omitted because she was thrown by also writing *nos* (the raised clitic indirect object of *tomar*) immediately after the verb? In (4), similarly, there is a construction which would surely have been deemed inelegant stylistically: two prepositions (*de* and *en*) appear together. This is no doubt the consequence of Teresa's having foregrounded in her mind the relationship of prayer and so delayed linearly the infinitive complement of *tener vergüenza de* (*tornarme a llegar* [...]); but might she not have revised this sentence to make it stylistically more satisfactory (as suggested in brackets) if it had been possible to redraft it, or, indeed, if she had not been writing so quickly in the first place?

> (4) [...] que ya yo tenía vergüenza de en tan particular amistad como es tratar de oración tornarme a llegar a Dios (*Vida* 7.1)[19]
>
> (= que ya yo tenía vergüenza de tornarme a llegar a Dios en tan particular amistad como es tratar de oración)

Octavio de Toledo's researches suggest that she is likely to have been very aware of such features.[20]

Another natural consequence of this mode is the lack of cohesion which is strikingly evident in Teresa's writing. Her propensity to ellipsis has often been noted, but we can be more discriminating about the nature of this: I will look at just one phenomenon which features very frequently in the *Libro de la vida*. While it is of course normal in Spanish for a verb not to have an overt subject when the subject is clear from the discourse, subjects are usually expressed for purposes of contrastive stress; however, Teresa often omits them in such cases. In (5), despite the fact that there is a strong contrast made between Teresa's mother and Teresa herself and between mother and children, the only stressed subject pronoun used is *yo* (shown in bold; I indicate absent subject pronouns in square brackets and the contrastive stress which an English reader would add orally by underlinings in the Cohen translation).[21] Indeed, one notes how very often translations of Teresa expand significantly on the original for precisely such reasons of clarity (raising, incidentally, interesting questions as to how appropriate they actually are as translations).

> (5) [Mi madre] Era aficionada a libros de caballerías, y no tan mal [ella] tomaba este pasatiempo como **yo** le tomé para mí; porque [ella] no perdía su labor, sino [nosotros] desenvolvíamonos para leer en ellos, y por ventura [ella] lo hacía para no pensar en grandes trabajos que [ella] tenía, y ocupar sus hijos, que no anduviesen en otras cosas perdidos. (*Vida* 2.1)[22]

> [She was very fond of books of chivalry, and this amusement did not have the bad effect on <u>her</u> that it came to have on <u>me</u>, because <u>she</u> never neglected her duties for it. But <u>we</u> were always making time for reading, and she let us, perhaps in order to distract her mind from her great sufferings, or perhaps merely for the sake of amusing her children and keeping them from pursuing other wickednesses.][23]

Another example of failure to indicate contrastive stress, this time with an object pronoun, is:

> (6) [...] por esto no me nombro, ni a nadie [...] (*Vida* 10.7)[24]
>
> (= no me nombro [ni a mí] ni a nadie)

Lack of clear subject anaphoric reference is also apparent in the use of some infinitive structures in place of full clauses, e.g.

> (7) Yo soy muy aficionada a San Agustín, porque el monesterio adonde estuve seglar era de su Orden; y también por haber sido pecador [...] (*Vida* 9.7)[25]
>
> (= porque [San Agustín] había sido pecador)

In (7), the understood subject of *haber sido pecador* must be *San Agustín* rather than, as would normally expected in such a construction, the subject of the sentence (*yo*). It is of course unambiguously interpretable because of the gender agreement (*pecador* rather than *pecadora*).

Another feature determined by the mode of Teresa's writing is that a complex construction may not be completed, but may give way to another, so creating a syntactic solecism. In (8), an instance which is celebrated for its difficulty of interpretation, we see the apparent lack of an apodosis corresponding to the protasis *si me ayudo al principio...* shown in bold (it might plausibly be *yo saldré / el alma saldrá con ello*). But Teresa tries to add as a parenthesis the fearfulness which attends the commencement of any task and the expression of the notions, first, that God wishes the soul to feel fear, and, second, that the greater the fear, the greater the reward will be. So the potential first apodosis becomes the protasis of a new conditional sentence (*si sale con ello*, also in bold).

> (8) Porque ya tengo espiriencia en muchas que, **si me ayudo al principio a determinarme a hacerlo** (que, siendo sólo por Dios, hasta encomenzarlo[26] quiere — para que más merezcamos — que el alma sienta aquel espanto, y mientras mayor, **si sale con ello**, mayor premio y más sabroso se hace después) [...] (*Vida* 4.2)[27]

Some of these features, especially constructional solecism, parallel what we know about spontaneous spoken discourse in modern Spanish, but the kind of ellipsis I have described, in which clear anaphoric reference is compromised, is not on the whole paralleled in speech. Nor does it seem to be associated with any of the textual traditions with which Santa Teresa was likely to have been familiar. It is not even a feature of everyday correspondence: although Fernández Alcaide mentions subject ellipsis as a feature of the sixteenth-century private letters she analyses,[28] closer inspection of the texts reveals that there is rarely the same level of difficulty of interpretation as is the case in the *Libro de la vida*. I therefore incline to the conclusion that what we are seeing here is more a function of the idiosyncratic mode of composition than either mimesis of the spoken language or the following of a particular tradition of discourse.

2.2 Tenor

Secondly, we should consider the parameter of **tenor**, or relation between (in this case) writer and reader. Indeed, Víctor García de la Concha called attention to the importance of taking the nature of the addressee into account in any analysis of Teresa's style.[29] As is well known, the *Libro de la vida* has a very specific and, in the context of Golden Age literary production, a relatively unusual overall tenor (indeed, Lázaro Carreter interestingly pointed out that there was no precedent in literature in Castilian for such autobiography):[30] the autobiographical account of her life and spiritual development directed to her confessor, Padre García de Toledo, who is often directly addressed (as *vuestra merced*):

> (9) No sé si digo desatinos; si lo son, **vuesa merced** los rompa; y si no lo son, **le** suplico ayude a mi simpleza con añidir aquí mucho [...] (*Vida* 7.22)[31]

Accordingly, first-person forms (verbs, pronouns, possessives) are very frequent, and first-person narrative predominates. But there is also frequent third-person reference to God, other third-person narrative, and many parenthetical passages in which the tenor essentially changes and Teresa addresses God directly in the second person *vos* form (10a). God is also addressed indirectly in the third person (10b), which is consistent with the direct addressing of Padre García de Toledo.

> (10a) ¡Oh Señor mío!, pues parece **tenéis determinado** que me salve, plega a vuestra Majestad sea ansí; y de hacerme tantas mercedes como me **habéis hecho**, ¿no **tuviérades** por bien — no por mi ganancia, sino por **vuestro** acatamiento — que no me ensuciara tanto posada adonde tan continuo **habíades** de morar? (*Vida* 1.8)[32]

> (10b) **Sea** bendito por todo y **sírvase** de mí, por quien Su Majestad **es**, que bien **sabe** mi Señor que no pretendo otra cosa en esto, sino que **sea** alabado y engrandecido un poquito de ver que en un muladar tan sucio y de mal olor hiciese huerto de tan suaves flores. (*Vida* 10.9)[33]

Sensitive to her habit of digressing and changing tenor, Teresa shows herself aware of the need for textual cohesion in her discourse by the use of 'signposts' such as *tornando a lo que decía, como ahora diré, como después diré*. Although these might seem to be formulae which follow an existing textual tradition, the evidence of

CORDE for the period 1400 to 1570 appears to show that these are peculiar to, or at least particularly favoured by Teresa. For *tornando a lo que decía* there are only six tokens returned, all from the *Libro de la vida*. Of the fourteen tokens of *como ahora/agora diré*, nine are from the *Libro de la vida* and five from Gonzalo Fernández de Oviedo's *Historia general y natural de las Indias*. *Como después diré* yields twenty-three tokens, eight from the *Libro de la vida* and seven from Francisco Cervantes de Salazar's *Crónica de la Nueva España*, with all other examples from technical texts or correspondence.

Of particular interest with regard to the achievement of textual cohesion is Teresa's use of such discourse markers. I want to focus on just one of these, *pues*, which had a number of different discourse functions in sixteenth-century Spanish. Teresa uses it in what may be regarded as a 'commentary' function, introducing a sentence which is an elaboration or explanation of the preceding discourse (what Cano Aguilar has designated the *pues* 'reactivo' [reactive] and Martínez García the *pues* 'fático' [phatic].[34] In this sense it is used clause-initially; it is not equivalent to *de modo que* and does not express literal consequence, but rather has the value of *en este caso* 'in that case; that being the case', indicating that the speaker is bearing the preceding discourse in mind, and corresponds to English 'so', 'well', 'indeed'). Teresa uses *pues* in this way as a general indication that the ensuing material indeed coheres with what has gone before (11):

> (11) Señalé con unas rayas las partes que eran y dile el libro para que él y el otro clérigo que he dicho, santo y siervo de Dios, lo mirasen y me dijesen lo que había de hacer [...]. **Pues** como di el libro y hecha relación de mi vida y pecados, lo mijor que pude por junto (que no confesión por ser seglar; más bien di a entender cuán ruin era) los dos siervos de Dios miraron con gran caridad y amor lo que me convenía. (*Vida* 23.12; 14)[35]

> [I underlined the relevant passage and gave him the book, so that he and that cleric I have mentioned, a holy man and a servant of God, might look at it, and tell me what I ought to do. (...) **Well**, when I had handed him the book, and given him the best account I could of my life and sins — not in confession, since he was a layman, although I fully explained to him how wicked I was — these two servants of God considered with great charity and love what would be best for me.]

In a study of the register value of discourse markers in sixteenth-century Spanish, I found that some texts were sharply differentiated by this usage.[36] In Tomás de Mercado's *Suma de tratos*, a treatise on the ethics of business practice,[37] it was almost completely absent. On the other hand, Fray Luis de Granada's *Guía de pecadores*, a text with which Teresa was almost certainly familiar,[38] has a similar propensity for this function of *pues* for the purpose of introducing a comment (12a) or a parenthetical remark (12b):

> (12a) [...] el teólogo escolástico no se contenta con el lugar de en medio, sino pone su silla sobre todos; y a ninguno le faltan razones, y grandes razones, para creer que su ciencia es la mejor y más necesaria. **Pues** esto que se halla en las ciencias tan descubiertamente, se halla en las virtudes, aunque más disimuladamente [...] (Fray Luis de Granada, *Guía de pecadores*, I, p. xvi)

> [(...) **For [indeed]** what is found so openly in the sciences is also found in virtues, though more covertly.]

> (12b) Lea quien pudiere los Opúsculos de san Buenaventura, que fue un doctor tan señalado en letras, en devoción, en religión, en prudencia de gobernar — **pues** a los trece años de su profesión fue general de su orden, y después obispo y cardenal — , y ahí verá cuántas maneras de potajes hace este santo de la vida y pasión de Cristo [...] (Fray Luis de Granada, *De doce singulares provechos...*, I)

> [(...) **indeed**, thirteen years after taking his vows he was the General of his Order (...)]

A very similar usage is found in Lope de Rueda's plays, where it typically introduces a speaker's comment on the basis of the instruction just received or the information just given, and signals the beginning of a new conversational turn which elaborates on the previous one. In (13a) Ginesa is acceding to Socrato's request, indicating that she accepts the reasons he gives for it, and in (13b) she asks for further information about what has happened to Pablos, for an explanation of how he came to fall, to which he has alluded rather casually.

> (13a) SOCRATO. No quiero por agora, sino por vida vuestra, ama, que os entréis allá dentro, y le aconsejéis de vuestra parte lo que mejor os paresciere, pues veis que le cumple, y aderéçame essa casa, que yo quiero ir a verme con essos señores.
> GINESA. **Pues** yo me entro, señor. (Lope de Rueda, *Camila*)[39]
> [(...) **Well (in that case)**, I'll go in.]

> (13b) PABLOS. [...] que creo que se me ha mudado el tono de la voz, como la color de los vestidos con la caída que di.
> GINESA. **Pues** ¿cómo caístes, o quién os hizo caer? (*ibid.*)
> [(...) **So (then)**, how did you fall (...)?]

While this feature in Teresa appears, then, to owe something to the spoken language, it is also possible that she is reflecting the tradition of discourse of direct address represented by Fray Luis de Granada.[40] But it is also apparent that such a strategy, the need to make links within a discourse that is very prone to parenthesis, is necessitated by the tenor of her writing.

2.3 Field

The third parameter to be considered is **field**, or, in simple terms, subject matter. Again, this is of considerable significance in the *Libro de la vida*, where Teresa is often struggling (and surely that is not too extreme a term) to convey experiences which are literally beyond conventional words. On the lexical level, Teresa appears very sophisticated (albeit with due self-depreciation and attribution of any such sophistication to God). Consider the richness of the semantic field of mystical experience represented by the words in bold in (14) and the clarity of the spatio-temporal distinctions made by the words in bold underline:

> (14) Querría saber declarar con el favor de Dios la diferencia que hay de **unión** a **arrobamiento** u **elevamiento** u **vuelo** que llaman **de espíritu** u

arrebatamiento, que todo es uno. Digo que estos diferentes nombres todo es una cosa, y también se llama **éstasi**. Es grande la ventaja que hace a la unión. Los efectos muy mayores hace, y otras hartas operaciones, porque la unión parece **principio** y **medio** y **fin** y lo es en lo interior; mas ansí como estotros fines son más alto grado, hace los efetos **interior** y **esteriormente**. Declárelo el Señor, como ha hecho lo demás, que, cierto, si Su Majestad no me hubiera dado a entender por qué modos y maneras se puede algo decir, yo no supiera. (*Vida* 20.1)[41]

Where she has more obvious difficulty is with syntactic complexity, which is also to be understood as a performance difficulty against the background of the mode of her writing. Looking at the structure of (15a), we can see that opacity of the section in bold is caused by the construction of a complex comparison with elision of some key elements, which are represented more fully in (15b), where coreference is shown by subscripts. Again, an English translation (15c) is compelled to fill in the missing material (shown in square brackets).

(15a) Paréceme que el demonio ha usado de este ardid como cosa que muy mucho le importa: **que se ascondan tanto de que se entienda que de veras quieren procurar amar y contentar a Dios, como ha incitado se descubran otras voluntades mal honestas, con ser tan usadas que** ya parece se toma por gala y se publican las ofensas que en este caso se hacen a Dios. (*Vida* 7.21)[42]

(15b) [...] (el demonio) [ha incitado que]
　　(tanto) [los que de veras quieren procurar amar y contentar a Dios] se escondan de que se entienda [su voluntad$_i$]
　　(como) [los que tienen voluntades$_j$ malhonestas] se descubran.
　　Estas voluntades$_j$ son tan usadas que [...].

(15c) [(The devil) uses them (to persuade) (men) who truly desire to love and please God to conceal *(omission in the translation)* their intentions, while he incites (others) to make open show of their evil purposes. (This state of things) is now so usual that (...).][43]

Thus the field of the *Libro de la vida* requires a sophisticated, even technical, level of discourse from which Teresa does not shy away, even if she sometimes cannot in a linear mode of composition handle its hierarchical syntactic complexity. As an indication of this, consider the frequency of comparative constructions, an indication of which is the presence of the elements *tan* and *tanto*, etc., in samples of the *Libro de la vida* and three other sixteenth-century texts in Table B). The frequency of *tan* in the *Libro de la vida* is significantly higher.

	Tan		*tanto* etc		Sample
Lazarillo	27	2.67	36	3.56	10,125
Vida	67	6.65	20	1.98	10,081
Suma	33	3.26	20	1.98	10,125
Acosta	20	1.94	25	2.42	10,331

TABLE B: *tan* and *tanto*, etc., in four sixteenth-century text samples

3 Towards the Subconscious?

Beyond the particular demands of mode, tenor and field which fashion Teresa's discourse, we can examine more deeply ingrained, systematic, features of her writing in an attempt to identify the traditions of discourse against which she wrote, and make quantitative comparisons across a range of texts. I want to indicate briefly how this might be done, and the kinds of results we might obtain, for just two features which I have found to be syntactic hallmarks of her writing, and not just in the *Libro de la vida*, although I shall continue to take this text as my basic reference point. I have used for this purpose the texts listed in the Appendix, which represent a number of genres across the sixteenth century.[44]

3.1 Relatives

Elsewhere I have shown that choice of relative pronoun has almost certainly been dependent on register since at least the fifteenth century.[45] My study of this group of sixteenth-century texts confirms this view.

3.1.1 'El cual', etc.

Considering first *el cual*, etc., José Luís Girón Alconchel, quoting Lapesa, says that *el cual* became fashionable in the fifteenth century as a literary and emphatic relative, and Beatriz Arias Álvarez observes that *el qual* is more prevalent in Golden Age written texts of a legal nature.[46] The forms involving *cual* had advantages for use in complex discourse since they marked gender and number and so were transparent in making reference to their antecedent. In Rueda, I found that the use of *el cual*, etc., as a relativizer appears to have been at least an **indicator** of upper-class speech, as can be clearly seen from Table C.[47]

	el cual, etc	Sample (words)	Frequency ptw
Upper classes	26	11,747	2.21‰
Shepherds	22	8,675	2.54‰
Subtotal	48	20,422	2.35‰
Middle classes	9	9,467	0.95‰
Lower classes	5	16,563	0.30‰

TABLE C: use of *el cual*, etc., in the prose dramas of Lope de Rueda[48]

Now, as can be seen from Table D, Teresa is very distinctive in not using forms in *el cual*, etc., and actually shows an even lower frequency than the middle- and lower-class characters in Rueda. This must raise the question as to whether for her the feature is a **marker**, i.e. a feature to be avoided because it has social or stylistic significance. It is inconceivable that she would not have been aware of it passively.

	el cual, etc.	*la cual*	*los cuales*	*las cuales*	*lo cual*	Total	Sample (words)	Freq. ptw
Amadís	28	18	13	4	14	77	127,982	0.60‰
Guevara	69	109	56	42	50	326	79,579	4.10‰
Osuna	173	128	72	61	235	669	96,601	6.93‰
Diálogo	4	1	13	5	0	23	38,732	0.59‰
Lazarillo	23	8	6	7	8	52	18,563	2.80‰
Vida	*1*	*2*	*1*	*0*	*0*	*4*	*113,829*	*0.04‰*
Suma	72	75	104	66	381	698	250,755	2.78‰
Moradas	*0*	*0*	*1*	*0*	*0*	*1*	*58,383*	*0.02‰*
Acosta	45	34	10	15	55	159	98,113	1.62‰

TABLE D. *el cual*, etc. in sixteenth-century texts

Some concomitant features of Teresa's use of relatives correspond to modern spoken rather than written usage, although similar statistics are extremely laborious to obtain for the sixteenth century. For example, the treatment of prepositions with relatives, which has come to be one of the preferred functions of *el cual*, etc., in written usage[49] and which predated the later use of *el que*, etc., is rendered in a number of alternative ways (16) (in each of the examples in (16) the antecedent is underlined and the sequence preposition + relative pronoun is shown in bold, with absence of a preposition by Ø). The preposition may not be present at all, but pragmatically understood (16a). Most often, the preposition is combined with the simple *que* (16b).

(16a) En la casa Ø **que** era monja no se prometía clausura. (*Vida* 4.5)[50]

(16b) [...] ha parecido que se podrá declarar algo de cuatro grados de oración, **en que** el Señor, por su bondad, ha puesto algunas veces mi alma. (*Vida* 11.8)[51]

Teresa also uses resumptive pronouns (17), the effect of which is to make the reference of the relative pronoun clear in the same way as *el cual*, etc., because the resumptive pronoun (also indicated in bold) indicates not only gender and number but also the function of the relativized element within the relative clause.[52]

(17) No he conocido persona que de veras le sea devota y haga particulares servicios, **que** no **la** vea más aprovechada en la virtud [...] (*Vida* 6.7)[53]

A final, particularly interesting, strategy of Teresa's is to place the preposition before the antecedent (18).

(18) [...] a decirme **en** el peligro **que** andaba [...] (*Vida* 6.4)[54]

(= a decirme el peligro en que andaba)

This seems to be a minority construction in the sixteenth century, though it is very laborious to establish statistics (as an indication, in the CORDE corpus, *en el peligro que* in the function of *el peligro en que* shows fourteen instances in the sixteenth century as against four of *en el peligro en que* (one of these is also from *Vida*) and

421 of *el peligro en que*).⁵⁵ Teresa seems to have a certain propensity towards the construction: I have found four examples of the relatively common sequence *de la manera que* used in the sense of *la manera de que* (19) in *Vida* and two in *Moradas*, while none of the other texts in my sample record this construction at all.

(19) Pues veamos ahora **de la manera que** se puede regar [...] (*Vida* 11.7)⁵⁶

(= [...] la manera de que [...])

Neither have I been able to establish a clear social value for this construction: there is only one example in Rueda, from an upper-class (shepherd) character (20), which suggests that it belongs to a cultured rather than a spoken register, though this cannot be conclusive evidence.

(20) y **de lo que** yo más preciarme debo (Lope de Rueda, *Tymbria*, Sulco)

(Note also in this example the inversion of the auxiliary [*debo*] and the infinitive [*preciarme*], which is a characteristic of 'rhetorical', upper-class, style.) A plausible conclusion is that although the construction was perhaps an indicator of cultured usage, it did not have the status of a marker, and that accordingly Teresa does not strive to suppress it.

3.1.2 'Quien', 'quienes'

In the use of *quien* (though not the innovation *quienes*, which in the texts I have surveyed only achieves any significant frequency in *Suma*,⁵⁷ Teresa again shows a certain individuality, since both *Vida* and *Moradas* show, along with *Suma*, a distinctively high frequency for this relative (Table E). The use of *quien* as a prepositional object relative may have provided another strategy to compensate for Teresa's resistance to *el cual*, etc., and similar conclusions can be drawn: *quien* was not a marker of cultured usage.

	Ø	*como*	*A*	*De*	*con*	*en*	*Por*	*para*	other	Total prep.	Total	Sample	Freq ptw	*quienes*
Amadís	30	8	37	12	16	3	16	1	2	87	125	127,982	0.98‰	0
Guevara	17	2	16	8	6	1	1	1	2	35	54	79,579	0.68‰	2
Osuna	14	5	15	2	2	0	0	0	0	19	38	96,601	0.39‰	0
Diálogo	8	1	8	1	4	0	0	0	0	13	22	38,732	0.57‰	0
Lazarillo	6	3	6	1	2	1	0	0	1	11	20	18,563	1.08‰	0
Vida	98	35	116	25	27	3	10	5	0	186	319	113,829	2.80‰	0
Suma	384	14	187	73	21	15	10	8	4	318	716	250,755	2.86‰	65
Moradas	54	8	64	12	7	3	5	3	0	94	156	58,383	2.67‰	0
Acosta	32	3	23	14	0	5	1	2	1	46	81	98,113	0.83‰	2

TABLE E. *quien (quienes)* in sixteenth-century texts

3.1.3 'cuyo', etc.

Teresa is a relatively low user of *cuyo*, etc., which, like *el cual*, etc., is associated with more formal usage in modern Spanish and may also have been in the sixteenth century. Again, I have been unable to draw any conclusions about its register value in the sixteenth century on the basis of the Rueda material, since there are only three instances of *cuyo*, etc., in all: two in the upper-class/shepherd characters and one in a lower-class character; both the former are instances of *cuyo* used as a transition relative, which is in itself a feature associated with formal usage (21).

> (21) [...] mi amada hija Florentina, la cual [...] me fue robada de Viana, un pueblo donde yo nascí, por **cuya** falta mi mijo adoptivo he con harto trabajo criado (Rueda, *Armelina*, 4)

In Table F we can note that the highest users of *cuyo*, etc., are Tomás de Mercado in the technical *Suma de tratos* (by some margin), Guevara, and Osuna, followed by Acosta, all of whom are associated with a more formal mode of discourse.

	cuyo, etc	Sample	Freq. ptw
Amadís	11	127,982	0.09
Guevara	33	79,579	0.41
Osuna	60	96,601	0.62
Diálogo	3	38,732	0.08
Lazarillo	1	18,563	0.05
Vida	*8*	*113,829*	*0.07*
Suma	186	250,755	0.74
Moradas	*5*	*58,383*	*0.09*
Acosta	32	98,113	0.33

TABLE F. *cuyo*, etc., in sixteenth-century texts

Overall, I suggest that Teresa is avoiding relative constructions which for her are markers of formal written language, sometimes at the expense of clarity, but that she does not avoid those which are only indicators.

3.2 'Que'-deletion

The second feature to which I want to call attention is a phenomenon I call *que*-deletion. By *que*-deletion, I mean the omission, or apparent omission, of the *que* complementizer in such sentences as (22b) by comparison with (22a) (in (22) and (23), I indicate a deleted/omitted *que* by double strike-through):

> (22a) **Rogamos que** disculpen las molestias
>
> (22b) **Rogamos que** disculpen las molestias

Que-deletion is an interesting phenomenon in the history of Castilian because it appears to rise and fall in popularity relatively quickly. As Octavio de Toledo has perceptively pointed out in his study of syntactic amendments Teresa made to the *Camino de perfección*, in which she both adds and suppresses *que*, its omission conforms to the principle of the avoidance of the superfluous while its inclusion conforms to the principle of clarity.[58] *Que*-deletion in Santa Teresa occurs with very many verbs (23a–b) and even with adjectives (23c):[59]

(23a) [...] porque días había que **deseaba que** fuera posible a mi estado andar pidiendo por amor de Dios y no tener casa ni otra cosa [...] (*Vida*, 35.2)[60]

(23b) [...] porque un espíritu tan disgustado de ira pone el demonio, que **parece** a todos **que** me querría comer [...] (*Vida* 30.13)[61]

(23c) [...] muy **contenta (de) que** se ofreciese algo en que yo padeciese por Él y le pudiese servir, me fui [...] (*Vida* 36.11)[62]

	Parecer					*querer*					
	Quedel	Que	Total	Freq. ptw	% quedel of total	quedel	que	Total	Freq. ptw	% quedel of total	Sample
Amadís	1	41	42	0.33‰	2.38%	2	58	60	0.47‰	3.33%	127,982
Guevara	0	6	6	0.08‰	0%	0	25	25	0.31‰	0%	79,579
Osuna	2	30	32	0.33‰	6.25%	1	22	23	0.24‰	4.35%	96,601
Diálogo	12	31	43	1.11‰	27.91%	5	36	41	1.06‰	12.20%	38,732
Lazarillo	1	9	10	0.54‰	10.00%	1	7	8	0.43‰	12.50%	18,563
Vida	360	155	515	4.52‰	**69.90%**	60	51	111	0.98‰	**54.05%**	113,829
Suma	23	62	85	0.34‰	27.06%	36	22	58	0.23‰	62.07%	250,755
Moradas	73	117	190	3.25‰	**38.42%**	6	44	50	0.86‰	12.00%	58,383
Acosta	18	75	93	0.95‰	19.35%	3	18	21	0.21‰	14.29%	98,113

TABLE G. *Que*-deletion in sixteenth-century texts (complements of *parecer* and *querer*)

Table G shows the striking frequency of *que*-deletion in Teresa, most especially in *Libro de la vida*, though it will be noted that *Las moradas* stands in second place in terms of the proportion of *que*-deleted instances of complements of *parecer*. Establishing the social/stylistic level of *que*-deletion has not proved straightforward, not least because, perhaps surprisingly, it has received relatively little attention as a syntactic feature. Keniston suggestively points out that Santa Teresa, in using *que*-deletion so prodigally, cannot be reflecting popular usage, since *que*-deletion is rare in Lope de Rueda.[63] Indeed, what we see from Table H is that the text to which Teresa comes closest statistically is the *Suma de tratos*, and so in this case she shares her predilection with the most formal level of technical writing in the Castilian of her day.

4 Conclusions

This has of necessity been a very partial survey of what I have suggested are some of the distinctive linguistic features of Teresa's writing, and a consistent conclusion may seem unreachable. But I would suggest that really that is the point: Teresa's writing will not, and indeed *a priori* would not be expected to, fit one particular tradition of discourse. It is certainly not equatable with 'spontaneous' spoken language, nor indeed to my mind can it be appropriately characterized as 'llaneza': the demands of field show a sophistication of lexis and syntactic construction that is not mirrored in everyday speech, and the *que*-deletion which is such a striking feature of her writing is more associated with technical writing than with vernacular usage.[64] However, it is possible that Teresa deliberately steered clear of features such as the *el cual* and *cuyo* relatives that she recognized as markers of the formal written language. A number of features which might be thought of as originating in the spoken language (absence of explicit anaphoric reference, syntactic solecism) are more likely to have been the result of the very distinctive mode and tenor of her writing (and indeed *que*-deletion might also fall into this category as having a similar advantage of economy). Finally, we must also not discount the possibility of certain features (the formulae marking cohesion, for example) being particular to herself, part of the creativity which notably manifested itself in her mastery of the field to which her writing pertained. Almost certainly, however, further comparative investigation of features of her writing with other sixteenth-century texts, particularly manifestations of 'practical literacy', will put the study of her 'style' on a rigorous empirical basis.

Appendix

Amadís = Garci Rodríguez de Montalvo, *Amadís de Gaula*, Libro Primero <www.ladeliteratura.com.uy/biblioteca/amadis.pdf> [accessed 15 February 2015]. (First published Zaragoza 1508, though based on versions dating from many years previously.)

Guevara = Antonio de Guevara, *Libro primero de las epístolas familiares, edición digital basada en la edición de Madrid, Aldus, 1950–1952*. <http://www.cervantesvirtual.com/obra/libro-primero-de-las-epistolas-familiares--2>. (1526) [accessed 22 August 2015]

Osuna = *Tratados I–X* of Francisco de Osuna, *Tercer abecedario espiritual, estudio histórico y edición crítica por Melquíades Andrés*, Biblioteca de Autores Cristianos, 333 (Madrid: Editorial Católica, 1972). (1527)

Valdés = Juan de Valdés, *Diálogo de la lengua. Edición, introducción y notas de Juan M. Lope Blanch*, Clásicos Castalia, 11 (Madrid: Castalia, 1976). (1535)

Lazarillo = Anon., *Lazarillo de Tormes. Edición de Francisco Rico*. 2nd edn (Madrid: Cátedra, 1987), and <http://www.cervantesvirtual.com/obra-visor/la-vida-de-lazarillo-de-tormes-y-de-sus-fortunas-y-adversidades--0/html/fedb2f54-82b1-11df-acc7-002185ce6064_2.html#I_0_>. (1554) [accessed 22 August 2015]

Vida = Dámaso Chicharro, ed., *Santa Teresa de Jesús: Libro de la Vida*, 10th edn (Madrid: Cátedra, 1994) (1562)

Suma = Tomás de Mercado: *Suma de tratos y contratos, edición digital basada en la edición de Madrid, Instituto de Estudios Fiscales, Ministerio de Economía y Hacienda, 1977* <http://www.cervantesvirtual.com/obra/suma-de-tratos-y-contratos--0>, Parts I and II. (1571) [accessed 22 February 2012]

Moradas = Santa Teresa de Jesús, *Las moradas o castillo interior*, in *Obras completas*, ed. by Efrén de la Madre de Dios and Otger Steggick, Biblioteca de Autores Cristianos, 212, 8th edn (Madrid: Editorial Católica, 1986), pp. 469–583. (1577)

Acosta = José de Acosta: *Escritos menores, edición digital a partir de* Obras del P. José de Acosta, Madrid, Atlas, 1954, pp. 250–386. <http://www.cervantesvirtual.com/obra-visor-din/escritos-menores--0/html/fee5cdd8–82b1–11df-acc7–002185ce6064.html> (1569–95) [accessed 15 March 2015]

Notes to Chapter 13

1. A. Sánchez Moguel, *El lenguaje de Santa Teresa de Jesús: juicio comparativo de sus escritos con los de san Juan de la Cruz y otros clásicos de su época* (Madrid: Imprenta Clásica Española, 1915); Ramón Menéndez Pidal, 'El estilo de Santa Teresa', in *La lengua de Cristóbal Colón: la lengua de santa Teresa y otros estudios sobre el siglo XVI*, Colección Austral, 228 (Madrid: Espasa-Calpe, 1942), pp. 119–42.
2. Fernando Lázaro Carreter, 'Fray Luis y el estilo de Santa Teresa', in *Homenaje a Gonzalo Torrente Ballester* (Salamanca: Biblioteca de la Caja de Ahorros y Monte de Piedad, 1981), pp. 463–69; 'Santa Teresa de Jesús, escritora (El "Libro de la vida")', in *Actas del Congreso Internacional Teresiano*, ed. by Teófanes Egido Martínez, Víctor García de la Concha and Olegario González de Cardedal (Salamanca: Universidad de Salamanca, 1983), pp. 11–27; Hans Flasche, 'Syntaktische Untersuchungen zu Santa Teresa de Jesús', in *Gesammelte Aufsätze zur Kulturgeschichte Spaniens 15 Band*, ed. by Johannes Vincke (Münster: Aschendorffsche Verlagsbuchhandlung, 1960), pp. 151–74; Flasche, 'Considerações sobre a estrutura da frase espanhola analisada na autobiografia de Santa Teresa', *Boletim de Filologia*, 19 (1961), 177–86.
3. Luisa López Grigera, 'Historia textual: textos literarios (Siglo de Oro)', in *Historia de la lengua española*, ed. by Rafael Cano Aguilar, 2nd edn (Barcelona: Ariel, 2005), pp. 701–28.
4. Álvaro S. Octavio de Toledo y Huerta, 'Santa Teresa y la mano visible: sobre las variantes sintácticas del *Camino de perfección*', in *Así se van las lenguas variando: nuevas tendencias en la investigación del cambio lingüístico en español*. ed. by Mónica Castillo Lluch and Lola Pons Rodríguez, Fondo hispánico de lingüística y filología, 5 (Bern: Peter Lang, 2011), pp. 241–304.
5. A conspicuous exception is María Jesús Mancho Duque, '*El Camino de perfección*: génesis y aspectos lingüísticos' (Alicante: Biblioteca Virtual Miguel de Cervantes, at <http://www.cervantesvirtual.com/nd/ark:/59851/bmc12695>, 2008) [accessed 4 April 2015].
6. Johannes Kabatek, 'Tradiciones discursivas y cambio lingüístico', *Lexis*, 29 (2005), 151–77.
7. See Peter Koch and Wulf Oesterreicher, 'Sprache der Nähe — Sprache der Distanz. Mündlichkeit und Schriftlichkeit im Spannungsfeld von Sprachtheorie und Sprachgeschichte', *Romanistisches Jahrbuch*, 36 (1985), 15–43.
8. Wulf Oesterreicher, 'Textos entre inmediatez y distancia comunicativas: el problema de lo hablado escrito en el Siglo de Oro', in *Historia de la lengua española*, ed. by Rafael Cano Aguilar, pp. 729–69 (p. 755).
9. Christopher J. Pountain, 'Las distintas gramáticas de los relativos españoles', in *Actas del VII Congreso Internacional de Historia de la Lengua Española (Mérida, Yucatán)*, ed. by Concepción Company Company and José G. Moreno de Alba, 2 vols (Madrid: Arco, 2008), I, 967–80; 'Variation in Address Forms in Sixteenth-Century Spanish Prose Drama', in *Stvdia Lingvistica in honorem Mariae Manoliu*, ed. by Sanda Reinheimer-Rîpeanu (Bucharest: Editura Universității din București, 2009), pp. 282–93; 'Dislocación popular y dislocación culta en la comedia en prosa del Siglo de Oro español', in *Pragmatique historique et syntaxe / Historische Pragmatik und Syntax. Actes de la section du même nom du XXXIè Romanistentag allemand / Akten der gleichnamigen Sektion des XXXI. Deutschen Romanistentags (Bonn, 27.9.–1.10.2009)*, ed. by Barbara Wehr and Frédéric Nicolosi (Frankfurt am Main: Peter Lang, 2012), pp. 140–56; 'Valores sociolingüísticos y funcionales de los posesivos en el español peninsular del siglo XVI', in *Actas del VIII Congreso Internacional de Historia de la Lengua Española (Santiago de Compostela, 14–18 de septiembre de 2009)*, ed. by Emilio Montero, 2 vols (Santiago de Compostela: Meubook, 2012), I, 1059–72; '*Que*-deletion: The Rise and Fall of a Syntactic Fashion', in *En memoria de tanto miragre: estudos dedicados*

ó profesor David Mackenzie, ed. by Francisco Dubert García, Gabriel Rei-Doval, and Xulio Sousa (Santiago de Compostela: Universidade de Santiago de Compostela, Servizo de Publicacións e Intercambio Científico, 2015), pp. 143–59.
10. This is what Peter Burke calls 'practical literacy'. Peter Burke, 'The Uses of Literacy in Early Modern Italy', in *The Social History of Language*, ed. by Peter Burke and Roy Porter, Cambridge Studies in Oral and Literate Culture, 12 (Cambridge: Cambridge University Press, 1987), pp. 21–42 (p. 24).
11. Real Academia Española, Banco de datos (CORDE) [en línea]. Corpus diacrónico del español. <http://www.rae.es> [accessed 22 August 2015]; Mark Davies, *Corpus del Español: 100 million words, 1200s–1900s* (2002–). <http://www.corpusdelespanol.org> [accessed 22 August 2015].
12. Hans Flasche, 'Syntaktische Untersuchungen', pp. 158–59.
13. Teresa de Jesús, *Libro de la vida*. Page references are given to the edition by Dámaso Chicharro (Madrid: Cátedra: 2014), henceforth *Vida*. Prólogo, p. 117.
14. *Vida* 3.2, p. 130.
15. Per thousand words, also indicated by the per mille sign (‰).
16. M. A. K. Halliday, *Language as Social Semiotic: The Social Interpretation of Language and Meaning* (London: Arnold, 1978), pp. 31–35.
17. *Vida* Epílogo, p. 482.
18. *Vida* 10.6, p. 186.
19. *Vida* 7.1, p. 156.
20. Octavio de Toledo y Huerta, 'Santa Teresa y la mano visible'.
21. *The Life of Saint Teresa of Ávila by herself*, translated with an Introduction by J. M. Cohen (London: Penguin, 1957).
22. *Vida* 2.1, pp. 123–24; trans. by Cohen, *The Life of Saint Teresa of Ávila*, p. 26.
23. Another source of anaphoric vagueness here, this time verbal, is the reference of the general verb *hacía*. Does it actually mean 'let' as Cohen translates it (i.e. *nos dejaba leer*), or does it refer to the act of reading (i.e. *leía*)? There is no way of knowing.
24. *Vida* 10.7, p. 188.
25. *Vida* 9.7, p. 180.
26. The valency of *encomenzar* is also problematic: perhaps the subject *el alma* is to be understood.
27. *Vida* 4.2, pp. 134–35.
28. Marta Fernández Alcaide, *Cartas de particulares en Indias del siglo XVI: edición y estudio discursivo*, Textos y Documentos Españoles y Americanos, 6 (Madrid: Iberoamericana; Frankfurt a.M.: Vervuert, 2009), pp. 113–15.
29. Víctor García de la Concha, *El arte literario de Santa Teresa*, Letras e Ideas: Maior, 13 (Barcelona: Ariel, 1978), p. 190, quoted in Rafael Lapesa, 'Estilo y lenguaje de Santa Teresa en las Exclamaciones del alma a su Dios', in *Aureum Saeculum Hispanum. Beiträge zu Texten des Siglo de Oro. Festschrift für Hans Flasche zum 70. Geburtstag*, ed. by Karl-Hermann Körner and Dietrich Briesemeister (Wiesbaden: Steiner, 1983), pp. 125–40 (p. 125).
30. Lázaro Carreter, 'Santa Teresa de Jesús, escritora', p. 19.
31. *Vida* 7.22, p. 168.
32. *Vida* 1.8, p. 122.
33. *Vida* 10.9, p. 189.
34. Rafael Cano Aguilar, 'La sintaxis del diálogo en el Quijote (1615)', *Boletín de la Real Academia Española*, 85 (2005), 133–55 (p. 137); Hortensia Martínez García, 'Del "pues" «temporal» al causal y contrastivo', in *Actas del Congreso de la Sociedad Española de Lingüística, XX Aniversario, Tenerife, del 2 al 6 de abril de 1990*, ed. by María Ángeles Álvarez Martínez, 2 vols (Madrid: Gredos, 1990), II, 599–610 (p. 600).
35. *Vida* 23.12, 14, pp. 300–01; translated by Cohen, *The Life of Saint Teresa of Ávila*, pp. 166–67.
36. Christopher J. Pountain, 'Variation and the Use of Discourse Markers in Sixteenth-century Spanish', to appear in *Studies in Historical Ibero-Romance Morphosyntax*, ed. by Miriam Bouzouita, Ioanna Sitaridou and Enrique Pato (Amsterdam: Benjamins).
37. See Appendix.
38. Fray Luis de Granada, *Guía de pecadores*, 1556 <http://biblioteca.universia.net/html_bura/ficha/

params/title/guia-pecadores-cual-trata-copiosamente-grandes-riquezas-hermosura-virtud-camino/id/52557546.html> [accessed 28 August 2013].
39. *Teatro español del Siglo de Oro* (Madrid: Chadwyck-Healey Espanã) at <http://teso.chadwyck.co.uk/> [accessed 27 July 2004]. Examples are cited in a normalized spelling.
40. See also Santiago U. Sánchez Jiménez, 'Marcadores discursivos en el teatro de Lope de Rueda', in *Actas del VII Congreso Internacional de Historia de la Lengua Española (Mérida, Yucatán)*, ed. by Concepción Company Company and José G. Moreno de Alba, 2 vols (Madrid: Arco, 2008), I, 2163–88 (p. 2175).
41. *Vida* 20.1, p. 263.
42. *Vida* 7.21, pp. 167–68.
43. Trans. by Cohen, *The Life of Saint Teresa of Ávila*, p. 59.
44. It would clearly also be of great interest to compare Santa Teresa's work with other 'convent writing', especially that of those who might be viewed as her precursors (I am grateful to Trevor Dadson for suggesting this line of enquiry). Unfortunately, however, such texts are difficult to access, still less available in a reliably edited digital format which would permit comparable linguistic analysis. A text of potentially great relevance which is available in what is obviously a somewhat modernized form, the *Conhorte* of Madre Juana de la Cruz (Inocente García de Andrés, *'El Conhorte': Sermones de una mujer. La Santa Juana (1481–1534)* (Madrid: Fundación Universitaria Española and Universidad Pontificia de Salamanca, 1999), shows no obvious similarities with the features I am about to discuss here, and is in any case in a completely different tenor (sermons directed at a mixed congregation). Madre Juana's autobiography, apparently written at her deathbed dictation by a Sor María Evangelista, referred to by García de Andrés for convenience as *Vida y fin*, is a hitherto unedited manuscript (Escorial Library MS K-III-13). But even if such autobiographical texts were more easily available, it is doubtful whether they would have formed plausible models for Teresa: Ronald E. Surtz, *Writing Women in Late Medieval and Early Modern Spain: The Mothers of Saint Teresa of Avila* (Philadelphia: University of Pennsylvania Press, 1995), observes that 'Teresa de Cartagena, Constanza de Castilla, María de Ajofrín, María de Santo Domingo, and Juana de la Cruz were Saint Teresa's "mothers" only in the sense that they preceded her in time. They probably did not know about one another, and Teresa never speaks of them. Even if we allow that she may have heard about them — Juana de la Cruz was quite well known — it is unlikely that Teresa ever read their writings', p. 127.
45. Christopher J. Pountain, 'Las distintas gramáticas'.
46. José Luis Girón Alconchel, 'Las oraciones de relativo II. Evolución del relativo compuesto el que, la que, lo que', in *Sintaxis histórica de la lengua española. Segunda parte: La frase nominal*, ed. by Concepción Company Company, 2 vols (Mexico City: UNAM and Fondo de Cultura Económica, 2009), II, 1479–1590 (p. 1492); Rafael Lapesa, ' "El", "la", "lo" como antecedente de relativo en español', in *Estudios de morfosintaxis histórica del español*, ed. by Rafael Cano Aguilar and María Teresa Echenique Elizondo, Biblioteca Románica Hispánica: II, Estudios y Ensayos, 418 (Madrid: Gredos, 2000), pp. 388–401 (pp. 390–92); Beatriz Arias Álvarez, 'Estudio histórico de los relativos en español', in *II Encuentro de lingüistas y filólogos de España y México. Salamanca 25–30 noviembre de 1991*, ed. by Alonso Alegría, Beatriz Garza Cuarón, and José A. Pascual (Salamanca: Junta de Castilla y León and Universidad de Salamanca, 1994), pp. 413–22 (p. 418).
47. William Labov, *Sociolinguistic Patterns* (Philadelphia: University of Pennsylvania Press, 1972), p. 314. In Labov's conception of the terms, an indicator is a variable to which no social interpretation is attached and which is usually stable: speakers tend to be unaware of indicators. A marker is a variable to which social interpretation is attached, and of which speakers are aware.
48. Shepherds in the pastoral dramas were scored separately because they are not *a priori* upper-class characters. However, as might be expected from the pastoral convention, their linguistic behaviour is quite clearly comparable with that of other upper-class characters, in this and several other features. These figures are a refinement of Pountain, 'Las distintas gramáticas', Cuadro 5 (p. 976).
49. In an examination of the seventy-two instances of *el cual* in *Suma*, twenty-nine were the object of a preposition, twenty-eight were used in isolation and fifteen with a following noun (the so-called 'transition' relative, which is now obsolete).

50. *Vida* 4.5, p. 136.
51. *Vida* 11.8, p. 194.
52. While purists often consider resumptive relatives (see Pountain, 'Las distintas gramáticas', p. 969) in the Romance languages and in English, they appear frequently in speech. See R. J. C. Smits, *Eurogrammar: The Relative and Cleft Constructions of the Germanic and Romance Languages* (Dordrecht: Foris, 1989), p. 57. Their usage is quite clearly rule-governed; see José María Brucart, 'La estructura del sintagma nominal: las oraciones de relativo', in *Gramática descriptiva de la lengua española*, ed. by Ignacio Bosque and Violeta Demonte, 3 vols (Madrid: Espasa, 1999), I, 395–522 (pp. 405–08).
53. *Vida* 6.7, p. 153.
54. *Vida* 6.4, p. 152.
55. Hayward M. Keniston, *The Syntax of Castilian Prose* (Chicago, IL: Chicago University Press, 1937), p. 179.
56. *Vida* 11.7, p. 194.
57. Keniston, *The Syntax of Castilian Prose*, p. 171, dates its appearance at 1573.
58. Octavio de Toledo y Huerta, 'Santa Teresa y la mano visible', pp. 264–68. Valdés commended *que*-deletion for its economy (whilst not always practising it himself, as can be seen in Table G: see also Kormi Anipa, *The Grammatical Thought and Linguistic Behaviour of Juan de Valdés*, LINCOM Studies in Romance Linguistics, 55 [Munich: LINCOM Europa, 2007]):

> VALDÉS. Diríale primeramente que guardasse lo que al principio dixe de los artículos, porque esto pertenece assí para el hablar bien como para el escrivir. Avisaríale más que no curasse de un *que* superfluo que muchos ponen tan continamente, que me obligaría quitar de algunas escrituras, de una hoja, media dozena de *quees* superfluos.
> MARCIO. Dadnos algunos exemplos para que entendamos esso.
> VALDÉS. De refrán no se me ofrece ninguno que tenga este *que* demasiado, y creo lo causa la brevidad con que stán escritos, pero, si miráis en lo que leéis, <u>hallaréis ser verdad lo que os digo en partes semejantes que ésta: *creo que será bien hazer esto*, adonde aquel *que* stá superfluo, porque diría mejor: *creo será bien hazer esto*.</u> [my underlining]

59. Pountain, '*Que*-deletion'.
60. *Vida* 35.2, p. 414.
61. *Vida* 30.13, p. 360.
62. *Vida* 36.11, p. 427.
63. Keniston, *The Syntax of Castilian Prose*, p. 676.
64. A similar general view has recently been put forward by Nieves Baranda Leturio and María Carmen Marín Pina, 'El universo de la escritura conventual femenina: deslindes y perspectivas', in their *Letras en la celda: cultura escrita en los conventos femeninos en la España moderna*, Tiempo emulado, 32 (Madrid: Iberoamericana-Vervuert, 2014), pp. 11–45: 'En general [la escritura conventual femenina] es una producción plasmada en formas que se mueven a caballo entre la oralidad y la escritura y toman elementos de ambas, como sucede con la Vida de Teresa de Jesús [...]. [Estas mujeres] ignoran los aspectos más complejos de los marcos genéricos y que los trasladan a sus escritos con mucha laxitud, lo que por un lado sitúa sus textos en los márgenes de la cultura letrada, pero por otro les proporciona una cierta libertad expresiva, ajena a las cortapisas que una cultura fuertemente generizada imponía a las mujeres. Lo mismo se puede decir de la retórica, ya que la carencia de una práctica en los usos cultos se suple con fórmulas de cuño popular oral [...]' (pp. 12–13).

BIBLIOGRAPHY

Primary Sources

ABELARD, *De auctoritate vel dignitate ordinis sanctimonialium (The Authority and Dignity of Nuns)*, ed. by J. T. Muckle, 'The Letter of Heloise on Religious Life and Abelard's First Reply', *Medieval Studies*, 17 (1995), 253–81

ALFONSO EL SABIO, *Las siete partidas del Rey don Alfonso el Sabio, cotejadas con varios códices antiguos por la Real Academia de la Historia, II: Partida segunda y tercera* (Madrid: Imprenta Real, 1807)

ALONSO DE CARTAGENA, *El oracional*, ed. by Silvia González-Quevedo (Valencia: Albatros, 1983)

——*A Cicerón, Libro de los oficios. Texto y concordancias del De officiis de Cicerón: traducción castellana por Alonso de Cartagena. MS. 7815, Biblioteca Nacional de Madrid*, ed. by María Morrás (Madison, WI: HSMS, 1989)

ALONSO DE MADRID, *Arte para servir a Dios* (Palma: En la Emprenta de la Vidua Guasp, 1685)

ANA DE JESÚS, *Escritos y documentos*, ed. by A. de Fortes and R. Palmero (Burgos: Monte Carmelo, 1996)

AQUINAS, THOMAS, ST, *Summa Theologicae*, XLII: *Courage*, trans. by Anthony Ross OP and P. G. Walsh (London: Blackfriars in conjunction with Eyre & Spottiswoode; New York: McGraw-Hill, 1966)

AUGUSTINE OF HIPPO, ST, *Confessions*, trans. by J. G. Pilkington (Edinburgh: T. &T. Clark, 1876)

——*Sancti Aureli Augustini, Corpus Scriptorum Ecclesiasticum Latinorum*, ed. by J. Zycha (Prague: Tempsky, 1894; repr. 1972)

——LATIN TEXTS, *Corpus Christianorum, series Latina*, 39, ed. by E. Dekkers and J. Fraipont (Turnhout: Brepols, 1955– present)

——*St Augustine's Confessions*, trans. by W. Watts, Loeb Classical Library, 26 (London: Heinemann, 1977)

——*Meditaciones, Soliloquios, Manual, Suspiros*, trans. by Ambrosio Montesino (Mexico: Aguilar, 1978)

——*Confessions*, trans. by James J. O'Donnell, 3 vols (Oxford: Clarendon Press, 1992)

——*The Works of Saint Augustine: A Translation for the Twenty-first Century*, ed. by John E. Rotelle, trans. by Maria Boulding and Edmund Hill, 6 vols (Hyde Park, NY: New City Press, 2000)

BARNES, JONATHAN, ed., *The Complete Works of Aristotle: The Oxford Translation* (Princeton, NJ: Princeton University Press, 1984)

BARONIUS, CAESAR, ed., *Martyrologium Romanum ad novam kalendarii rationem ... restitutum Gregorii XII jussu ditum* (Rome: Ex Typographia Dominici Basæ, 1586)

Breviarium iuxta ordinale novarumque ordinationum stilum Fratrum Sacri Ordinis Gloriosissimae Dei Genitricis Semperque Virginis Mariae de Monte Carmeli (Venice: Bartholomaeus de Blavis & Soc., 1481)

Breviarium Carmelitanum cum annotationibus in margine ad facillime omnia que in ipso ad alias paginas remittuntur inuenienda (Venice: Lucantonij de Giunta, 1543)

Breviarium Carmelitanum secundum usum Ecclesiae Hierosolymitanae et Cominici Sepulchri. Nunc recens sub R. P. Ioanne Baptista Rubeo .... solerti cura et diligentia F. Iacobi Maistret ... emendatum ac typu mandatum ... (Lyons: Apud Ioannem Stratium, 1575)

Breviarium antiquae professionis regularium Beatissimae Dei Genitricis Semperq. Virginis Mariae de Monte Carmelo ex usu et consuetudine approbata Hierosolymitanae Ecclesiae et Dominici Sepulchri superrime iussu ... Ioan. Baptistae Caffardi ... reformatum excusum (Venice: Apud Iuntas, 1579)

CARDUCHO, VICENTE, and FRANCISCO MARTÍNEZ, *Dialogos de la pintura: su defensa, origen, esse[n]cia, definicion, modos y differencias* (Madrid: Francisco Martínez, 1633)

—— *Diálogos de la pintura: su defensa, origen, esencia, definición y diferencias*, ed. by Francisco Calvo Serraller (Madrid: Ediciones Turner, 1979)

CAREW, RICHARD (trans.), *The Examination of Men's Wits*, ed. by Rocío G. Sumillera, MHRA Tudor and Stuart Translations, 17 (London: MHRA, 2014)

CONSTANZA DE CASTILLA, *Book of Devotions: Libro de devociones y oficios*, ed. by Constance L. Wilkins, Exeter Hispanic Texts, 52 (Exeter: Exeter University Press, 1998)

CÓRDOBA, MARTÍN DE, *Jardín de nobles doncellas, Fray Martín de Córdoba: A Critical Edition and Study*, ed. by Harriet Goldberg (Chapel Hill: Department of Romance Languages and Literatures, University of North Carolina, 1974)

COVARRUBIAS HOROZCO, SEBASTIÁN DE, *Tesoro de la lengua castellana*, ed. by Ignacio Arellano and Rafael Zafra, Biblioteca Áurea Hispánica, 21 (Madrid: Iberoamericana-Vervuert, 2006)

Decrees of the Ecumenical Councils, ed. by Norman P. Tanner, 2 vols (London: Sheed and Ward, 1990)

FERNÁNDEZ ALCAIDE, MARTA, *Cartas de particulares en Indias del siglo XVI. Edición y estudio discursivo*, Textos y Documentos Españoles y Americanos, 6 (Madrid: Iberoamericana; Frankfurt am Main: Vervuert, 2009)

Fontes narrativi de S. Ignatio de Loyola et de Societatis Iesu initiis, ed. by Fernández Zapico, Dionysius and Cándido de Dalmases, 4 vols (Rome: Monumenta Historica Societatis Iesu, 1943)

GARCÍA DE ANDRÉS, INOCENTE, *'El Conhorte': Sermones de una mujer. La Santa Juana (1481–1534)* (Madrid: Fundación Universitaria Española and Universidad Pontificia de Salamanca, 1999)

GREGORY THE GREAT, ST, *Forty Gospel Homilies*, trans. by David Hurst (Kalamazoo, MI: Cistercian Publications, 1990)

HUARTE DE SAN JUAN, JUAN, *The Examination of Mens Wits*, trans. by Richard Carew (London: Adam Islip, 1594)

GUEVARA, ANTONIO DE, *Oratorio de religiosos y exercicio de virtuosos* (Anvers: Martin Nucio, c. 1550)

IGNACIO DE LOYOLA, SAN, *Obras completas. Edición manual*, ed. by Ignacio Iparraguirre and Cándido de Dalmases (Madrid: Biblioteca de Autores Cristianos, 1982)

JEROME, ST, *Letters and Select Works*, trans. by W. H. Fremantle, G. Lewis, and W. G. Martley (Oxford: Parker, 1893), <http://www.newadvent.org/fathers/3001.htm> [accessed 15 January 2016]

—— *Epístolas de San Hierónimo traduzidas en lengua castellana por Juan de Molina* (Valencia: Juan Jofre, 1520)

JERÓNIMO DE SAN JOSÉ, *Historia Del Carmen Descalzo [...]. Tomo Primero* (Madrid: Francisco Martínez, 1637)

JESÚS MARÍA, JUAN DE, *Compendium vitae beatae Virginis Teresiae* (Rome: Stefano Paolini, 1609)

JOHN OF THE CROSS, ST, *The Collected Works of St John of the Cross*, trans. by Kieran Kavanaugh and Otilio Rodriguez (Washington, DC: Institute of Carmelite Studies, 1994)

Juan de la Cruz, OP, *Diálogo sobre la necessidad y obligación y prouecho de la oración y diuinos loores* [...] (Salamanca: Juan de Cánova, 1555), repr. in *Tratados espirituales*, ed. by Vicente Beltrán de la Heredia (Madrid: Biblioteca de Autores Cristianos, 1962)

Juan de la Cruz, San, *Obras completas*, ed. by Eulogio Pacho (Burgos: Monte Carmelo, 1997)

Julian of Norwich, *Showings*, trans. by Edmund Colledge and James Walsh (Mahwah, NJ: Paulist Press, 1978)

Kempis, Thomas à, *Concordance to the Latin Original of the Four Books Given to the World as De imitatione Christi in 1440*, ed. by Rayner Storr (London: Oxford University Press, 1910)

—— *The Imitation of Christ*, trans. by Robert Jeffery (London: Penguin Books, 2013)

Laredo, Bernardino de, *Místicos Franciscanos*, ed. by Los redactores de "Verdad y Vida", 3 vols, Biblioteca de Autores Cristianos, 44 (Madrid: Editorial Católica, 1948), II: *Subida del Monte Sión*

—— *The Ascent of Mount Sion, Being the Third Book of the Treatise of that Name*, trans. by E. Allison Peers (London: Faber and Faber, 1952)

León, Luis de, *The Names of Christ*, trans. by Manuel Durán and William Kluback (London: SPCK, 1984)

—— *Obras completas de Fray Luis de León*, ed. by Félix García, 4th edn, 2 vols (Madrid: Biblioteca de Autores Cristianos, 1967)

Lezana, Juan Bautista de, and Luca Ciamberlano, *Annales sacri, prophetici, et Eliani Ordinis Beatae Virginis Mariæ de Monte Carmeli*, 4 vols (Rome: Typis Mascardi, 1645–56)

Lope de Vega y Carpio, Félix, *Vida y muerte de Santa Teresa de Jesús. Commedia inédita. Introduzione, edizione e commento a cura di Elisa Aragone* (Florence: Casa Editrice d'Anna, 1970)

Luis de Granada, *Libro de oración y meditación en la cual se trata de la consideración de los principales misterios de nuestra fe* (Zaragoza: en la oficina de Medardo Heras, n.d.)

—— *Manual de diuersas oraciones y spirituales exercicios* (Anvers: Juan Bellero, 1558)

—— *Guía de pecadores*, ed. by Ignacio Arellano (Madrid: Homo Legens, 2012)

—— *The Sinners' Guide: A Worke Contayning the Whole Regiment of a Christian Life, Devided into Two Books*, trans. by Francis Meres (London: Richard Field in St Paule's Church-yard at the sign of the Beare, 1614)

Mendoza, Fray Íñigo de, *Dechado y regimiento de príncipes* (Zamora: Antonio de Centenera, 1493)

Missale secundum usum Carmelitarum (Venice: Lucantonij de Giunta, 1504)

Missale secundum usum Carmelitarum ... non paucis imaginibus depictum (Venice: Lucas Antonius de Giunta, 1509)

Missale Ordinis Carmelitarum (Brescia: Bonino de' Bonini, 1490)

Monsignano, Eliseo, and G. M. Ximenes, eds, *Bullarium Carmelitanum*, 4 vols (Rome: Hermathenea, 1715–18, 1768)

—— *On the Account of the World's Creation Given by Moses*, trans. by F. Colson and G. Whitaker, Loeb Classical Library, 226 (London: Heinemann, 1929)

Ockham, William of, *Opera Theologica*, ed. by G. Gál, S. Brown, G. Etzkorn, and F. Kelley, 4 vols (St Bonaventure, NY: St Bonaventure University, 1967–85)

Osuna, Francisco de, *Tercer abecedario spiritual. Estudio histórico y edición crítica por Melquíades Andrés*, Biblioteca de Autores Cristianos, 592 (Madrid: Editorial Católica, 1972)

—— *The Third Spiritual Alphabet*, trans. by Mary E. Giles (New York: Paulist Press, 1981)

—— *Tercer abecedario espiritual de Francisco de Osuna*, ed. by Saturnino López Santidrián (Madrid: Biblioteca de Autores Cristianos, 1998)

Pacheco, Francisco, *Arte de la pintura*, ed. by Bonaventura Bassegoda i Hugas (Madrid: Cátedra, 1990)

Papenbroeck, Daniel, 'De Beato Alberto ex Canonico Regulari Episcopo Primum

Vercellensi, dein Patriarcha Hierosolymitano, Legato Apostolico, et Legislatore Ordinis Carmelitici. Ann. Mccxiv', in *Acta Sanctorum*, ed. Bollandists (Antwerp: Apud Ioannem Meursium, 1643–1794), pp. 769–802

PHILO OF ALEXANDRIA, *On the Confusion of Tongues*, trans. by F. Colson and G. Whitaker, Loeb Classical Library, 227 (London: Heinemann, 1929)

—— *Allegorical Interpretation of Genesis 2,3*, trans. by F. Colson and G. Whitaker, Loeb Classical Library, 226 (London: Heinemann, 1929)

PLOTINUS, *Plotinus, The Enneads*, trans. by A. H. Armstrong, Loeb Classical Library, 440–45, and 468, 7 vols (London: Heinemann, 1966–88)

PORPHYRY, *On the Life of Plotinus and the Order of his Books*, trans. by A. H. Armstrong, Loeb Classical Library, 440 (Cambridge, MA: Harvard University Press, 1966)

Procesos de beatificación y canonización de Santa Teresa de Jesús, ed. by Silverio de Santa Teresa, 3 vols (Burgos: Monte Carmelo, 1935)

Procesos de beatificación y canonización de la Madre Teresa de Jesús, ed. by Julen Urkiza, 6 vols (Burgos: El Monte Carmelo, 2015–16)

QUEVEDO, FRANCISCO DE, *Memorial por el patronato de Santiago y por todos los santos naturales de España*. Madrid, 1628, Biblioteca Nacional Madrid, Sección de Manuscritos, MS R/11465

Relación de la solemnidad con que se han celebrado en la ciudad de Barcelona las fiestas a la Beatificación de la Madre S. Teresa de Iesvs, ed. by Joseph Dalmau (Barcelona: Sebastian Matevad, 1615)

RIBERA, FRANCISCO DE, *Vida de la Madre Teresa de Jesús* (Salamanca: Pedro Lasso, 1590)

—— *La vida de la Madre Teresa de Jesús*, ed. by Jaime Pons (Barcelona: Gustavo Gilí, 1908)

—— *La vida de la Madre Teresa de Jesús*, ed. by José A. Martínez Puche (Madrid: Edibesa, 2004)

—— *Vida de Santa Teresa de Jesús, fundadora de las Descalzas y Descalzos Carmelitas*, ed. by Inocente Palacios de la Asunción (Madrid: Librería de Francisco Lizcano, 1863)

SAN BERNARDO, FRAY JUAN DE, *Chronica de la vida admirable y milagrosas haçanas de el Admirable Portento de la Penitencia S. Pedro de Alcántara* [...] (Naples: En la empresa de Geronimo Fasulo, 1667)

SAN JOSEPH, ANTONIO DE, ed., *Cartas de Santa Teresa de Jesús, Madre y Fundadora de la Reforma de la Orden de Nuestra Señora del Carmen, de la Primitiva Observancia*, 4 vols (Madrid: Don Joseph Doblado, 1771)

SÁNCHEZ, PEDRO LUIS, *Triangulo de las tres virtudes theologicas, fe, esperança, y caridad, y Cuadrangulo de las quatro cardinales, prudencia, templança, iusticia, y fortaleza* (Toledo: Tomás de Guzmán, 1595)

TERESA DE CARTAGENA, *Arboleda de los enfermos y Admiraçión operum Dey*, ed. by Lewis Joseph Hutton, *Boletín de la Real Academia Española*, Anejo 16 (Madrid: BRAE, 1967)

TERESA DE JESÚS, SANTA, *Las obras de la Santa Madre Teresa de Jesús fundadora de la reformación de las descalças y descalços de N. Señora del Carmen*, 3 vols (Antwerp: Plantin, 1630)

—— *The Flaming Hart, or, The Life of the Gloriovs S. Teresa*, trans. by Tobie Matthew (Antwerp: Meursius, 1642)

—— *The Way of Perfection*, in *The Second Part of the Works of the Holy Mother St Teresa of Jesus*, trans. by Abraham Woodhead (London, 1675)

—— *The Letters of Saint Teresa. A Complete Edition Translated from the Spanish and Annotated by the Benedictines of Stanbrook*, 4 vols (London: Thomas Baker, 1919–24)

—— *The Life of Saint Teresa of Ávila by herself*, translated with an Introduction by J. M. Cohen (London: Penguin, 1957)

—— *La poesía de Santa Teresa*, ed. by Ángel Custodio Vega (Madrid: Biblioteca de Autores Cristianos, 1972)

―― *The Collected Works of St Teresa of Avila*, ed. and trans. by Kieran Kavanaugh and Otilio Rodriguez, 3 vols (Washington, DC: Institute of Carmelite Studies, 1976–85)
―― *Libro de la vida*, ed. by Otger Steggink (Madrid: Castalia, 1986)
―― *Obras completas*, ed. by Efrén de la Madre de Dios and Otger Steggink, Biblioteca de Autores Cristianos, 212 (Madrid: Editorial Católica, 2015)
―― *Santa Teresa de Jesús. Obras completas*, ed. by Alberto Barrientos, 5th edn (Madrid: Editorial de Espiritualidad, 2000)
―― *The Collected Letters of St Teresa of Avila*, trans. by Kieran Kavanaugh, 2 vols (Washington, DC: Institute of Carmelite Studies, 2001–07)
―― *The Complete Works of St Teresa of Avila*, trans. and ed. by E. Allison Peers, 3 vols (London: Sheed and Ward, 1946; repr. London and New York: Burns & Oates, 2002)
―― *Camino de perfección*, ed. by Salvador Ros García, 4th edn (Madrid: San Pablo, 2008)
―― *Santa Teresa. Obras completas*, ed. by Tomás Álvarez (Burgos: Monte Carmelo, 2014)
―― *Libro de la vida*, ed. by Dámaso Chicharro, 17th edn, Letras Hispánicas, 98 (Madrid: Cátedra, 2014)
―― *Libro de la vida*, ed. by Fidel Sebastián Mediavilla (Madrid: Real Academia Española, 2014)
―― *Las moradas del castillo interior*, ed. by Dámaso Chicharro, 2nd edn, Clásicos de Biblioteca Nueva, 11 (Madrid: Biblioteca Nueva, 2015)
―― *Obras completas: edición manual*, ed. by Efrén de la Madre de Dios and Otger Steggink, Biblioteca de Autores Cristianos, 212 (Madrid: Editorial Católica, 1986)
VARIOUS, *Tratados de erudición de varios autores*, MS 1713, Biblioteca Nacional de España, fols 246^r–2449^v
VIERGE MARIE, DANIEL DE LA, *Speculum Carmelitanum, sive historia Eliani Ordinis Fratrum Beatissimae Virginis Mariae de Monte Carmelo*, 4 vols (Antwerp: Typis Michaelis Knobbari, 1680)
VILLENA, ISABEL DE, '*Vita Christi', compost per Isabel de Villena, abadessa de la Trinitat de Valencia, ara novament publicat segons l'edició de l'any 1497*, ed. by Ramón Miquel y Planas, 2nd edn, 3 vols, Biblioteca Catalana (Barcelona: Casa Miquel-Rius, 1916)
WESSELS, GABRIEL, ed., *Acta Capitulorum Generalium Fratrum B.V. Mariae de Monte Carmelo*, 2 vols (Rome: Apud Curiam Generalitiam, 1912, 1934)
YEPES, DIEGO DE, *Vida, virtudes y milagros, de la Bienaventurada Virgen Teresa de Jesus, Madre y fundadora de la nueva Reformación de la Orden de Los Descalços y Descalças de Nuestra Señora del Carmen* (Zaragoza: Angelo Tauanno, 1606)
―― *Vida, virtudes, y milagros de la bienaventurada virgen Teresa de Jesus* (Lisbon: Pedro Craesbeeck, 1614)
―― *Vida, virtudes y milagros de la bienaventurada virgen Teresa de Jesús*, ed. by Manuel Diego Sánchez (Madrid: Editorial de Espiritualidad, 2015)
ZIMMERMAN, BENEDICT MARY OF THE CROSS, *Ordinaire de l'Ordre de Notre-Dame du Mont Carmel par Sibert De Beka (vers 1312). Publié d'après le manuscrit original et collationné sur divers manuscrits et imprimés* (Paris: Picard, 1910)

Secondary Sources

AHLGREN, GILLIAN T. W., 'Negotiating Sanctity: Holy Women in Sixteenth-century Spain', *Church History*, 64 (1995), 373–88
―― *Teresa of Avila and the Politics of Sanctity* (Ithaca, NY: Cornell University Press, 1996)
―― *Entering Teresa of Avila's 'Interior Castle': A Reader's Companion* (Mahwah, NJ: Paulist Press, 2005)
―― *Enkindling Love: The Legacy of Teresa of Ávila and John of the Cross* (Minneapolis, MN: Fortress Press, 2016)

ALEGRE CARVAJAL, ESTHER, 'Ana de Mendoza y de la Cerda, princesa de Éboli y duquesa de Pastrana (Cifuentes, 1540–Pastrana, 1592)', *Damas de la Casa de Mendoza*, ed. by Alegre Carvajal, pp. 578–617
—— 'Grupos aristocráticos y práctica urbana: la ciudad nobiliaria de los Mendoza. "Imagen distintiva" de su linaje y de su red de poder', in *Familia, valores y representaciones*, ed. by Joan Bestard and Manuel Pérez García (Murcia: Editum, 2010), pp. 31–47
——, ed., *Damas de la Casa de Mendoza. Historias, leyendas y olvidos* (Madrid: Polifemo, 2014)
—— 'El encuentro y la ruptura entre Teresa de Jesús y la Princesa de Éboli: ¿Una cuestión de enfrentamiento personal o un asunto de estrategia política?', *eHumanista*, 24 (2013), 466–78
ÁLVAREZ, TOMÁS, *Estudios teresianos*, 3 vols (Burgos: Editorial Monte Carmelo, 1995–96)
—— *Comentarios a las obras de Santa Teresa: Libro de la vida, Camino de perfección, Castillo interior* (Burgos: Monte Carmelo, 2005)
—— 'Jesucristo en la vida y la enseñanza de Teresa', in *Diccionario de Santa Teresa*, ed. by Álvarez, pp. 363–74
ANDRÉS ORDAX, SALVADOR, 'Iconografía Teresiana-Alcantarina', *Boletín del Seminario de Estudios de Arte*, 48 (1982), 301–26
ANDREWS, JEAN, OLIVER NOBLE WOOD, and JEREMY ROE, eds, *On Art and Painting: Vicente Carducho and Baroque Spain* (Cardiff: University of Wales Press, 2016)
ANGULO ÍÑIGUEZ, DIEGO, and ALFONSO E. PÉREZ SÁNCHEZ, *Historia de la pintura española. Escuela madrileña del primer tercio del siglo XVII* (Madrid: Instituto Diego Velázquez, 1969)
ANIPA, KORMI, *The Grammatical Thought and Linguistic Behaviour of Juan de Valdés*, LINCOM Studies in Romance Linguistics, 55 (Munich: LINCOM Europa, 2007)
ARCHER, ROBERT, *The Problem of Woman in Late Medieval Hispanic Literature* (Woodbridge: Tamesis, 2005)
ARIAS ÁLVAREZ, BEATRIZ, 'Estudio histórico de los relativos en español', in *II Encuentro de lingüistas y filólogos de España y México. Salamanca 25–30 noviembre de 1991*, ed. by Alonso Alegría, Beatriz Garza Cuarón, and José A. Pascual (Salamanca: Junta de Castilla y León and Universidad de Salamanca, 1994), pp. 413–22
BALDWIN, JOHN W., *The Scholastic Culture of the Middle Ages, 1000–1300* (Lexington, MA: Heath, 1971)
BARCELÓ DE TORRES, EDUARDO, and LETICIA RUIZ GÓMEZ, eds, *La recuperación de El Paular* (Madrid: Ministerio de Educación, Cultura y Deporte, 2013)
BARANDA LETURIO, NIEVES, and MARÍA CARMEN MARÍN PINA, 'El universo de la escritura conventual femenina: deslindes y perspectivas', in their *Letras en la celda: cultura escrita en los conventos femeninos en la España moderna*, Tiempo emulado, 32 (Madrid: Iberoamericana-Vervuert, 2014), pp. 11–45
BASSEGODA I HUGAS, BONAVENTURA, 'Observaciones sobre el *Arte de la Pintura* de Francisco Pacheco como tratado de iconografía', *Cuadernos de Arte e Iconografía*, 2 (1989), 185–96
—— 'Las tareas intelectuales del pintor Francisco Pacheco', *Symposium Internacional Velázquez. Actas. Sevilla, 8–11 noviembre de 1999*, ed. by Alfredo J. Morales and Carlos Sánchez de las Heras (Seville: Junta de Andalucía, Consejería de Cultura, 2004), pp. 39–46
BATAILLON, MARCEL, *Les Jésuites dans l'Espagne du XVIe siècle*, ed. by Pierre-Antoine Fabre (Paris: Les Belles Lettres, 2009)
BENÍTEZ BLANCO, VICENTE, 'Evocación de la santidad: los relicarios del convento madrileño del Corpus Christi, vulgo "Las Carboneras"', in *El culto a los santos cofradías, devoción, fiestas y arte*, ed. by F. Javier Campos y Fernández de Sevilla (San Lorenzo del Escorial: Ediciones Escurialenses, 2008), pp. 739–58
BERBARA, MARIA, '"Esta pena tan sabrosa": Teresa of Avila and the Figurative Arts', in *The Sense of Suffering: Constructions of Physical Pain in Early Modern Culture*, ed. by Jan Frans van Dijkhuizen and Karl A. E. Enenkel, Intersections, 12 (Leiden: Brill, 2009), pp. 267–97

BERESFORD, ANDREW M., and LESLEY K. TWOMEY, eds., 'Visions of Hagiography' (special edition), *La corónica*, 43 (2013)

BEUTLER, WERNER, *Vicente Carducho en El Paular* (Cologne: Verlag Locher, 1998)

BIERNOFF, SUZANNAH, 'Carnal Relations: Embodied Sight in Merleau-Ponty, Roger Bacon, and St Francis', *Journal of Visual Culture*, 4.1 (2005), 39–52

—— 'Seeing and Feeling in the Middle Ages', in *Visual Sense: A Cultural Reader*, ed. by Elizabeth Edwards and Kaushik Bhaumik (Oxford: Berg, 2008), pp. 51–57

—— *Sight and Embodiment in the Middle Ages* (Basingstoke: Palgrave Macmillan, 2002)

BILINKOFF, JODI, 'Elite Widows and Religious Expression in Early Modern Spain: The View from Avila', in *Widowhood in Medieval and Early Modern Europe*, ed. by Sandra Cavallo and Lyndan Warner (London: Longman, 1999), pp. 181–92

—— *The Avila of Saint Teresa: Religious Reform in a Sixteenth-century City* (Ithaca, NY: Cornell University Press, 1989)

BOAGA, EMANUELE, *Celebrare i nostri Santi* (Rome: Edizione Carmelitane, 2009)

BOASE, ROGER, *The Troubadour Revival: A Study of Social Change and Traditionalism in Late Medieval Spain* (London: Routledge and Kegan Paul, 1978)

BOYCE, JAMES, 'The Feasts of Saints Elijah and Elisha in the Carmelite Rite: A Liturgico-Musical Study', in *Master of the Sacred Page. Essays and Articles in Honor of Roland E. Murphy, O.Carm., on the Occasion of His Eightieth Birthday* (Washington, DC: The Carmelite Institute, 1997), pp. 155–88

—— *Carmelite Liturgical Spirituality* (Melbourne: Carmelite Communications, 2000)

—— *Carmelite Liturgy and Spiritual Identity: The Choir Books of Krakow* (Turnhout: Brepols, 2008)

BRINE, KEVIN R., ELENA CILETTI, and HENRIKE LÄHNEMANN, eds, *The Sword of Judith: Judith Studies across the Disciplines* (Cambridge: Open Book Publishers, 2010)

BRUCART, JOSÉ MARÍA, 'La estructura del sintagma nominal: las oraciones de relativo', in *Gramática descriptiva de la lengua española*, ed. by Ignacio Bosque and Violeta Demonte, 3 vols (Madrid: Espasa, 1999), I, 395–522

BURKE, PETER, 'The Uses of Literacy in Early Modern Italy', in *The Social History of Language*, ed. by Peter Burke and Roy Porter, Cambridge Studies in Oral and Literate Culture, 12 (Cambridge: Cambridge University Press, 1987), pp. 21–42

BYNUM, CAROLINE WALKER, *Christian Materiality: An Essay on Religion in Late Medieval Europe* (New York: Zone, 2011)

CAMILLE, MICHAEL, 'Before the Gaze: The Internal Senses and Late-Medieval Practices of Seeing', in *Visuality Before and Beyond the Renaissance: Seeing as Others Saw*, ed. by Robert S. Nelson (Cambridge: Cambridge University Press, 2000), pp. 197–223

CANO AGUILAR, RAFAEL, 'La sintaxis del diálogo en el Quijote (1615)', *Boletín de la Real Academia Española*, 85 (2005), 133–55

CANTERA BURGOS, FRANCISCO, *Alvar Garcia de Santa Maria: Historia de la judería de Burgos y de sus conversos más egregios* (Madrid: Instituto Arias Montano, 1952)

CARRERA, ELENA, *Teresa of Avila's Autobiography: Authority, Power and the Self in Mid-Sixteenth-Century Spain* (Oxford: Legenda, 2005)

—— 'The Emotions in Sixteenth-century Spanish Spirituality', *Journal of Religious History*, 31.3 (2007), 235–52

—— 'Embodied Cognition and Empathy in Cervantes's *El celoso extremeño* (1613)', *Hispania*, 97.1 (2014), 113–24

CASTRO, AMÉRICO, 'Teresa la Santa', in his *Santa Teresa y otros ensayos*, Hombres, Hechos e Ideas, 23 (Madrid: Alfaguera, 1972), pp. 59–66

CASTRO, JUAN NICOLAU, 'Santa Teresa en el arte español', *Toletum: Boletín de La Real Academia de Bellas Artes y Ciencias Históricas de Toledo*, 15 (1984), 111–25

CATURLA, MARÍA LUISA, 'Documentos en torno a Vicente Carducho', *Arte Español*, 26 (1968), 145–22
CERTEAU, MICHEL DE, *The Mystic Fable. I: The Sixteenth and Seventeenth Centuries* (Chicago, IL: Chicago University Press, 1992)
CHENU, MARIE-DOMINIQUE, *Nature, Man, and Society in the Twelfth Century: Essays on New Theological Perspectives in the Latin West* (Toronto: University of Toronto Press, 1997)
CLARK, MARY T., *Augustine* (London and New York: Continuum, 1994)
CLASSEN, CONSTANCE, *Worlds of Sense: Exploring the Senses in History and Across Cultures* (London: Routledge, 1993)
CONDE, CARMEN, 'La escritura de santa Teresa y su amor a los libros', *Boletin del Museo e Instituto 'Camón Aznar': obra social de la Caja de Ahorros de Zaragoza, Aragón y Rioja*, 10 (1983), 5–14
COOLIDGE, GRACE, *Guardianship, Gender, and the Nobility in Early Modern Spain* (Farnham: Ashgate, 2010)
COOLMAN, BOYD TAYLOR, *Knowing God by Experience: The Spiritual Senses in the Theology of William of Auxerre* (Washington, DC: Catholic University of America Press, 2004)
COPSEY, RICHARD, ED. and TRANS., *The Ten Books on the Way of Life and Great Deeds of the Carmelites (Including the Book of the First Monks). A Medieval History of the Carmelites Written c.1385 by Felip Ribot, O.Carm.* (Faversham: British Province of Carmelites, 2005)
CORELLA, JESÚS, 'Consolación', in *Diccionario de Espiritualidad Ignaciana*, ed. by Castro, pp. 413–24
COULTER, DALE M., 'Contemplation as "Speculation": A Comparison of Boethius, Hugh of St Victor, and Richard of St Victor', in *From Knowledge to Beatitude: St Victor, Twelfth-century Scholars, and Beyond. Essays in Honour of Grover A. Zinn, Jr*, ed. by E. Ann Matter and Lesley Smith (Notre Dame, IN: University of Notre Dame Press, 2012), pp. 204–28
CRAWFORD VOLK, MARY, *Vicente Carducho and Seventeenth-Century Castilian Painting* (London and New York: Garland Publishing, 1977)
CRUZ, TOMÁS DE LA, and SIMEÓN DE LA SAGRADA FAMILIA, *La reforma teresiana. Documentario histórico de sus primeros días* (Rome: Teresianum-Desclée, 1962)
DADSON, TREVOR J., 'The Education, Books and Reading Habits of Ana de Mendoza y de la Cerda, Princess of Éboli (1540–1592)', in *Women's Literacy in Early Modern Spain and the New World*, ed. by Anne J. Cruz and Rosilie Hernández-Pecoraro (Aldershot, UK; Burlington, VT: Ashgate, 2011), pp. 79–102
—— 'Tradición y reforma en la vida espiritual de la princesa de Éboli', in *Rostros, relatos e imágenes de Teresa de Jesús. Reflexiones en el V Centenario de su nacimiento*, ed. by Esther Alegre Carvajal, *eHumanista*, 33 (2016), 230–45
—— AND HELEN H. REED, *Epistolario e historia documental de Ana de Mendoza y de la Cerda, princesa de Éboli* (Madrid: Iberoamericana-Vervuert, 2013)
DALMASES, CÁNDIDO DE, 'Santa Teresa y los jesuitas. Precisando fechas y datos', *Archivum Historicum Societatis Iesu*, 35 (1966), 347–78
—— 'Cetina, Diego de', in *Diccionario Histórico de la Compañía de Jesús*, ed. by Charles O'Neill and Joaquín María Domínguez, 4 vols (Rome: Institutum Historicum Societatis Iesu; Madrid: Universidad Pontificia Comillas, 2001)
DAVIES, MARK, *Corpus del Español: 100 Million Words, 1200s–1900s* (2002–). <http://www.corpusdelespanol.org> [accessed 22 August 2015]
DELGADO, EDUARDO, and EDUARDO LAMAS, 'La serie de dibujos de Vicente Carducho con los Padres de la Iglesia: nuevos elementos', *Anales de Historia del Arte*, 23 (2013), 89–97
DENERY, DALLAS G., *Seeing and Being Seen in the Later Medieval World: Optics, Theology and Religious Life* (Cambridge: Cambridge University Press, 2005)
DEWEY, JOHN, *The Quest for Certainty* (New York: Putnam, 1960)

DEYERMOND, ALAN D., '"El convento de dolençias": The Works of Teresa de Cartagena', *Journal of Hispanic Philology*, 1 (1976–77), 19–29
—— 'Spain's First Women Writers', in *Women in Hispanic Literature: Icons and Fallen Idols*, ed. by Beth Miller (Berkeley: University of California Press, 1983), pp. 27–52
—— 'La Biblia en la poesía de Juan del Encina', in *Poética figural: usos de la Biblia en la literatura medieval española* (Salamanca and Oxford: Sociedad de Estudios Medievales y Renacentistas, 2015), pp. 155–73
DHÔTEL, JEAN-CLAUDE, 'Les Confesseurs jésuites de Thérèse de Jésus', in *Mystique et pédagogie spirituelle: Ignace, Thérèse, Jean de la Croix*, ed. by Centre Sèvres (Paris: Médiasèvres, 1992), pp. 21–27
DICKEN, E. W. TRUEMAN, *The Crucible of Love: A Study of the Mysticism of St Teresa of Jesus and St John of the Cross* (London: Darton, Longman and Todd, 1963)
Diccionario de Espiritualidad Ignaciana, ed. by José García de Castro (Burgos: Monte Carmelo, 2007)
Diccionario de Santa Teresa: doctrina e historia, ed. by Tomás Álvarez (Burgos: Monte Carmelo, 2006)
Diccionario Histórico de la Compañía de Jesús, ed. by Charles O'Neill and Joaquín María Domínguez, 4 vols (Rome: Institutum Historicum Societatis Iesu; Madrid: Universidad Pontificia Comillas, 2001)
DRONKE, PETER, *Women Writers of the Middle Ages: A Critical Study of Texts from Perpetua (d. 203) to Marguerite Porete (d. 1310)* (Cambridge: Cambridge University Press, 1984)
—— 'Les Cinq Sens chez Bernard Sylvestre et Alain de Lille', *Micrologus*, 10 (2002): 1–14
EDWARDS, ELIZABETH, and KAUSIK BHAUMIK, *Visual Sense: A Cultural Reader* (Oxford: Berg, 2008)
EDWARDS, JOHN, *Inquisition* (Stroud: Tempus, 1999)
ELIZALDE, IGNACIO, 'Teresa de Jesús y los jesuitas', in *Teresa de Jesús. Estudios histórico-literarios* (Rome: Teresianum, c.1982), pp. 151–75
ELLIOTT, J. H., *The Count-Duke of Olivares: The Statesman in an Age of Decline* (New Haven, CT: Yale University Press, 1986)
EMONET, PIERRE, 'Indiferencia', in *Diccionario de Espiritualidad Ignaciana*, 2 vols (Bilbao: Ediciones Mensajero; Santander: Sal Terrae, 2007), II, 1015–22
ENGEN, JOHN VAN, *Sisters and Brothers of the Common Life: The Devotio Moderna and the World of the Late Middle Ages* (Philadelphia: University of Pennsylvania Press, 2008)
ETCHEGOYEN, GASTON, *L'Amour divin* (Bordeaux: Bibliothèque de l'École des Hautes Études Hispaniques, 1923)
FAESEN, ROB, 'The Grand Silence of St Joseph: Devotion to St Joseph and the Seventeenth-Century Crisis of Mysticism in the Jesuit Order', in *Joseph of Nazareth through the Centuries*, ed. by Joseph F. Chorpenning (Philadelphia, PA: Saint Joseph's University Press, 2011), pp. 137–50
—— 'A French Mystic's Perspective on the Crisis of Mysticism: Jean-Joseph Surin (1600–1665)', in *Mysticism in the French Tradition: Eruptions from France*, ed. by Louise Nelstrop and Bradley B. Onishi (Farnham: Ashgate, 2015), pp. 149–67
FINDLEN, PAULA, and HANNAH MARCUS, 'Science under Inquisition: Heresy and Knowledge in Catholic Reformation Rome', *Isis*, 103 (2012), 376–82
FINK DE BACKER, STEPHANIE, *Widowhood in Early Modern Spain: Protectors, Proprietors, and Patrons* (Leiden and Boston, MA: Brill, 2010)
FLASCHE, HANS, 'Syntaktische Untersuchungen zu Santa Teresa de Jesús', in *Gesammelte Aufsätze zur Kulturgeschichte Spaniens 15 Band*, ed. by Johannes Vincke (Münster: Aschendorffsche Verlagsbuchhandlung, 1960), pp. 151–74
—— 'Considerações sobre a estrutura da frase espanhola analisada na autobiografia de Santa Teresa', *Boletim de Filologia*, 19 (1961), 177–86

Freud, Salomon, *Sefer ha-Yesodot. Buch der Elemente: Ein Beitrag zur jüdischen Religionsphilosophie des Mittelalters* (Frankfurt: J. Kaufmann, 1900)
Fuente, Vicente de la, ed., *Escritos de Santa Teresa*, 2 vols (Madrid: M. Rivadeneyra, 1861–62)
Galilea, Segundo, *The Future of Our Past: The Spanish Mystics Speak to Contemporary Spirituality* (Notre Dame, IN: Ave Maria Press, 1985)
Gannon, Mary Ann Ida, 'The Active Memory of Sensation in St Augustine', *The New Scholastic*, 30 (1956), 154–80
García de la Concha, Víctor, *El arte literario de Santa Teresa* (Barcelona: Ariel, 1978)
Gavrilyuk, Paul L., and Sarah Coakley, eds, *The Spiritual Senses: Perceiving God in Western Christianity* (Baltimore, MD: Johns Hopkins University Press, 2011)
Gilson, Étienne, *Introduction á l'étude de saint Augustine* (Paris: Vrin, 1943)
Girón Alconchel, José Luis, 'Las oraciones de relativo II. Evolución del relativo compuesto el que, la que, lo que', in *Sintaxis histórica de la lengua española. Segunda parte: La frase nominal*, ed. by Concepción Company Company, 2 vols (Mexico City: UNAM and Fondo de Cultura Económica, 2009), II, 1479–1590
Gómez, Pedro, '"*Accende lumen sensibus*": una aproximación filosófico-teológica a la doctrina de los sentidos en la teología monástica medieval', *Teología y vida*, 49.4 (2008), 749–69
González y González, Nicolás, *El monasterio de la Encarnación de Ávila*, 2 vols (Ávila: Caja de Ávila, 1976–77)
Gray, Patrick, *Godly Fear: The Epistle to Hebrews and Greco-Roman Critiques of Superstition* (Atlanta, GA: Society of Biblical Literature, 2003)
Graziano di S. Teresa, 'Il Codice Di Avila', *Ephemerides Carmeliticae*, 9 (1958), 442–52
Hadot, Pierre, *Philosophy as a Way of Life: Spiritual Exercises from Socrates to Foucault.* (Oxford: Blackwell, 1995)
Hahn, Cynthia, '*Visio Dei*: Changes in Medieval Visuality', in *Visuality Before and Beyond the Renaissance: Seeing as Others Saw*, ed. Robert S. Nelson (Cambridge: Cambridge University Press, 2000), pp. 169–96
Halliday, M. A. K., *Language as Social Semiotic: The Social Interpretation of Language and Meaning* (London: Arnold, 1978)
Hamburger, Jeffrey F., *Nuns as Artists: The Visual Culture of a Medieval Convent* (Berkeley: University of California Press, 1997)
—— 'Speculations on Speculation: Vision and Perception in the Theory and Practice of Mystical Devotion', in *Deutsche Mystik im abendländischen Zusammenhang: Neu erschlossene Texte, neue methodische Ansätze, neue theoretische Konzepte, Kolloquium Kloster Fischingen 1998*, ed. by Walter Haug and Wolfram Schneider-Lastin (Tübingen: Niemayer, 2000), pp. 353–408
—— and Anne-Marie Bouché, eds, *The Mind's Eye: Art and Theological Argument in the Middle Ages* (Princeton, NJ: Princeton University Press and the Department of Art and Archeology, 2006)
Hapsburg, Max von, 'Introduction', in Thomas à Kempis, *The Imitation of Christ*, trans. by Robert Jeffery (London: Penguin, 2013)
Hardman, Anne, *Life of the Venerable Anne of Jesus* (London: Sands, 1932)
Hatzfeld, Helmut, *Estudios literarios sobre la mística española*, 2nd edn, Biblioteca Románica Hispánica, 16, II: Estudios y Ensayos (Madrid: Gredos, 1968)
—— *Santa Teresa de Ávila*, TWAS, 79 (New York: Twayne, 1969)
Heller-Roazen, Daniel, 'Common Sense: Greek, Arabic, Latin', in *Rethinking the Medieval Senses: Heritage/Fascinations/Frames*, ed. by Stephen G. Nichols, Andreas Kablitz, and Alison Calhoun, pp. 30–50
Herraiz García, Maximiliano, *Sólo Dios basta: claves de la espiritualidad teresiana* (Madrid: Editorial de la Espiritualidad, 1980)

Hidalgo Ogáyar, Juana, 'La familia Mendoza, ejemplo de patronazgo femenino en la edad moderna', in *Familias, jerarquización y movilidad social*, ed. by Giovanni Levi y Raimundo A. Rodríguez Pérez (Murcia: Editum, 2010), pp. 297–309
Hillgarth, J. N., *The Spanish Kingdoms 1250–1516*, 3 vols (Oxford: Clarendon Press, 1978), II: *1410–1516 Castilian Hegemony*
Howe, Elizabeth Teresa, *Mystical Imagery: Santa Teresa de Jesús and San Juan de la Cruz*, Series II: Romance Languages and Literatures, 76 (New York: Peter Lang, 1988)
—— 'Sor Teresa de Cartagena and *entendimiento*', *Romanische Forschungen*, 108 (1996), 133–45
—— 'Zenobia or Penelope? Isabel la Católica as Literary Archetype', in *Isabel la Católica, Queen of Castile: Critical Essays*, ed. by David A. Boruchoff (New York: Palgrave Macmillan, 2003), pp. 91–102
—— *Education and Women in the Early Modern Hispanic World* (Aldershot, UK; Burlington, VT: Ashgate, 2008)
Howells, Edward, *John of the Cross and Teresa of Ávila: Mystical Knowing and Selfhood* (New York: Crossroad, 2002)
Huélamo San José, Ana María, 'El devocionario de la domínica Sor Constanza', *Boletín de la Asociación Española de Archiveros, Bibliotecarios, Museólogos y Documentalistas*, 42 (1992), 133–47
Iglesias, Ignacio, 'Santa Teresa de Jesús y la espiritualidad ignaciana', *Manresa*, 54 (1982), 291–311
Iparraguirre, Ignacio, *Historia de los Ejercicios de San Ignacio*, 3 vols (Bilbao: Mensajero; Rome: Instiutum Historicum Societatis Iesu, 1955)
Ivens, Michael, *Understanding the Spiritual Exercises: Text and Commentary* (Leominster: Gracewing, 1998)
—— *Keeping in Touch: Posthumous Papers on Ignatian Topics*, ed. by Joseph A. Munitiz (Leominster: Gracewing, 2007)
Jiménez Delgado, José, 'Las citas latinas de santa Teresa', *Revista Helmántica*, 24 (1983), 339–49
Jorge, Enrique, 'El P. Diego de Cetina confiesa y dirige a Santa Teresa de Jesús', *Manresa*, 24 (1952), 115–25
Kabatek, Johannes, 'Tradiciones discursivas y cambio lingüístico', *Lexis*, 29 (2005), 151–77
Kallenberg, Arie Paschalis, 'Le Culte liturgique d'Élie dans l'Ordre du Carmel', in *Élie le Prophète*, II, *Études Carmélitaines*, 34 (1956), 134–50
—— *Fontes Liturgiae Carmelitanae* (Rome: Institutum Carmelitanum, 1962)
Kamen, Henry, *Spain, 1469–1714: A Society of Conflict*, 2nd edn (London: Longman, 1991)
Kavanaugh, Kieran, 'Introduction', in Francisco de Osuna, *The Third Spiritual Alphabet*, trans. by Mary E. Giles (Mahwah, NY: Paulist Press, 1981)
Keller, Hildegard Elisabeth, 'Blinded Avengers: Making Sense of Invisibility in Courtly Epic and Legal Ritual', in *Rethinking the Medieval Senses: Heritage/Fascinations/Frames*, ed. by Stephen G. Nichols, Andreas Kablitz, and Alison Calhoun, pp. 218–62
Kemp, Simon, and Garth J. O. Fletcher, 'History of Psychology: The Medieval Theory of the Inner Senses', *The American Journal of Psychology*, 106.4 (1993), 559–76
Keniston, Hayward M., *The Syntax of Castilian Prose* (Chicago, IL: Chicago University Press, 1937)
Kenney, John Peter, *The Mysticism of Saint Augustine: Rereading the Confessions* (London: Routledge, 2005)
—— *Contemplation and Classical Christianity: A Study in Augustine* (Oxford: Oxford University Press, 2013)
Kim, Yonsoo, *El saber femenino y el sufrimiento corporal de la temprana Edad Moderna. Arboleda de los enfermos y Admiraçión Operum Dey de Teresa de Cartagena* (Córdoba: Universidad de Córdoba, Servicio de Publicaciones, 2008)

—— 'Writing to Survive and Heal: Teresa de Cartagena's Life and Works', in her *Between Desire and Passion: Teresa de Cartagena* (Leiden: Brill, 2012), pp. 11–34
KINKADE, RICHARD P., and JOHN A. ZAHNER, 'Pero López de Ayala's Translation of the *Magna moralia*', in *Homenaje a Don Agapito Rey: trabajos publicados en su honor*, ed. by Josep Roca-Pons (Bloomington, IN: Indiana University, 1980), pp. 131–48
KOCH, PETER, and WULF OESTERREICHER, 'Sprache der Nähe — Sprache der Distanz. Mündlichkeit und Schriftlichkeit im Spannungsfeld von Sprachtheorie und Sprachgeschichte', *Romanistisches Jahrbuch*, 36 (1985), 15–43
KUBLER, GEORGE, 'Vicente Carducho's Allegories of Painting', *The Art Bulletin*, 47 (1975), 439–45
KÜPPER, JOACHIM, 'Perception, Cognition, and Volition in the Arcipreste de Talavera', in *Rethinking the Medieval Senses: Heritage/Fascinations/Frames*, ed. Stephen G. Nichols, Andreas Kablitz, and Alison Calhoun, pp. 119–53
LABOV, WILLIAM, *Sociolinguistic Patterns* (Philadelphia: University of Pennsylvania Press, 1972)
LAPESA, RAFAEL, 'Estilo y lenguaje de Santa Teresa en las Exclamaciones del alma a su Dios', in *Aureum Saeculum Hispanum. Beiträge zu Texten des Siglo de Oro. Festschrift für Hans Flasche zum 70. Geburtstag*, ed. by Karl-Hermann Körner and Dietrich Briesemeister (Wiesbaden: Steiner, 1983), pp. 125–40
—— '"El", "la", "lo" como antecedente de relativo en español', in *Estudios de morfosintaxis histórica del español*, ed. by Rafael Cano Aguilar and María Teresa Echenique Elizondo, Biblioteca Románica Hispánica: II, Estudios y Ensayos, 418 (Madrid: Gredos, 2000), pp. 388–401
LARRAÑAGA, VICTORIANO, *La espiritualidad de San Ignacio de Loyola: estudio comparativo con la de Santa Teresa de Jesús* (Madrid: A. C. N. de Casa de San Pablo, 1944)
LAWRANCE, JEREMY, 'Vicente Carducho and the Spanish Literary Baroque', in *On Art and Painting: Vicente Carducho and Baroque Spain*, ed. by Jean Andrews, Oliver Noble Wood and Jeremy Roe (Cardiff: University of Wales Press, 2016), pp. 19–70
LÁZARO CARRETER, FERNANDO, 'Fray Luis y el estilo de Santa Teresa', in *Homenaje a Gonzalo Torrente Ballester* (Salamanca: Biblioteca de la Caja de Ahorros y Monte de Piedad, 1981), pp. 463–69
—— 'Santa Teresa de Jesús, escritora (El "Libro de la vida")', in *Actas del Congreso Internacional Teresiano*, ed. by Teófanes Egido Martínez, Víctor García de la Concha, and Olegario González de Cardedal (Salamanca: Universidad de Salamanca, 1983), pp. 11–27
LEHFELDT, ELIZABETH, *Religious Women in Golden Age Spain: The Permeable Cloister* (Aldershot: Ashgate, 2005)
LENTES, THOMAS, '"As Far as the Eye Can See": Rituals of Gazing in the Late Middle Ages', in *The Mind's Eye: Art and Theological Argument in the Middle Ages*, ed. by Jeffrey E. Hamburger and Anne-Marie Bouché, pp. 360–73
LINDBERG, DAVID C., ed., *John Pecham and the Science of Optics: Perspectiva communis* (Madison: University of Wisconsin Press, 1970)
—— 'Lines of Influence in Thirteenth-Century Optics: Bacon, Witelo and Pecham', *Speculum*, 46.1 (1971), 66–83
—— 'The Intromission-Extramission Controversy in Islamic Visual Theory: Alkindi versus Avicenna', in *Studies in Perception in the History of Philosophy and Science*, ed. by Peter K. Machamer and Robert G. Turnbull (Columbus: Ohio State University Press, 1978), pp. 137–59
—— *Theories of Vision from Al-Kindi to Kepler* (Chicago, IL: University of Chicago Press, 1976)
—— and KATHERINE H. TACHAU, 'The Science of Light and Colour', in *The Cambridge History of Science*, ed. by David C. Lindberg and Michael H. Shank (Cambridge: Cambridge University Press, 2013), II: *Medieval Science*, pp. 486–511

LLAMAS MARTÍNEZ, ENRIQUE, *Santa Teresa de Jesús y la Inquisición española* (Madrid: CSIC, 1971)
—— *Santa Teresa de Jesús. Obras completas* (Madrid: Editorial de Espiritualidad, 1984)
—— 'Poesías', in *Introducción a la lectura de Santa Teresa*, 2nd edn (Madrid: Editorial de Espiritualidad, 2002), pp. 607–10
LLAMAS, ROMÁN, *Biblia en Santa Teresa* (Madrid: Editorial de Espiritualidad, 2007)
LOOTENS, MATTHEW, 'Augustine', in *The Spiritual Senses: Perceiving God in Western Christianity*, ed. by Paul L. Gavrilyuk and Sarah Coakley (Baltimore, MD: Johns Hopkins University Press, 2011), pp. 56–70
LÓPEZ BARALT, LUCE, 'Simbología mística musulmana en San Juan de la Cruz y Santa Teresa de Jesús', *Nueva Revista de Filología Hispánica*, 30.1 (1981), 21–91
LÓPEZ GRIGERA, LUISA, 'Historia textual: textos literarios (Siglo de Oro)', in *Historia de la lengua española*, ed. by Rafael Cano Aguilar, 2nd edn (Barcelona: Ariel, 2005), pp. 701–28
LOUTH, ANDREW, *The Origins of the Christian Mystical Tradition: From Plato to Denys* (Oxford: Oxford University Press, 2007)
LUBAC, HENRI DE, *Medieval Exegesis*, trans. by Mark Sebanc (Grand Rapids, MI, and Edinburgh: Eerdmans, 1998), I: *The Four Senses of Scripture*
MADRE DE DIOS, EFRÉN DE LA, and OTGER STEGGINK, *Tiempo y vida de Santa Teresa*, 3rd edn, Biblioteca de Autores Cristianos, Maior, 52 (Madrid: Editorial Católica, 1996)
MADRUGA REAL, A., *Arquitectura barroca salmantina: las agustinas de Monterrey* (Salamanca: Centro de Estudios Salmantinos, 1983)
MANCHO DUQUE, MARÍA JESÚS, 'El *Camino de perfección*: génesis y aspectos lingüísticos' (Alicante: Biblioteca Virtual Miguel de Cervantes, at <http://www.cervantesvirtual.com/nd/ark:/59851/bmc12695>, 2008) [accessed 4 April 2015]
MANERO SOROLLA, MARÍA PILAR, 'La Biblia en el Carmelo femenino: la obra de María de San José (Salazar)', in *Actas del XII Congreso de la Asociación Internacional de Hispanistas. Birmingham 1995*, ed. by Jules Whicker, 7 vols (Birmingham: University of Birmingham, 1998), III: *Estudios Áureos II*, pp. 52–58
—— 'On the Margins of the Mendozas: Luisa de la Cerda and María de San José (Salazar)', in *Power and Gender in Early Modern Spain*, ed. by Helen Nader, pp. 113–31
MÁRQUEZ, ANTONIO, *Los alumbrados: orígenes y filosofía, 1525–1559* (Madrid: Taurus, 1972)
MARTÍN GONZÁLEZ, JUAN JOSÉ, 'El Convento de San José de Ávila (patronos y obras de arte)', *Boletín del Seminario de Estudios de Arte*, 45 (1979), 349–76
MARTÍNEZ GARCÍA, HORTENSIA, 'Del "pues" «temporal» al causal y contrastivo', in *Actas del Congreso de la Sociedad Española de Lingüística, XX Aniversario, Tenerife, del 2 al 6 de abril de 1990*, ed. by María Ángeles Álvarez Martínez, 2 vols (Madrid: Gredos, 1990), II, 599–610
MARTÍNEZ MILLÁN, JOSÉ, 'Grupos de poder en la corte durante el reinado de Felipe II: la facción ebolista, 1554–1573', in *Instituciones y elites de poder en la Monarquía Hispana durante el siglo XVI*, ed. by J. Martínez Millán (Madrid: Universidad Autónoma de Madrid, 1992), pp. 137–97
MATARASSO, PAULINE, ed., *The Cistercian World: Monastic Writings of the Twelfth Century* (London: Penguin, 1993)
MATTER, E. ANN, and LESLEY SMITH, eds, *From Knowledge to Beatitude: St Victor, Twelfth-century Scholars, and Beyond. Essays in Honour of Grover A. Zinn, Jr.* (Notre Dame, IN: University of Notre Dame Press, 2012)
MATTHEWS, GARETH B., 'Medieval Theory of Vision', in *Studies in Perception in the History of Philosophy and Science*, ed. by Peter K. Machamer and Robert G. Turnbull (Columbus: Ohio State University Press, 1978), pp. 87–99

Mayer, Thomas F., *The Roman Inquisition: A Papal Bureacracy and its Laws in the Age of Galileo* (Philadelphia: University of Pennsylvania Press, 2013)
McGinn, Bernard, *The Presence of God: A History of Western Christian Mysticism*, I: *The Foundations of Mysticism* (London: SCM, 1991)
—— 'Thomas Gallus and Dionysian Mysticism', *Studies in Spirituality*, 8 (1998), 81–96
—— '*Visio Dei*: Seeing God in Medieval Theology and Mysticism', in *Envisaging Heaven in the Middle Ages*, ed. by Carolyn Muessig and Ad Putter (London: Routledge, 2007), pp. 15–33
—— 'Humans as *Imago Dei*: Mystical Anthropology Then and Now', in *Sources of Transformation: Revitalizing Christian Spirituality*, ed. by Edward Howells and Peter Tyler (London: Bloomsbury, 2010), pp. 19–40
—— 'True Confessions: Augustine and Teresa of Avila on the Mystical Self', in *Teresa of Avila: Mystical Theology and Spirituality in the Carmelite Tradition*, ed. by Edward Howells and Peter Tyler (London: Routledge, 2017), pp. 9–29
Melián, Elvira M., 'Santiago contra Santa Teresa: Beatriz Ramírez de Mendoza o la redención de cautivos', *Clepsydra. Revista de Estudios de Género y Teoría Feminista*, 8 (2009), 29–46
Menéndez Pidal, Ramón, 'El estilo de Santa Teresa', in *La lengua de Cristóbal Colón: la lengua de santa Teresa y otros estudios sobre el siglo XVI*, Colección Austral, 228 (Madrid: Espasa-Calpe, 1942)
Miguéliz Valcarlos, Ignacio, 'Bustos relicarios italianos en el Museo Lázaro Galdiano', *Goya: Revista de Arte*, 310 (2006), 3–10
Moreno Cuadro, Fernando, 'En torno a las fuentes iconográficas de Tiepolo para la "Visión teresiana" del Museo de Bellas Artes de Budapest', *Archivo Español de Arte*, 82 (2009), 243–58
—— 'La serie de la transverberación de Santa Teresa con las dos Trinidades derivada de Wierix. Acerca de una pintura de Francisco Rizi', *Goya: Revista de Arte*, 341 (2012), 312–23
—— 'San Pedro de Alcántara y la transverberación teresiana en la estampa alemana del último Barroco', *Cauriensia: Revista Anual de Ciencias Eclesiásticas*, 7 (2012), 421–32
—— 'Iconografía de los testigos de los procesos teresianos: a propósito de Adrian Collaert y la iconografía de la Capilla Cornaro', *Archivo Español de Arte*, 87 (2014), 29–44
Mujica, Barbara, 'Performing Sanctity: Lope's Use of Teresian Iconography in *Santa Teresa de Jesús*', in *A Companion to Lope de Vega*, ed. by A. Samson and J. Thacker, Colección Támesis, Serie A, 260 (Woodbridge: Tamesis, 2008), pp. 183–98
—— 'Encuentro de santos: Francisco de Borja y Teresa de Jesús', in *Francisco de Borja y su tiempo: política, religión y cultura en la Edad Moderna*, ed. by Enrique García Hernán and María Pilar Ryan (Valencia: Albatros / Rome: Institutum Historicum Societatis Iesu, 2012), pp. 745–53
Müller, Jan-Dirk, 'Blinding Sight: Some Observations on German Epics of the Thirteenth Century', in *Rethinking the Medieval Senses: Heritage/Fascinations/Frames*, ed. by Stephen G. Nichols, Andreas Kablitz, and Alison Calhoun (Baltimore, MD: Johns Hopkins University Press, 2008), pp. 206–17
Mullins, Patrick, *St Albert of Jerusalem and the Roots of Carmelite Spiritualilty*. Institutum Carmelitanum, Textus et Studia Historica Carmelitana, 34 (Rome: Edizioni Carmelitane, 2012)
—— *The Carmelites and St Albert of Jerusalem: Origins and Identity*, Institutum Carmelitanum, Textus et Studia Historica Carmelitana, 38 (Rome: Edizioni Carmelitane, 2015)
Nader, Helen, *The Mendoza Family in the Spanish Renaissance, 1350–1550* (New Brunswick, NJ: Rutgers University Press, 1979)
——, ed., *Power and Gender in Early Modern Spain: Eight Women of the Mendoza Family, 1450–1650* (Urbana and Chicago: University of Illinois Press, 2004)

NELSON, ROBERT S., *Visuality Before and Beyond the Renaissance: Seeing as Others Saw* (Cambridge: Cambridge University Press, 2000)

NEVILLE, DAVID O., 'The Bodies of the Bride: The Language of Incarnation, Transcendence, and Time in the Poetic Theology of Mechthild of Magdeburg', *Mystics Quarterly*, 34.1/2 (2008), 1–34

NEWHAUSER, RICHARD G., 'Optics and the Science of the Senses', *The Senses and Society*, 5 (2010), 28–44

NEWMAN, BARBARA, 'Divine Power Perfect in Weakness: St Hildegard on the Frail Sex', in *Medieval Religious Women: Peaceweavers*, ed. by J. A. Nichols and Lillian Thomas Shank (Kalamazoo, MI: Cistercian Publications, 1987), pp. 103–22

—— *From Virile Woman to WomanChrist: Studies in Medieval Religion and Literature* (Philadelphia: University of Pennsylvania Press, 1995)

NICHOLS, STEPHEN G., '"The Pupil of Your Eye": Vision, Language, and Poetry in Thirteenth-century Paris', in *Rethinking the Medieval Senses: Heritage/Fascinations/Frames*, ed. by Stephen G. Nichols, Andreas Kablitz and Alison Calhoun (Baltimore, MD: Johns Hopkins University Press, 2008), pp. 286–307

—— ANDREAS KABLITZ, and ALISON CALHOUN, eds, *Rethinking the Medieval Senses: Heritage/Fascinations/Frames* (Baltimore, MD: Johns Hopkins University Press, 2008)

O'CALLAGHAN, JOSEPH F., *A History of Medieval Spain* (Ithaca, NY: Cornell University Press, 1975)

OCTAVIO DE TOLEDO Y HUERTA, ÁLVARO S., 'Santa Teresa y la mano visible: sobre las variantes sintácticas del *Camino de perfección*', in *Así se van las lenguas variando: nuevas tendencias en la investigación del cambio lingüístico en español*, ed. by Mónica Castillo Lluch and Lola Pons Rodríguez, Fondo hispánico de lingüística y filología, 5 (Bern: Peter Lang, 2011), pp. 241–304

OESTERREICHER, WULF, 'Textos entre inmediatez y distancia comunicativas: el problema de lo hablado escrito en el Siglo de Oro', in *Historia de la lengua española*, ed. by Rafael Cano Aguilar, 2nd edn (Barcelona: Ariel, 2005), pp. 729–69

OLMO LETE, GREGORIO DE, 'La Biblia en la literatura espiritual del Siglo de Oro', in *La Biblia en la literatura española*, II: *Siglo de Oro*, ed. by Rosa Navarro Durán (Madrid: Editorial Trotta, 2008), pp. 101–79

ONG, WALTER, *Ramus, Method, and the Decay of Dialogue* (Cambridge, MA: Harvard University Press, 1958)

O'REILLY, TERENCE, 'The Spiritual Exercises and Illuminism in Spain: Dominican Critics of the Early Society of Jesus', in *Ite Inflammate Omnia. Selected Historical Papers from Conferences Held in Loyola and Rome in 2006*, ed. by Thomas M. McCoog (Rome: Institutum Historicum Societatis Iesu, 2010), pp. 210–15

—— 'Joseph Veale and the History of the Spiritual Exercises', *Milltown Studies*, 66 (2010), 1–18

—— 'Early Printed Books in Spain and the *Exercicios* of Ignatius Loyola', *Bulletin of Spanish Studies*, 89.4 (2012), 635–64

PABLO MAROTO, DANIEL DE, *Lecturas y maestros de Santa Teresa* (Madrid: Editorial de Espiritualidad, 2009)

PALEOTTI, GABRIELE, *Discourse on Sacred and Profane Images* (Los Angeles, CA: Getty Research Institute, 2012)

PALOMINO DE CASTRO Y VELASCO, ANTONIO, and NINA A. MALLORY, *Vidas* (Madrid: Alianza Editorial, 1986)

PASCUAL CHENEL, ÁLVARO, and ÁNGEL RODRÍGUEZ REBOLLO, *Vicente Carducho. Dibujos. Catálogo razonado* (Madrid: Centro de Estudios Europa Hispánica, Biblioteca Nacional de España, Museo del Prado, 2015)

PASTORE, STEFANIA, *Una herejía española. Conversos, alumbrados e inquisición (1449–1559)* (Madrid: Marcial Pons Historia, 2010)

Pearson, Hilary E., 'Teresa de Cartagena: A Late Medieval Woman's Theological Approach to Disability' (unpublished DPhil, University of Oxford, 2011)
Peers, E. Allison, *Spanish Mysticism: A Preliminary Survey* (London: Methuen, 1924)
—— 'Introduction', in Bernardino de Laredo, *The Ascent of Mount Sion*, trans. by E. Allison Peers (London: Faber and Faber, 1952)
Pérez, Joseph, *Teresa de Ávila y la España de su tiempo*, 2nd edn (Madrid: Algaba Ediciones, 2015)
Pérez Sánchez, Alfonso Emilio, 'Pintura madrileña del siglo XVII: "Addenda"', *Archivo Español de Arte*, 49 (1976), 293–326
Perry, Mary Elizabeth, *Gender and Disorder in Early Modern Seville* (Princeton, NJ: Princeton University Press, 1990)
Pinilla Martín, María José, 'La ilustración de los escritos teresianos: grabados de las primeras ediciones', *Boletín del Seminario de Estudios de Arte*, 74 (2008), 185–202
—— 'Arte efímero en Valladolid con motivo de la beatificación de Teresa de Jesús', *Boletín del Seminario de Estudios de Arte*, 75 (2009), 203–14
—— 'Dos "Vidas Gráficas" de Santa Teresa de Jesús: Amberes 1613 y Roma 1655', *Boletín del Seminario de Estudios de Arte*, 79 (2013), 183–202
—— 'Una aproximación a la iconografía de Santa Teresa', *Patrimonio Histórico de Castilla y León*, 54 (2015), 63–66
Portús, Javier, 'Painting and Poetry in the Diálogos', in *On Art and Painting: Vicente Carducho and Baroque Spain*, ed. by Jean Andrews, Oliver Noble Wood, and Jeremy Roe (Cardiff: University of Wales Press, 2016), pp. 71–90
Poska, Allyson M., *Women and Authority in Early Modern Spain: The Peasants of Galicia* (Oxford: Oxford University Press, 2005)
Pountain, Christopher J., 'Las distintas gramáticas de los relativos españoles', in *Actas del VII Congreso Internacional de Historia de la Lengua Española (Mérida, Yucatán)*, ed. by Concepción Company Company and José G. Moreno de Alba, 2 vols (Madrid: Arco, 2008), I, 967–80
—— 'Variation in Address Forms in Sixteenth-Century Spanish Prose Drama', in *Stvdia Lingvistica in honorem Mariae Manoliu*, ed. by Sanda Reinheimer-Rîpeanu (Bucharest: Editura Universităţii din Bucureşti, 2009), pp. 282–93
—— 'Dislocación popular y dislocación culta en la comedia en prosa del Siglo de Oro español', in *Pragmatique historique et syntaxe / Historische Pragmatik und Syntax. Actes de la section du même nom du XXXIè Romanistentag allemand / Akten der gleichnamigen Sektion des XXXI. Deutschen Romanistentags (Bonn, 27.9– 1.10.2009)*, ed. by Barbara Wehr and Frédéric Nicolosi (Frankfurt am Main: Peter Lang, 2012), pp. 140–56
—— 'Valores sociolingüísticos y funcionales de los posesivos en el español peninsular del siglo XVI', in *Actas del VIII Congreso Internacional de Historia de la Lengua Española (Santiago de Compostela, 14–18 de septiembre de 2009)*, ed. by Emilio Montero, 2 vols (Santiago de Compostela: Meubook, 2012), I, 1059–72
—— '*Que*-deletion: The Rise and Fall of a Syntactic Fashion', in *En memoria de tanto miragre: estudos dedicados ó profesor David Mackenzie*, ed. by Francisco Dubert García, Gabriel Rei-Doval, and Xulio Sousa (Santiago de Compostela: Universidade de Santiago de Compostela, Servizo de Publicacións e Intercambio Científico, 2015), pp. 143–59
Rahner, Karl, 'La Doctrine des "sens spirituels" au Moyen Âge: en particulier chez Saint Bonaventure', *Revue d'Ascétique et de Mystique*, 14 (1933), 263–99
Raynaud, Dominique, 'Effets de réseau dans la science pré-institutionnelle: le cas de l'optique médiévale', *European Journal of Sociology*, 42.3 (2001), 483–505
Reed, Helen H., and Trevor J. Dadson, *La princesa de Éboli. Cautiva del rey. Vida de Ana de Mendoza y de la Cerda (1540–1592)* (Madrid: Marcial Pons Historia-Centro de Estudios Europa Hispánica, 2015)

Rivera-Cordero, Victoria, 'Spatializing Illness: Embodied Deafness in Teresa de Cartagena's *Arboleda de los enfermos*', *La corónica*, 37.2 (2009), 61–77

Rodríguez, José Vicente, '*Nada de turbe, / nada te espante...* (Parte I)', *San Juan de la Cruz*, 30 (2013–14), 323–31

Roest, Bert, *Order and Disorder: The Poor Clares between Foundation and Reform* (Leiden: Brill, 2013)

Rorem, P., *Pseudo-Dionysius. A Commentary on the Texts and an Introduction to their Influence* (Oxford: Oxford University Press, 1993)

Rubio Ávila, María Belén, 'María de Mendoza y de la Cerda (Utiel, c. 1522–Madrid, 15 de julio de 1567)', in *Damas de la Casa de Mendoza*, ed. by Esther Alegre Carvajal, pp. 561–76

Ruether, Rosemary Radford, 'Misogynism and Virginal Feminism in the Fathers of the Church', in her *Religion and Sexism: Images of Woman in the Jewish and Christian Traditions* (New York: Simon and Schuster, 1974), pp. 150–83

Ruiz Jurado, M., 'Álvarez, Baltasar', in *Diccionario Histórico de la Compañía de Jesús*, ed. by O'Neill and Domínguez, I, 91–93

Saggi, Ludovico, 'La mitigazione del 1432 della Regola Carmelitana: tempo e persone', *Carmelus*, 5 (1958), 2–39

Sánchez Jiménez, Santiago U., 'Marcadores discursivos en el teatro de Lope de Rueda', in *Actas del VII Congreso Internacional de Historia de la Lengua Española (Mérida, Yucatán)*, ed. by Concepción Company Company and José G. Moreno de Alba, 2 vols (Madrid: Arco, 2008), I, 2163–88

Sánchez Moguel, A., *El lenguaje de Santa Teresa de Jesús: juicio comparativo de sus escritos con los de san Juan de la Cruz y otros clásicos de su época* (Madrid: Imprenta Clásica Española, 1915)

Santa Teresa, Silverio de, ed., *Obras de Santa Teresa de Jesús*, 9 vols (Burgos: Monte Carmelo, 1915–24)

——*Historia del Carmen Descalzo en Espáña, Portugal y América*, 15 vols (Burgos: Monte Carmelo, 1935–52)

Schribner, Robert W., 'Popular Piety and Modes of Visual Perception in Late-Medieval and Reformation Germany', *Journal of Religious History*, 15 (1989), 448–69

Seidenspinner-Núñez, Dayle, '"But I Suffer not Woman to Teach": Two Women Writers in Late Medieval Spain', in *Hers Ancient and Modern: Women's Writing in Spain and Brazil*, ed. by Catherine Davies and Jane Whetnall, Manchester Spanish and Portuguese Studies, 6 (Manchester: University of Manchester, Department of Spanish and Portuguese, 1997), pp. 1–14

——, ed., *The Writings of Teresa de Cartagena* (Cambridge: Brewer, 1998)

——and Yonsoo Kim, 'Historicizing Teresa: Reflections on New Documents Regarding Sor Teresa de Cartagena', *La corónica*, 32.2 (2004), 121–50

Serrano, R. P. L., *Los conversos D. Pablo de Santa María y D. Alfonso de Cartagena* (Madrid: Instituto Arias Montano, 1942)

Shore, Paul, 'The *Vita Christi* of Ludolph of Saxony and its Influence on the *Spiritual Exercises* of Ignatius of Loyola', in *Studies in the Spirituality of Jesuits*, 30.1 (1998), <https://ejournals.bc.edu/ojs/index.php/jesuit/article/viewFile/3970/3534> [accessed 15 February 2016]

Silva, José Filipe, and Juhana Toivanen, 'The Active Nature of the Soul in Sense Perception: Robert Kilwardby and Peter Olivi', *Vivarium*, 48 (2010), 245–78

Smith, Mark A., 'Getting the Big Picture in Perspectivist Optics', *Isis*, 4 (1996), 568–89

——*Sensing the Past: Seeing, Hearing, Smelling, Touching, Tasting in History* (Berkeley: University of California Press, 2008)

Smits, R. J. C., *Eurogrammar: The Relative and Cleft Constructions of the Germanic and Romance Languages* (Dordrecht: Foris, 1989)

Steggink, Otger, *La reforma del Carmelo español. La visita canónica del General Rubeo y su encuentro con Santa Teresa (1566–1567)* (Rome: Institutum Carmelitanum, 1965)

Surtz, Ronald E., 'Image Patterns in Teresa de Cartagena's *Arboleda de los enfermos*', in *La Chispa 87: Selected Proceedings. The Eighth Louisiana Conference on Hispanic Languages and Literatures, Tulane University, Louisiana, 1987*, ed. by Gilbert Paolini (New Orleans, LA: Tulane University Press, 1987), pp. 297–304

—— 'The New Judith: Teresa de Cartagena', in his *Writing Women in Late Medieval and Early Modern Spain: The Mothers of Saint Teresa of Avila* (Philadelphia: University of Pennsylvania Press, 1995), pp. 21–40

—— *Writing Women in Late Medieval and Early Modern Spain: The Mothers of St Teresa of Ávila* (Philadelphia: University of Pennsylvania Press, 1995)

—— 'Iberian Holy Women', *Medieval Holy Women in the Christian Tradition, c. 1100–1500*, ed. by Alastair Minnis and Rosalynn Voaden, Brepols Essays in European Culture, 1 (Turnhout: Brepols, 2010), pp. 499–525

Tachau, Katherine H., 'Seeing as Action and Passion in the Thirteenth and Fourteenth Centuries', in *The Mind's Eye: Art and Theological Argument in the Middle Ages*, ed. by Jeffrey E. Hamburger and Anne-Marie Bouché, pp. 336–59

—— *Vision and Certitude in the Age of Ockham: Optics, Epistemology, and the Foundations of Semantics, 1250–1325*, Studien und Texte zur Geistesgeschichte des Mittelalters, 22 (Leiden: Brill, 1988)

Teatro español del Siglo de Oro (Madrid: Chadwyck-Healey Españá) at <http://teso.chadwyck.co.uk/>

Thøfner, Margit, 'How to Look Like a (Female) Saint: The Early Iconography of St Theresa of Avila', in *Female Monasticism in Early Modern Europe: An Interdisciplinary View*, ed. by Cordula van Wyhe (Aldershot: Ashgate, 2008), pp. 59–80

Thompson, Colin P., *The Poet and the Mystic: A Study of the Cántico Espiritual of San Juan de la Cruz* (Oxford: Oxford University Press, 1977)

—— 'Seeing the Unseen: The Representation of Visions in Golden Age Painting and Writing', *Bulletin of Hispanic Studies*, 86.6 (2009), 797–809

Tovar Martín, Virginia, 'Noticias documentales sobre el convento madrileño de Las Carboneras y sus obras de arte', *Boletín del Seminario de Estudios de Arte*, 38 (1972), 413–25

Trapè, A. 'VI: Saint Augustine', in *Patrology, IV: The Golden Age of Latin Patristic Literature from the Council of Nicea to the Council of Chalcedon*, ed. by A. Di Berardino (Westminster: Christian Classics, 1986)

Trillia, Raquel, 'Teresa de Cartagena: Agent of Her Own Salvation', *Revista Canadiense de Estudios Hispánicos*, 32 (2007), 51–70

Twomey, Lesley K., *The Fabric of Marian Devotion in Isabel de Villena's Vita Christi*, Colección Támesis, Série A: Monografías, 313 (Woodbridge: Boydell & Brewer, 2013)

—— 'The Aesthetics of Beauty in the Writings of Cloistered Women in Late Medieval and Golden Age Spain (Constanza de Castilla, Teresa de Cartagena, Isabel de Villena, and Teresa de Ávila)', *e-humanista*, 43 (2016), 50–68

—— 'Court and Convent: Senses and Spirituality in Hispanic Medieval Women's Writing', in *The Routledge Companion to Iberian Studies*, ed. by Javier Muñoz-Basols, Laura Lonsdale, and Manuel Delgado (Abingdon: Routledge, 2017), pp. 65–78

Tyler, Peter M., *Sources of Transformation: Revitalizing Christian Spirituality*, ed. by Peter M. Tyler and Edward Howells (London: Bloomsbury Continuum, 2010)

—— *The Return to the Mystical: Ludwig Wittgenstein, Teresa of Avila and the Christian Mystical Tradition* (London: Continuum, 2011)

—— *Teresa of Avila: Doctor of the Soul* (London: Bloomsbury Continuum, 2013)

—— 'To Centre or Not to Centre: Saints Teresa of Avila and John of the Cross and the "Centre of the Soul"', in *Christian Mysticism and Incarnational Theology: Between Transcendence and Immanence*, ed. by Louise Nelstrop and Simon D. Podmore (Farnham: Ashgate, 2013), pp. 177–90

—— *The Pursuit of the Soul: Psychoanalysis, Soul-Making and the Christian Tradition* (Edinburgh: T. & T. Clark, 2016)
VANCE, EUGENE, 'Seeing God: Augustine, Sensation, and the Mind's Eye', in *Rethinking the Medieval Senses: Heritage, Fascinations, Frames*, ed. by Stephen G. Nichols, Andreas Kablitz, and Alison Calhoun, pp. 13–29
VANHOYE, ALBERT, *El mensaje de la Carta de los Hebreos* (Estella: Editorial Verbo Divino, 2006)
VAQUERO SERRANO, MARÍA DEL CARMEN, 'Books in the Sewing Basket: María de Mendoza y de la Cerda', in *Power and Gender in Early Modern Spain*, ed. by Nader, pp. 93–112
—— *En el entorno del Maestro Alvar Gómez; Pedro del Campo, María de Mendoza, y los Guevara* (Toledo: Oretania Ediciones, 1996)
—— 'La ilustre y hermosísima María de Mendoza: nuevos datos de su vida y poemas del humanista Alvar Gómez a ella', *Lemir*, 19 (2015), 9–68
VAUGHAN, ROBERT ALBERT, *Hours with the Mystics*, 2 vols (London: John W. Parker, 1856)
VEALE, JOSEPH, 'Dominant Orthodoxies', *Milltown Studies*, 30 (1992), 43–65, reprinted in his collected essays, *Manifold Gifts* (Oxford: Way Books, 2006), pp. 127–49
WARNING, RAINER, 'Seeing and Hearing in Ancient and Medieval Epiphany', in *Rethinking the Medieval Senses: Heritage/Fascinations/Frames*, ed. by Stephen G. Nichols, Andreas Kablitz, and Alison Calhoun, pp. 102–116
WEBER, ALISON, *Teresa of Avila and the Rhetoric of Femininity* (Princeton, NJ: Princeton University Press, 1990)
—— 'Saint Teresa's Problematic Patrons', *Journal of Medieval and Early Modern Studies*, 29.2 (1999), 357–79
—— 'Spiritual Administration: Gender and Discernment in the Carmelite Reform', *The Sixteenth Century Journal*, 31.1 (2000), 123–46
——, ed., *María de San José Salazar, 'Book for the Hour of Recreation'* (Chicago, IL: University of Chicago Press, 2002)
—— 'Los jesuitas y las carmelitas descalzas en tiempos de San Francisco de Borja: amistad, rivalidad y recelos', in *Francisco de Borja y su tiempo: política, religión y cultura en la Edad Moderna*, ed. by Enrique García Hernán and María Pilar Ryan (Valencia: Albatros / Rome: Institutum Historicum Societatis Iesu, 2012), pp. 103–13
WEISS, JULIAN, 'Vernacular Commentaries and Glosses in Late Medieval Castile, II: A Checklist of Classical Texts in Translation', in *Medieval Hispanic Studies in Memory of Alan Deyermond*, ed. by Andrew M. Beresford, Louise M. Haywood, and Julian Weiss, Colección Támesis Série A: Monografías, 315 (Woodbridge: Boydell & Brewer, 2013), pp. 237–71
WILLIAMS, ROWAN, *Teresa of Avila* (London: Geoffrey Chapman, 1991)
WILSON, CHRISTOPHER, 'Teresa of Ávila vs. the Iconoclasts: Convent Art in Support of a Church in Crisis', in *Imagery, Spirituality, and Ideology in Baroque Spain and Latin America*, ed. by Jeremy M. N. Roe and Marta Bustilllo (Newcastle: Cambridge Scholars Press, 2010), pp. 45–57
WOOLGAR, C. M., *The Senses in Late Medieval England* (New Haven, CT: Yale University Press, 2006)
ZAMORA CALVO, MARÍA JESÚS, 'Demonología y misticismo: Teresa de Jesús', *Alpha*, 31 (2010), 147–61

INDEX

abstinence 15
　fasting 15
action 32, 34, 38–40, 82, 84, 87. 88, 94, 119, 137–38, 144, 153, 154, 157, 160, 196, 204, 209
　call to 1, 11
　God's 35–36, 101, 103, 115–16, 209
　prophetic 138, 144
　see also Martha (Bethany)
activity 34–36, 38–40, 201, 211
　God's (divine) 35–36, 38–39, 136, 141
　active 7–8, 33–35, 86–87, 143, 153, 171, 180, 204, 207
Alba de Tormes (Carmelite convent) 43, 54
Alba, Duke of, Fernando Álvarez de Toledo (1507–1582) 50, 54
　Alba faction 45, 54
Albert of Jerusalem, St, Law-giver and Patriarch (†1214) 14–25, 27
　Formula of Life 14, 15, 18, 20, 22, 26, 27
Albert of Trapani (Sicily), St, OCarm (c. 1250–1306) 17, 19, 62, 63
Alcalá de Henares (convent) 17, 20, 23, 42, 45, 55, 115
Alcántara, Peter of, St (1499–1562) 39, 61–62, 177, 180
　Libro de la oración 181
　Tratado de la oración y meditación 181
Alfonso X, King of Castile and León (1221–84) 150
　Siete partidas 150
alumbrados 44, 56, 169, 186
　alumbradismo 178
Ambrose, St (340–397) 184
America 158
　Native Americans 125
Ana de Jesús Lobera (1545–1621) 4, 5, 12, 60, 62, 75
Anastasius, St (†628) 17–18
Angelus of Sicily, St, OCarm (†1220) 16–17, 19
Anthony of Padua, St (1195–1231) 61, 176
Aquinas, Thomas, St (1225–74) 150, 151, 153, 157, 158, 163, 165
Aristotle (b. 353 BC) 152, 162, 165, 194, 203–04
Augustine, St (354–430) 2, 32, 41, 66, 91, 93, 94–99, 101, 103–05, 112, 135, 176–77, 183, 184, 197, 200, 204
　Confessions 2, 32, 95–98, 112, 176–77, 183, 184, 197, 209
　De Genesi ad Litteram 95–97
　De Trinitate 95–99
　Homily on the Psalms 96–97
　Homilies on John 97
　Meditations 177
　translation of 177

Augustinian 1, 91–93, 95, 99, 100, 104–05
Augustinian Order 2, 5
　Augustinian canon 181
　Augustinian friar 1, 174
　Augustinian nuns 42, 61, 168
autobiography, 2, 155, 177, 218
　spiritual, see St Teresa, autobiography
Auxerre, William of (1140/50–1231?) 196
Ávila 2, 4, 17, 19, 21, 30, 36, 38–39, 42–43, 45, 47, 60, 108, 168, 172, 176, 180
　Bishop of 21, 46

Bacon, Roger (born c. 1210) 194, 198, 205, 208
　see optics
Beata 85
beauty 5, 93, 95, 100, 124, 136, 206, 210
benefaction 42, 44, 83
　benefactors 42–44, 49, 50
　see patronage
Berthold, St (†1195), first Prior of Mount Carmel 15–18, 26
Bible 80, 169, 170, 172, 173, 183, 184, 187, 188
　Polyglot Bible 169
　vernacular 80, 169, 172
　Vulgate 175, 184, 186
　quotations from 184
　reading of 81, 169, 173
　translations of 169, 175
Biblical characters
　Abraham 178
　Adam 6, 84, 178, 197
　Andrew, St 178
　Bartholomew, St 86
　David 171, 172, 178
　Esau 178
　Eve 178
　Good Samaritan 178
　Jacob 171, 178
　Jonah 171–72
　Joseph 172
　Lot 178
　Lot's wife 171
　Man healed (Siloam) 173
　Paul, St 170–72, 173, 174, 192
　Peter, St 86, 171, 172, 178, 187, 195
　penitent thief 83
　penitent woman 83
　Pharisee and publican 83

Prodigal Son 83, 143
Samaritan woman 82, 84, 172, 174
Simon, the Pharisee 83, 84, 86
Tax-Collector 83
Wise and foolish virgins 172
Biblical locations:
  Calvary 172
  Gethsemane (garden of) 10, 37, 82, 112, 132, 165, 172
  Red Sea 80, 172
  Tabor 172
body 4, 142, 147, 160, 196–200, 203, 206, 210
  eyes 195–97, 199, 206
Boethius (c. 475–526) 168, 184
  Consolations 168
books 135, 157, 175–76, 183, 186, 209
  good 2, 34, 168–69, 175, 176, 179, 181, 186
  pious 158
  of chivalry 168, 175, 177, 184
  banning of 39, 114, 169
    see Index (Valdés)
Borja, Francisco de (1510–72) 44, 46, 56, 117
Brocard, St (d. 1231), second Prior of Mount Carmel 15–17
butterfly (metaphor) 34–35, 106, 182

Cano, Alonso (1601–1667) 66, 209
Carducho, Vicente (c. 1576–1638) 59–77
Carmel (also Mount) 14, 15–18, 20–22, 24, 26, 27, 86, 88
Carmelite (Order) 2, 6, 7, 14–31, 45–47, 49–52, 60, 62, 63, 90, 114, 133, 164, 181, 187
  Discalced 6, 12, 17, 18–20, 42, 53, 55, 63, 64, 72, 108, 164
  breviary 16–17
  Constitutions 3, 16, 19–20, 22–25, 175
  friars 17, 19, 21, 22, 24, 47–49, 51, 64, 130, 194
  novice 53, 109, 115, 200
  nuns 17–18, 20–25, 29, 30, 36, 42, 50, 52, 57, 108, 109, 120, 178–80, 199, 201
  dowry of 22, 42
  Rule 14, 15, 18–26, 42, 110, 161
    primitive 18, 20, 21, 25, 43
    observance of 110
    Spanish translation of 19
    see Innocent IV, Eugene IV
  saints 16–18
    see also St Albert, St Angelus, St Berthold, St Brocard, St Cyril, St Hilarion, St Euphrasia
Carmelites (Reformed) 2, 49, 50, 86
  life 81
  tradition 14–31
Cartagena, Alonso de, Bishop of Burgos (1384–1456) 168, 184, 186, 192
Cartagena, Teresa de (born c. 1435) 167, 183–85, 206, 210
castle (metaphor) 2, 5, 34–36, 86, 100, 143, 182

Catherine of Siena, St (1347–86) 176
censors 8
Cepeda y Ahumado, Lorenzo de (brother of Teresa) 48
Cepeda y Ahumado, Rodrigo de (brother of Teresa) 126, 157–58, 175
Cerda, Ana de la, see Éboli
Cerda, Luisa de la, daughter of Duke of Medinaceli 45, 46, 47, 49, 50, 53, 56
Cetina, Diego de (1531–1568) 108, 115–18, 121, 155, 165
charity 50, 52, 57, 71, 99, 138, 219
Christ 1, 8–10, 21, 30–31, 32, 34, 36, 68, 70, 71, 72, 73, 80, 82, 83–89, 96, 97, 137, 141, 142, 147, 150, 155, 156, 158, 159, 171, 172, 176, 181, 182, 187, 195–96, 198–99, 201, 203–05, 207, 210
  at the column 10, 66–68, 71, 72, 73, 138
  body of 133
  call of 86
  companionship of 36, 147
  death of 157
  friendship with 124
  kinship with 85, 89
  humanity of 112–13, 116, 142, 202
  identification with 99
  images of 112, 113, 201
  imitation of 105, 156
  incarnate 142
  presence of 99, 108, 112–13
  tears of 165
  union with 99, 141
  wounds of 36, 70–72, 112
  risen 151, 159
  see Passion
Church 1, 2, 4, 6–9, 12, 15, 21, 30, 44, 52, 81, 89, 99, 114, 121, 125, 143, 150, 160, 163, 169, 173, 174, 179
  defence of 150
  divisions in 89, 121, 125, 139, 169
  Fathers of 2, 183
churchmen 8, 9, 199
Cisneros, Francisco Jiménez de, Cardinal (1436–1514) 169, 177, 181
Clare, St (1194–1253) 25, 66
commission 61, 72, 73
Communion, Holy 61, 62, 130, 132, 158
  see also Eucharist
community 2, 7, 8, 9, 26, 55, 81, 85–87, 89, 115, 127, 143, 145–46, 181
  apostolic 86
  life 2, 7, 8, 87
  of grace 89
compassion 84, 137, 141
confession 6, 34, 91, 99, 104, 105, 115, 128, 177, 218
  confess 6, 167, 197, 201
  confessor 2, 3, 6, 12, 21, 47, 56, 90, 91, 108–09, 111, 115, 119–20, 152, 155, 158, 159, 161, 165, 167, 174, 178, 179, 196, 203, 218

consolation 10, 43, 50–51, 53, 101, 115–16, 122, 154, 159
see also joy
Constanza de Castilla (1354–1478) 194, 205, 212
contemplation 3, 10, 15, 18, 26, 34, 59, 84, 86–89,
94–96, 98–100, 103–04, 109, 111–14, 116–17, 120,
137, 146, 162, 177, 207
inner 94–95, 99, 103, 105
intellectual 162
contemplate 93, 96, 136, 142
contemplative 84, 85, 86–89, 96, 111, 120–21
and active 86
calling 1, 81, 85, 87, 89
community 88
gifts 86, 87, 117
insight 96
life 3, 82, 84, 87, 89, 94, 171, 177
maturation 89
saints 176
silence 87, 88
female contemplative 87, 88
women contemplatives 84, 85
see Meditation, Prayer, and Recollection
convent (or monastery) 2, 3, 9, 42–44, 46–47, 49–54,
55, 57, 63, 66, 69, 73, 87, 110, 151, 158, 160, 175,
176, 178, 180, 183, 184, 194, 199, 230
as burial place 42, 43, 55
construction:
bell-tower 21, 30
cell 22, 30, 71
chantry 42
chapel 21, 42, 43, 62
cloister 21, 30, 183
dormitory 21, 22, 25, 30
garden (orchard) 21, 30, 50, 52
oratory 36, 70, 180
poultry house 21, 30
refectory 21, 30
Discalced 3, 159, 160, 161
reformed 20, 21, 23, 49, 156–57, 173, 175, 180
de la Imagen (Alcalá) 20, 23
of the Carmen 62
of Corpus Christi 66
of the Incarnation 16, 17, 19–22, 25, 30, 42, 43, 158,
159, 172
of Las Carboneras 66–67, 73, 74, 76
of St Joseph (San José, Ávila) 2, 4, 7, 21, 30, 34, 36,
38–39, 43, 52, 60, 62, 64, 65, 66, 68, 72, 73, 74,
125, 126, 151, 159–60, 161, 176, 178
strict life at 161
of St Joseph (Pastrana) 52
of Our Lady of Grace (Santa Maria de Gracia) 42, 168
Las Huelgas 183
of Augustinian Recollect nuns 61, 168
conversion 32, 34, 36–38, 40, 173, 176–77, 197
convert 56, 177
Counter-Reformation 85

courage 8, 38, 40, 118, 141, 144, 150–65
inner 153
model of 163
cross 10, 35–36, 40, 82, 83, 97, 116, 129–31, 143, 155,
156, 197
crucifixion 10, 66, 69, 84
with the Virgin and St John 66
curiosity 200–01
Cyril of Alexandria, St (c. 376–444) 17, 18
Cyril of Constantinople, St (†1234) 15, 16, 17, 22
Cirilo (see Gracián) 17
Catalina de San Cirilo 17
Nicolás de San Cirilo 17
Colegio de San Cirilo (Carmelite College, Alcalá)
17, 45

Dávila, Jerónimo (active 1560s) 68, 72–73
Daza, Gaspar (Ávila) (†1592) 38, 115, 158
death 1, 3–4, 5, 6, 10, 16–19, 33–36, 42–43, 45, 51,
53–54, 56, 60, 64, 66, 83, 96, 120, 137, 157, 162–
63, 168, 180, 186, 197
fear of 83, 162
of St Teresa 1, 3–6, 16–18, 43, 54, 64, 66, 121
deification 95, 99, 105
delight 74, 100, 102–03, 110, 113–14, 129–31, 138, 139,
194, 200
see also joy, consolation
determination 9, 36, 136, 145, 151, 152, 157, 162–63
Devil 6, 15, 38, 71, 77, 113–14, 154, 156, 158, 159, 161,
173, 176, 196, 207, 221
demonic 6, 11, 158
diabolical 180, 191
Devotio moderna 181
Dionysius the Areopagite (first century AD) 91, 93,
102
Dionysian 92, 103
Pseudo-Dionysius 205, 212
discipline 53, 155, 180
divine 6, 17, 24, 32, 33–35, 36, 39–49, 72, 88–89, 92,
94, 95–98, 103, 105, 111, 113, 116, 119, 129, 132,
133, 141, 142, 143, 145, 151, 154, 157, 162, 199, 205
companionship 39–40
light 205
presence 32, 34–35, 142
providence 24
Divinity 112–13, 116, 142
Dominic Guzmán, St (1170–1221) 66
Dominican Order 14, 28, 43, 45, 77, 111, 114, 151, 181,
183, 203
Duruelo (Carmelite monastery) 20, 43, 45

Éboli, Prince of, Ruy Gómez de Silva (1516–1573)
45–48, 56
faction 44–46, 54, 56
Éboli, Princess of, Ana de Mendoza y de la Cerda
(1540–1592) 45–48, 49–50, 53–55, 57, 58

ecstasy 32–33, 36–40, 94, 97–99, 103–04, 143
  Ictus cordis 97
education:
  of St Teresa 2, 42, 168, 182
  of other women 184–85
Elijah 6, 14, 15–19, 25, 27, 28, 80, 171, 187
  Elijan succession 14, 17, 19, 21, 25
Elisha, St 6, 15–19, 25, 28
embodiment 140, 161, 166
emotions 70, 71, 73, 74, 92, 103, 159
enclosure 16, 21, 43, 85, 199
  cloistered 193–94
  enclosed 7, 16, 110
Erasmus of Rotterdam (c.1466–1536) 44, 181
Eros 93, 96, 100–03
  erotic 93, 95, 102
Eucharist 62, 89, 128, 130, 132, 133
  desecration of 128, 130
  eucharistic 132
  theology of 89
Eugene IV, Pope (1383–1447) 22, 23, 25
  Rule 22, 25
Euphrasia, St (380–410) 17–18

family 2, 3, 44–46, 85, 87, 88, 89, 137, 138, 172, 183–84
fear 5, 6, 35, 36, 38, 40, 73, 83, 113–15, 160, 163, 165, 196
Ferdinand I, King of Aragon (1452–1516) 169, 181, 199
fortitude 40, 150–51, 153, 158
founding (convents, houses, Order) 3, 6, 42–43, 45–50, 53–54, 66, 159, 175
  foundation 2, 3, 5, 6, 14, 17, 20–21, 23, 32, 34, 36, 38–39, 86, 146, 151, 178, 180
  founder/foundress 50, 108, 157
  see Alcalá de Henares, Alba de Tormes, Duruelo, Malagón, Medina del Campo, Pastrana, Salamanca, Toledo, Valladolid
Francis, St (1181–1226) 59, 61, 66, 176
  apparition of Christ to 66
Franciscan Order 14, 44, 49, 70, 177, 180, 181, 182, 183, 193–94, 208
  Discalced/Observant 5, 25, 27, 177, 180
  reformed 44
  Poor Clare 6, 183
  Third Order 60

garden, watering (metaphor) 129, 178–79, 182
Gerson, Jean (1363–1429) 91–92, 93, 104
God (the Father, the One) 1, 5, 7–9, 10, 15, 16, 20–21, 24, 32–40, 47, 49, 60, 64, 66, 69, 70, 71, 73, 82, 93–96, 98–100, 102, 105, 107, 109–20, 124–32, 136–46, 152–59, 162, 165, 171, 172, 174, 175–78, 179, 180, 189, 200–02, 205–06, 216–21
  absence of 144
  communion with 21
  companionship of 38, 40, 41, 144
  constancy of 140, 141
  conversation with 8, 15, 146
  experience of 40, 73, 97, 135, 139–40, 146
  friendship with 139, 140, 141
  generosity of 139, 140, 146
  gift from 10, 111–13, 117, 127, 129, 162–78
  image (sculpture) of 6–7, 21, 64, 95, 98, 201, 203
  incarnate 142, 144
  indwelling of Christ with 82, 83, 86
  intimacy with 114, 119, 139–40, 144, 145
  knowledge of 109, 193–94, 199, 200, 202
  mystery of 139
  partnership with 135, 138, 139, 141, 143, 146
  presence of 35, 37–38, 109, 117, 137, 138, 140, 197, 206
  relationship with 125, 127, 128, 135, 138, 139, 141, 144, 145, 146, 176
  search for 88, 97
  self-realization in 136
  tenderness of 129, 140, 144
  thirst for 135
  unity with (the One) 94
  will of 17, 35, 38, 82, 84, 116, 118, 119, 204
  word of 9
  see also union
grace 5–7, 32, 85, 96, 101, 103, 140, 142, 143, 144, 146, 151, 152, 162
Gracián, Jerónimo (1545–1614) 17, 27, 58, 126–27, 156, 187–89
Granada, Luis de, fray (1504–1588) 45–46, 181–82, 191
Gregory, St, the Great (540–604) 66, 170, 176, 183, 184, 185
  Moralia 170, 176, 183, 184, 185, 186
  Flores de los Morales de Job, translation, Pero López de Ayala 186
Grosseteste, Robert (1175–1293) 92, 194, 198–99, 211
Guevara, Antonio de (1480–1545) 177, 180, 191, 225, 227
  The Oratory of Religious 180
Guzmán, Aldonza de 21, 30
Guzmán, Fernán Pérez de (1376–1468) 168

Hail Mary 80, 109, 169
  Ave Maria 9
heart 103, 109, 112–13, 120, 140, 143, 178, 197, 201–02, 204–05
  my heart (endearment) 160
  weak 158
Heaven 1, 6, 15, 16, 18, 37, 98, 100, 128, 130, 135, 155, 171, 195, 202
Hell 20, 101, 116, 125
hermit 14, 15, 18, 20, 21, 24, 53
  hermitage 15, 52, 72–73
Hilarion, St (291–371), anchorite 15, 17–19, 25
honesty 7, 11, 135
honour 10, 16, 17, 21, 49, 88
Huarte de San Juan, Juan (1529–1588) 153, 164–65

humility 7–11, 86, 98, 131, 135, 155, 167, 184
  lack of 9
  humble 26, 31, 70, 98, 108, 117
humour 7, 124, 126, 135

Ignatius Loyola, St (1419–1556) 45, 108, 115–21, 123, 142, 181
  Spiritual Exercises 108, 115, 116–20
illness 2, 51, 154–55, 158, 163, 168, 183
illuminist, see *alumbrado*
imagination 2, 8, 112, 140, 161, 195–96, 201–03, 206
Incarnation 7, 33, 40, 140, 142, 165
income 23–25, 43, 57, 112, 180
  rent 50, 54, 57
Index (Valdés) 39, 100, 114, 165, 169, 173, 178, 181, 182
Innocent IV, Pope (in office, 1243–54) 14, 18, 20, 23, 25, 29
  Rule of 19, 20, 23, 25, 29
  Spanish translation of 19
Inquisition 7, 44, 56, 81, 114, 116, 129, 167, 169, 170, 174, 175, 179, 181, 186, 199
  Inquisitor 56, 169, 174
Interior Castle, see St Teresa, Works, *Interior Castle*
introspection 94, 135
Isabella, Queen of Castile (1451–1504) 56, 151, 164, 169, 181, 199

Jerome, St (c. 342–420) 66, 158, 168, 176, 184
  Letters 168, 176
  translated 176
Jesuit Order 3, 6, 38–39, 54, 56, 57, 108, 140, 142, 155, 158, 159, 165, 181
John of the Cross, St (1549–1608) 2, 4, 20, 45, 57, 80, 83, 84, 88, 91, 99, 109, 111, 117, 119, 120, 175, 205, 212
John the Baptist, St 15, 66
John the Evangelist, St 130, 172
journey 7, 33, 43, 46, 52, 85, 86, 88–89, 99, 101, 104, 125, 136
joy 15, 109–10, 113–16, 124, 127, 131, 140, 143, 144, 145, 147, 157, 172

Kempis, Thomas à (1380–1471) 181
  Imitation of Christ 121, 173, 181
knowledge 97–98, 109, 111, 130, 136, 169, 175, 176, 187, 193, 194, 197, 199–98, 202, 206
  lack of 196, 206, 209

Laredo, Bernardino de (1482–1540) 177, 179, 182
  Ascent of Mount Zion 179
Latin 3, 6, 17, 19–20, 24, 29, 45, 81, 85, 100, 117, 165, 168, 170–76, 183–84, 186–87, 192
  quotations in 170, 171, 172, 173, 174
  read 183–84
  understanding of 170
Latinism 178
León, Fray Luis de (1527–1591) 1, 5, 174

letrados 77, 178
Library 60, 168, 169, 184, 185
Life, see Teresa, St, works, *Book of her Life*
liturgy 16, 17, 93, 114, 173, 174
  Creed 174
  (Divine) Office 3, 16, 100, 103
  Magnificat 171, 174
  Missal 17, 18, 27, 28, 184
  liturgical books 80
Lord's Prayer 9, 82, 132, 169
  Our Father 9, 81, 85, 127
  Pater Noster 9, 124, 127
love 7–11, 34–35, 37, 39, 60, 70–71, 83, 87, 88, 92–96, 98, 99, 102, 111, 116, 119–20, 125, 128, 130, 131, 135, 156–57, 161–62, 171–73, 179, 180, 182, 202
  courtly 175, 182
  mutual 127
  transformative 143
  acts of 156, 162
  in action 125
  of God 37, 119–20, 141–42, 175, 180
  beloved 10, 138, 172, 202
  love-exchange 102
  loved 98
  lover 35, 98, 138, 162, 202, 206
  see also *Eros*
Ludolph of Saxony (the Carthusian, 1295–1378) 121, 173, 181, 183
  Life of Christ (Vita Christi) 121, 173, 181, 183
luteranos 2, 12, 71, 81
Lutheranism 169

Madrid, Alonso de (c. 1485–1510) 177, 180
  The Art of Serving God 180
Malagón (Carmelite convent) 17, 43, 45–47, 49–51, 53
manliness 151–53
María de Jesús Yepes (Foundress at Alcalá, Beata, 1522–1580) 20, 23–25
María de San José Salazar (1548–1603) 52, 126
  Libro de recreaciones 52, 55
marker (discourse) 222, 224, 230
Martha, St (of Bethany) 34, 83, 84, 125, 171
Mary (of Bethany) 34, 83, 84, 125, 171
Mary Magdalene, St 83, 84, 86, 87, 88, 90, 132, 171
Mass 17, 18, 42–44, 47, 50, 57, 61, 90, 132
  of St Gregory 207
Medina del Campo (Carmelite convent) 43, 45–46, 49
Medinaceli, Duke of, Juan de la Cerda (1483–1544) 45
meditation 8, 10, 60, 85, 109, 112–13, 116, 121, 142, 159, 181
  on Christ at the column 10
  meditate 8, 159
  see also prayer
Mélito, Count of, Diego Hurtado de Mendoza (1469–1536) 42, 45

Mélito, Countess of, Catalina de Silva (1518–1576) 42, 45
memory 98, 104, 110, 142, 172, 173, 178, 202
Mendoza y Sarmiento, Álvaro Hurtado de, Bishop of Ávila (†1586) 46
Mendoza y Sarmiento, María de, Marchioness of Camarasa (1523–1589) 42, 45, 46, 50
metaphor 178, 182, 193, 206
miracle, see Teresa, St
Montesinos, Fray Ambrosio de (1450–1514) 169, 173, 177, 181
    Life of Christ (translation) 181
    Meditaciones, soliloquios, manual y suspiros 177
mortification 71, 87, 154, 155, 156, 158, 161, 162, 163
mysticism 44, 121, 138, 206
    mystic 11, 114, 140, 205
    mystical 1, 11, 21, 35, 41, 60, 100, 105, 109, 120–21, 125, 130, 132, 169, 177, 181, 205
        ecstasy 32–33
        experience 1, 15, 183, 195, 220
        life 138, 144
        raptures 159
        theology 37, 92, 103, 104, 109, 111, 178–79
        tradition 1, 103
        see also prayer

Neoplatonism 93, 95
    Neoplatonist 93, 95
    Neoplatonic 92, 93, 94, 95–96, 100, 102, 103, 193

obedience 14, 16, 20–21, 100, 129, 157
    disobedient 3, 146
Ockham, William of (1287–1347) 199, 200
Olivares, Count-Duke of (1587–1645) 45, 60
optics 193–96, 198–99, 202–03, 205–06, 207, 208
    see Sight, Bacon, Ockham
Osuna, Francisco de (1492–c. 1540) 44, 80, 83, 91, 93, 104, 108, 112–14, 116, 117, 167, 177–79, 182
    Third Spiritual Alphabet 44, 91, 92, 104, 167, 168, 177, 178, 180
    teaching of 108, 114, 116

Pacheco, Francisco (1564–1644) 67, 68, 74
Padilla, Juan de (1468–1520) 168
    Retablo de la vida de Cristo 168
pain 10, 36, 110, 111, 141, 154–58, 161–62
    fear of 83, 162
Passion (of Christ) 8, 9, 80, 108, 112, 114, 116, 117, 132, 150, 159, 181
passions 151–52, 164
passivity 33–34, 41
    passive 34, 38, 117, 142, 204, 207
    see activity
Pastrana (Carmelite convent) 5, 42–58
    closure of the convent 49, 50, 53
patronage 42–44, 50, 54, 55, 57, 69, 85, 87, 89
    patron 44, 45, 50, 54, 57
    see Aldonza de Guzmán, Guiomar de Ulloa

Pecham, John (c. 1230–1292) 194, 198, 205, 208
    see Optics
penance 18, 118, 155–56, 159, 161, 163
perception, theory of 195, 203–04
perfection 5, 6, 16, 27, 38, 59, 69, 111, 114, 136, 160, 163
    imperfection 71, 110–11
perseverance 9, 11, 130
    persevere 2, 114, 118, 130, 163
Philip II (1527–1598) 3, 12, 45–47, 51–52, 53, 56, 152
Philip III (1578–1621) 59
Philip IV (1605–1665) 59
Plato (429?–347? BC) 93–96, 106, 150, 164, 194
    Platonic 91, 96, 99, 101–02, 104–05, 160, 162
    Platonists 96–97, 103, 162
Plotinus (204–270) 93–97, 104
    Plotinian 95–96, 97, 103–04
possessions 25, 197–98, 210, 211
    see income
poverty 2, 15, 18, 25, 43, 57, 86, 89, 180
Prádanos, Juan de (1521–97) 108, 118, 120
prayer 1, 2, 3, 7, 8, 9, 11–12, 15, 33, 36–38, 40, 42–44, 51, 55, 71, 72, 82–88, 90, 103–04, 108–21, 124–25, 127, 129–30, 132, 135, 136, 138–39, 142, 146, 154, 170, 172, 177, 179, 195, 201, 203, 216
    contemplative 82, 86, 169, 177, 178
    evangelical 81
    Ignatian 120
    imaginative 8
    infused 142
    interior 81, 85, 88, 90
    liturgical 85
    mental 8, 9, 85, 86, 108, 109, 111, 113, 114, 139, 169
    personal 132
    silent 44
    Teresian 124
    vocal 8, 9, 12, 139, 169
    books on 2, 39, 108, 112, 114, 135, 181
    experience of 108–09, 179–80
    first stage of 179–80
    four waters of 33, 36, 38
    fourth degree of 179
    gifts of 86
    how to pray 124
    journey of 125
    life of 2, 7, 8, 11, 83, 103, 160, 168, 177
    path of 167
    teacher of 7
    teaching on 2, 7, 8, 11, 124, 168, 178–79
    way of 37, 81, 132
    with Scripture 141
    of offering 124
    of quiet 37, 131, 174
    of recollection 91, 178, 179
    see also contemplation, meditation, Hail Mary, Lord's Prayer

preaching, women's 7, 160
  prohibition of 7, 160
property 14, 23, 24
Protestant 7, 114, 169, 173
psyche 93–94, 96, 106
  see also soul
Purgatory 42, 52, 159
purification 84, 94, 104, 205

reason 34–36, 49, 96, 112, 159, 162, 178, 202–03
  ratio 95–96
  reasoning 92, 179
recollection 9–10, 81, 91, 107, 116, 131–32, 178–79
  recollected 103
  see Prayer
reform 2, 18, 20, 29, 39, 42, 44–47, 49, 50, 52, 54, 56, 57, 60, 90, 108, 126, 133, 144, 156, 169, 170, 177, 180, 181, 182, 199, 211
  Carmelite 4, 7, 10, 12, 20, 27, 60, 108
  Discalced 2, 42, 108, 156
  Franciscan 25, 177
Reformation 81, 173
register 213–14, 219, 222, 224–25
revelation 2, 4, 7, 142, 143, 151, 154, 195, 199
rhetoric 83, 90, 184, 185, 213, 224
  rhetorical devices 167
  rhetorical methods 183
  rhetorical style 224
Ribera, Francisco de (1537–1591) 3–4, 27, 60–61, 67, 118, 151, 152, 157, 163
Ribot, Felip (Philip), OCarm (†1398) 14–16, 19–21, 25, 26, 29
  Ten Books on the Way of Life and Great Books of the Carmelites 15–16, 19, 21, 25
  Spanish translation of 19, 25

Sagredo, Gerard, St (*c.* 980–1046) 17–18
saints 4, 5, 16–19, 61, 67, 69, 76
  lives of 2, 4, 6, 157, 175–76, 26
  martyrdom of 1
Salamanca 4, 43, 54, 69, 99, 115, 164, 184
Salcedo, Francisco de (Ávila) (d. 1580) 38, 47, 114–15
salvation 96, 116, 125, 126, 184
scandal 53, 57, 84, 86–87, 88
Scripture 80, 99, 100, 135, 141, 169, 172, 173, 175, 178, 179, 183–84, 192
  approach to 178, 183
  ban on 173, 174–75
  Gospels 15, 81, 85, 89, 170, 171, 172, 173, 175, 181, 184
  Greek 96
  Hebrew 80, 96
  Holy 173, 179
  New Testament 80, 169, 170–71, 172, 175, 184
  Old Testament 14, 19, 25, 80, 169, 171, 184
  reader of 80
  reading of 169
  vernacular translations 169, 173, 174, 175, 181

books:
  Acts 173, 188
  Corinthians 15, 170, 188
  Exodus 24, 80, 171, 187–88
  Ezekiel 80
  Galatians 41, 170
  Hebrews 124, 134, 157, 165
  Isaiah 80
  Job 80, 150, 170, 172, 176, 184, 188
  John 81–84, 86, 124, 135–36, 171–72, 174, 175, 187–88
  I John 135, 171
  Luke 80, 83, 84, 175
  Mark 80, 81, 90, 170
  Matthew 80–85, 170, 175, 187–88
  I Peter 124, 171, 187
  Philippians 170, 171, 174, 187, 189
  Proverbs 64, 90, 130, 150, 171, 187
  Psalms 80, 170, 171, 172, 173, 174, 175, 183, 187, 188, 189
  Romans 170, 188
  Song of Songs 60, 80, 88, 90, 142, 171, 172, 174, 175, 183, 187
self 7, 88, 89, 95–96, 100, 105, 126, 139–40, 145, 156, 175, 201
  displacement of 88
  journey into the 7
  self-abandonment 35–36
  self-abnegation 143
  self-absorption 147, 201
  self-analysis 7
  self-awareness 125
  self-control 94
  self-depreciation 8, 220
    self-depreciatory 167, 179
  self-disclosure 135
  self-emptying 84
  self-flagellation 154, 161
  self-knowledge 131, 135, 136
  self-laceration 176
  self-loss 40
  self-regard 120
  self-understanding 32, 33, 35, 40
senses 97, 110, 140, 193–95, 197, 200, 204, 206–07
  common sense 195, 197, 209
  bodily/corporeal 97, 195, 197, 200, 204
  inner/interior 194–95, 197, 204
  mind's eye 198, 206, 211
sight 193–94, 197–98, 209
  seeing 193–200, 203–06
  spiritual 195, 207, 211
silkworm (metaphor) 34–36, 172
sin 101, 111, 114, 118, 136, 144, 176, 197, 198, 200, 205, 206
  sinner 54, 83, 88, 130
  sinful 83, 114, 117, 200, 206
solitude 10, 15, 18, 20–21, 29, 82, 112, 167

soul 5, 7, 8, 10, 16, 26, 32, 34–41, 42, 44, 50, 52, 57, 73, 83, 86, 88–89, 91–105, 108–12, 114, 116–17, 119–21, 130, 131, 132, 136, 137, 141–44, 146, 147, 159, 173, 178, 179, 182, 195–99, 201–06, 211, 217
  ascent of the 94, 95, 99, 103
  dark night of the 111, 120
  divinization of the 96
  eyes of the 73, 195–99, 203–04, 206, 211
Spirit, Holy 6, 59, 64, 66, 112, 129–30, 133, 146, 154, 159, 165, 178, 181, 205
spirit/spirits 94, 106, 113, 115, 117
  Evil 115
spirituality 1, 33, 44, 57, 95, 106, 136–38, 139, 145
  false 138, 201
  development, spiritual 167, 176, 179, 182, 183, 218
  spiritual 44, 59–61, 69, 71–72, 74, 81, 83–87, 89, 91, 94, 97–104, 106, 108, 111–12, 114, 115, 120, 167, 169, 171, 181, 183, 188, 191
    advisers 154, 155, 163, 180
    books 81, 100, 167–69, 173, 183, 186
    direction 114
    director 39, 91, 118, 120, 158
    experience 183, 191
    formation 85
    gifts 103, 120
    growth 7, 87, 137
    intimacy 86
    journey 89
    joy 114, 116
    life 2, 7, 11, 101–03, 108, 110, 138, 174, 176
    light 198–99, 211
    longing 84
    marriage 104
    practice 94, 145
    sacrifice 124
    warrior 18
    wisdom 7, 179
suffering 10, 36, 83, 84, 88, 111, 137, 138, 150, 154, 156, 157, 163, 172, 183, 197, 210

teaching 1, 2, 6, 10, 11, 34, 36, 39, 80, 83, 92, 108, 113, 116, 117, 124, 139, 160, 168, 172, 174, 177, 178, 179, 182, 194, 208
  Christian 160
  evil 3
  prohibition of women's 2, 6, 174
  University 80, 208
  on prayer 2, 36, 91, 124, 172, 178
tears 10, 36, 70, 112, 165
Teresa, St (1515–82):
  autobiography 32, 36, 60, 63–64
    see also autobiography
  beatification of 3, 12, 150, 151, 162, 163
    beatified 163
  biography of 3, 32, 61–62, 73, 76, 152, 164
    biographer of 3, 5, 53–54, 61, 118, 155, 157, 158
  canonization of 3, 5, 6, 61, 73, 76, 151, 155–56, 164
  canonized 163, 180
  hagiography of 53, 76
  language, spoken 214, 218, 220, 223–24, 227
  life, early (adolescence) 2, 17, 55, 100, 111, 120, 157, 168, 175, 177, 200
  miracles of 3–6
  sanctity of 3, 4, 6, 152
  writing 1–4, 7, 39, 41, 43, 47, 49, 91, 111, 121, 125, 135, 136, 138, 151, 157, 159, 162–63, 167, 169–70, 172, 174–75, 177–83, 185, 193, 203, 205, 206, 213–16, 220–22, 226–27
    style of 213–15, 218, 224, 227
    sophisticated 214, 220, 221, 227
  works:
    Book of Foundations 2, 3, 5, 11, 18, 49–50, 53, 77, 84, 85, 170, 171, 174, 180
    Book of her Life 1, 2, 4, 7, 11, 28, 32–34, 36–41, 50, 59, 61, 64, 70, 71, 73, 81, 82, 91, 99, 101, 103, 109–20, 129, 132, 133, 135, 139, 146, 151, 154, 156, 157, 158, 159, 162, 163, 167, 170, 172, 173, 174, 175, 176, 177, 179, 180, 182, 189, 195–203, 206, 214, 215
    Constitutions 17, 27, 170, 180, 182
    'In God's hands' (poem) 172
    Interior Castle 3, 5, 7, 18, 33–37, 39, 41, 81, 82, 83, 84, 87, 88, 99, 100, 101–06, 124, 125, 129, 132, 136, 137, 138, 141, 142, 144, 145, 170, 171, 173, 174, 189, 195, 201–02, 204, 206
      Second Mansions 35
      Third Mansions 34–35
      Fourth Mansions 101, 137
      Fifth Mansions 36, 141, 151, 201, 202
      Sixth Mansions 102, 132, 143, 202
      Seventh Mansions 34, 41, 125, 141, 143, 171, 173
    Letters 18, 47, 53, 56, 57, 58, 126, 127, 128, 133, 155, 156
    Meditations 3, 60, 82, 172, 173, 174, 175, 189
    'On the way to heaven' (poem) 18
    'Soul, seek yourself in me' (poem) 84, 201
    Soliloquies 33, 82, 83, 130, 131, 170, 172
    Spiritual Testimonies 33, 38, 83, 133, 171, 174, 189
    Way of Perfection 2, 7, 9, 11, 18, 80–86, 87, 90, 91, 124, 126, 127, 128, 132, 136, 144, 151, 156, 160–62, 163, 170, 171, 173
Toledo (Carmelite convent) 43–50
Tomás de Jesús Sánchez Dávila (1563–1624) 12
transformation 34–36, 40, 120
transverberation 37, 60, 64, 65, 101, 104
  see ecstasy
Trinity 59, 95–96, 98, 103, 105, 124, 127–29, 130–32
  Trinitarian 86
  Triune 98–99

Ulloa, Guiomar de 21, 30, 39

union 33–35, 38–40, 86–88, 93, 96, 101–05, 116, 137, 141–42, 172, 179, 201, 220–21
   contemplative 87
   preparation for 33
Valdés, Fernando de (1483–1568) 39, 100, 169, 178, 180, 213
   see Index
Valladolid (Carmelite convent) 43, 45–47, 49–51, 189
Vega, Pedro de la (†1541) 176
   Flos sanctorum 176
Victorine Order 92, 103
   tradition 92, 103
Villena, Isabel de (1430–1490) 194, 197, 199, 206, 208, 210
Virgin Mary 16, 59, 62, 84, 171
   Vision of the Virgin and St Joseph 62–63
   Virgin of Mercy 64
   Virgin of Mount Carmel 20–21
virtue 8, 9, 10, 83, 95, 114, 119, 137, 150–53, 200
   feminine 151, 164
virtues 3, 5, 8, 92, 104, 146, 150
   cardinal 150
   moral 92, 95, 152
vision 2, 4, 5, 7, 11, 20, 21, 39, 62, 63, 64, 66, 67, 72, 73, 74, 76, 101, 109, 154, 158, 159, 162, 180, 191, 193–207
vocation 40, 81, 85, 108

water, living (metaphor) 9, 125, 172, 188
Way of Perfection, see Teresa, St, works, *Way of Perfection*
wisdom 7, 105, 109, 117, 120, 136, 137, 146, 150, 179, 183, 197, 202
women 2, 6, 7, 8, 9, 11, 12, 20, 21, 38, 42–46, 52–53, 55–57, 83–85, 86, 89, 90, 114, 145, 152, 158, 159, 160, 164, 167, 168, 172, 174, 175, 184, 194, 197, 199, 205, 206, 210
   lay 81
   speaking in Church 2
   widow 21, 43, 50, 51, 53
   see also preaching, prohibition of and teaching, prohibition of
works, good (or virtuous) 33, 34, 104, 137–38, 143, 211

Yepes, Diego de, confessor to Philip II (1529–1613) 5–6, 12, 60–61, 73, 152, 155, 156, 163, 164

Zurbarán, Francisco de (1598–1664) 66

CPSIA information can be obtained
at www.ICGtesting.com
Printed in the USA
BVHW011442141220
595676BV00008B/664